MORAL ISSUES and MOVIES

An Introduction to Ethical Theories and Issues Through the Lens of Film

Joseph M. FORTE

Kendall Hunt
publishing company

Book Team
Chairman and Chief Executive Officer Mark C. Falb
President and Chief Operating Officer Chad M. Chandlee
Vice President, Higher Education David L. Tart
Vice President of Operations Kevin Johnson
Senior Managing Editor Greg DeRosa
Acquisitions Editor Daniel Pinto
Director of Publishing Services Wendy Jochum
Publishing Specialist Supervisor Carrie Maro
Senior Publishing Specialist Beth Trowbridge
Rights and Permissions Specialist Carla Kipper
Cover Designer Heather Richman

Kendall Hunt
publishing company
www.kendallhunt.com
Send all inquiries to:
4050 Westmark Drive
Dubuque, IA 52004-1840

ISBN 978-1-7924-3312-2

Published in the United States of America

I dedicate this book to the people I love, most especially my dear wife and daughters who were so patient and understanding about the work involved in this project.

Special thanks go to the publishing team at Kendall Hunt, the contributors, and reviewers, all of whom graciously and generously contributed their time and expertise to enriching this project.

CONTENTS

Chapter 6: Euthanasia and Assisted Suicide 97

> Recommended viewing: *The Elephant Man* (1980), *Million Dollar Baby* (2004), *The Walking Dead*, Season Two (2011), *Breaking Bad* (2009, Season Two, Episodes Twelve and Thirteen)

Chapter 7: Environmental Ethics: Dominion and Harmony 115
Co-Authored with Mark Sentesy

> Recommended Viewing: *An Inconvenient Truth* (2006), *An Inconvenient Sequel* (2017), *Cooked: Survival by Zip Code* (2018), *Cowspiracy* (2014), *Years of Living Dangerously* (2014), *Avatar* (2009)

Chapter 10: Just War Theory 193

Prerequisite viewing: Some or all of *The Vietnam War* (2017) by Burns and Novick

Chapter 11: Capital Punishment 221

Prerequisite viewing: *Dead Man Walking* (1995);
Recommended viewing: *Making a Murderer* (2015, 2018)

ABOUT THE AUTHOR

Joseph M. Forte, PhD
Assistant Professor of Philosophy
Rivier University

Background

Dr. Joseph M. Forte teaches ethics courses at Rivier University that are part of the core curriculum. He specializes in ancient philosophy, and has published on the ethics of Plato as well as the Scholarship of Teaching and Learning. His university-level teaching spans over thirteen years, with much of it focused on ethics.

He lived in New York City (the Bronx) until college and currently lives in North Berwick, Maine, with his family.

Degrees

PhD, The Catholic University of America
MA, Boston College
BA, College of the Holy Cross

Teaching

- Rivier University
- Merrimack College
- Northeast Catholic College
- Boston College
- Bridgewater State University
- Southern New Hampshire University
- The Catholic University of America
- Prince George's Community College

Courses Taught

- Love and Hope in the Good Life
- Theories of Ethics
- Contemporary Moral Issues
- Philosophy Through Film
- Dignity, Work, Vocation
- Epistemology
- Metaphysics
- Modern Continental Philosophy
- The Philosophy and Theology of St. Thomas Aquinas

- Aristotelian Logic
- The Medieval Flowering of Christendom
- Greece, Rome, and the Birth of Christianity
- Ancient Greece and Philosophical Inquiry
- Foundations of Logical Reasoning
- Philosophy of the Person
- The Classical Mind
- The Modern Mind
- Introduction to Ethics
- Introduction to Critical Thinking
- Introduction to Philosophy

Publications

- "Hope in Plato's Myth of Er," *Philosophical News* 17 (2020): 33–57.
- "A Model for Linking Interdisciplinary Courses Using Minimal Additional Preparation," *Insight. Rivier Academic Journal* 15 (2019).
- Commentary on Ewegen's 'A Man of No Substance: The Philosopher in Plato's *Gorgias*,' *Proceedings of the Boston Area Colloquium in Ancient Philosophy* 33 (2018): 113–117.
- Review of *The City-State of the Soul* by Kevin Crotty, *Review of Metaphysics* 71 (2017): 376–377.
- Review of *Quest for the Good Life* by Oyvind Rabbas, Eyolfur Emilsson, Hallvard Fossheim, and Miira Tuominen, *Review of Metaphysics* 70 (2017): 576–579.
- "Explaining Hope in Plato's *Philebus*," *International Philosophical Quarterly* 56 (2016): 283–295.
- "Plato's Efforts at Political Recuperation in *Republic* 6": Commentary on "Plato's *Republic* and the Politics of Convalescence" by Jacob Howland in *American Dialectic* 1 (2010): 1–17.

Web

- LinkedIn: https://www.linkedin.com/in/joseph-forte-71b9224/
- Twitter: @JosephFortePh1
- YouTube: https://www.youtube.com/channel/UCesv7S7ZaH55TTOU4fzjw8g?view_as=subscriber
- Academia.edu: https://rivier.academia.edu/JosephForte
- Rivier University: https://www.rivier.edu/directory/joseph-forte/

ACKNOWLEDGMENTS

Contributors

Chapter 7: Environmental Ethics
Mark Sentesy, PhD
Assistant Professor of Philosophy and Classics and Ancient Mediterranean Studies
The Pennsylvania State University

Chapter 8: Animal Ethics
Lucille Thibodeau, p.m., PhD, FOCAE
Fellow of the Oxford Centre for Animal Ethics
Professor of English, Emerita
Writer-in-Residence
Rivier University

Reviewers

Chapter 1
Jeffrey Dirk Wilson, PhD
Collegiate Associate Professor
School of Philosophy
The Catholic University of America

Chapter 2
William Wians, PhD
Professor of Philosophy
Merrimack College

Chapters 3 and 4
Francis Fallon, PhD
Assistant Professor of Philosophy
St. John's University

Chapter 5
Melinda M. Luther DNP, RN, CNE
Associate Professor
Rivier University

Chapters 5 and 6
Cynthia Cameron, PhD
Assistant Professor of Religious Studies
Rivier University

Chapter 8
Max Reinhold, MSc
Infectious Disease Prevention Coordinator
Maine Centers for Disease Control

Chapters 9 and 10
Nicole Loring, PhD
Assistant Professor of Political Science
Rivier University

Martin Menke, PhD
Professor of History, Department Coordinator
Rivier University

Chapter 11
Eric Gentes, JD
Professor and Director, Criminal Justice
Rivier University

Appendix
Video co-creator:
Maria Jacobs
Contract Coordinator
New England College

INTRODUCTION

I.1 Why the "Lens of Film"?

This textbook is designed to aid the reader's learning in the field of ethics by providing a robust context to serve as a springboard, or foothold, for their study. The book is designed not only to facilitate the understanding of philosophical concepts, texts, issues, authors, and historical periods, but most importantly, to facilitate readers' thinking thoroughly, authentically, and carefully about questions relevant to living a good life.

The core of most chapters is a set of curated excerpts from perennial or "classic" texts—many of which are considered "great books." Typically, an instructor will provide contextual background for primary source reading to the best of their ability, and perhaps recommend questions for students to keep in mind as they read philosophy that is mostly new to them. This is often not a sufficient foundation for enabling even diligent students to grasp the material well enough in order to deeply engage with the questions raised. By employing popular films as lenses through which the reader may gain a better grasp of philosophical content, this book bolsters the aforementioned foundation. Each film is not only selected thoughtfully and carefully, but each chapter draws connections between the films and the philosophical content in a way that is intended to provoke readers to develop connections of their own. The book offers additional support with fundamentals by way of explanations, commentary, annotations, glossaries, and an appendix of information about the philosophers and historical periods discussed. For those who want to read more than just short excerpts of each "great book," each chapter, as well as the Instructor's Supplement, provides recommendations of and links to freely available translations and editions for further exploration of the books discussed and excerpted.

I.2 Resources in This Book

Additional resources—contextual framework—that this textbook provides for aiding the readers' understanding of perennial thinkers, texts, concepts, and debates in the history of ethics:

- **Explanations** of some of the many possible connections between the films and philosophical content of each chapter, written in **simple, accessible prose,** designed to encourage the reader to develop their own connections
- A **glossary of terminology** in each chapter
- **Annotations** and **commentary** to explain possibly confusing aspects of excerpts from classic philosophy texts
- **Carefully selected, relevant images, including charts, graphs, and famous works of art**
- **Questions for consideration** and discussion to conclude each subsection
- **Links to vetted internet sources** to provide context and avenues for further learning
- **An appendix of biographical and historical background information** relevant to each chapter, which includes not only text, but **videos** co-created by the author and curated from the web
- A concise **introduction to logic**, focusing on the basic parts of an argument (see especially Chapters 2, 5, and 9), as well as a number of informal fallacies (spread across multiple chapters), integrated seamlessly into the text
- An **Instructor's Supplement** to serve as a pedagogical resource, with extensive suggestions about how to use the textbook effectively

I.3 How to Use This Book

Each chapter begins with a note to the reader about which films are necessary ("prerequisite") for understanding the chapter's content, and which are simply recommended. Readers, then, should be prepared to watch at least one film before or during their reading of each chapter. The easiest way to do this is to look up each film on a site like justwatch.com to see what streaming services host each film for free, for rent, or for purchase. IMDb.com is a great resource for information about each film, including words of caution about possibly disturbing content. This book, and the films in it, are not intended for children. Its subject matter is not fitting for those under the age of seventeen or eighteen. Each chapter includes questions to keep in mind while viewing. The reader is also encouraged to consult the appendix each time a famous philosopher is first mentioned, and to consult the glossary each time an unfamiliar term is first used, in order to develop the necessary context for understanding each chapter. After reading each subsection, the reader is encouraged to write down their thoughts about the questions for consideration that are included. Therefore, the attentive reader should approach the book ready to write as they read. Finally, readers who are especially interested in the content of each chapter can use the resources curated for further exploration, most of which are freely available online, to extend their learning.

I.4 Intended Learning Outcomes

The following outcomes are not exhaustive. In fact, it may well be the case that it is impossible to develop a complete set of learning outcomes for any philosophical text or course.

Chapters 1–4: Unit 1: Ethical Theories

i. Readers will engage in the discovery of ethical nuance, including the breadth and depth of the foundations of ethical thinking and action.
ii. Readers will have the opportunity to live more reflectively; to give in to fewer snap judgments and ideologies.
iii. Learners will improve in their understanding of themselves, others, and the world.
iv. The reader will develop their connections to something larger than themselves.
v. The reader will develop their active reading, critical thinking, and creative thinking skills.
vi. The learner will hone and develop their thoughts and opinions about humanity's greatest, most fundamental questions, including: How shall we live? What is the good life? What is the highest good? What is the best foundation for ethical character and action? How are ancient, medieval, and modern ethical theories similar and different? How are they reconciled, if at all? Why is human life so valuable?

Chapters 5–11: Contemporary Moral Issues/Applied Ethics: Unit 2: Bioethics, and Unit 3: Ethics and Politics

i. Learners will engage in the discovery of both the difficulty and the possibility of applying ethical theory to practice, and the importance of such application.
ii. The reader will improve in their ability to address real-world problems thoughtfully and systematically, rather than reactively.
iii. The book prompts readers to live more reflectively; to give in to fewer snap judgments and closed-minded ideologies.
iv. Learners will engage in the life-long commitment to understanding self, others, and the world.
v. The reader will develop the ability to identify weaknesses in *ad hoc* opinions and fallacious reasoning, beginning to see how the aforementioned denigrates society. Readers will develop and begin to use tools to resist poor reasoning and its effects.
vi. Learners will cultivate their connection to something larger. They will be provoked to effect well-informed positive change. They will have the opportunity to become better citizens through this book and the exercises it prompts.

vii. Readers will develop in their active reading, critical thinking, and creative thinking skills.

viii. Readers will hone and develop their thoughts and opinions about humanity's greatest, most fundamental questions, including: How shall we live? What is the good life? How is philosophy best applied to the moral problems of today? What is the relationship between man's political life and man's ethical life? Why is human life so valuable?

An additional, and very significant, learning outcome for the entire book is for readers to come away with the desire to read and study more philosophy than just what is excerpted, summarized, or explained in what follows.

UNIT 1

Ethical Theories

CHAPTER 1

Plato's Virtue Ethics through Film

Prefatory Note

The reader is encouraged to watch the films discussed in this chapter before reading it—especially *The Matrix* (1999).[1] For one, the chapter contains spoilers. Also, having familiarity with the films will greatly enhance one's reading experience. While watching both films, consider the following questions:

QUESTIONS FOR CONSIDERATION

a. How does the main character change throughout the film? Is he better off in the end than he was in the beginning? Why or why not?
b. Does the main character help, or even save, others in the film? If so, why is he able to do that? If not, why not?

1.1 Introduction

Virtue ethics was the first ethical theory on the scene in Western philosophy.[2] In the modern period, several other ethical theories emerged, most notably Immanuel Kant's deontological ethics and the utilitarianism of Jeremy Bentham

VIRTUE ETHICS
A theory of ethics that focuses on attaining virtue in order to live well, which involves achieving happiness; Socrates, Plato, and Aristotle are father figures to this theory, which many subsequent philosophical schools and philosophers took up and expanded upon, notably the Stoics and Thomas Aquinas.

ETHICAL THEORY
A systematic approach to living well; a systematic approach to character-building; a philosophy focused on the foundations of moral decision-making, not necessarily the practice or application of such decisions.

WESTERN PHILOSOPHY
The intellectual tradition, including schools of thought and individual thinkers, of European origin; currently includes American philosophy as well.

1. Go to a website like https://www.justwatch.com/ for information about which streaming services have each film, and whether or not it is free, for rent, or for purchase.
2. This book mainly focuses on Western thought. Henceforth, any reference to philosophy in general should be understood as referring to Western philosophy, rather than the thought of the East or anywhere else.

MODERN PERIOD
The time spanning roughly the Renaissance to the twentieth century; follows the ancient and medieval periods.

DEONTOLOGICAL ETHICS
Kantian ethical theory; the ethics developed by Immanuel Kant in the eighteenth century, based on his revolutionary metaphysics and epistemology; the highest command of this theory is expressed in the categorical imperative.

UTILITARIANISM
The ethical theory Jeremy Bentham and John Stuart Mill articulated in the nineteenth century; core doctrine is to maximize happiness, where happiness is pleasure.

SUBFIELD OR SUBDISCIPLINE OF PHILOSOPHY
An area within the larger field of philosophy; as neurology is to medicine, so is metaphysics to philosophy; examples of such parts or components of philosophy include but are not limited to ethics, epistemology, political philosophy, philosophy of science, philosophy of education, and philosophy of religion.

EPISTEMOLOGY
The study of knowledge, including its causes and its effects.

METAPHYSICS
The study of being, of existence, of reality; according to Aristotle, it is the study that goes beyond that of the physical.

POLITICAL PHILOSOPHY
The study of human communities, including but not limited to cities, city-states, and nation-states; studies, among other things, the possible forms of government, and the roles of all people within it.

and John Stuart Mill.[3] From Socrates's initiating the very existence of the field of ethics, to Kant's take on it about two thousand years later, virtue ethics was dominant. Philosophers before Socrates mainly focused on the philosophy of nature, seeking out the essential physical elements of the natural world. It was Socrates who really began the millenia-long inquiry into what the good life is, and how we should act if we want to live it. These are the core questions of ethics, perhaps the most important **subfield or subdiscipline of philosophy**. Since Socrates didn't write anything down, most of what we know (technically, what we think we know) about his thought comes from Plato, his most famous follower. Plato's contributions to virtue ethics span a large portion of his corpus.[4] The textual selection below—the famous "Allegory of the Cave"—is only one small part of one dialogue[5] in the massive body of work we attribute to Plato. Furthermore, the allegory below has significant philosophical implications not only on ethics, but **epistemology**, **metaphysics**, **political philosophy**, and other subdisciplines of philosophy. Though the following has an ethical emphasis, this chapter will cover aspects of the allegory's implications on other subfields as well.

1.2 The Metaphysics and Morals of *The Matrix*

Mr. Thomas A. Anderson becomes Neo (Keanu Reeves), a.k.a. "The One," in *The Matrix* (1999),[1] through a journey from ignorance to knowledge. He transitions from the world of appearances—the matrix—to the real world; from dissatisfaction to hopeful confidence; and from slavery to freedom. His path was not initially clear to him, and it took a great struggle for him to see the way forward. In fact, he

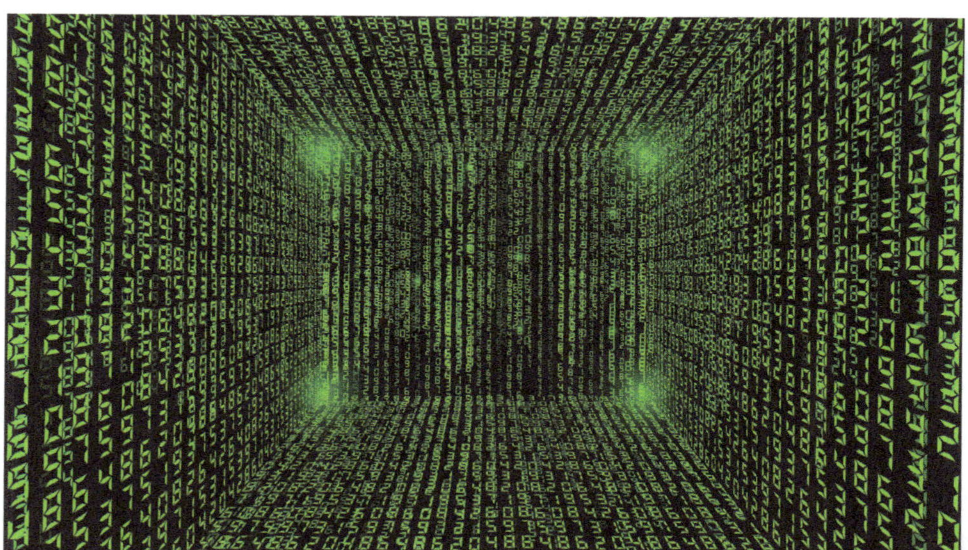

3. For information about the philosophical thinkers and epochs mentioned, please see the appendix of biographies.
4. Corpus = A body, in this case, of work
5. A conversation; a literary genre that reads like the script of a play, but typically does not serve as such

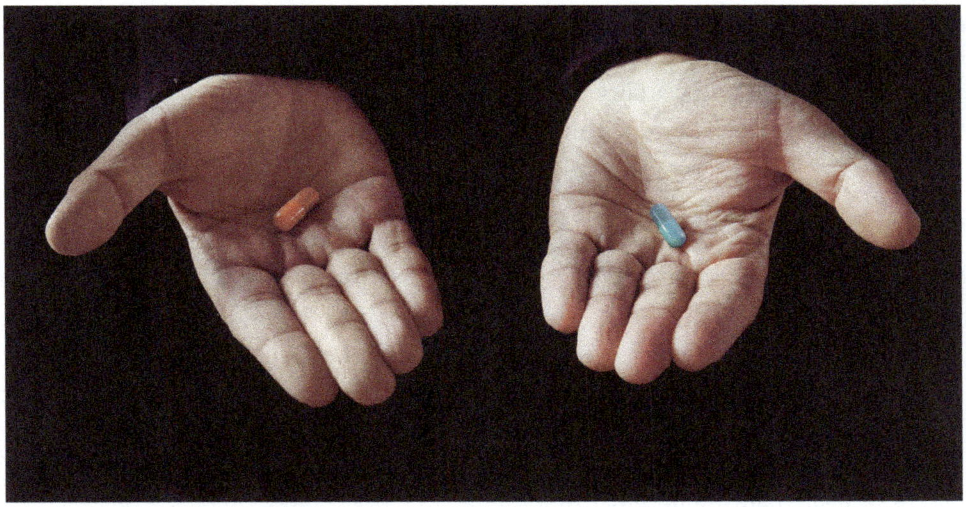

needed to die and come back to life to become who he was born to be. His rebirth was the final transformative step, burying Mr. Anderson for good, to fully become "The One." Not only did his intellectual journey save him from ignorance, delusion, and enslavement, but it saved others as well.

We all live in the matrix, but we can be saved too, if we can follow the model Neo has set for us. For those who are interested in deriving the "messages" of the film, this seems to be a significant one, especially when considering this film alongside Plato's "Allegory of the Cave."

Anderson/Neo/The One initially leads a boring life in the matrix, dissatisfied with his day job and interested in something more. He's also a hacker who shows a keen interest in a mysterious figure known only as Morpheus. A woman named Trinity (Carrie-Anne Moss) comes into Anderson's life and delivers him to Morpheus (Laurence Fishburne). Morpheus lets Anderson choose whether he will awaken to reality or remain ignorant and deluded in the familiar world of the matrix. From Morpheus, and with the support of Trinity and others, Anderson learns that what he views as his reality is actually a dream world induced by artificially intelligent beings that have taken over the world, and that use humans as an energy source. Anderson has spent his whole life in a womb-like vat, with his head plugged into the matrix: a computer-driven alternate world that only exists in the minds of those who are asleep and plugged into it. It is a world of appearances; a fake; a shadow world. The lives of all humans in the matrix, which includes most humans, is a total farce. They think they are living lives that matter, but it's all just an elaborate hoax perpetuated by evil beings who control their existence with the help of agents who easily overpower humans. The agents dominate humans by the cold, brute execution of robot-driven rules. Neo gradually learns not only the truth about his former fake existence, but also that he may be "The One"—namely, the person chosen to save humankind. After his initial awakening, Neo is in a highly unsettled state of shock, depicted in his vomiting scene. After settling down, Neo begins learning a lot in a very short time, and quickly demonstrates his uncanny ability to handle large doses of knowledge in the exponentially fast-paced learning environment that those aboard the Nebuchednezzar set up. The latter is the ship manned by those who are

JUSTICE
One of the four virtues central not only to Plato's virtue ethics, but also that of Aristotle and others; often called one of the "cardinal virtues"; the most discussed virtue of Plato's *Republic* and famously difficult to define; necessary for living a good life according to Plato's *Republic;* involves doing good toward oneself and others.

THE GOOD LIFE
The life well-led; the happy life, where happiness means more than mere amusement or enjoyment; the life of virtue.

SOUL
According to many ancient and medieval philosophers, the immaterial and immortal essence of a human being; According to Plato, it is composed of three aspects or characters: rational, spirited, and appetitive, in order from best to worst.

METAPHORS: SYMBOLS
Symbols; non-literal representations; example: "The Lord is my shepherd" does not mean that God is *literally* a shepherd and I am *literally* a sheep, but that God guides me and protects me in the manner that a shepherd does to his flock.

PHILOSOPHER
A person who studies philosophy; in Plato's *Republic,* someone who is in the highest class of the city and who rules the city; in Plato's *Republic,* someone who has undergone and succeeded at the most extensive, rigorous, and selective course of study possible; in Plato's *Republic* and other dialogues, a lover of wisdom.

WISDOM
One of the four virtues central not only to Plato's virtue ethics, but also to that of Aristotle and others; often called one of the "cardinal virtues"; not equivalent to knowledge, but bears an important relationship to it; necessary for living a good life according to Plato's *Republic.*

free, in that they are out of the matrix. Though he initially is not powerful enough to overcome Morpheus in their training simulations, by the end of the film, Neo gains the knowledge and ability not only to be superior to Morpheus, but to easily overpower the ever-present, seemingly unbeatable agents.

1.3 Introduction to Plato's Cave

Plato's allegory about the cave is arguably the most famous example of Plato's philosophical imagery, and it occurs in the middle books of the *Republic,* Plato's most famous work. The *Republic,* or "*Politeia*" in Greek, is a fictional dialogue depicting an all-night conversation of Socrates and his friends. It is written like a play, with some characters resembling real people, including Socrates and Glaucon.[6] The conversation really gets going when those who are present urge Socrates to discuss the nature of **justice**, and its relationship to **the good life**. In Book Two, Socrates proposes that they build an imaginary city, from scratch, designed to illustrate the nature of justice. (Instead of chapters, the dialogue is divided into "books.") The city starts off quite idyllic and quickly becomes rather disturbing. (357b–383c) Socrates seems to be doing this knowing that the city he's designing is far from ideal, replete with radical censorship, lies implemented by the government, and a eugenics program that includes not only government-induced public sex but the possibility of incest. Also, children whom people have outside the guidelines set by the rulers are either aborted or left to die. (373b–462a) While reading all of this, the reader is periodically reminded that this is a fictional city meant to illustrate the nature of justice. Why use such deviance to shed light on justice? Socrates tells us that the city is meant to be understood in relation to the human **soul**. (368c–369b) In other words, it is a kind of metaphor for justice and injustice in the soul. There may be good reason, then, not to take the political proposals as literal recommendations for constituting a real city, though there is great debate about this among scholars. Some or all of the political proposals very well may be elaborate **metaphors** that are not so devious when applied to an individual soul in a symbolic way.[7] The ruler of the city is supposed to be a **philosopher**—a lover of **wisdom**, which, when applied symbolically to the soul, seems to mean that wisdom or reason should govern one's psyche.

6. Glaucon, the character in Plato's *Republic,* is probably based on a real person: Plato's brother, who had the same name. The character plays a central role in the dialogue, initially by framing the argument in Book Two that prompts Socrates to create the hypothetical city. Later, Glaucon is Socrates's main interlocutor (conversation partner) in the "Allegory of the Cave." Plato portrays Glaucon as a friend to Socrates. The former is generally receptive to Socrates's arguments throughout the *Republic.*
7. Ancient interpreters of Plato were the first to read the work of Plato figuratively or allegorically. The following contemporary Plato scholars are just a few of many who stand by a symbolic or non-literal interpretation of parts or all of Plato's *Republic:* Eva Brann, *The Music of the Republic* (Philadelphia: Paul Dry Books, 2004); Martin Heidegger, "Plato's Doctrine of Truth," in Pathmarks, ed. William McNeill (Cambridge: Cambridge University Press, 1998); Stanley Rosen, *Plato's Republic: A Study* (New Haven: Yale University Press, 2008); Eric Voegelin, *Plato* (Columbia, MO: University of Missouri Press, 1957).

QUESTIONS FOR CONSIDERATION

a. Why is a philosopher best suited to lead others?
b. How does a philosopher come to be?
c. Taken figuratively, those questions can be re-phrased to read: (i) Why is reason, in the form of wisdom, best suited for ruling the soul, as opposed to its other components, like the emotions and base appetites? (ii.) How does one come to develop true wisdom?

BASE APPETITES
The desires for food, drink, and sex.

The "Allegory of the Cave," excerpted below, offers answers to these questions. It contains many metaphors. In this famous ancient story, a chained prisoner in a state of deep delusion about his own existence is set free and has a long and difficult journey to freedom and enlightenment, after which he is able to save others from ignorance and slavery. (*Republic* 514a–521b)[8]

© delcarmat/Shutterstock.com

1.4 Annotated Excerpts from Plato's "Allegory of the Cave"

(*The narrator is the character Socrates, who is the first to speak. The character to whom he is speaking is Glaucon.*)

> Imagine human beings living in an underground, cavelike dwelling, with an entrance a long way up, which is both open to the light and as wide as the cave itself. They've been there since childhood, fixed in the same place, with their necks and legs fettered, able to see only in front of them, because their bonds prevent them from turning their heads around. Light is provided by a fire

8. See Plato, Republic, trans. G. M. A. Grube (Indianapolis: Hackett, 1992). All page numbers appear in parentheses and as Stephanus page numbers. This is the method of citation that Plato scholars commonly use. It is useful for the reader in that they can find the exact page regardless of the translation they use. These page numbers are typically visible in the margins of the text. If the translation the reader chooses does not have such page numbers listed, it is advisable to select a different version.

burning far above and behind them. Also behind them, but on higher ground, there is a path stretching between them and the fire. Imagine that along this path a low wall has been built, like the screen in front of puppeteers above which they show their puppets.

I'm imagining it.

Then also imagine that there are people along the wall, carrying all kinds of artifacts that project above it—statues of people and other animals, made out of stone, wood, and every material. And, as you'd expect, some of the carriers are talking, and some are silent.

It's a strange image you're describing, and strange prisoners.

They're like us. Do you suppose, first of all, that these prisoners see anything of themselves and one another besides the shadows that the fire casts on the wall in front of them?

How could they, if they have to keep their heads motionless throughout life?

What about the things being carried along the wall? Isn't the same true of them?

Of course.

And if they could talk to one another, don't you think they'd suppose that the names they used applied to the things they see passing before them?

They'd have to.

And what if their prison also had an echo from the wall facing them? Don't you think they'd believe that the shadows passing in front of them were talking whenever one of the carriers passing along the wall was doing so?

I certainly do.

Then the prisoners would in every way believe that the truth is nothing other than the shadows of those artifacts.

They must surely believe that.

Consider, then, what being released from their bonds and cured of their ignorance would naturally be like if something like this came to pass. When one of them was freed and suddenly compelled to stand up, turn his head, walk, and look up toward the light, he'd be pained and dazzled and unable to see the things whose shadows he'd seen before. What do you think he'd say, if we told him that what he'd seen before was inconsequential, but that now—because he is a bit closer to **the things that are** and is turned towards **things that are more**—he sees more correctly? Or, to put it another way, if we pointed to each of the things passing by, asked him what each of them is, and compelled him to answer, don't you think he'd be at a loss and that he'd believe that the things he saw earlier were truer than the ones he was now being shown?

THE THINGS THAT ARE/THE THINGS THAT ARE MORE

In Plato's *Republic,* entities that are more real and true, and that occupy a higher level of being; often called "Ideas" or "Forms"; divine entities that serve as standards and causes; example: the "Form" of a circle is a perfect circle. It exists as a mental concept and is the standard against which all circles are judged. It is also the source of circularity for all things. The "Form" of a circle is more than any ordinary physical circle. It is an immaterial entity of a higher order of being. The examples from the *Republic* include the "Forms" of beauty, goodness, and justice.

Much truer.

And if someone compelled him to look at the light itself, wouldn't his eyes hurt, and wouldn't he turn around and flee towards the things he's able to see, believing that they're really clearer than the ones he's being shown?

He would.

© Yannick Martinez/Shutterstock.com

And if someone dragged him away from there by force, up the rough, steep path, and didn't let him go until he had dragged him into the sunlight, wouldn't he be pained and irritated at being treated that way? And when he came into the light, with the sun filling his eyes, wouldn't he be unable to see a single one of the things now said to be true?

He would be unable to see them, at least at first.

I suppose, then, that he'd need time to get adjusted before he could see things in the world above. At first, he'd see shadows most easily, then images of men and other things in water, then the things themselves. Of these, he'd be able to study the things in the sky and the sky itself more easily at night, looking at the light of the stars and moon, than during the day, looking at the sun and the light of the sun.

Of course.

Finally, I suppose, he'd be able to see the sun, not images of it in water or some alien place, but the sun itself, in its own place, and be able to study it.

Necessarily so.

And at this point he would infer and conclude that the sun provides the seasons and the years, governs everything in the visible world, and is in some way the cause of all the things that he used to see.

It's clear that would be his next step.

What about when he reminds himself of his first dwelling place, his fellow prisoners, and what passed for wisdom there? Don't you think that he'd count himself happy for the change and pity the others?

Certainly.

And if there had been any honors, praises, or prizes among them for the one who was sharpest at identifying the shadows as they passed by and who best remembered which usually came earlier, which later, and which simultaneously, and who could best divine the future, do you think that our man would desire these rewards or envy those among the prisoners who were honored and held power? Instead, wouldn't he feel, with Homer, that he'd much prefer to 'work the earth as a serf to another, one without possessions,' and go through any sufferings, rather than share their opinions and live as they do?

I suppose he would rather suffer anything than live like that.

Consider this too. If this man went down into the cave again and sat down in his same seat, wouldn't his eyes—coming suddenly out of the sun like that—be filled with darkness?

They certainly would.

And before his eyes had recovered—and the adjustment would not be quick—while his vision was still dim, if he had to compete again with the perpetual prisoners in recognizing the shadows, wouldn't he invite ridicule? Wouldn't it be said of him that he'd returned from his upward journey with his eyesight ruined and that it isn't worthwhile even to try to travel upward? And, as for anyone who tried to free them and lead them upward, if they could somehow get their hands on him, wouldn't they kill him?

They certainly would.

This whole image, Glaucon, must be fitted together with what we said before. The **visible realm** should be likened to the prison dwelling, and the light of the fire inside it to the power of **the sun**. And if you interpret the upward journey and the study of things above as the upward journey of the soul to the **intelligible realm**, you'll grasp what I hope to convey, since that is what you wanted to hear about. Whether it's true or not, only the god knows. But this is how I see it: In the **knowable realm**, the **form of the good** is the last thing to be seen, and it is reached only with difficulty. Once one has seen it, however, one must conclude that it is the cause of all that is correct and beautiful in anything, that it produces both light and its source in the visible realm, and that in the intelligible realm it controls and provides truth and understanding, so that anyone who is to act sensibly in private or public must see it. (514a–517c)

[. . .]

It is our task as founders, then, to compel the best natures to reach the study we said before is the most important, namely, to make the ascent and see the good. But when they've made it and looked sufficiently, we mustn't allow them to do what they're allowed to do today.

What's that?

To stay and refuse to go down again to the prisoners in the cave and share their labors and honors, whether they are of less worth or of greater. (519c–d)

[. . .]

(We'll say to them) each of you in turn must go down to live in the common dwelling place of the others and grow accustomed to seeing in the dark. When you are used to it, you'll see vastly better than the people there. And because you've seen the truth about fine, just, and good things, you'll know each image for what it is and also that of which it is the image. Thus, for you and for us, the city will be governed, not like the majority of cities nowadays, by people who fight over shadows and struggle against one another in order to rule—as if that were a great good—but by people who are awake rather than dreaming. . . (520c)[2]

VISIBLE REALM
That which is physically visible, with the human eye; anything we know about this realm only amounts to opinion and does not actually count as knowledge, according to Socrates in Plato's *Republic*.

THE SUN
The physical sun is a simile for the "Form" or "Idea" of the Good; just as the physical sun is the cause of so much in nature, as well as the source of light, the Good is the cause of beauty and truth.

INTELLIGIBLE/KNOWABLE REALM
That which is immaterial, mental, and invisible; where truly knowable objects—the "Forms" or "Ideas"—reside.

FORM OF THE GOOD
The Form of the Good is the source or cause of everything that exists; it makes truth knowable; it is divine and immaterial, as opposed to the physical sun; the "Form" or "Idea" that is superior to all others.

1.5 Plato's Cave in Relation to *The Matrix*

Plato's vivid set of metaphors above begins with a description of prisoners chained up deep down in the darkest part of a cave-like place. Their shackles not only bolt them to the ground, but they are designed to keep their whole bodies, including their heads, fixed facing one position for their whole lives. They face the cave wall, on which there is a kind of play happening, composed of shadows and complete with sound effects, all created by puppeteers at some distance behind the prisoners. The puppeteers' light source is a fire, presumably because they are too far into the cave to use sunlight. The prisoners think that the shadows in front of them are reality. This shadow show in the cave is what is real to the prisoners. For them, it is all that is real and true. The prisoners are completely ignorant of anything that may exist outside of it. Somehow, one of the prisoners is freed, turns around and sees what has been creating the shadows, and immediately wants to go back to the familiar world of slavery that he[3] came from. But, someone else—a guide; a teacher; perhaps a philosopher—turns the freed prisoner back around and drags him up a long, steep path with difficult terrain, until they are out of the cave. Once emerged into the real world, the prisoner needs time to adjust his eyes, and so, he views reality there by nightlight at first. Eventually, he is able to see the outside world in full sunlight, at which point he must be compelled to return to his original home among the prisoners and try to save them.

Socrates explicitly links this set of metaphors to those of the Sun (506b–509b) and **"The Divided Line,"** (509b–511e) which both occur in the preceding book of the *Republic.* (517a-b) The implication, then, is that the prisoners, when chained up, are in a state of ignorance, and at best, can engage in a sort of **conjecture** about the truth. Socrates dramatically portrays this by saying that they pass their time trying to guess what shapes will come next in the shadow show, giving out awards for those who guess the best. (516c–d) They are in a state of extreme delusion, just like everyone trapped in the matrix. Not only are they in a state of ignorance, but they are ignorant of their ignorance. They are merely the subjects of deviant masters, and they participate out of a narrow-mindedness induced by their nightmare-like existence as slaves. The prisoner who has just been freed, and who glimpses the puppet show that has been the source of his entire world until now, is like Anderson when he first meets Morpheus and initially boards the Nebuchednezzar. Both are out of their comfort zones—which is an understatement—and there is a strong urge to go back to what is perceived as safe and familiar—to blissful ignorance. It is at this stage that the prisoner and Neo are still ignorant of a great deal but are no longer deluded about their own ignorance. Urged on by their guides, they both move forward in their journey to knowledge and freedom, despite the perceived risks involved. Just as the prisoner has a long, difficult journey out of the cave, so does Neo in that he learns a great deal in a relatively short period of time and has to fight his way to **self-actualization**.

Once the escaped prisoner emerges from the cave, there is still an adjustment period to this new and unfamiliar world. The prisoner cannot view the landscape of the outside world in the full light of the Sun right away, so he navigates by moonlight (reflected sunlight). (516a–b) Similarly, Neo does not initially succeed in his battles with the agents. Even though he is done training and has begun his real trials, he still has doubts about the true nature of his existence. Just as the escapee no longer needs his guide once out of the cave, neither does Neo need Morpheus's intensive mentorship as he did earlier. Once the freed prisoner's eyes are adjusted to the moonlight in the outside world, he transitions to navigating the world of the real and true in the full light of the Sun. He eventually is able to gaze at the Sun itself. (516b) It is at this point that the allegory depicts the elimination of doubt and ignorance. It is also at this point that the escaped slave has achieved the greatest kind of knowledge possible: knowledge that is oriented to the source and summit of truth and goodness. In this way, the escapee-turned-philosopher has an enlightened

THE DIVIDED LINE
Socrates describes this **simile** at the end of Book Six, right before the "Allegory of the Cave." A line, divided into four unequal segments, represents four stages or levels of knowledge: conjecture, belief, thought, and contemplation, in order from lowest to highest. Knowledge of the physical world is really just opinion, represented in the two lowest levels: **conjecture** (baseless opinion) and belief (true opinion). The two higher levels represent knowledge, which is of the intelligible or immaterial. True knowledge transcends the physical world. What we can know in the truest sense is vast compared with what we can know about the physical world.

SIMILE
Symbol or representation that uses "like" or "as"; example: The sunlight is like the truth; just as the sunlight is the means by which all physical things are visible, the truth is the means by which all things are known.

SELF-ACTUALIZATION
Typically associated with modern psychology, indicating self-knowledge and fulfillment of individual potential.

perspective of all things. He has a comprehensive worldview. This enlightenment enables the former slave to return to the cave and save others. The philosopher who attains true wisdom is most capable of educating others, and of serving as a leader to others. This leader is happy when outside the cave, in that he despises his former way of life. (516d–e) However, others urge him to go back and be among those in extreme delusion to save them from their intellectual impoverishment. (519c–520e) While the man of wisdom tries to save others, the ignorant hate him and try to kill him. (517a) While wisdom has the power to make someone good and just, ignorance leads to injustice. Neo incrementally gains the enlightened perspective that he needs to have in order to defeat the agents. He has to undergo a sort of death in order to fully emerge as his true self, just as the escapee undergoes a sort of death when he firmly renounces his former way of life and expunges all doubt and ignorance from his soul. The climax of Neo's intellectual perspective coincides with the climax of his physical ability and his suitability to save mankind. This multifaceted climax is dramatically portrayed by his single-handed domination of Agent Smith (Hugo Weaving). Neo can stop bullets effortlessly, and he has an unmatched power to repulse the robotic forces that continuously try to enslave mankind. Though the enlightened thinker who returns to the cave does have a unique ability to save those trapped inside, he does not do so effortlessly. The task is difficult and the risks are great. In this way at least, there is not a perfect correspondence between the Wachowski's *The Matrix* and Plato's allegory. Nonetheless, by drawing out the many parallels between the two, one gains an enlightened perspective about the rich philosophical content of both.

The aspects of the cave story that convey ethical insights point to the central doctrine that knowledge and wisdom lead to the good life, which includes not only individual happiness, but goodness toward others.[9] Knowledge can save one's own soul and can enable one to save others. The ethical implications of *The Matrix* are similar. By emerging from delusion and renouncing ignorance, one can live an authentic life that involves a superior ability to help others. Whether everyone is destined to become the ultimate mentor and leader like the fully enlightened philosopher, or an all-powerful sage like Neo, remains in question. One notable feature of *The Matrix* on this topic is that it portrays other enlightened individuals who are not as great as Neo, but who have nonetheless emerged from complete ignorance and can play important roles in changing others' lives for the better. Cypher (Joe Pantoliano) memorably uses his position of power to betray his enlightened brothers and sisters for the benefit of the agents. It is eventually clear that this is to his own detriment. In this way, the film implies that knowledge does not always equal goodness. Just as the freed prisoner can turn back, so can we. Just as Cypher was able to use his ability for harm, so are we. The film and the allegory both imply **free will**. We are responsible for our choices, at least once we have the opportunity to be freed from intellectual slavery.

FREE WILL
Denotes the ability to make choices with some degree of independence from factors that might otherwise determine one to act in a certain way.

9. This is one conception of the virtue of justice offered in the *Republic*.

QUESTIONS FOR CONSIDERATION

a. Is it true that knowledge leads to goodness?
b. Do you prefer to live as an ignorant person in the cave/matrix, or as an enlightened individual?
c. Which character(s) in the "Allegory of the Cave," if any, correspond with the character of Cypher in *The Matrix*? Why? What does this correspondence possibly mean for us here and now?
d. Can *anyone* become a sage-savior like Neo and the philosopher when they have fully reached their true potential, or is this destiny only for "the One"?
e. Is everyone capable of emerging from their slave-like existence in the cave/matrix to become like those aboard the Nebuchadnezzar? Do you need to be a rebel to be free?
f. Is it always wrong to live in ignorance?
g. Is it ANY kind of learning that has the power to free us? Is there a difference between learning and indoctrination in this regard? Between information and knowledge?
h. Do we really have free will?
i. What is an intellectual life, compared to a life that is focused on the physical?
j. When is Neo just receiving information, and when is he starting to really gain knowledge?

INDOCTRINATION
Similar to brainwashing; a method of persuasion that eliminates free thought.

1.6 James Cameron's *Avatar*

Another film that speaks to these ethical themes is James Cameron's *Avatar* (2009).

The main character, Jake Sully (Sam Worthington), is a paraplegic veteran of the US Marine Corps who is sent to Pandora, a distant planet in a distant future. Jake is to fill his dead brother's shoes in a mission to extract a natural resource ("unobtanium") and bring it back to Earth, which has been depleted of its own natural resources. The mission has a component that involves a partnership between a corporate entity and the US military, as well as a second, more diplomatic, component composed of experts on the biology and culture of Pandora. Jake becomes a part of the latter, though he seriously lacks their knowledge and training. Jake and his team get hooked up to MRI-like machines that enable human minds to occupy and control avatars.[10] The latter resemble the natives of Pandora—the Na'vi—in body size, general shape, and skin color, but their faces incorporate facial features of the humans piloting them. The human pilot's body lies down and enters a sleeping state in its dream machine, while the human mind roams Pandora embodied as an avatar capable of living among the natives. Those in the military wing of the human operation see the natives as savages deserving of human domination, while the diplomatic wing, including Dr. Grace Augustine (Sigourney Weaver), champions a nuanced, more comprehensive understanding of the value of Na'vi life. This is perhaps afforded by the perspective they gain by being able to live among the natives. Dr. Grace Augustine and her teammate Norm Spellman (Joel David Moore) discern an elaborate network of neural connections between the Na'vi and the life forms of Pandora. We learn that the Na'vi are highly intelligent and have a

10. Avatars = Alternate identities; representations of identity that diverge from the latter but that might bear some resemblance to it.

©Justyna Sobesto/Shutterstock.com

well-developed culture that centers around a deeply rooted harmony with nature. The corporate/militant humans remain blinded to this truth because of their limited perspective, which focuses only on the physical appearance of the Na'vi, rather than their unique intelligence and culture. Colonel Miles Quaritch (Stephen Lang) initially befriends Jake, and Jake expresses his sympathy to the Colonel's military perspective. Through a difficult journey from ignorance to knowledge—both about himself and the natives of Pandora—Jake Sully decides to renounce the ways of the Colonel and the corporate boss, Parker Selfridge (Giovanni Ribisi). Jake's decision is due in large part to the imminent threat the Na'vi face from the humans, as well as Jake's love for Neytiri, a Na'vi (Zoe Saldana). As an avatar, Jake fought against the humans to try and save the Na'vi. Like the freed prisoner who returns to the cave to save others, Jake does so at great risk to his life. Ultimately, Jake is essentially killed for his decision. However, through a spiritual ritual, Jake's **mind**/soul is reborn in his avatar, while his human body remains dead.[11]

MIND
In ancient and medieval philosophy it is similar in many ways to the soul, as opposed to the brain; different from but related to the body in various ways, depending on the philosopher.

Like Neo, Jake is reborn. Like Neo and the freed prisoner, Jake chooses a life of truth and goodness, rather than deception and evil, all as a result of the tortuous journey from delusion to self-awareness. Transitioning from tunnel vision to comprehensive vision, and from conjecture to wisdom, Jake is reborn as a better version of himself. On the surface, he experiences physical improvements in that he is no longer a paraplegic, but upon deeper reflection, one can discern that the more substantial improvement is in his intellect. He opens his mind to a way of living that is humble in relation to nature, rather than dominating (see Chapter Seven for more on this theme). Rather than manipulating and consuming natural resources with ever-larger machines as the physically focused humans do, the Na'vi live in a way that is guided by their minds and their extensively complex interconnectedness toward harmony with nature.

11. An excellent philosophical text on the distinction between the mind and body, and the subjection of the latter to the former, is Rene Descartes's *Meditations on First Philosophy.*

QUESTIONS FOR CONSIDERATION

a. Is Jake Sully a rebellious traitor, or a savior? Or both?
b. What does *The Matrix* suggest about the power of the mind? *Avatar?*

1.7 Resources for Further Study

1.7.1 Links to Free Versions of Plato's *Republic*

a. Highly recommended:

A translation, accompanied by a Greek edition and an authoritative commentary are freely available through Perseus Project:

Plato. *Plato in Twelve Volumes,* Vols. 5 & 6. Translated by Paul Shorey. Cambridge: Harvard University Press, 1969. http://www.perseus.tufts.edu/hopper/text?doc=Perseus%3Atext%3A1999.01.0168%3Abook%3D1

b. Recommended:

Plato. *Republic.* Translated by Francis MacDonald Cornford. Oxford: Oxford University Press, 1941. http://faculty.smcm.edu/jwschroeder/Web/ETHR1002/Global_Jutice_Readings_files/3.PlatoRepblic.pdf

c. Not recommended: The many free versions of the Jowett translation available.

1.7.2 Recommended Print Translations of the *Republic*

a. Plato. *Republic.* Translated by Allan Bloom. New York: Basic Books, 1968.
b. Plato. *Republic.* Translated by G. M. A. Grube, rev. C. D. C. Reeve. Indianapolis: Hackett, 1992.
c. Plato. *Republic.* Translated by G. M. A. Grube, rev. C. D. C. Reeve. In *Plato. Complete Works,* edited by John M. Cooper, 971–1223. Indianapolis: Hackett, 1997.

Endnotes

1. All information about the film's actors and production details is from IMDb: https://www.imdb.com/title/tt0133093/
2. Plato, *Republic,* trans. G. M. A. Grube, 186–192.
3. The use of masculine pronouns here is simply for the sake of convenience, in that it mirrors the language Plato uses. Women are by no means excluded from Plato's allegory though. In fact, in the *Republic,* Plato depicts Socrates and his friends agreeing that women can serve alongside men in the running of the city. (451d–457c) Other chapters in this book will favor feminine pronouns and feature female authors more prominently.

Chapter 2

Aristotle's Virtue Ethics through Film

2.1 Introduction

Aristotle's works on ethics have one main goal: to show the reader how to live a happy life. To do so, a person must develop the habits of character that form the basis of virtue. One key indication that a person has developed the right character is their ability to face hardships and misfortune. Another is that their life is enriched with friends who are as good as they are themselves.[1]

Aristotle[2] wrote several significant works on ethics, the most notable and authoritative of which is his *Nicomachean Ethics*, which bears the name of both his father and his son. Unlike Plato's ethics, a student can grasp the essentials of Aristotle's work on the topic by focusing intensively on this single text. The authority and comprehensiveness of the *Nicomachean Ethics* are so well accepted that it is customary to refer to it simply as Aristotle's *Ethics*. Aristotle's writing style is not as dramatic and poetic as Plato's. Unlike his teacher Plato, who wrote dialogues, Aristotle wrote in treatise form, which means that his work is a series of arguments for his claims. Though some scholars regard the *Ethics* as a compilation of notes taken by his best students, each chapter contains such logically arranged arguments on so many relevant topics, many scholars agree that one can read and re-read this text for a lifetime while constantly being delighted by its nuances. Simultaneously, Aristotle's main lessons are accessible to the intelligent first-time reader, and it has a great deal to offer for *any* student, regardless of their level of expertise in ancient philosophy. These are all among the reasons why many consider *Nicomachean Ethics* to be a "**great book**," like Plato's *Republic,* which is discussed in Chapter One.

GREAT BOOK
Though many associate this term with the "Great Books" movement championed by Mortimer Adler, many others (including this textbook) simply use this term to refer to classic texts that have stood the test of time and are widely regarded as life-changing in their effects on readers. Such books are conducive to re-reading because of their depth of insight and other factors. Nearly all of the excerpts in this textbook are from such books. Recommendations for further reading, including links to free versions, are in place to encourage the reader to explore these perennially relevant texts more deeply.

1. Special thanks to reviewer William Wians for the wording of this opening and helpful recommendations throughout.
2. Please see the appendix for information about Aristotle, ancient Greece, and ancient philosophy.

Among the multitude of rich topics from the *Ethics* that one can gain insight to through film, this chapter first focuses on the role of habit in the formation of virtue, and the significant way in which virtue contributes to happiness. Next, the chapter treats Aristotle's account of friendship, including its relationship to the virtue of justice. The final sections consider the nature of vice according to Aristotle.

2.2 The Virtuous Life of Forrest Gump

Though it is not *essential* to watch *Forrest Gump* in order to follow the next few sections of the chapter, the upcoming sections contain spoilers. The reader is advised to view the film before reading further in order to achieve the fullest possible experience of this chapter. Locate the film on streaming platforms by going to a site like justwatch.com. While watching, consider the following questions: a. Is Forrest a good man? Why or why not? b. Is he brave? c. Does he have good relationships with his friends? d. Does he deserve to be successful? Why or why not?

© Anton_Ivanov/Shutterstock.com

Directed by Robert Zemeckis, and starring Tom Hanks, *Forrest Gump* (1994)[1] portrays the life of a man with below average IQ who far exceeds society's expectations of him by developing virtuous habits and living by simple mantras of practical wisdom: "Stupid is as stupid does." "Life is like a box of chocolates. You never know what you're gonna get." Though he is neither the politician Aristotle idealizes, nor the god-like sage who lives a life of theoretical wisdom, it is clear that Forrest Gump resembles many essential features of Aristotle's theory of the virtuous person.

Forrest develops virtuous habits so well that he becomes an All-American college football star, a celebrated ping-pong player, and a famous cross-country runner. He maintains several meaningful friendships throughout his life, doing such good for his friends that their relationship with him sustains them, even in times of extraordinary adversity.

© Keith Tarrier/Shutterstock.com

Though dismissed by many critics as superficial and sentimental when it was first released, *Forrest Gump* illustrates, sometimes to a surprising degree, main themes from Aristotle's ethics. As we shall see, Forrest has the virtue of justice, in that he does good for others by loving them as his friends. Forrest bears his own misfortune well. He doesn't allow it to ruin his life. He manages wealth with excellence, exhibiting the virtue of generosity. Perhaps most notable is the courage Forrest displays on his tour in Vietnam, earning him the Medal of Honor for saving many of his fellow soldiers.

2.3 Annotated Excerpts from *Nicomachean Ethics*

The following excerpts provide an elementary sketch of Aristotle's conception of happiness as well as four of the virtues that constitute a happy, or blessed, life.

2.3.1 An Account of Happiness: Book One, Chapters Seven and Ten[2]

Chapter Seven

[. . .]

[. . .] The chief good is evidently something final. Therefore, if there is only one final end, this will be what we are seeking, and if there are more than one, the most final of these will be what we are seeking. (1097a)

The page number in parentheses is a "Bekker" number, corresponding to a widely accepted, standardized pagination of Aristotle's Greek text. Such a standardized, official system enables readers of different translations to refer to passages efficiently and effectively. Both translations used in this chapter, and any good translation, lists the Bekker page numbers throughout the text, usually in the margins, in addition to pagination specific to the edition.

END
Goal; as opposed to a means.

[. . .]

Now such a thing happiness, above all else, is held to be; for this we choose always for itself and never for the sake of something else, but honour,[3] pleasure, reason, and every virtue we choose indeed for themselves (for if nothing resulted from them we should still choose each of them), but we choose them also for the sake of happiness, judging that by means of them we shall be happy. (1097a–1097b)

[. . .]

For just as for a flute-player, a sculptor, or any artist, and in general, for all things that have a function or activity, the good and the 'well' is thought to reside in the function, so it would seem to be for a human being,[4] if he has a function. [. . .] What, then, can this be? Life seems to be common even to plants, but we are seeking what is peculiar to a human being. Let us exclude, therefore, the life of nutrition and growth. Next there would be a life of perception, but it also seems to be common even to the horse, the ox, and every animal. There remains, then, an active life of the element that has a rational principle. [. . .] Now if the function of a human being is an activity of the soul which follows or implies a rational principle, [. . .] and the function

3. Ross uses British spelling, which occasionally differs from American spelling, as in the case of the word "honor."

4. Wians, in correspondence with me, recommends the translation "human being" instead of "man," which Ross uses here and elsewhere.

of a good human being to be the good and noble performance of these (actions), [. . .] human good turns out to be activity of the soul in accordance with virtue [. . .].

But we must add 'in a complete life.' For one swallow does not make a summer, nor does one day; and so too one day, or a short time, does not make a human being blessed or happy. (1097b–1098a)

> Besides "noble," another good defining word for virtue is "excellence." In fact, it may aid one's understanding of the translation to mentally substitute "excellence" for "nobility."
>
> Notice that Aristotle has led up to this **conclusion** through a series of supporting claims, or **premises**. The premises and conclusion together form an **argument**.

CONCLUSION
The main point of the argument; its main claim; the statement that is the logical result of the premises; the statement or proposition the premises claim to support.

PREMISES
The statements or propositions being claimed to support the conclusion; an argument must have at least one of these, but it can also have many more.

ARGUMENT
At its core, according to logicians, is at least one statement or proposition being claimed to support another one; note that this is much different from the definition of this term in normal, everyday English.

PROPOSITION
Synonymous with "statement," it is a claim that may or may not occur as a complete sentence; an argument contains at least two propositions: a premise and a conclusion; one proposition on its own does not constitute an argument.
Example A: All wars are unfortunate.
Example B: In light of the fact that all wars are unfortunate, . . .

> Aristotle defines happiness, then, as the activity of the soul in line with reason exercised over a complete life. He later adds that it requires sufficient external goods, like basic necessities for living. (1097a–1099b) This conception of happiness is much different from what we moderns often mean by the word. Other modern English equivalents may include "flourishing" or "well-being." Another notable addition is: "All who are not maimed as regards their potentiality for virtue may win it by a certain study and care." (1099b) This implies that someone like Forrest Gump, who lacks some natural intelligence, but who is not "maimed" in their ability to be virtuous, may achieve it with effort according to Aristotle.

[. . .]

Chapter Ten

[. . .]

[. . .] (The happy human being) will bear the chances of life most nobly and altogether decorously, if he is 'truly good' [. . .]

Now many events happen by chance, and events differing in importance; small pieces of good fortune or of its opposite clearly do not weigh down the scales of life one way or the other, but a multitude of great events if they turn out well will make life happier (for not only are they themselves such as to add beauty to life, but the way a human being deals with them may be noble and good), while if they turn out ill they crush and maim happiness; for they both bring pain with them and hinder many activities. Yet even in these nobility shines through, when a human being bears with resignation many great misfortunes, not through insensibility to pain but through nobility and greatness of soul.[5] (1100b)

[. . .]

5. A synonym for "greatness of soul" is magnanimity, which is the virtue of doing good on a large scale. It might be interesting to investigate Aristotle's treatment of this virtue in Book Four to see whether it accurately describes Forrest Gump.

QUESTIONS FOR CONSIDERATION

a. Does Forrest Gump live a happy life, according to Aristotle's conception of happiness above?
b. Do you agree with Aristotle that many major misfortunes ruin one's ability to be happy? Consider someone like Socrates, Jesus, or Gandhi. Two related films include *Jesus of Nazareth* (1977) and *Gandhi* (1982).

2.3.2 An Account of Virtue General, Including Remarks about Temperance and Courage

Excerpts from *Nicomachean Ethics* Book Two, Chapters One, Two, and Three[3]

Chapter One

[. . .]

[. . .] The virtues arise in us neither by nature nor against nature. Rather, we are by nature able to acquire them, and we are completed through habit.

[. . .] Virtues, [. . .] we acquire, just as we acquire crafts, by having first activated them. For we learn a craft by producing the same product that we must produce when we have learned it; we become builders, for instance, by building, and we become harpists by playing the harp. Similarly, then, we become just by doing just actions, temperate by doing temperate actions, brave by doing brave actions. (1103a–1103b)

[. . .]

[. . .] To sum it up in a single account: a state [of character] results from [the repetition of] similar activities. (1103b)[6]

[. . .]

QUESTIONS FOR CONSIDERATION

a. Does Forrest exemplify one who develops excellence through the repetition of similar activities (that is, "habit")? Why or why not?
b. Do you agree with Aristotle that virtue is acquired and not something we are born with? Consider virtuosos.
c. What is more important in developing expertise? Inborn talent or practice? Nature or nurture?

Chapter Two

[. . .]

[. . .] Both excessive and deficient exercise ruin bodily strength, and, similarly, too much or too little eating or drinking ruins health, whereas the proportionate amount produces, increases, and preserves it.

6. Another film to consider, which comically portrays the relationship between repetition, virtue, and happiness, is *Groundhog Day* (1993).

The same is true, then, of temperance, bravery, and the other virtues. For if, for instance, someone avoids and is afraid of everything, standing firm against nothing, he becomes cowardly; if he is afraid of nothing at all and goes to face everything, he becomes rash. Similarly, if he gratifies himself with every pleasure and abstains from none, he becomes intemperate; if he avoids them all, as boors do, he becomes some sort of insensible human being. Temperance and bravery, then, are ruined by excess and deficiency, but preserved by the mean. (1104a)

QUESTION FOR CONSIDERATION

a. Do you agree with Aristotle that excess and deficiency ruin strength and health? Consider bodybuilders, professional athletes, and Olympians. NB: Aristotle explains in Book Two, Chapter Six that the mean in virtue is relative, meaning that what counts as intermediate differs from person to person. For example, what seems like excessive eating or training to a normal person will not be extreme to a world-class athlete.

BRAVERY
The virtue of courage; consists in the attainment of a mean between fear and confidence; best exemplified by a soldier facing death with the proper mixture of caution and boldness.

TEMPERANCE
The virtue of moderation; consists in a mean between excess and deficiency with regard to bodily appetites according to Aristotle; involves, for instance, eating the right amount of the right food at the right time consistently, and feeling pleasure while doing so.

VICE
The complete opposite of virtue; worse than incontinence because the person with this character no longer feels pained about their evil ways; they may even wrongfully assume that vice is good, because they feel pleasure (albeit passing) doing it. Such a person may be incurable and beyond all hope, though this is not necessarily the case for all vicious people, according to Aristotle.

Chapter Three

But we must take someone's pleasure or pain following on his actions to be a sign of his state. For if someone who abstains from bodily pleasures enjoys abstinence itself, he is temperate; if he is grieved by it, he is intemperate. Again, if he stands firm against terrifying situations and enjoys it, or at least does not find it painful, he is brave; if he finds it painful, he is cowardly. [. . .]

For pleasure causes us to do base actions, and pain causes us to abstain from fine ones. That is why we need to have had the appropriate upbringing—right from early youth, as Plato says—to make us find enjoyment or pain in the right things; for this is the correct education. (1104b)

[. . .]

Virtue, then, according to Aristotle is acquired through habit, and is a mean (intermediate or mid-point) between an excess and a deficiency. The two examples he gives so far are temperance (moderation) and courage (bravery). Temperance is a mean between excess and deficiency in that it is temperate not to eat or drink too much or too little, but just the right amount. The same would go for other bodily appetites like sex. Courage is a mean in that if we are rash (overconfident, fearless, not careful, very angry), we are not courageous, just as if we are cowardly (overly fearful and cautious). Being brave then is an intermediate between rashness and cowardice. Furthermore, a sign that we really have one of these virtues is that we feel pleasure, or at least are not pained, when we exercise it. If it feels good to eat the right amount, for instance, then that is a sign of temperance. If one takes pleasure, however, in eating the wrong amount, then that is a sign that pleasure has corrupted one's development of the virtue of temperance. It is a sign of vice, which in this case is intemperance.

QUESTIONS FOR CONSIDERATION

a. Does Forrest have an upbringing conducive to virtue, in Aristotle's sense of the word? Why or why not?
b. Does Forrest experience pleasure when he displays his virtue, or is he pained when he does so? What does your answer to this indicate about whether or not Aristotle would consider him to be truly virtuous?

2.3.3 Generosity: Excerpts from *Nicomachean Ethics* Book Four, Chapter One[4]

Next let us discuss generosity. It seems, then, to be the mean about wealth [. . .].

Both wastefulness and ungenerosity are excesses and deficiencies about wealth. Ungenerosity is always ascribed to those who take wealth more seriously than is right. [. . .] (1119b)

[. . .]

Whatever has a use can be used either well or badly; riches are something useful; and the best user of something is the person who has the virtue concerned with it. Hence the best user of riches will be the person who has the virtue concerned with wealth; and this is the generous person.

Using wealth seems to consist in spending and giving, whereas taking and keeping seem to be possessing rather than using. That is why it is more proper to the generous person to give to the right people than to take from the right sources and not from the wrong sources.

[. . .] Moreover, thanks go to the one who gives, not to the one who fails to take, and praise goes more [to the giver]. Besides, not taking is easier than giving, since people part with what is their own less readily than they avoid taking what is another's. [. . .]

Actions in accord with virtue are fine, and aim at the fine. Hence the generous person will also aim at the fine in his giving, and will give correctly; for he will give to the right people, the right amounts, at the right time, and all the other things that are implied by correct giving. Moreover, he will do this with pleasure, or at any rate without pain; for action in accord with virtue is pleasant or at any rate painless, and least of all is it painful. (1120a)

[. . .]

QUESTIONS FOR CONSIDERATION

a. Is Forrest generous, according to Aristotle's conception of the term?
b. What do you think about Aristotle's statement that taking wealth too seriously is a deviation from generosity, and hence, vicious? Consider *The Wolf of Wall Street* (2013) and/or *A Christmas Carol* (1951).

2.3.4 Friendship: Excerpts from *Nicomachean Ethics* Book Eight, Chapters One, Two, and Three[5]

Chapter One

[. . .]

[. . .] The justice that is most just seems to belong to friendship. (1155a)

[. . .]

Chapter Two

[. . .]

[. . .] Friendship is said to be reciprocated goodwill.

[. . .] Friends are aware of the reciprocated goodwill. (1155b)

> Reciprocation—equality—is necessary for friendship. Real friendships are not one-sided or parasitical according to Aristotle. This is part of the reason why friendship exemplifies the virtue of justice.

Chapter Three

[. . .] Friendship has three species, corresponding to the three objects of love. For each object of love has a corresponding mutual kind of loving, combined with awareness of it.

But those who love each other wish goods to each other [only] insofar as they love each other. Those who love each other for utility love the other not in his own right, but insofar as they gain some good for themselves from him. The same is true of those who love for pleasure; for they like a witty person not because of his character, but because he is pleasant to them.

> Neither one of these kinds of friendship is exemplified well by an erotic or romantic relationship according to Aristotle. He considers such relationships to be prone to inequality, and equality or reciprocity is a necessary condition for all three types of friendship discussed here. It's important to keep in mind, then, that he's not focusing on sexual relationships in these excerpts.

Those who love for utility or pleasure, then, are fond of a friend because of what is good or pleasant for themselves, not insofar as the beloved is who he is, but insofar as he is useful or pleasant. Hence these friendships as well [as the friends] are coincidental, since the beloved is loved not insofar as he is who he is, but insofar as he provides some good or pleasure.

And so these sorts of friendships are easily dissolved, when the friends do not remain similar [to what they were]; for if someone is no longer pleasant or useful, the other stops loving him. (1156a)

> Though these first two types of friendship are inferior to the third kind, they are still good, and are still important for living a happy life, with the friendship of pleasure out-ranking that of utility. By "utility," he doesn't mean "using" someone in the way we normally use that term.

JUSTICE
The virtue of character that involves giving what is owed or ensuring that people have what they deserve. Often considered one of the four "cardinal" virtues (along with temperance, bravery, and wisdom), Aristotle treats this virtue extensively not just in Book Eight, but in Book Five.

TEMPERANCE
The virtue of moderation; consists in a mean between excess and deficiency with regard to bodily appetites according to Aristotle; involves, for instance, eating the right amount or the right food at the right time consistently, and feeling pleasure while doing so.

BRAVERY
The virtue of courage; consists in the attainment of a mean between fear and confidence; best exemplified by a soldier facing death with the proper mixture of caution and boldness.

WISDOM
For Aristotle, there are at least two main kinds: practical and theoretical. The practical kind, known as prudence, involves the application of knowledge and is critical to attaining virtues of character like temperance and bravery. For instance, knowing that lean meat is better for one's health than fatty meat aids one in the attainment of moderate eating habits. Theoretical wisdom is the highest kind of wisdom and is god-like according to Aristotle. It is akin to contemplation and does not involve the application of knowledge. Rather, it considers knowledge that is valuable in and of itself. Note that knowledge and wisdom are not the same thing according to Aristotle.

QUESTION FOR CONSIDERATION

a. There are a series of premises here resulting in the conclusion that friendships of utility and pleasure are easily dissolved. Can you identify and number the premises? Hint: one occurs after the conclusion.

[. . .]

[. . .] But complete friendship is the friendship of good people similar in virtue; for they wish goods in the same way to each other insofar as they are good, and they are good in their own right. [Hence they wish good to each other for each other's own sake.] Now those who wish goods to their friend for the friend's own sake are friends most of all; for they have this attitude because of the friend himself, not coincidentally. Hence these people's friendship lasts as long as they are good; and virtue is enduring.

Each of them is both good without qualification and good for his friend, since good people are both good without qualification and advantageous for each other. They are pleasant in the same ways too [. . .].

It is reasonable that this sort of friendship is enduring, since it embraces in itself all the features that friends must have. [. . .]

These kinds of friendships are likely to be rare, since such people are few. Further, they need time as well, to grow accustomed to each other [. . .] (1156b)

b. Aristotle argues here for the conclusion that this third type of friendship is the best one. Can you identify and number the premises in Aristotle's argument? All of them form the substantial list of criteria that must be fulfilled for a friendship to fit the description of this third kind. This is complete or true friendship—friendship in its fullest sense.

Chapter Four

[. . .]

[. . .] The same people do not become friends for both utility and pleasure. For things that [merely] coincide with each other are not very regularly combined. (1157a)

QUESTIONS FOR CONSIDERATION

a. What kind of friendship would Aristotle say Forrest has with Bubba? With Lt. Dan? With Jenny?
b. Do you agree with Aristotle that there are three main kinds of friendship? Why or why not?

c. Do you have friendships in your own life that fit the criteria for any of the primary kinds of friendship according to Aristotle? If so, which ones have improved or enhanced your life the most? Why?
d. Do you think it's possible to develop any of the types of friendship above through social media? Is in-person interaction necessary for any of them? For all of them? Is it beneficial but not necessary? Why or why not?
e. Do you think that the third kind of friendship (the best one) correlates at all with the modern conception of a long-term, committed romantic relationship?

2.4 *Nicomachean Ethics* and *Forrest Gump*

Forrest Gump employs basic reason[7] in his efforts to develop virtues and live a happy life. He fulfills this important component of Aristotle's definition of happiness from Book One, Chapter One above. He also resembles the happy person in that he bears misfortune very well, and does not let it ruin his life. When Bubba (Mikyelti Williamson) dies in battle, Forrest mourns him but then turns to ping-pong, becoming an international star. When Jenny (Robin Wright) leaves him abruptly after they express their love for one another, Forrest runs, and he becomes famous for this too. However, viewers of the film do not get to see Gump's entire life, and Aristotle adds the significant qualifier to his conception of happiness, that one can only be pronounced happy once one's life is complete.

QUESTION FOR CONSIDERATION

a. The question still remains then, did Forrest Gump lead a life of happiness in the Aristotelian sense?[8]

In real life, one does not become a collegiate athlete simply from inborn talent, but the playful montage in the film might give one the impression that Forrest Gump does. He definitely has a natural talent for running, but it is arguable that only after executing this talent repeatedly throughout his early life that his running ability earns him a place on a college football team, and eventually to stardom. Aristotle argues that virtue is acquired, not inborn, in Book Two, Chapter One above.

7. That is, a level of reason attainable by the vast majority of adults, regardless of education; Aristotle wants happiness to be widely attainable, rather than just available to elites who reach enlightenment. He seems to think the latter is a drawback of Plato's ethics, and so, if one can argue successfully that Forrest attains happiness in the Aristotelian sense, Aristotle is vindicated in a way.
8. To fully answer this question, one needs to consider not only the excerpts above, but also Aristotle's discussion of external goods in Book One, Chapter Eight.

b. Does Forrest Gump become a great runner through practice, through natural talent, or both? What does this mean for the correspondence between the film and Aristotle's *Ethics*?

Later in life, Gump uses his running ability to cope with the devastation of Jenny's abrupt departure, and once again does it with such persistence and regularity over such a long period of time that he runs across the entire continental United States several times! He inspires many others with his dedication.[9]

© Catuncia/Shutterstock.com

© jdross75/Shutterstock.com

While in recovery from a bullet wound sustained in the Vietnam War, Forrest receives a comically simple set of instructions about how to play ping-pong. Zemeckis employs another montage to show the progression from Forrest's initial discovery of his natural ability for ping-pong, to his repetitive, mind-numbing practice regimen, to his impressive displays against Chinese players on the international stage for this sport. *Forrest Gump* convincingly illustrates what Aristotle's *Ethics* argues: that diligent practice over a long period of time is necessary for success.

Forrest develops and exhibits the virtue of courage during his Vietnam War service. He follows Lieutenant Dan Taylor's (Gary Sinise) orders dutifully, without being overly cautious and fearful on the one hand, and without being rash and overconfident on the other. In this way, he hits the proper mean between extremes and exhibits courage according to Aristotle in Book Two, Chapter One above. Forrest steadily marches through the jungle with his comrades, knowing that danger can strike at any time. When someone is needed to check a potentially lethal tunnel, Lt. Dan calls Gump over, and Forrest obeys dutifully and calmly. When they walk into an ambush, sustaining many casualties, Private Gump retreats, but returns several times to bring the wounded to safety. He sustains a bullet wound to his buttocks in the process, but he does not allow it to stop him. At least part of the reason for this is that he thinks "something bit" him. One could call his courage into question here, in that he was not fully aware that he had been shot. So the case could be made that he did not knowingly face the possibility of death with regard to this particular aspect of the situation. One could also question his courage because Lt. Dan asks him not to save him, but only to save himself. Perhaps Gump's return to the active battle scene after this, knowing that an air strike is imminent, counts as rash. However, the film portrays his subsequently being lauded as a hero and receiving the Medal of Honor.

9. Thereby showing an aspect of the relationship between excellence and leadership, which Aristotle treats in Chapters Ten and Eleven of Book Eight, not excerpted above.

c. **Given all of this, does Forrest Gump satisfy Aristotle's requirements for courage?[10] Why or why not?**
d. **What is your assessment of Aristotle's definition of courage?**

Forrest does not complain. He does not whine. In fact, he often seems content, and even pleased, with his virtuous actions. He therefore exhibits an important characteristic of the virtuous person, according to Book Two, Chapter Three above: that one feels pleasure, or at least does not experience pain, while doing virtuous things. Even after sustaining his bullet wound, which clearly hurts initially, Forrest focuses on the positive aspects of the situation: the ice cream and the White House visit!

Forrest Gump is generous. When he becomes rich through a series of fortunate coincidences, he views his wealth as a means to satisfy the problem of needing money to live. Since he has what he needs in order to live the simple life he desires, he gives the rest of the money away. He clearly satisfies the criterion of not taking wealth too seriously (Book Four, Chapter One above). Also, he gives money to Bubba's family because he believes he owes it to his fallen comrade, who inspired Forrest's shrimp business, through which Forrest became rich. It changes Bubba's family's life for the better. As always, he feels pleasure doing this, which is an indicator that he possesses the virtue of generosity.

e. **The question remains: Does Forrest give the right amount, for the right reasons, to the right people (see Book Four, Chapter One above)? Why or why not?**

Gump's friendships with Jenny and Bubba begin similarly, when Jenny and Bubba give Forrest the dignity of moving over so that he has somewhere to sit on the bus. In this sense, the two fulfill a need of Forrest's, not just for a space on the bus, but for acceptance. Bubba's actions in this regard are particularly poignant, given the setting and the characters' backgrounds: Jim Crow laws were in effect not long before the two encounter one another, and Forrest is named after a famous KKK leader. Yet Bubba, an African American man from the southern US who has probably experienced racial oppression for his own life, moves over and gives Forrest a seat next to him. The bus, furthermore, prompts one call to mind Rosa Parks and her famous fight against segregation. Bubba clearly needs someone to talk to and lean on, and Forrest does those things for him. Jenny, in turn, needs Forrest's companionship, stability, and kindness.

10. In order to answer this question fully, one needs to consider not only the excerpts above, but Aristotle's further treatment of courage in Book Three, Chapters Six through Nine.

f. Would these relationships count as friendships of utility according to Aristotle (Book Eight, Chapter One above)?

In both relationships, the parties enjoy one another's company, thus resembling the friendship of pleasure. Additionally, Jenny becomes a better person because of Forrest, and he learns about romantic love because of her. Whether or not this relationship, or any that Gump develops, counts as a true or complete friendship in the Aristotelian sense, is difficult to say. According to Aristotle, both parties in such a friendship are good people, and they make each other more virtuous. It is not clear whether Jenny is good in the Aristotelian sense, nor is it clear that she makes Forrest more virtuous.

g. Does Jenny leaving Forrest make him more virtuous, because it prompts him to run? If so, is this one way that she makes Forrest a better person?[11]

Jenny is the one who initially urges Forrest to run as a child, after all. True friendships take a long time to develop, last a long time, and are very rare according to Aristotle. These qualifications seem to fit Gump's relationships with Jenny and Bubba.

h. Is Jenny a virtuous person, in the Aristotelian sense? Bubba? Lt. Dan? Forrest Gump's mother?
i. Considering the lives of Forrest Gump and his friends, does one need to attain the level of knowledge required to emerge from "the cave" into "the sunlight" (see Chapter One) in order to become virtuous? In order to lead others? To be truly happy?
j. Does Forrest's relationship with Jenny fully satisfy Aristotle's criteria for a true friendship?
k. What about his friendship with Bubba?
l. His friendship with Lt. Dan?[12]

In any case, it is clear that Forrest develops friendships that resemble the primary kinds Aristotle identifies, and therefore, Mr. Gump could accurately be described as just in the Aristotelian sense.

11. Wians, in a correspondence with me, prompts the reader to deeper reflection, saying: "Yes, he runs after she leaves, and so in a sense because she leaves. But he does not embrace running as a good in itself until later. There's a very Aristotelian point here about how something external could be internalized."
12. To answer these questions thoroughly, consider not only the excerpts from Book Eight, Chapters One through Four above, but the entirety of Chapter Four, as well as Chapters Five through Eight, and Book Nine, Chapters One, Three, Four, and Five.

2.5 The Vicious Life of Frank Sheeran in Martin Scorcese's *The Irishman* (2019)

What follows contains spoilers, and assumes that the reader has seen the film. Seeing *The Irishman* before reading further is strongly recommended. It should be available on Netflix, but one can nonetheless locate it on streaming services using a website like justwatch.com.

While watching, consider the following questions: a. Is Frank Sheeran happy in the Aristotelian sense? Is he virtuous? Why or why not? b. Does he have good reasons for doing some of the bad deeds he commits? c. Does Frank have good friendships? Do any of them fit the three primary kinds Aristotle describes?

Martin Scorcese's depiction of Frank Sheeran's life can be understood as a dramatic portrayal of Aristotelian vice and unhappiness, explained below.

"Whatever happens, happens." Frank Sheeran (Robert DeNiro) tells Russell Bufalino (Joe Pesci) that this is what he thinks about having carried out orders to kill prisoners of war when he served in World War II. He says nothing about having any internal conflict at the time, nor does he indicate any remorse. It is this same saying that seems to guide him throughout the film, since he indicates no hesitation, internal turmoil, or regret for any of the killings he methodically carries out[13] (perhaps with one exception). He's rewarded with respect for carrying out such orders, and the powerholders in the criminal underworld actually have a dinner and award ceremony in his honor at one point, with Jimmy Hoffa (Al Pacino) as the keynote speaker. Even at the end of his life, when Frank is trying to repair his relationship with his daughter Peggy (Anna Paquin), his apology for his actions is superficial and half-hearted. After he confesses his sins to a priest (Jonathan Morris), he does not shed a tear, even when provoked to think about the families of his victims. When federal agents ask him to tell them what he knows about the disappearance of Jimmy Hoffa for the sake of the Hoffa family, Frank gives them no information, even though everyone else involved in the hit is deceased and Frank is near the end of his life.

INCONTINENCE
Weakness of will according to Aristotle; the state of character that involves knowing what virtuous action is but consistently failing to enact it; the person in this state feels pained at their failure, and so has hope for moving toward virtue.

VICE
The complete opposite of virtue; worse than incontinence because the person with this character no longer feels pained about their evil ways; they may even wrongfully assume that vice is good, because they feel pleasure (albeit passing) doing it. Such a person may be incurable and beyond all hope, though this is not necessarily the case for all vicious people, according to Aristotle.

© kcube/Shutterstock.com

© Tinseltown/Shutterstock.com

© DFree/Shutterstock.com

13. In a correspondence with me, Wians pointed out that this is notable because it is a key marker in the movement from **incontinence** to **vice**, according to Aristotle.

2.6 Vice According to Aristotle

2.6.1 A Summary of *Nicomachean Ethics* Book Seven, Chapters Seven, Eight, Nine, and Fourteen: Vice and Related Conditions

In Book Seven, Aristotle explains conditions that are distinct from vice, as well as vice itself. Incontinence, or weakness, is different from vice, in that the incontinent person knows what virtue is, understands that it is good, but repeatedly tries and fails to attain virtue. The weak or incontinent person would appropriately feel pained about these failures. The vicious person, on the other hand, no longer recognizes virtue as worth seeking. This person repeatedly fails to attain virtue, but was not really trying to, and so would not be pained to fail in this way. In fact, just as the virtuous person takes pleasure in doing the right thing, the vicious person takes pleasure in doing vice, or at least is not pained by it. Unlike the incontinent, the vicious feel no remorse. In this way, those who are vicious may be rather hopeless and incurable. (1150a, 1150b–1151a, 1152a, 1154a)

2.6.2 A Summary of *Nicomachean Ethics* Book Eight, Chapters One, Four, Eight, and Thirteen; Book Nine, Chapters Two, Three, and Four: Vice and Friendship

Vicious people also cannot have the best kind of friendship, which Aristotle describes as the true or complete friendship of good people. This is because vicious people cannot be friends with someone else for the other person's sake. (1157a) Vicious people have severe difficulties developing and maintaining any of the three primary kinds of friendship, for a number of reasons (1159b): One is that the vicious are prone to accusations, which dissolve friendships. (1163a) Another is that they are not reliable with regard to reciprocation and equality. (1165a) Yet another reason is that vicious people simply are not lovable and ought not to be loved. (1165b) Finally, those who are vicious cannot properly love themselves, which is a necessary precursor to real friendship. This is because deep down, they actually hate their lives and seek to ruin themselves. So, the relationships of vicious people mainly involve keeping company with people to pass the time with, which enables the lack of self-reflection necessary to maintain a life of vice. (1166b) The difficulties that vicious people have with friendship contribute to the unhappiness of their lives, since friendship, according to Aristotle, is necessary for happiness. (1155a)

2.7 Aristotle and *The Irishman*

Sheeran fits the description of the vicious person from Book Seven above, but questions remain about whether or not his friendships fit Aristotle's Book Eight portrayal of this topic in relation to vice. Frank has a great deal of difficulty maintaining positive relationships with his daughters, and he abruptly leaves his first wife (Aleksa Palladino). He also kills at least two people with whom he had what seemed to be friendships. However, his friendship with Russell seems quite genuine in that it is reciprocal, involves a kind of loving admiration and/or respect, and lasts for a long time. Frank's friendship with Hoffa seems similar, at least until Frank abruptly ends it.

QUESTIONS FOR CONSIDERATION

a. Does Frank have friendships of utility and pleasure? Does he have difficulties developing and maintaining these friendships?
b. Do Frank and Russell respect each other for the good person each can become?
c. Does Frank Sheeran have any true/complete friendships?
d. Does he have friendships that consist merely in passing the time with others, so that he can avoid facing harsh truths about his life?
e. How do Forrest Gump's friendships compare to those of Frank Sheeran?
f. Is there a real danger of becoming incurably vicious and destroying one's life as well as the lives of others as a result of an initial process of numbing or desensitization? Consider addictions.
g. If someone like Frank Sheeran was encouraged to have a formal education in some form, and he chose that path for his post-war life, could that have saved him and everyone he killed?

2.8 Resources for Further Study

2.8.1 Links to Free Online English Translations of *Nicomachean Ethics*

http://classics.mit.edu/Aristotle/nicomachaen.html

http://www.perseus.tufts.edu/hopper/text?doc=Perseus%3Atext%3A1999.01.0054

2.8.2 Recommended Print Translations of *Nicomachean Ethics*

Aristotle. *Nicomachean Ethics*. Translated by Robert C. Bartlett and Susan D. Collins. Chicago: University of Chicago Press, 2011.

Aristotle. *Nicomachean Ethics*. Translated by Terence Irwin. Indianapolis: Hackett, 1999, 2019.

Endnotes

1. All details about films' production, cast, and crew are from IMDb.com.
2. Aristotle, *Nicomachean Ethics*, trans. W. D. Ross (Clarendon Press: 1908).
3. Aristotle, *Nicomachean Ethics*, trans. Terence Irwin (Indianapolis: Hackett, 1999).
4. Also from Irwin's translation.
5. Also translated by Irwin.

Chapter 3

Natural Law and Deontological Ethics through the Lens of *The Good Place*

3.1 Introduction

In addition to explaining two key ethical theories, this chapter provides critical background for Chapters Four through Eleven. Those chapters will regularly use the content of this one. There is more to ethical theory after Aristotle than natural law, deontological ethics, and utilitarianism. However, it would go beyond the scope of this book to do justice to all of them.[1]

3.2 Natural Law

3.2.1 Overview of the Development of Natural Law

Ancient thinkers after Aristotle, as well as **medieval** philosophers, developed virtue ethics under the influence of **Epicureanism** and **Stoicism**, as well as Judaism

ANCIENT PERIOD
Generally considered to be from the time of the Pre-Socratics (late 600s–400s BCE) up until the fall of Rome (476 CE), according to historians of philosophy.

MEDIEVAL PERIOD
Widely agreed to span from the fall of Rome (476 CE) to the beginning of the Renaissance in the 1300s.

EPICUREANISM
Ancient Greek school of thought founded by Epicurus (341–270 BCE); focused on attainment of pleasure as happiness, not to be confused with crude hedonism, which pursues pleasure indiscriminately and could result in more pain than pleasure; mental pleasures are superior to physical pleasures, according to Epicureans. Famous adherents include Lucretius (c. 99–c. 51 BCE).

1. One prominent example is egoism, championed by Ayn Rand in the twentieth century. *See Internet Encyclopedia of Philosophy*, s.v. "Egoism," accessed October 2, 2020, https://www.iep.utm.edu/egoism/ and Ibid., s.v. "Ayn Rand (1905–1982)," accessed October 2, 2020, https://www.iep.utm.edu/rand/. Another example is social contract theory, explained briefly in this chapter. Additionally, **relativism** and **Social Darwinism** have been highly influential in recent years and the theories in this book can be understood as critical responses to both.

Christianity and Islam.[2] One major development includes the theory of natural law. Stoic philosophers articulated an early form of this ethical theory, and it saw further notable development in the work of Augustine of Hippo, but its most highly regarded exposition occurs in the writing of Thomas Aquinas.

> Please see the appendix for brief biographies of Augustine, Aquinas, and the other philosophers discussed in this chapter.

© Savvapanf Photo/Shutterstock.com

© mojahata/Shutterstock.com

© Amedeo Zullo/Shutterstock.com

© Bill McKelvie/Shutterstock.com

3.2.2 The Stoic Origins of Natural Law

The Hymn to Zeus by Cleanthes includes the lines: ". . .There is no greater prize, neither for mortals nor for gods, than to praise with justice the common law forever."[1] Writing about the ethics of Zeno and other Stoics, Stobaeus discusses virtues and writes, "The goal of all these virtues is to live consistently with nature. Each

MORAL RELATIVISM
Implies that ethics or morals ought to be determined on an individual basis, rather than on a universal one; says that each person decides what is right for them individually; a doctrine or belief that ethics is subjective rather than objective; when taken to an extreme, any act is morally permissible as long as the person doing it thinks it's right for them. Relativism generally was initially made famous by the Pre-Socratic philosopher Protagoras, to whom is attributed the saying "Man is the measure of all things."

SOCIAL DARWINISM
applied to ethics; The theory that it is best for only the strongest and most capable to thrive, while those who seem weaker do not. Those who have more deserve more, while the 'have nots' deserve their status because of their weakness.

STOICISM
School of thought founded by Zeno of Citium (c. 344–c. 262 BCE); the school's ethical teachings focused on the attainment of tranquility by controlling the passions. Its natural philosophy included the idea of a guiding principle or force that governs all things. Its philosophy of nature and ethical teachings converge on the notion of a natural or common law, explained below. Famous adherents include (in chronological order) Cleanthes, Chrysippus, Cicero, Seneca, Epictetus, and Marcus Aurelius (121–180 CE).

2. Christianity originated with the life of Jesus, who was born sometime between 4 BCE and 7 CE, and who was crucified probably around 29–30 CE. See Britannica, s.v., "The relation of the early church to the career and intentions of Jesus," accessed October 2, 2020, https://www.britannica.com/topic/Christianity/The-relation-of-the-early-church-to-the-career-and-intentions-of-Jesus. For further reading, see Mark Goodacre, "Jesus," *British Broadcasting Company*, 2014, https://www.bbc.co.uk/religion/religions/christianity/history/jesus_1.shtml. Islam originated with the prophet Muhammad, born in Mecca at around 570 CE. See "History of Islam," *BBC World* Service, 2002, https://www.bbc.co.uk/programmes/p03qtyj4. He died on June 8, 632. For a detailed timeline of his life, see "Muhammad: Legacy of a Prophet," *Public Broadcasting System*, accessed October 2, 2020, https://www.pbs.org/muhammad/timeline_html.shtml.

3. Icthus, ancient Christian symbol.

one enables man to achieve this [goal] in its own way; for [man] has from nature inclinations to discover what is appropriate and to stabilize his impulses and to stand firm and to distribute [fairly]."[2] Stobaeus adds: "Zeno defined the goal thus: 'living in agreement.' This means living according to a single and consonant rational principle, since those who live in conflict are unhappy."[3] Cleanthes's use of the term "common law," Zeno's thoughts about "inclinations" from nature that enable us to do good, and Zeno's idea about living in accord with a "rational principle," are all clear precursors to Aquinas's famous articulation of the natural law.

© Shyshko Oleksandr/Shutterstock.com[4]

3.2.3 Introduction to Aquinas on Natural Law

© Eric Letourneau/Shutterstock.com

It is critical to recognize Aquinas's influences, which include not only the Stoics, but Plato, Aristotle, Christian scripture (the Bible), Islamic philosophy, as well as others. Though some count the theory of natural law as an ethical theory independent of virtue ethics, it is clear in Aquinas's work that his explanation of natural law occurs within his Christianized version of Aristotle's virtue ethics. The excerpts below are from Aquinas's *Summa Theologiae*, also known as the *Summa Theologica*, which is his most famous and highly referenced work. It contains four large volumes of the most concise versions of Aquinas's thoughts about theology and philosophy. He wrote it for students of these subjects. More elaborate expositions of his ideas are in other works, such as the *Summa Contra Gentiles*. Rather than being divided into chapters, each volume of *The Summa Theologica* contains dozens of questions, subdivided into

4. The Stoa of Attalos in Athens, Greece. The Stoics got their name from the time they spent doing philosophy amidst the Stoa.

articles. Furthermore, the volumes are numbered as follows: I-I, I-II, II-II, and III. This is because Aquinas divided the second part into two volumes, while the first and third parts are one volume each.[5]

3.3 Annotated Excerpts from Aquinas on Natural Law (Drawn from *Summa Theologica* I-II: Question 91, Article Two and Question 94, Article Two)

After explaining eternal law in Volume I-II, Question 91, Article One, Aquinas begins Article Two by quoting the Bible on the topic of natural law (specifically *Romans*, Chapter Two Verse Fourteen). Referring to non-Jews, or Gentiles, Aquinas writes, "Although they have no written law, yet they have the natural law, whereby each one knows, and is conscious of, what is good and what is evil."[4]

> In saying this, Aquinas is claiming that *all* people are governed by natural law and that it is inherent in human nature itself.

Later in Article Two, Aquinas provides this explanation of natural law, in relation to **eternal law**:

ETERNAL LAW
The source of natural law; governs the universe; superior to natural law.

PROVIDENCE
The care, guidance, and protection of the universe by God.

ENDS
Synonym: goals; antonym: means.

> Wherefore, since all things subject to Divine **providence** are ruled and measured by the eternal law, as was stated above (Article 1); it is evident that all things partake somewhat of the eternal law, in so far as, namely, from its being imprinted on them, they derive their respective inclinations to their proper acts and **ends**.

> The ends or goals, in other words, of all things, exist because of eternal law, not natural law.

> Now among all others, the rational creature is subject to Divine providence in the most excellent way, in so far as it partakes of a share of providence, by being provident both for itself and for others.

> The human being, "the rational creature," shares in divine providence as its subject or recipient.

> Wherefore it has a share of the Eternal Reason, whereby it has a natural inclination to its proper act and end: and this participation of the eternal law in the rational creature is called the natural law.

> Though the end or goal of a human being has its source in eternal law, the way in which a rational creature shares in eternal law is called "natural law."

5. The full name of each volume is "The First Part of the First Part," "The Second Part of the First Part," "The Second Part of the Second Part," and "The Third Part."

Hence the Psalmist after saying (Ps. 4:6): 'Offer up the sacrifice of justice,' as though someone asked what the works of justice are, adds: 'Many say, Who showeth us good things?' in answer to which question he says: 'The light of Thy countenance, O Lord, is signed upon us':

> Clearly Aquinas relies on the testimony of a faith-based source (the Bible) in order to convey his understanding of natural law.

thus implying that the light of natural reason, whereby we discern what is good and what is evil, which is the function of natural law, is nothing else than an imprint on us of the Divine light.

> Aquinas describes reason as "light" to indicate that it illuminates truth. The light of natural reason is a share of, or a reflection of, divine light. Thinking about the light sources of Plato's "Allegory of the Cave" from Chapter One can aid in one's understanding of this part of the excerpt.

DIVINE LIGHT
The reasoning or thought of God; the source of human knowledge; natural light is humanity's share of divine light.

It is therefore evident that the natural law is nothing else than the rational creature's participation of the eternal law.[5]

> Natural law is based on eternal law, and human law is based on natural law, according to Questions 93–95 of the *Summa Theologica*. Yet another kind of law Aquinas discusses in this section of the *Summa* is divine law.

In Question 94, Article Two, Aquinas explains the precepts of natural law:

Now a certain order is to be found in those things that are apprehended universally. For that which, before aught else, falls under apprehension, is 'being,' the notion of which is included in all things whatsoever a man apprehends.

UNIVERSALLY
Everywhere and at all times; antonym: particularly.

> The fact that we exist—that we are—is our most fundamental realization, or "apprehension."

Wherefore the first indemonstrable principle is that 'the same thing cannot be affirmed and denied at the same time,' which is based on the notion of 'being' and 'not-being': and on this principle all others are based, as is stated in Metaph. iv, text 9.

> Aquinas is here referring to Book Four of Aristotle's *Metaphysics* and the "Principle of Non-Contradiction," which basically states that a thing cannot both be something and also not be that very thing at the same time in the same way. For example, it cannot be both 9:14 a.m. right now and also not be 9:14 a.m. right now.

INDEMONSTRABLE
A point or claim so obvious that it does not need proof or argument in order to be accepted.

PRACTICAL REASON
According to Aquinas, it is "directed to action," in contrast to speculative or theoretical reason, which pertains to the intellectual realm in such a way that it is not oriented toward actions in the physical world.

Now as 'being is the first thing that falls under the apprehension simply, so 'good' is the first thing that falls under the apprehension of the practical reason, which is directed to action: since every agent acts for an end under the aspect of good.

> Just as our existence is a basic or foundational realization, so is the notion of goodness.

Consequently the first principle of practical reason is one founded on the notion of good, viz. that 'good is that which all things seek after.' Hence this is the first precept of law, that 'good is to be done and pursued, and evil is to be avoided.' All other precepts of the natural law are based upon this: so that whatever the practical reason naturally apprehends as man's good (or evil) belongs to the precepts of the natural law as something to be done or avoided.

> Here, Aquinas uses basic principles of reasoning to arrive at the fundamental claim that according to natural law, human beings must seek to do good and avoid evil. First: We acknowledge the truth of existence. Second: We acknowledge the truth of the Principle of Non-Contradiction. Third: We acknowledge the notion of goodness. Fourth: We arrive at the first, or foundational, principle of natural law: pursue good and avoid evil.

Since, however, good has the nature of an end, and evil, the nature of a contrary, hence it is that all those things to which man has a natural inclination, are naturally apprehended by reason as being good, and consequently as objects of pursuit, and their contraries as evil, and objects of avoidance.

> Goodness is a proper natural end or goal, but evil is not, because of its very nature. So, it is natural—or inherent in human nature—to pursue good and shun evil.

Wherefore according to the order of natural inclinations, is the order of the precepts of the natural law.

> The natural law fundamentally dictates that pursuing natural inclinations is good, and therefore is to be sought after, while that which is unnatural is evil and is to be avoided.

Because in man there is first of all an inclination to good in accordance with the nature which he has in common with all substances: inasmuch as every substance seeks the preservation of its own being, according to its nature: and by reason of this inclination, whatever is a means of preserving human life, and of warding off its obstacles, belongs to the natural law.

> The primary example of the specific natural "inclinations" Aquinas has in mind is to preserve life, including one's own life.

Secondly, there is in man an inclination to things that pertain to him more specially, according to that nature which he has in common with other animals: and in virtue of this inclination, those things are said to belong to the natural law, 'which nature has taught to all animals' [. . .], such as sexual intercourse, education of offspring and so forth.

> Here, Aquinas reasons that we should look to the larger animal kingdom to observe the natural inclination for sexual intercourse, which is therefore good, as well as the natural inclination to educate one's offspring.

> Thirdly, there is in man an inclination to good, according to the nature of his reason, which nature is proper to him: thus man has a natural inclination to know the truth about God, and to live in society: and in this respect, whatever pertains to this inclination belongs to the natural law; for instance, to shun ignorance, to avoid offending those among whom one has to live, and other such things regarding the above inclination.[6]

The method Aquinas employs, which involves using observations of the physical world as evidence on which to base one's philosophical claims, is empirical. Aristotle also proceeded empirically in his thought, as well as John Locke (discussed below) and John Stuart Mill (Chapter Four).

EMPIRICISM
The method that uses observations of the physical world—data gathering—as evidence on which to base one's claims.

Other significant natural inclinations include seeking truth and knowledge, avoiding ignorance, and seeking to live in harmony with others in society.

Aquinas adds to the list of what is prescribed by natural law in the third article of Question 94:

> If then we speak of acts of virtue, considered as virtuous, thus all virtuous acts belong to the natural law. For it has been stated (Article 2) that to the natural law belongs everything to which a man is inclined according to his nature. Now each thing is inclined naturally to an operation that is suitable to is according to its form: thus fire is inclined to give heat. Wherefore, since the rational soul is the proper form of man, there is in every man a natural inclination to act according to reason: and this is to act according to virtue.
>
> Consequently, considered thus, all acts of virtue are prescribed by the natural law: since each one's reason naturally dictates to him to act virtuously.[7]

Aquinas is referring to the idea, rooted in Aristotle, that the human soul is composed of both rational and non-rational powers or capabilities.

Recall Chapter Two and Aristotle's argument that the distinguishing function of a human being is reason, and virtue is a state of excellence in regard to the activity of reason. Aquinas is saying here that it is a proper natural inclination, and therefore an inherent good, to pursue virtue.

Though there is much more to what Aquinas has to say about natural law, the excerpts above show the basic outline of his theory on law, the essence of natural law, and its main corresponding rules.

QUESTIONS FOR CONSIDERATION

a. Are matters of faith the only basis for natural law according to Aquinas, or does he defend and explain it with reason as well?
b. What are the stated rules of natural law, according to Aquinas? What other rules might they imply?

3.4 Locke and Natural Law

Though John Locke wrote in the 1600s[6] and can be considered a **social contract theorist** with regard to his ethics, he bases his notion of **rights** on the "law of nature," which bears distinct similarities to the accounts of natural law above. The law of nature is foundational to Locke's argument against **absolutist monarchs** in the *Second Treatise of Government*, which is, in turn, foundational to modern democracies throughout the world. Locke explains it, as follows, in the sixth section of the second chapter:

SOCIAL CONTRACT THEORIST
Ethicists whose theory focuses on an agreement to leave the state of nature and endow a leader or government with power; actions are right insofar as they accord with this collective agreement and its corresponding laws; well-known examples include Hobbes, Locke, Rousseau, and Rawls.

RIGHTS
That for which human beings are owed protection because of the very nature of humanity; according to Thomas Jefferson (derived from Locke), life, liberty, and the pursuit of happiness are essential human rights.

ABSOLUTIST MONARCHS
Kings, queens, and/or emperors whose authority throughout their kingdom or empire is essentially boundless; examples include kings who were thought to have a divine right to rule over everything and everyone in their kingdom, in every way; according to Locke, such power often includes the arbitrary taking of life, liberty, and/or property from people by the monarch. In the *First Treatise of Government*, as well as in the *Second Treatise*, Locke famously argues against such rule as well as its supposed divine origins.

> The state of nature has a law of nature to govern it, which obliges every one: and reason, which is that law, teaches all mankind, who will but consult it, that being all equal and independent, no one ought to harm another in his life, health, liberty, or possessions: for men being all the workmanship of one omnipotent, and infinitely wise maker; all the servants of one sovereign master, sent into the world by his order, and about his business; they are his property, whose workmanship they are, made to last during his, not one another's pleasure [. . .][8]

It's very important not to confuse the state of nature with the law of nature. The former is basically an elaborate thought experiment about the state human beings are in when they are not part of a society with a civil government. The law that applies in that natural state is the law of nature. It is basic. It is so fundamental in fact, that it must be enforced in all circumstances, especially including when people are in a society with a civil government. An excellent show that thematically treats these concepts is *The Walking Dead*, created by Frank Darabont and Angela Kang, aired 2010–2020 on AMC, https://www.imdb.com/title/tt1520211/.

Just as in Aquinas's articulation of natural law, Locke's law of nature prescribes that we preserve life. Also similar to Aquinas is that Locke uses a faith-based, or theological, claim as support for his argument. For Locke, the claim is that we are God's property. We cannot mistreat God's property. This includes not only harming others, but also ourselves, as Locke explains later. We commit a grave offense against the law of nature, and therefore against God, if we commit suicide, give ourselves over to slavery, or harm ourselves deliberately in other ways.[9]

According to Locke, people have a natural right to life, liberty, and property because of the law of nature.

6. Reminder: Please see the appendix of biographies for background on Locke and the Enlightenment.

QUESTION FOR CONSIDERATION

a. Is there any reason to follow the natural law, either according to Aquinas or to Locke, if one does not believe in God?

© Freeda Michaux/Shutterstock.com[7]

3.5 *The Good Place* (2016–2020) and Non-Consequentialism

© VGstockstudio/Shutterstock.com

© PR Image Factory/Shutterstock.com

Why do you do good and avoid evil? Is it because you feel a sense of duty or obligation to do certain things and avoid others? Is it to produce good consequences and avoid negative ones? It is common for parents and educators to teach children by means of rewards and punishments. When your motivation stems from a desire for approval, for a good grade or performance review, or from the pleasure that might result from an action, you are driven by consequences. Insofar as Aristotle's virtue ethics aims at the goal of happiness, it is **consequentialist**. Insofar as it considers virtue valuable in itself—that is, for its own sake, regardless of consequences, Aristotle's virtue ethics is **non-consequentialist**.[8] For Aquinas, people ought to be virtuous because they seek happiness, especially supernatural happiness, which is with God in Heaven for eternity. Additionally though, it is clear that for Aquinas, human beings have an inherent obligation to obey the natural law. He does not argue that observing

CONSEQUENTIALIST
When the value of an action depends on its results or outcomes.

NON-CONSEQUENTIALIST
When the value of an action depends on its motivation or principles, regardless of its consequences.

7. An artist's rendering of a section from Michaelangelo's sixteenth-century painting on the Sistine Chapel ceiling in Vatican City.
8. The same could be said for Stoic ethics.

© djgis/Shutterstock.com

© Kathy Hutchins/Shutterstock.com

the precepts of the natural law is contingent on any considerations about the consequences that might result from that obedience. It is somewhat difficult then, and perhaps anachronistic,[9] to try and categorize virtue ethics, including natural law ethics, as consequentialist or non-consequentialist.

Immanuel Kant's ethics, also known as deontological ethics, is emphatically non-consequentialist. John Stuart Mill's utilitarian ethics, on the other hand, is clearly consequentialist and is the subject of the next chapter. Both ethical theories, furthermore, do not rely on faith in God for the justification of their core principles.

> It is recommended to view at least this one episode before reading further. For one, what follows contains spoilers. Also, one's reading and learning experience will benefit from having familiarity with the show. Of course, seeing all of the episodes prior to and including this one would be best. Go to a website like https://www.justwatch.com/ for information about which streaming services have *The Good Place,* and whether or not it is free, for rent, or for purchase.

DICHOTOMY
A duality such that there are only two options or entities; black or white, with no gray area.

Many episodes of *The Good Place* play with the **dichotomy** between consequentialism and non-consequentialism. The show consistently uses Kantian ethics as a framework for the rules of afterlife punishments and rewards. The episode "Jeremy Bearimy"[10] stands out in its substantive treatment of Kantian non-consequentialism. *The Good Place* begins with four people dying and going to what they think is heaven. Their journey takes a few twists and turns through two seasons and the first three episodes of Season Three, before they find themselves doomed to hell. Their fate is sealed because they find out how the afterlife system of rewards and punishments actually works. Once this occurs, their motivations for doing good are corrupted, because it is no longer possible for them to do good simply and purely for its own sake. The latter is what scores points for admittance into heaven, hence their being doomed to hell for eternity. One of the doomed humans, Eleanor Shellstrop (Kristen Bell), immediately heads to a bar after her fate is sealed. She demands a free margarita for her birthday, even though it's not her birthday. Though the bartender does give her the drink she desires, he points out the problematic nature of her demand for exceptionalism, showing Eleanor and the audience that making oneself an exception to the rules is wrong. Eleanor subsequently begins to do good deeds to cope with her impending doom, just as two of the other main characters do: Tahani Al-Jamil (Jameela Jamil) and Jason Mendoza (Manny Jacinto). Throughout the episode, these characters realize the value of doing good for its own sake. Another main character, Chidi Anagonye (William Jackson Harper), who is an ethics professor, gives a brief overview of ethical theory after engaging in some comically idiotic activities to cope with his ultimate fate being sealed.

9. Appropriate or proper to one time but wrongly applied to another.

3.6 Introduction to Kantian Ethics

Kant developed his own theory of ethics that is non-consequentialist, **non-empirical**, and explicitly distinct from virtue ethics. His theory, also known as **deontological ethics**, gets its name from its basis in **metaphysics**. The term "**ontological**" indicates a relation to being or existence, which is what metaphysics studies. Kantian metaphysics, which is intertwined with Kant's **epistemology**, involves what is now known as the "**Copernican Turn**." Kant refers to it as "The Copernican Revolution in Philosophy," because he thinks that what his philosophy does to transform human beings' understanding of their relationship with the world is on par with the revolutionary change in cosmic perspective that Copernican astronomy prompted.

Based on his careful observation and study of the Solar System, Nicolaus Copernicus theorized that Earth orbits the sun (**heliocentrism**), rather than the other way around (**geocentrism**). At the time during which he lived, people thought that humanity was at the center of the Solar System—a privileged place—with the Sun and all of the planets orbiting Earth. Altering one's perspective to a heliocentric model meant that Earth, and humanity with it, no longer occupied such a special astronomical position. Copernicus's radical change in perspective was not easily accepted.[10]

© vector punch/Shutterstock.com

© Johan Swanepoel/Shutterstock.com

What is so radical about Kant's epistemological metaphysics to make it comparable to Copernicus? Influenced by Rene Descartes, David Hume, and many others, Kant theorized that one cannot know things-in-themselves, also known as "**noumena**." Rational beings can only know what the mind processes through its experience with the world. Human beings can know things in the world only as the mind engages with and interprets them. The knowable, which Kant refers to as "**phenomena**," excludes anything that the mind does not have an experience of—namely, things as they are in themselves, independent of the mind. The reality, then,

NON-EMPIRICAL
Not based on the study or observation of physical reality or the natural world.

DEONTOLOGICAL ETHICS
Metaphysical ethics; ethics essentially based on an understanding of being or existence; synonymous with Kantian ethics.

METAPHYSICS
Study of being or existence; could include the study of God; sometimes called "First Philosophy"; asks and attempts to answer questions such as: What is being? What is existence? How is existence related to essence? What is the source of existence?

ONTOLOGICAL
Indicates a relation to being or existence; to metaphysics.

EPISTEMOLOGY
Study or theory of knowledge; asks and attempts to answer questions such as: What is knowledge? How is knowledge attained? How is knowledge related to information? To wisdom? To ignorance? What kinds of knowledge are there?

COPERNICAN TURN
The name of Kant's philosophical revolution; a revolution in thought; a reorientation of basic assumptions about one's relationship to the world.

HELIOCENTRISM
The theory that Earth orbits the Sun, with the latter as the center of the Solar System.

GEOCENTRISM
The theory that the Sun orbits Earth, with the latter as the center of the Solar System.

NOUMENA
The unknowable, according to Kant; things-in-themselves.

PHENOMENA
The knowable, according to Kant; things as they are according to the mind.

10. For more information about Copernicus, see: "Nicolaus Copernicus," Khan Academy, accessed October 2, 2020, https://www.khanacademy.org/partner-content/big-history-project/big-bang/how-did-big-bang-change/a/nicolaus-copernicus-bh.

that human beings tend to think they know objectively, really is rather subjective. Kant does not go as far as saying that all that humans think is real is really just "in our heads," though. Kant does not negate the existence of a real world external to the human mind. Rather, he radically alters the way human beings ought to perceive and understand themselves and everything around them. The exact nature of the existence of things—what they are independent of the mind—is unknown. The implication of this theory is that **empiricism**, or data-gathering based on observation of the natural world, is not as reliable as previously thought. All observations are interpreted by the mind, and therefore are somewhat subjective. There is no such thing as completely objective data based on observation if one follows Kant.

EMPIRICISM
The approach that takes as its foundation or basis the study or observation of the natural, physical world; favored by Aristotle, Aquinas, Locke, and many others.

***A PRIORI* REASON**
Synonym: "pure reason"; antonym: empirical or *a posteriori* reason; reasoning that is prior to and independent of human experience; Kant wants to favor this instead of the empirical because it is more certain in that it is not based on experience of the physical world.

PURE REASON
(Au – Please complete)

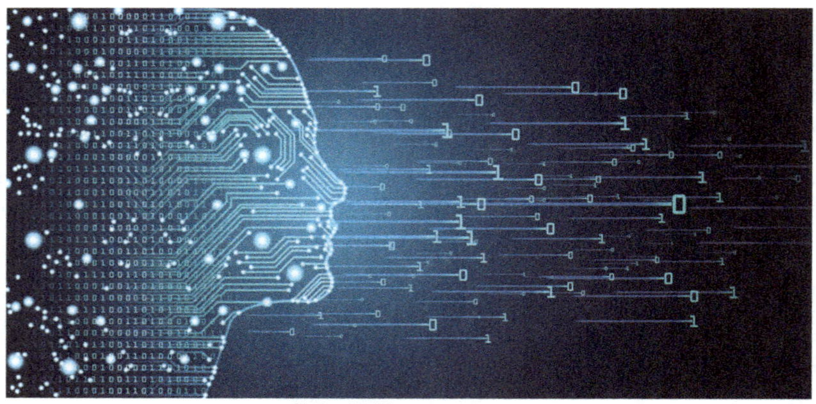

© Ryzhi/Shutterstock.com

Ethics prior to Kant was all empirically based. Because empiricism is not as reliable as previously thought, and because ethics is of the utmost importance to humanity, Kant argues that ethical theory cannot be based on empiricism. Kant's argument in this regard, and the foundations of his ethical theory, occur in *The Grounding for the Metaphysics of Morals*, which often goes by other translations from the original German, including *The Fundamental Principles of the Metaphysic of Morals*. The non-empirical knowledge that Kant favors in the development of his ethics is formed by ***a priori* reason,** also known as "**pure reason**": reasoning that is prior to and independent of human experience. An approximate analogy for the *a priori*

© IIerlok_xolms/Shutterstock.com

is mathematical truth, like the idea of a triangle or any geometric shape, which one can grasp purely based on reason, independent of experience. In other words, one does not have to perceive a physical triangle with one's senses in order to understand what a triangle is. One can grasp its essence *a priori*. Anything known empirically is "**a posteriori,**" since it is formed by experience, therefore occurring after such experience.

In the first section of the *Grounding for the Metaphysics of Morals* (henceforth, simply *The Grounding* or *The Foundation*), Kant uses *a priori* reason to arrive at the core principle or commandment of his ethics: the categorical imperative. In the second section, Kant argues for the primacy of pure reason in the foundations of ethics, and also develops a reformulation of the **categorical imperative**. This reformulation is essentially an implication of the categorical imperative, and it commands certain behavior just as the first formulation does. Though there are other implications (or articulations) of the categorical imperative in *The Grounding*, the following excerpts focus on the two that are most fundamental to Kantian ethics, as well as the radically new process of ethical decision-making that results from these imperatives.

A POSTERIORI REASON
Synonym: empirical reason; antonym: *a priori* or pure reason; it is formed by experience, therefore occurring after such experience. There is a place for it in Kantian ethics, but only secondarily. It should not be the basis for something as important to humankind as ethics. Kant does not want to use it as the basis for fundamental ethical principles, but it can be useful to determine how to live in accord with such principles.

CATEGORICAL IMPERATIVE
The highest command of reason, as established by pure or a priori reason, which is of greater certitude than the empirical; all other ethical principles, according to Kant, stem from it. Its primary formulation dictates that one should only act in such a way that the maxim or principle of one's action can be taken up by everyone at all times.

3.7 Excerpts from *Foundation for the Metaphysic of Morals*

First Section

> Nothing can possibly be conceived in the world, or even out of it, which can be called good, without qualification, except a good will.

> The notion that goodness has inherent value is foundational for Kant, just as it is for Aquinas, interestingly.

> Intelligence, wit, judgment and the other talents of the mind, however they may be named, or courage, resolution, perseverance, as qualities of temperament, are undoubtedly good and desirable in many respects; but these gifts of nature may also become extremely bad and mischievous if the will which is to make use of them, and which, therefore, constitutes what is called character, is not good. It is the same with gifts of fortune. Power, riches, honour, even health, and the general well-being and contentment with one's condition which is called happiness, inspire pride, and often presumption, if there is not a good will to correct the influence of these on the mind, and with this also to rectify the whole principle of acting and adapt it to its end.[11]

> For clarification: One can misuse courage, say, by initiating unjust aggression, whereas a good will is always good, regardless of circumstances. One can use power well, or poorly, unlike a good will, which is always good, without needing conditions added to it. A good will is what makes virtues like courage good, or qualities like power.[12]

VOLITION
Willing, as in pertaining to the will; if one wills to be good, it is of one's volition to be good.

[. . .]

A good will is good not because of what it performs or effects, not by its aptness for the attainment of some proposed end, but simply by virtue of the volition; that is, it is good in itself, and considered by itself is to be esteemed much higher than all that can be brought about by it in favour of any inclination, nay even of the sum total of all inclinations.[13]

For clarification: By "inclinations," Kant means feelings or desires. Because a good will is good in itself, it is good simply in its willing (its volition), regardless of consequences or outcomes.

[. . .]

For as reason is not competent to guide the will with certainty in regard to its objects and the satisfaction of all our wants (which it to some extent even multiplies), this being an end to which an implanted instinct would have led with much greater certainty; and since, nevertheless, reason is imparted to us as a practical faculty, i.e., as one which is to have influence on the will, therefore, admitting that nature generally in the distribution of her capacities has adapted the means to the end, its true destination must be to produce a will, not merely as a means to something else, but good in itself, for which reason was absolutely necessary. This will then, though not indeed the sole and complete good, must be the supreme good and the condition of every other, even of the desire of happiness.[14]

For clarification: Kant does not want to eliminate happiness from ethics, but he wants it to be conditioned by a principle of good will. Happiness, then, is a *secondary* good for Kant. It is not the highest good for him, as it is for Aristotle.

[. . .]

We have then to develop the notion of a will which deserves to be highly esteemed for itself and is good without a view to anything further [. . .]. In order to do this, we will take the notion of duty, which includes that of a good will, although implying certain subjective restrictions and hindrances. These, however, far from concealing it, or rendering it unrecognizable, rather bring it out by contrast and make it shine forth so much the brighter.

[. . .]

MAXIM
Principle; intention.

[. . .] It is a duty to maintain one's life; and, in addition, everyone has also a direct inclination to do so. But on this account the often anxious care which most men take for it as no intrinsic worth, and their maxim has no moral import. They preserve their life as duty requires, no doubt, but not because duty requires. On the other hand, if adversity and hopeless sorrow have completely taken away the relish for life; if the unfortunate one, strong in mind, indignant at his fate rather than desponding or dejected, wishes for death, and yet preserves his life without loving it—not from inclination or fear, but from duty—then his maxim has a moral worth.[15]

For clarification: Inclinations, like virtues, are not good in themselves. Nor are desires for particular consequences. All of these are good only insofar as they stem from a good will. The decision to preserve one's life because it feels good to do so, or because it will yield positive results, is not good in itself. This decision is only good, and therefore only has moral value, if it is done out of duty to a principle of good will. This is why the moral worth of the decision to preserve one's life despite misery is so clear—it is clearly done purely from duty and not because of other possibly bad motivations.

To be beneficent[11] when we can is a duty; and besides this, there are many minds so sympathetically constituted that, without any other motive of vanity or self-interest, they find a pleasure in spreading joy around them and can take delight in the satisfaction of others so far as it is their own work. But I maintain that in such a case an action of this kind, however proper, however amiable it may be, has nevertheless no true moral worth, but is on a level with other inclinations, e.g., the inclination to honour [. . .].[16]

For clarification: Being good toward others because it comes naturally, or because it feels good, has no moral worth. Being good towards others even when it is annoying, inconvenient, or painful, clearly has moral worth because it is done purely out of duty to a principle of good will.

To secure one's own happiness is a duty, at least indirectly; for discontent with one's condition, under a pressure of many anxieties and amidst unsatisfied wants, might easily become a great temptation to transgression of duty.[17]

For clarification: Being happy is not a primary goal of ethical decision-making according to Kant, but we do need to ensure our happiness so that we can achieve the primary goal of Kant's ethics: doing our duty as prescribed by the categorical imperative. [. . .]

11. That is, good.

© wavebreakmedia/Shutterstock.com

[. . .]

The second proposition is: That an action done from duty derives its moral worth, not from the purpose which is to be attained by it, but from the maxim by which it is determined, and therefore does not depend on the realization of the object of the action, but merely on the principle of volition by which the action has taken place, without regard to any object of desire. It is clear from what precedes that the purposes which we may have in view in our actions, or their effects regarded as ends and springs of the will, cannot give to actions any unconditional or moral worth. In what, then, can their worth lie, if it is not to consist in the will and in reference to its expected effect? It cannot lie anywhere but in the principle of the will without regard to the ends which can be attained by the action.[18]

For clarification: Calculations about effects, or consequences, do not have value in ethical decision-making because they can be corrupt. They are not necessarily good, unless founded on a principle of good will first and foremost. As long as that primary condition is satisfied, it is acceptable to make decisions using practical wisdom about consequences.

[. . .]

The third proposition, which is a consequence of the two preceding, I would express thus: Duty is the necessity of acting from respect for the law. I may have inclination for an object as the effect of my proposed action, but I cannot have respect for it, just for this reason, that it is an effect and not an energy of will. Similarly I cannot have respect for inclination, whether my own or another's; I can at most, if my own, approve it; if another's, sometimes even love it; i.e., look on it as favourable to my own interest. It is only what is connected with my will as a principle, by no means as an effect—what does not subserve my inclination, but overpowers it, or at least in case of choice excludes it from its calculation—in other words, simply the law of itself, which can be an object of respect, and hence a command.[19]

For clarification: Only a law that commands a good will can be an object of moral respect, unlike feelings, desires, or motivations about consequences, all of which can be corrupt because they are not necessarily founded on good will. Notice that he brings in the concept of duty first, and then the concept of law. This is arguably evidence of his *a priori* approach. [. . .]

Thus the moral worth of an action does not lie in the effect expected from it, nor in any principle of action which requires to borrow its motive from this expected effect. For all these effects—agreeableness of one's condition and even the promotion of the happiness of others—could have been also brought about by other causes, so that for this there would have been no need of the will of a rational being; whereas it is in this alone that the supreme and unconditional good can be found. The pre-eminent good which we call moral can therefore consist in nothing else than the conception of law in itself, which certainly is only possible in a rational being, in so far as this conception, and not the effect, determines the will. This is a good which is already present in the person who acts accordingly, and we have not to wait for it to appear first in the result.

But what sort of law can that be, the conception of which must determine the will, even without paying any regard to the effect expected from it, in order that this will may be called good absolutely and without qualification? As I have deprived the will of every impulse which could arise to it from obedience to any law, there remains nothing but the universal conformity of its actions to law in general, which alone is to serve the will as a principle, i.e., I am never to act otherwise than so that I could also will that my maxim should become a universal law.[20]

For clarification: This is the main formulation of the categorical imperative. One can rephrase it accordingly: Only act in such a way that the principles motivating your actions can be applied to everyone at all times; in other words, only act in accord with maxims that everyone can act on at all times. Kant explains in a part of Section Two not included here why this command is called the "categorical imperative." By "categorical," he means the opposite of hypothetical or conditional.

[. . .]

I do not, therefore, need any far-reaching penetration to discern what I have to do in order that my will may be morally good. Inexperienced in the course of the world, incapable of being prepared for all its contingencies, I only ask myself: Canst thou also will that thy maxim should be a universal law? If not, then it must be rejected.

Kant tells us the practical application of the categorical imperative: Discern the principle or maxim of your action (this is much different than the action itself), and then consider whether or not it can be taken up by everyone at all times. If it can't, don't act on that maxim. [. . .].[21]

© Igor Palamarchuk/Shutterstock.com

After initially explaining the categorical imperative, Kant uses the example of lying to illustrate the application of this supreme command of reason. When one lies, one wills that everyone adopt the *opposite* of the maxim of one's action. It is impossible to lie and also will that the principle or maxim motivating one's action be universally acceptable. If it was, the very act of lying would be destroyed. A lie is no longer a lie if everyone lies all the time, by default. A lie only functions when the assumption is that everyone tells the truth. Lying relies on making oneself an exception to the rule. This is precisely why it, and any other similar exceptionalism, is clearly forbidden by the categorical imperative.[22]

QUESTIONS FOR CONSIDERATION

a. What is the categorical imperative, in your own words, and what does it mean to live by it? Though you may think it is the same as the "Golden Rule"—to do unto other as you would have them do to you—it is not exactly the same, because of its focus on the principles of actions, rather than the actions themselves.
b. Is it plausible to live in such a way that one makes decisions primarily with regard to intentions, rather than consequences?
c. What should matter more to the morality of an action: Its intent or its consequences? Why?
d. What is the reasoning process Kant uses to justify the formulation of the categorical imperative?
e. Besides the clear example of telling a lie, what other specific actions are immoral according to the categorical imperative?
f. Are there actions that should be forbidden according to an ethical theory, but are not clearly banned by this initial formulation of the categorical imperative?

Second Section

[. . .]

[. . .] Unless we deny that the notion of morality has any truth or reference to any possible object, we must admit that its laws must be valid, not merely for men but for rational creatures generally, not merely under certain contingent conditions or with exceptions but with absolute necessity [. . .].[23]

> For clarification: Because Kantian moral principles are based on *a priori* principles of reason, Kantian morality is not contingent on factors in the physical world that are subject to change and interpretation. Kant's moral principles apply objectively to all rational beings (human beings) at all times. This is completely opposed to relativism. [. . .]

From what has been said, it is clear that all moral conceptions have their seat and origin completely a priori in the reason, and that, moreover, in the commonest reason just as truly as in that which is in the highest degree speculative; that they cannot be obtained by abstraction from any empirical, and therefore merely contingent, knowledge; that it is just this purity of their origin that makes them worthy to serve as our supreme practical principle, and that just in proportion as we add anything empirical, we detract from their genuine influence and from the absolute value of actions; that it is not only of the greatest necessity, in a purely speculative point of view, but is also of the greatest practical importance, to derive these notions and laws from pure reason, to present them pure and unmixed, and even to determine the compass of this practical or pure rational knowledge, i.e., to determine the whole faculty of pure practical reason; and, in doing so, we must not make its principles dependent on the particular nature of human reason, though in speculative philosophy this may be permitted, or may even at times be unnecessary; but since moral laws ought to hold good for every rational creature, we must derive them from the general concept of a rational being.[24]

> For clarification: The moral laws Kant reasons his way to are based on the very notion of rationality. Reason is the foundation—not faith, pleasure, or the desire for happiness. Because reason is the foundation for Kantian morality, Kant's moral laws apply to all reasoning beings. [. . .]

[. . .]

Supposing [. . .] that there were something whose existence has in itself an absolute worth, something which, being an end in itself, could be a source of definite laws; then in this and this alone would lie the source of a possible categorical imperative, i.e., a practical law.[25]

> For clarification: What is the source of rational laws? Reason. What is the source of reason? Rational beings (i.e., human beings, in a general sense). Human beings, then, are the source of moral laws. Moral laws are ends in themselves because they are based on good will. Therefore, human beings are ends in themselves.

Now I say: man and generally any rational being exists as an end in himself, not merely as a means to be arbitrarily used by this or that will, but in all his actions, whether they concern himself or other rational beings, must be always regarded at the same time as an end. All objects of the inclinations have only a conditional worth, for if the inclinations and the wants founded on them did not exist, then their object would be without value. But the inclinations, themselves being sources of want, are so far from having an absolute worth for which they should be desired that on the contrary it must be the universal wish of every rational being to be wholly free from them. Thus the worth of any object which is to be acquired by our action is always conditional. Beings whose existence depends not on our will but on nature's, have nevertheless, if they are irrational beings, only a relative value as means, and are therefore called things; rational beings, on the contrary, are called persons, because their very nature points them out as ends in themselves, that is as something which must not be used merely as means [. . .]. These, therefore, are not merely subjective ends whose existence has a worth for us as an effect of our action, but objective ends, that is, things whose existence is an end in itself. [. . .]

Feelings and objects are means, unlike people, who are ends. The former have value only conditionally, based on what they are used for and how they are used. The latter have value in and of themselves, regardless of circumstances, conditions, or outcomes.

[. . .]

If then there is a supreme practical principle or, in respect of the human will, a categorical imperative, it must be one which, being drawn from the conception of that which is necessarily an end for everyone because it is an end in itself, constitutes an objective principle of will, and can therefore serve as a universal practical law. [. . .] Accordingly the practical imperative will be as follows: So act as to treat humanity, whether in thine own person or in that of any other, in every case as an end withal, never as a means only.[26] [. . .]

For clarification: People are not means like money, which is used to obtain something. On the contrary, people are ends. People are valuable in themselves and ought to be treated as such. People may not be used.

QUESTIONS FOR CONSIDERATION

a. What does it mean to treat others as ends and never as means? What kinds of actions are clearly opposed to this second formulation of the categorical imperative?
b. What is the reasoning process Kant uses to justify the reformulation of the categorical imperative in Section Two?

3.8 "Jeremy Bearimy" and Kant

In the "Jeremy Bearimy" episode of *The Good Place*, humans are doomed to hell by a Kantian system of afterlife rewards and punishments when they find out that there is indeed an afterlife and that it has a certain judgment system. This is a mystery that humans are not supposed to know, according to the writers (Michael Schur and Megan Amram). The assumption is that it is intrinsic to the human condition not to be certain about the matter of judgment after death and the soul's post-mortem existence. Such intrinsic uncertainty allows humans to do good simply for its own sake—out of duty to a principle of good will, to use Kant's language. According to the episode, doing good that really counts involves doing it regardless of such consequences as the prospect of punishments and rewards after death.

QUESTIONS FOR CONSIDERATION

a. Does Kant agree with the notion that doing good only counts when it is done regardless of its possible consequences?
b. Based on what you can infer about Kant's ethics, would he agree with the idea that real goodness is not possible if one has certain knowledge of the afterlife and its justice system?
c. If all human beings actually could be certain of such an other-worldly justice system, would there be a need for deontological ethics?
d. Is Eleanor's behavior at the bar immoral from a Kantian standpoint? Why or why not?
e. Does the bartender's explanation to Eleanor resemble what you think Kant would say about the matter?
f. Michael, the reformed demon (Ted Danson) makes a few suggestions about how to handle the accidental revelations to the humans. Are any of these opposed to Kantian ethics? Why?

3.9 Resources for Further Study

3.9.1 Freely Available Online Sources

Aquinas, Thomas. *Summa Theologica*. Benzinger Brothers Edition. Translated by the Fathers of the English Dominican Province. 1947. https://www.ccel.org/ccel/aquinas/summa

Kant, Immanuel. *Fundamental Principles of the Metaphysic of Morals*. Translated by Thomas Kingsmill Abbott. http://www.gutenberg.org/files/5682/5682-h/5682-h.htm

Locke, John. *Second Treatise of Government*. 1690 edition. https://www.gutenberg.org/files/7370/7370-h/7370-h.htm

3.9.2 Recommended Print Translations of Stobaeus, Kant, and Aquinas, Respectively

Inwood, Brad, and L. P. Gerson, trans. *Hellenistic Philosophy. Introductory Readings* (2nd ed). Indianapolis: Hackett, 1997.

Kant, Immanuel. *Grounding for the Metaphysics of Morals*. Translated by James W. Ellington. Indianapolis: Hackett, 1993.

Kreeft, Peter, Ed. *Summa of the Summa*. San Francisco: Ignatius, 1990.

Endnotes

1. From Stobaeus's *Anthology*; see Brad Inwood and L. P. Gerson, trans. *Hellenistic Philosophy. Introductory Readings*, 2nd ed. (Indianapolis: Hackett, 1997), 140–141.
2. Ibid., 205.
3. Ibid., 211.
4. Thomas Aquinas, *Summa Theologica*, trans. The Fathers of the English Dominican Province (Benziger Bros., 1947), https://www.ccel.org/a/aquinas/summa/FS/FS091.html#FSQ91A-2THEP1.
5. Aquinas, ST I-II.91.2, https://www.ccel.org/a/aquinas/summa/FS/FS091.html#FSQ91A-2THEP1.
6. Aquinas, ST I-II.94.2, https://www.ccel.org/a/aquinas/summa/FS/FS094.html#FSQ94A-2THEP1.
7. Aquinas, ST I-II.94.3, https://www.ccel.org/a/aquinas/summa/FS/FS094.html#FSQ94A-3THEP1.
8. Locke, *Second Treatise of Government*, 2.6, https://www.gutenberg.org/files/7370/7370-h/7370-h.htm
9. Locke, *Second Treatise*, 4.23, https://www.gutenberg.org/files/7370/7370-h/7370-h.htm.
10. *The Good Place*, season 3, episode 4, directed by Trent O'Donnell, written by Michael Schur and Megan Amram, aired October 18, 2018, https://www.imdb.com/title/tt8601210/?ref_=ttep_ep4. All information about the shows discussed in this chapter is from IMDb. See https://www.imdb.com/.
11. Kant, *Foundation for the Metaphysic of Morals*, Section 1, p. 393.
12. All Kant excerpts are from: http://www.gutenberg.org/files/5682/5682-h/5682-h.htm.
13. Ibid., 394.
14. Ibid., 396.
15. Ibid., 397–398.
16. Ibid., 398.
17. Ibid., 399.
18. Ibid., 399–400.
19. Ibid., 400.
20. Ibid., 401–402.
21. Kant, *Foundation*, 403.
22. Ibid., 402–403.
23. Kant, *Foundation*, Section Two, p. 408.
24. Ibid., 411–412.
25. Ibid., 428.
26. Ibid., 428–429.

Chapter 4

Utilitarianism through the Lens of *The Good Place*

4.1 *The Good Place* and "The Trolley Problem"

"The Trolley Problem" episode of *The Good Place*[1] centers around the famous ethical dilemma in which one is to imagine oneself in a trolley headed directly toward five people, whom it will kill, unless one uses the controls to redirect the trolley onto another track, on which stands only one person whom it will kill.

> Philippa Foot, who invented the dilemma, and Judith Jarvis Thomson, deserve a great deal of the credit for this thought experiment's fame.[6]

> It is recommended, but not necessary, to view this episode before reading further. One's reading and learning experience will benefit from having familiarity with the show. Go to a website like https://www.justwatch.com/ for information about which streaming services have *The Good Place,* and whether or not it is free, for rent, or for purchase.

These are the only two choices. Michael magically places the hopelessly indecisive Chidi in that exact scenario, and repeats it several different times to torture Chidi, who presumably had inflicted the thought experiment on many students throughout his teaching career. The correct answer to the dilemma seems obvious: choose the track with one person on it in order to save the five. The core principle of utilitarianism would clearly be in agreement with that intuitive decision, because in utilitarianism, one is to maximize happiness (which is pleasure) for the greatest number of people. The dilemma becomes more complicated when one considers another scenario with key similarities and differences: Imagine you are a surgeon who can save five dying people by killing one healthy person to distribute their organs on the five. The healthy person has not consented to this, and is, in fact, unaware of it.[1] Michael comically tortures Chidi by placing him in this scenario too.

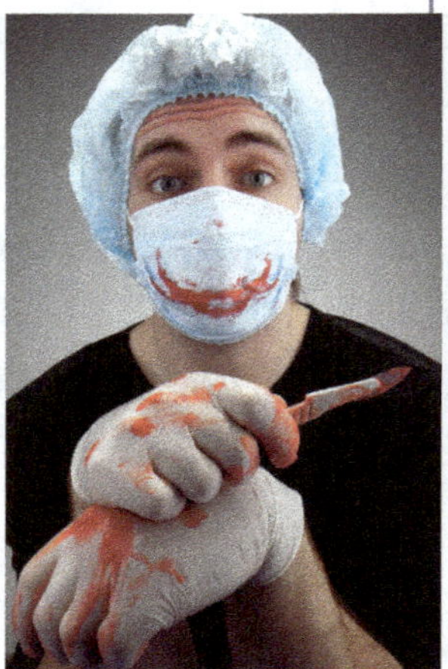

© Nomad_Soul/Shutterstock.com

© canadastock/Shutterstock.com

© Krakenimages.com/Shutterstock.com

QUESTIONS FOR CONSIDERATION

a. In the surgeon scenario, is it clear that one should be killed to save five?
b. Does the surgeon scenario cast doubt on the seemingly obvious decision to kill one and save five in the trolley case?

Though Philippa Foot intended for this example to be used in a debate about abortion, it also has clear value in the effort to understand utilitarianism. Utilitarianism understood one way seems to encourage the killing of one to save five in both scenarios, which would strike many reasonable people as morally questionable, if not reprehensible, though it may be difficult to explain why. For one, any reputable medical community would forbid the active killing of one person against their will in order to save five others. Utilitarianism, especially Mill's formulation of it, offers other guiding principles to reach clarity and perhaps even moral acceptability in both cases.

4.2 Introduction to Utilitarianism

Jeremy Bentham, who preceded John Stuart Mill, is the founder of the modern theory of utilitarianism. In *An Introduction to the Principles of Morals and Legislation*, Bentham identifies the core principle of his ethical theory as "**the principle of utility**":

THE PRINCIPLE OF UTILITY
According to Bentham, it "approves or disapproves" of actions based on their ability to maximize happiness, where happiness means pleasure.

> By the principle of utility is meant that principle which approves or disapproves of every action whatsoever, according to the tendency it appears to have to augment or diminish the happiness of the party whose interest is in question:

1. This addition is part of Foot's original explanation of the dilemma.

> or, what is the same thing in other words, to promote or to oppose that happiness. I say of every action whatsoever, and therefore not only of every action of a private individual, but of every measure of government.[2]

For Bentham, doing good means maximizing happiness, which he sees as pleasure. Furthermore, this principle applies not only to individuals, but to governments. Bentham goes on to explain what he means by pleasure, citing many different kinds. He emphasizes the quantity of pleasure more than its quality, famously saying that "push-pin" (a game) is as good as poetry. Also, he seems to focus on decision-making with regard to particular actions, rather than the establishment of general rules that can apply to many actions. For this reason, many consider Bentham to be an **act utilitarian**.

ACT UTILITARIAN
Calculates the happiness of individual acts and their consequences.

Mill develops utilitarianism by emphasizing the *quality* of pleasures and also by establishing general rules to maximize happiness for the greatest number of people. One can consider Mill to be a **rule utilitarian** for this reason. In Chapter One of *Utilitarianism*, Mill begins by explaining that much of his theory is not new. He credits Plato and the Epicureans for articulating precursors to utilitarianism. He then proceeds to distinguish himself from Kant, with whom he largely disagrees. The excerpted passages below are from Chapter Two, where one can see that like Bentham, Mill lays out the core principle of his ethical theory early on. He then argues for what he considers to be superior pleasures: intellectual, rather than physical pleasures. He also argues for several general rules, including some that are very familiar, which one can follow in order to be in line with his ethical theory.

RULE UTILITARIAN
Calculates the happiness of actions based on their association with rules, laws, or precedents; when the consequences of the rule or precedent maximizes happiness (pleasure), the associated action is deemed praiseworthy.

4.3 Annotated Excerpts from Mill's *Utilitarianism*

Chapter 2

[. . .]

The creed which accepts as the foundation of morals, Utility, or the Greatest Happiness Principle, holds that actions are right in proportion as they tend to promote happiness, wrong as they tend to produce the reverse of happiness. By happiness is intended pleasure, and the absence of pain; by unhappiness, pain, and the privation of pleasure.

GREATEST HAPPINESS PRINCIPLE
According to Mill, it obligates maximizing the greatest happiness for the greatest number of people.

> Mill's definition of happiness is arguably in tension with Aristotle's in the following way: Recall that the latter defines happiness (*eudaimonia*) as an activity of the soul in line with reason over a complete life, with sufficient external goods. Virtue is the perfection of activity in line with reason, and so, a complete life of virtue is a happy life. See *Nicomachean Ethics*, Book One, as well as Chapter Two above. One might object to this assessment of the conflict between Aristotle and Mill in the following way though, as Francis Fallon did in correspondence with me: If *eudaimonia* is intrinsically pleasant, and Mill admits higher forms of pleasure, then they can be read as compatible. Aristotle is incompatible with Bentham, of course. [. . .]

© mimagephotography/Shutterstock.com

© tommaso79/Shutterstock.com

Now, such a theory of life excites in many minds, and among them in some of the most estimable in feeling and purpose, inveterate dislike. To suppose that life has (as they express it) no higher end than pleasure—no better and nobler object of desire and pursuit—they designate as utterly mean and grovelling; as a doctrine only worthy of swine, to whom the followers of Epicurus were, at a very early period, contemptuously likened [. . .]

> He's explaining here that in its day, Epicureans were accused of being crude pleasure-seekers, willing to pursue any pleasurable activity no matter how immoral and seemingly subhuman. This is not an accurate view of Epicureanism or its modern relative, utilitarianism, according to Mill. Here he is trying to address and object to the possibility that utilitarianism could receive the same improper treatment as Epicureanism.

[. . .]

When thus attacked, the Epicureans have always answered, that it is not they, but their accusers, who represent human nature in a degrading light; since the accusation supposes human beings to be capable of no pleasures except those of which swine are capable. [...] The comparison of the Epicurean life to that of beasts is felt as degrading, precisely because a beast's pleasures do not satisfy a human being's conceptions of happiness. Human beings have faculties more elevated than the animal appetites, and when once made conscious of them, do not regard anything as happiness which does not include their gratification. [. . .] It is quite compatible with the principle of utility to recognize the fact, that some kinds of pleasure are more desirable and more valuable than others. It would be absurd that while, in estimating all other things, quality is considered as well as quantity, the estimation of pleasures should be supposed to depend on quantity alone.

© Chumash Maxim/Shutterstock.com

> So, what counts as pleasurable, and therefore constitutive of happiness, is not just any pleasure. Furthermore, a high quantity of pleasure is not necessarily a contributor to happiness. It's pleasures of a certain *quality* that Mill wants to argue for.

If I am asked, what I mean by difference of quality in pleasures, or what makes one pleasure more valuable than another, merely as a pleasure, except its being greater in amount, there is but one possible answer. Of two pleasures, if there be one to which all or almost all who have experience of both give a decided preference, irrespective of any feeling of moral obligation to prefer it, that is the more desirable pleasure.

> Mill's empirical approach is evident here. If most people consider one pleasure to be better than another, that is enough to deem the former to be superior. He's basically crowdsourcing the task of judging which pleasures are of the highest quality.

[. . .]

Now it is an unquestionable fact that those who are equally acquainted with, and equally capable of appreciating and enjoying, both, do give a most marked preference to the manner of existence which employs their higher faculties. Few human creatures would consent to be changed into any of the lower animals, for a promise of the fullest allowance of a beast's pleasures; no intelligent human being would consent to be a fool, no instructed person would be an ignoramus, no person of feeling and conscience would be selfish and base, even though they should be persuaded that the fool, the dunce, or the rascal is better satisfied with his lot than they are with theirs. [. . .] If they ever fancy they would, it is only in cases of unhappiness so extreme, that to escape from it they would exchange their lot for almost any other, however undesirable in their own eyes. A being of higher faculties requires more to make him happy, is capable probably of more acute suffering, and is certainly accessible to it at more points, than one of an inferior type; but in spite of these liabilities, he can never really wish to sink into what he feels to be a lower grade of existence. [. . .] It is better to be a human being dissatisfied than a pig satisfied; better to be Socrates dissatisfied than a fool satisfied. And if the fool, or the pig, is of a different opinion, it is because they only know their own side of the question.

> Mill thinks most people would prefer to live a life of long-lasting, deeply fulfilling pleasures, rather than a life filled with passing and superficial ones. The higher quality pleasures may involve more short-term dissatisfaction, but Mill thinks all would agree that this is a worthy price to pay for living a more fulfilling, and of course, more pleasant life.

[. . .]

It may be objected, that many who are capable of the higher pleasures, occasionally, under the influence of temptation, postpone them to the lower. But this is quite compatible with a full appreciation of the intrinsic superiority of the higher. Men often, from infirmity of character, make their election for the nearer good, though they know it to be the less valuable [. . .].

> One general rule of Mill's *Utilitarianism,* then, is to act in such a way that one maximizes higher quality pleasures, especially those of the intellect. Mill here allows for the possibility that those who generally do this may occasionally choose lower, more immediate pleasures, without abandoning their appreciation of the better pleasures. [. . .]

[. . .]

[. . .] Utilitarianism, therefore, could only attain its end by the general cultivation of nobleness of character [. . .]

> Another rule of utilitarianism, which is clearly related to the first, is to cultivate a noble character. Such a character is one that generally leads a person to value and to pursue consistently those pleasures of a higher quality. This includes cultivating the virtues, as Mill explains in Chapter Four.

According to the Greatest Happiness Principle, as above explained, the ultimate end, with reference to and for the sake of which all other things are desirable (whether we are considering our own good or that of other people), is an existence exempt as far as possible from pain, as rich as possible in enjoyments, both in point of quantity and quality [. . .].

[. . .]

[. . .] Next to selfishness, the principal cause which makes life unsatisfactory, is want of mental cultivation. A cultivated mind—I do not mean that of a philosopher, but any mind to which the fountains of knowledge have been opened, and which has been taught, in any tolerable degree, to exercise its faculties—finds sources of inexhaustible interest in all that surrounds it; in the objects of nature, the achievements of art, the imaginations of poetry, the incidents of history, the ways of mankind past and present, and their prospects in the future. [. . .]

> Mill does not want to be elitist and restrict the truly happy life to philosophers. Anyone with some education can potentially be opened to the riches of the intellectual life.

© IPGG/Shutterstock.com[3]

With regard to Mill's negative remark about selfishness, and the "ways of mankind," including their prospects: It is possible to expand upon this in the following way, as Fallon did in a correspondence with me—someone who is capable of taking pleasure in the pleasure of others has more opportunities for pleasure. This in turn motivates one to act for the greater good, by bringing closer together the greater good with one's own good.

Now there is absolutely no reason in the nature of things why an amount of mental culture sufficient to give an intelligent interest in these objects of contemplation, should not be the inheritance of every one born in a civilized country. [. . .] [. . .] Unless such a person, through bad laws, or subjection to the will of others, is denied the liberty to use the sources of happiness within his reach, he will not fail to find this enviable existence, if he escape the positive evils of life, the great sources of physical and mental suffering—such as indigence, disease, and the unkindness, worthlessness, or premature loss of objects of affection. [. . .]

It is possible for people to be closed out to the happy life Mill portrays because of a lack of opportunity; through bad fortune and/or poor government. Another rule, then, according to Mill's ethical theory, is for political communities and their leaders to foster the conditions for as many people as possible to be able to pursue rich intellectual lives.

[. . .]

In the golden rule of Jesus of Nazareth, we read the complete spirit of the ethics of utility. To do as one would be done by, and to love one's neighbor as oneself, constitute the ideal perfection of utilitarian morality. As the means of making the nearest approach to this ideal, utility would enjoin, first, that laws and social arrangements should place the happiness, or (as speaking practically it may be called) the interest, of every individual, as nearly as possible in harmony with the interest of the whole; and secondly, that education and opinion, which have so vast a power over human character, should so use that power as to establish in the mind of every individual an indissoluble association between his own happiness and the good of the whole [. . .]. [. . .][3]

2. Statue in Florence, Italy, of Leonardo da Vinci, famous painter, engineer, and inventor.

> Another rule: As individuals, we ought to do to others what we would want for ourselves. In this spirit, societies should foster the conditions for its people to live by this principle. This would be for the good (the happiness) of the whole. According to Fallon, in correspondence with me: One's happiness is no more or less important than another's, therefore we must treat others' happiness as equal to our own. This principle of equal treatment could serve as a fast refutation of egoism.

> It's clear here that though Mill does not rely on theological claims to support his ethical theory, his theory is consonant with core Christian values.

In Chapter Three, Mill argues that both internal and external sanctions (punishments) should enforce the rules of utilitarianism. Internally, one's conscience should be the guide. Externally, the force of society's praise or blame, as well as laws, are among the sanctions Mill considers. In Chapter Four, he argues that it is consistent with the principles of utilitarianism to seek the attainment of virtue, and furthermore, that one cannot have too much virtue. On the other hand, though money and fame can contribute to happiness, when pursued to excess, they are opposed to Mill's ethical theory because they make one "noxious" to society.

© UfaBizPhoto/Shutterstock.com

© Fancy Studio/Shutterstock.com

In Chapter Five, Mill treats the concept of justice:

DUTIES OF PERFECT OBLIGATION
Necessary responsibilities; associated with respecting people's rights.

DUTIES OF IMPERFECT OBLIGATION
Significant and good, but not necessary responsibilities; not associated with the respect for basic rights; sometimes referred to as supererogatory, which can also be used in other ways. Example: Doing volunteer work.

[. . .]

[. . .] Now it is known that ethical writers divide moral duties into two classes, denoted by the ill-chosen expressions, duties of perfect and of imperfect obligation; the latter being those in which, though the act is obligatory, the particular occasions of performing it are left to our choice; as in the case of charity or beneficence, which we are indeed bound to practise, but not towards any definite person, nor at any prescribed time. In the more precise language of philosophic jurists, duties of perfect obligation are those duties in virtue of which a correlative right resides in some person or persons; duties of imperfect obligation are those moral obligations which do not give birth to any right. [. . .] It seems to me that this feature in the case—a right in some person, correlative to the moral obligation—constitutes the specific difference between justice, and generosity or beneficence. Justice implies something which it is not

> only right to do, and wrong not to do, but which some individual person can claim from us as his moral right. [. . .]
>
> [. . .]
>
> To have a right, then is, I conceive, to have something which society ought to defend me in the possession of. If the objector goes on to ask why it ought, I can give him no other reason than general utility. [. . .]

> The final general rule to observe here is that we have a perfect obligation to respect and protect people's rights. Rights are determined by general utility, meaning that everyone has a right to the conditions, and the ability, to live happily. For Mill, a fairly high level of security is crucial, as well as education, among other things. For lists of human rights as officially determined by various political and legal bodies throughout the years, see: The US Bill of Rights, 1789, http://www.gutenberg.org/0/2/2-h/2-h.htm, The French Declaration of the Rights of Man, 1789, https://avalon.law.yale.edu/18th_century/rightsof.asp, and The United Nations' Universal Declaration of Human Rights, 1948, http://www.self.gutenberg.org/articles/eng/Universal_Declaration_of_Human_Rights.

QUESTIONS FOR CONSIDERATION

a. Why does Mill think it is better to consistently seek higher quality pleasures, even though lower, more physical, pleasures are easier to attain?
b. What does Mill mean when he says, "It is better to be a human being dissatisfied than a pig satisfied; better to be Socrates dissatisfied than a fool satisfied?" Do you agree? Why or why not?
c. What should governments do in order to create the conditions under which Mill's conception of a happy life is possible?
d. Why is the observance of the golden rule of Christianity in accordance with Mill's version of utilitarianism?
e. Why is it accurate to describe Mill's theory of ethics as consequentialist?

4.4 The Trolley Problem, Natural Law, Locke, Kant, and Utilitarianism

4.4.1 Philippa Foot and Double Effect

Philippa Foot, in examining the **doctrine of double effect**, asks the reader to suppose that "the driver of a runaway tram" can "only steer from one narrow track on to another; five men are working on one track and one man on the other; anyone on the track he enters is bound to be killed." She adds, "The question is why we should say, without hesitation, that the driver should steer for the less occupied track,"[4] given other similar scenarios, like the following:

DOCTRINE OF DOUBLE EFFECT
Says that doing an immoral act intentionally is ethically impermissible, unlike doing something good intentionally that has unintended immoral consequences, even when those results are foreseen.

> Why then do we not feel justified in killing people in the interests of cancer research or to obtain, let us say, spare parts for grafting on to those who need them? We can suppose, similarly, that several dangerously ill people can be saved only if we kill a certain individual and make a serum from his dead body.[5]

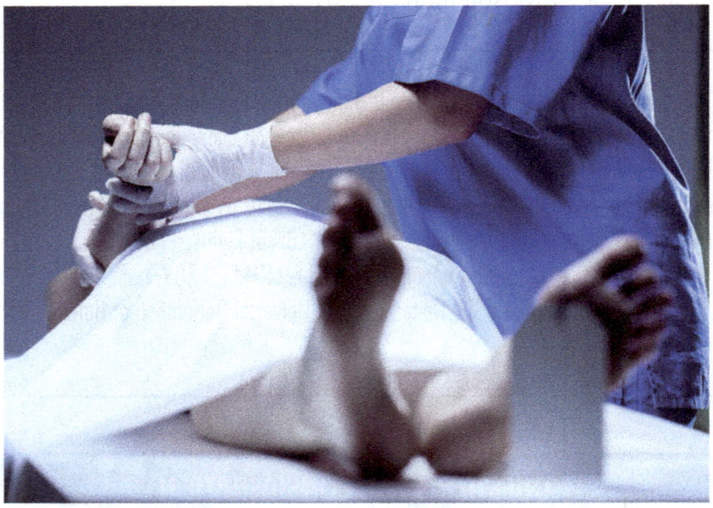

© Photographee.eu/Shutterstock.com

4.4.2 Natural Law and Foot's Scenarios

From the perspective of natural law, the most relevant precept to these invented scenarios is that against the killing of innocents. Recall from Chapter Three that the duty to preserve human life, which accords with a strong natural inclination, is fundamental according to Aquinas. In the tram example, someone will die; it is inevitable. Furthermore, the driver *finds* himself on the runaway tram. He does not set it in motion with the intent of killing someone. In the medical example, on the other hand, someone will kill one person to save several. The act of killing an innocent person is clearly forbidden by natural law.

QUESTIONS FOR CONSIDERATION

a. Given that natural law theorists like Aquinas want to preserve human life, would it be right according to him to kill one in order to save several others?
b. If it's always wrong to kill an innocent person according to natural law, does this mean that the tram driver is forbidden from steering the vehicle away from the five workers and toward the one?

The doctrine of double effect, which is often used in natural law ethics, distinguishes between the intent to kill and the intent to save. If one takes an action intended to save someone (or several people) that has the unintended (or not directly intended) consequence of killing someone else, that action is morally permissible according to the doctrine of double effect. On the other hand, intentionally killing an innocent person, even though it will save someone else, is impermissible. The most common contemporary example in which this doctrine is applied is that of abortion, discussed further in Chapter Five.

QUESTIONS FOR CONSIDERATION

a. Given the doctrine of double effect, what would natural law theorists say about the tram problem (a.k.a. the "Trolley Problem")?
b. What would natural law ethicists say about killing someone in a medical scenario in order to save others?
c. What is your assessment of the probable verdicts of natural law ethics on these invented scenarios?

4.4.3 Deontological Ethics, the Trolley, and the Devious Doctors

A brief recap of concepts from Chapter Three: The first formulation of the categorical imperative, according to Kant, asks the decision-maker to consider the maxim or principle of their action, and whether or not it can be adopted universally. Recall this commandment's prohibition against lying and other forms of exceptionalism. The second formulation dictates that human beings ought to be treated as ends, and never as means. In other words, people cannot be used the way that tools or money can.

QUESTIONS FOR CONSIDERATION

a. How could one phrase the maxims of the tram driver's possible actions?
b. What might the first formulation of the categorical imperative oblige the driver to do?
c. What is a viable way of articulating the doctors' possible maxims in the unwilling organ donor example? Would more than one maxim be involved? Would a principle of deception, of the donors by the medical professionals, be necessary?
d. What might the first formulation of the categorical imperative dictate about this scenario?
e. Would there be a clear verdict by the second formulation of the categorical imperative about the tram/trolley problem?
f. What would the second formulation of the categorical imperative dictate about the unwilling organ donor example?
g. If Chidi is a Kantian, does his indecision as the trolley driver accurately reflect the possible application of deontological ethics to the trolley/tram problem?

4.4.4 Utilitarianism, the Tram, and the Medical Mutilators

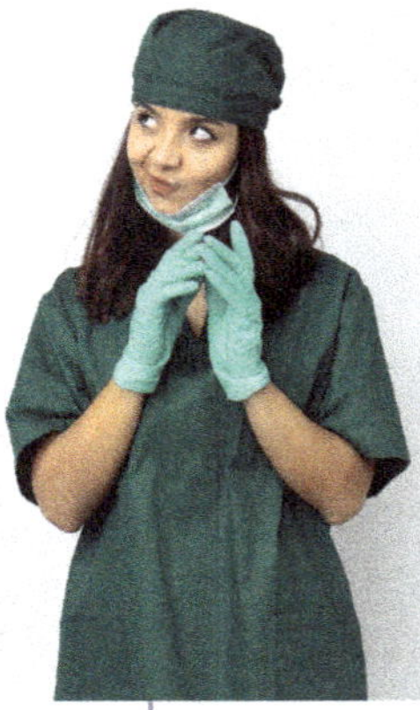

A strict act utilitarian, perhaps one following more in Bentham's footsteps than Mill's, would simply consider the amount of happiness (pleasure) that each decision would yield, and then opt for the course of action that maximizes the quantity of happiness. In both scenarios, the act utilitarian would weigh the pain and suffering of one person and their loved ones against the pain and suffering of several people and their loved ones. A rule utilitarian dedicated to the application of Mill's version of utilitarianism, on the other hand, would give serious weight to the following rules in considering Foot's examples: (1) Do to others what one would want done to oneself. (2) Do not violate people's rights. People have the rights that are needed to afford everyone the conditions necessary for living happily. Presumably, then, one would have the right to life, with possible exceptions, including situations in which one threatens others' lives.

QUESTIONS FOR CONSIDERATION

a. What would an act utilitarian decide is the best course of action for the driver? For the surgeons in the unwilling organ donor example?
b. What would a rule utilitarian decide is the best course of action for the driver? For the surgeons in the organ donor example?
c. What is your critical assessment of the different forms of utilitarianism when applied to Foot's examples?
d. Considering all of the ethical theories in this chapter, which one(s) do you think would be best for the tram/trolley driver to adopt? Why?
e. What about the surgeons and their possible organ donor—which theory or theories would be best?
f. Would you change your mind if the one worker alone on the track was someone you loved? Why? Why not?
g. What about if the potential non-consenting organ donor was one of your loved ones?
h. What if one of the people who could be saved by the unwitting donor is a person you love?
i. Recall the definition of moral relativism from Chapter Three: Should relativism have a place in the ethical decisions involved in Foot's examples?
j. Should there be impartial decision-makers who are appointed to set standards for such decisions? If so, what ethical theory or theories should they favor? Why?
k. Is it reasonable to employ a combination of ethical theories in one's decision-making?

4.5 Resources for Further Study

4.5.1 Freely Available Online Sources

Anscombe, G. E. M. "Who is Wronged? Philippa Foot on Double Effect: One Point." *Oxford Review* 5 (1967): 6. https://philarchive.org/rec/FOOTPO-2

Bentham, Jeremy. *An Introduction to the Principles of Morals and Legislation*. (1823). https://oll.libertyfund.org/titles/bentham-an-introduction-to-the-principles-of-morals-and-legislation

Foot, Philippa. "The Problem of Abortion and the Doctrine of Double Effect," *Oxford Review* 5 (1967): 1–5. https://philarchive.org/rec/FOOTPO-2

Mill, John Stuart. *Utilitarianism*. (1879). https://www.gutenberg.org/files/11224/11224-h/11224-h.htm

Wilson, James. "The Trolley Problem." *Psyche* (2020). https://aeon.co/essays/what-is-the-problem-with-ethical-trolley-problems

4.5.2 Books

Macleod, Christopher, and Dale Miller, eds. *A Companion to Mill*. London: Wiley-Blackwell, 2016.

Crisp, Roger. *Routledge Philosophy Guidebook to Mill*. London: Routledge, 1997.

Endnotes

1. *The Good Place*, season 2, episode 5, directed by Dean Holland, written by Michael Schur and Josh Siegal, aired October 19, 2017, https://www.imdb.com/title/tt6951978/?ref_=ttep_ep5. All information about the shows and films of this chapter is from IMDb. See https://www.imdb.com/.
2. Bentham, *An Introduction to the Principles of Morals and Legislation* (1823): I.II. From: https://oll.libertyfund.org/titles/bentham-an-introduction-to-the-principles-of-morals-and-legislation.
3. All excerpts of Mill's *Utilitarianism* are from: https://www.gutenberg.org/files/11224/11224-h/11224-h.htm.
4. In one of many responses to this article by well-known philosophers, Thomson refers to the tram scenario as the "trolley problem." See Thomson, 359.
5. Foot, 3.
6. See Foot, "The Problem of Abortion and the Doctrine of Double Effect," *Oxford Review 5* (1967): 1–5. Also see Thomson, "Turning the Trolley," *Philosophy and Public Affairs 36* (2008): 359–374.

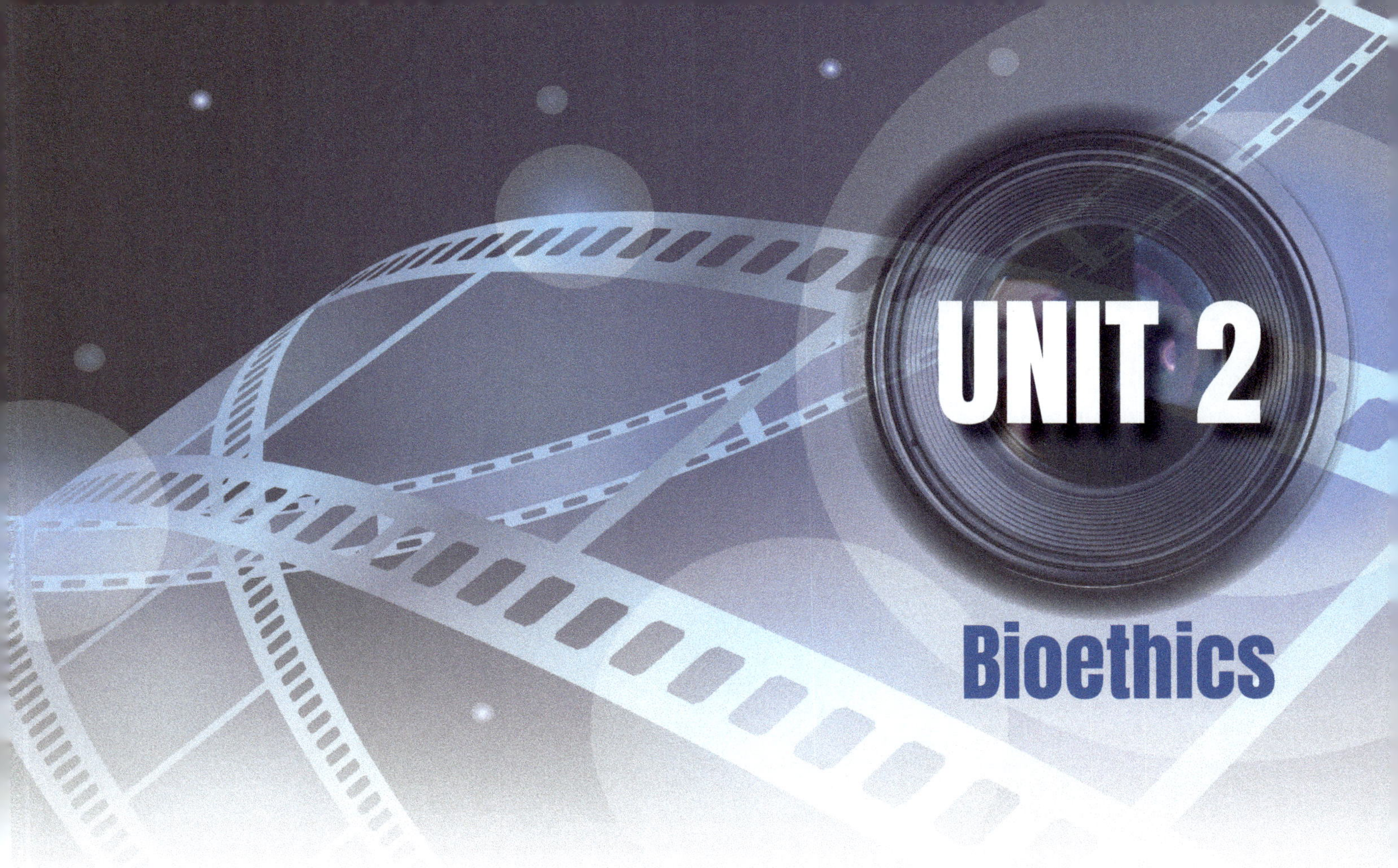

UNIT 2

Bioethics

Chapter 5

Abortion

5.1 Introduction

ABORTION
According to the CDC: "a legal induced abortion is defined as an intervention performed by a licensed clinician (e.g., a physician, a nurse-midwife, nurse practitioner, physician assistant) within the limits of state regulations that is intended to terminate a suspected or known ongoing intrauterine pregnancy and that does not result in a live birth."[50]

Abortion may very well be the most controversial issue of this book. Arguments for and against its legality and moral permissibility often start and end with emotionally-heated statements that resemble popular slogans: "Pro-choice = Pro-death!"; "Protect the Unborn!"; "Pro-choicers are murderers!"; "My body, my choice!"; "Respect a woman's right to choose!"; "Stop trying to control women's bodies!" Such tactics isolate each side of the debate from one another by demonizing one's opponents. They also commit logical fallacies and are therefore bad arguments. A tactic that argues by means of emotion commits the fallacy of appeal to pity. An argument that demonizes the personal character of one's opponent commits the ad hominem fallacy. One who uses a slogan to distract from the relevant premises commits the red herring fallacy, while one who unfairly reduces an argument to make it more vulnerable to attack commits the straw man fallacy.

Those in favor of abortion's legality, and who argue that it is morally permissible at least in some cases, identify as "pro-choice." They tend to be on the left of the political spectrum, and are mostly liberals. In recent years, the US Democratic Party has mostly represented such a position. Many utilitarians adopt this position.[1] The pro-choice argument focuses on a woman's right to privacy and bodily autonomy.[2] The pro-choice position defends the need to protect a woman's right to determine her own medical care, rather than having it determined for her. An example of a

> It is highly recommended to view the film before reading further. For one, what follows contains spoilers. Also, one's reading and learning experience will benefit from having familiarity with the movie. Go to a website like https://www.justwatch.com/ for information about which streaming services have *Juno*, and whether or not it is free, for rent, or for purchase.

1. See Chapter Four on utilitarianism.
2. The ability and freedom to determine what happens to one's body.

ARGUMENT[1]
At its core, according to logicians, is at least one statement or proposition being claimed to support another one; note that this is much different from the definition of this term in normal everyday English.

PROPOSITION
Synonymous with "statement," it is a claim that may or may not occur as a complete sentence; an argument contains at least two propositions: a premise and a conclusion; one proposition on its own does not constitute an argument.
Example A: All abortions are unfortunate.
Example B: In light of the fact that all abortions are unfortunate, . . .

PREMISES
The statements or propositions being claimed to support the conclusion; an argument must have at least one of these, but it can also have many more.

CONCLUSION
The main point of the argument; its main claim; the statement that is the logical result of the premises; the statement or proposition the premises claim to support.

LOGICAL FALLACIES
The technical term for mistakes in argumentation.

BAD ARGUMENTS
Technically, those that are either unsound or not cogent; a false premise, or premises that do not actually support the conclusion, are what can make an argument bad; fallacies make arguments bad.

APPEAL TO PITY
A.k.a. the fallacy of "appeal to emotion"; instead of supporting a conclusion with reasons, it relies on various emotions to persuade the listener; emotions cannot validly support a conclusion.
Example: Abortion is both sad and enraging, therefore it should be outlawed.

AD HOMINEM
A.k.a. the fallacy "argument against the person"; attacks a person's character rather than their argument when their character is not relevant to the argument.
Example: Pro-lifers hate women and want to control women's bodies, therefore abortion should be legal.

RED HERRING
Introduces an irrelevant premise intended to distract others from the argument.
Example: Washington is highly flawed, therefore late-term abortions should be legal.

STRAW MAN
Makes an argument more vulnerable to attack by unfairly simplifying it or misrepresenting it in some other way.
Example: Murder is wrong, therefore abortion is wrong.

PRO-CHOICE
In favor of keeping abortion legal and accessible.

LIBERALS
Different from classical liberalism; the left of the political spectrum; progressives; typically more interested in change and reform than conservatives; the Far Left is usually more associated with socialism than liberalism.

PRO-LIFE
Opposed to the legalization of abortion; in favor of imposing restrictions on access to abortion.

CONSERVATIVES
Opposite liberals on the political spectrum; on the right of the spectrum; typically in favor of smaller, more minimal government; the Far Right is usually more associated with radicals in favor of actions that most conservatives oppose.

leftist extremist on abortion is Peter Singer, who even justifies infanticide and the killing of people with disabilities.[1]

Those against the legality and permissibility of abortion identify as "**pro-life**," and tend to be on the right of the political spectrum. They are mostly **conservatives** and the US Republican Party (or GOP) has largely represented such a position in recent years, though the pro-life faction within the Democratic Party is not insignificant. Those who favor natural law ethics[3] typically adopt this conservative stance on abortion. Pro-life arguments largely focus on the defense of the right to life of the unborn, which they argue, outweighs a woman's right to privacy and self-determination. An example of Right-wing extremism with regard to abortion is those who bomb abortion clinics.

© mark reinstein/Shutterstock.com

© Xavier Ascanio/Shutterstock.com

© Kamaan Richards/Shutterstock.com

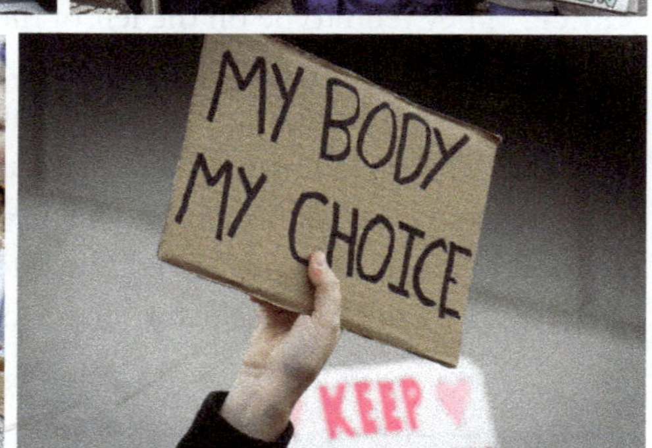

© Traci Hahn/Shutterstock.com

3. See Chapter Three on natural law ethics.

Some pro-lifers believe that abortion should be reduced by means other than making it illegal, on the grounds that such action may result in "underground" abortions that are much more dangerous to pregnant women. More preferable and effective abortion-reducing means, they argue, include social supports for women.

Those in-between the two typical pro-choice and pro-life stances are **moderates**. Though some moderates may "lean"[4] left or right, or "lean" Democrat or Republican, others are independent, and yet others identify with another party. Philosophical arguments about the morality of abortion are more complex than those typically given by those on the left or right. This chapter explores a range of such arguments, and considers questions and objections from across a wide swath of the political spectrum. In so doing, the chapter attempts to adopt a neutral, unbiased stance on the issue.

MODERATES
The middle of the political spectrum; sympathize with aspects of both conservatism and liberalism; the opposite of extremists or radicals.

QUESTION FOR CONSIDERATION

a. Reflect on your own personal stance before reading further. What is it? If you watched the film before beginning to read this, what was your stance before you watched the film? Keep that in mind as you read. Perhaps jot it down in a notebook or journal.

5.2 Background Information

5.2.1 The Stages of Fetal Development

Selections adapted from the work of the Cleveland Clinic.

First Trimester

Moment of fertilization: Genetic makeup of the unborn is complete, including its sex.[2]

Week 2: Most experts agree that **twinning** does not occur after this point.

Week 3: **Blastocyte** cells "form a little ball, or an **embryo**."[3]

Week 4: Primitive face has formed, circulation has begun, small heart-like tube has begun beating.

Week 6: Heartbeat can usually be detected.[4]

Week 7: First brain activity present; unborn may feel pain/have the ability to suffer/be **sentient**.[5]

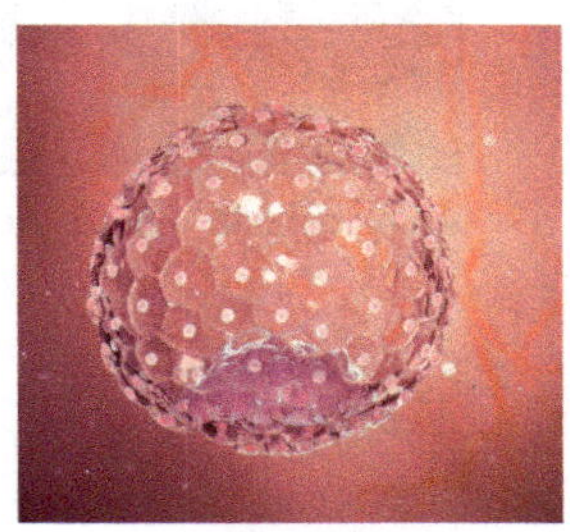

© SciePro/Shutterstock.com

A 3-D rendering of a blastocyst becoming an embryo.

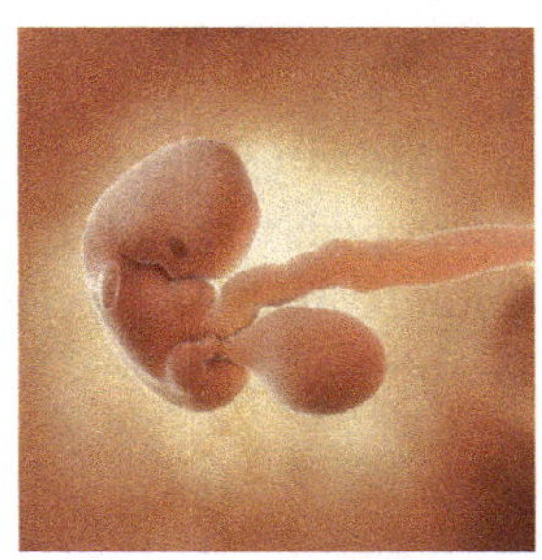

© SciePro/Shutterstock.com

A 3-D-rendered illustration of a late-stage embryo.

TWINNING
"When a single fertilized egg splits and develops into two fetuses [. . .] Genetically, the two babies are identical." Fraternal twins occur when two eggs are fertilized by different sperm.[51] There is widespread agreement that it occurs only before the two-week mark of pregnancy, though there are reasons to reconsider this consensus.[52]

BLASTOCYST
"A sphere of cells enclosing an inner mass of cells and a fluid-filled cavity."[53]

EMBRYO
"Characterized by cleavage, the laying down of fundamental tissues, and the formation of primitive organs and organ systems."[54]

SENTIENT
Able to think in some way; able to experience pain and pleasure; able to suffer.

4. Meaning to tend toward that side of the spectrum.

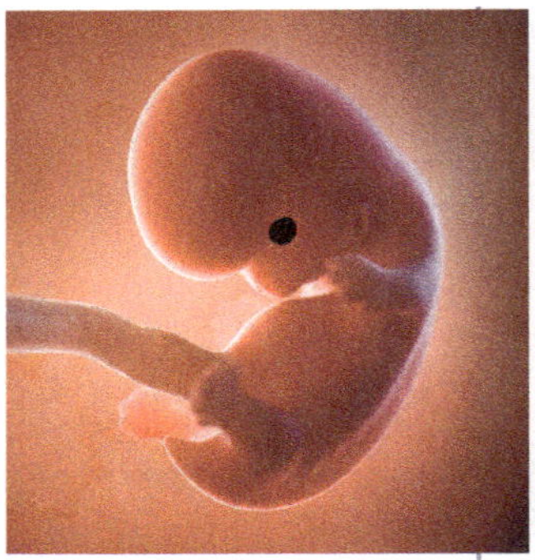

A 3-D-rendered illustration of an 8-week fetus.

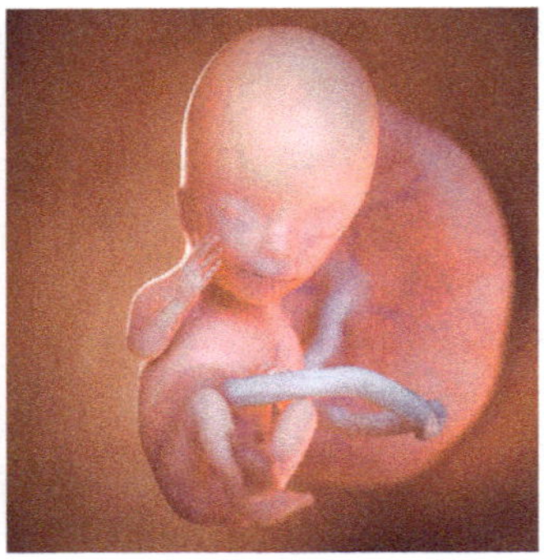

A 3-D-rendered image of a fetus at week 12.

Week 8: Embryo is now a **fetus**.

Week 12: Body is fully formed, includes most organs and extremities, as well as circulatory and urinary systems; unborn is around 4 inches long and weighs about 1 ounce; chance of miscarriage considerably drops.

FETUS
Has attained "the basic structural plan of its kind."[55]

Second Trimester

Month 4 (weeks 13–16): Can suck thumb, yawn, stretch, and make facial expressions; reproductive organs are fully developed; grows to about 6 inches and 4 ounces.

QUICKENING
The initial movements of the fetus felt by the mother; usually described as a "flutter."

Month 5 (weeks 17–20): **Quickening** occurs (able to feel fetus moving); hair begins to grow; grows to roughly 10 inches and .5–1 pound.

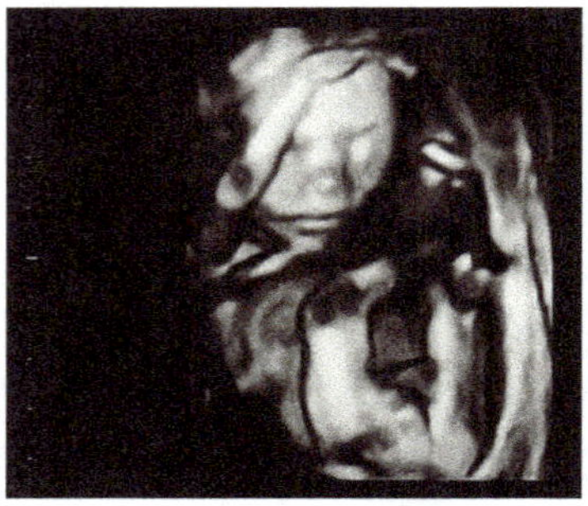

An ultrasound scan at week 18.

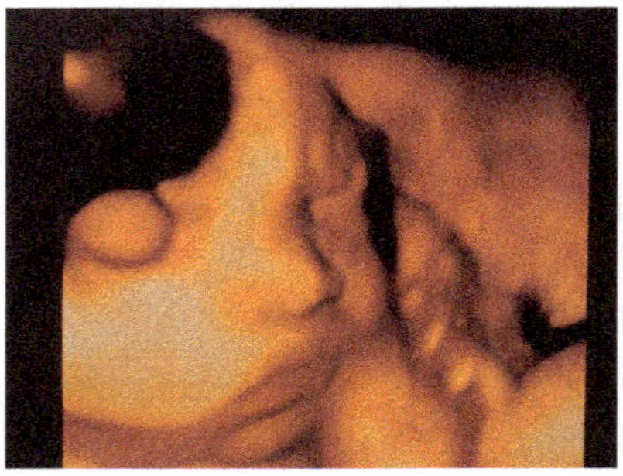

A 4-D ultrasound taken at 20 weeks.

VIABILITY
The stage of pregnancy at which the fetus can survive outside the womb with medical intervention.

Month 6 (weeks 21–24): Eyes begin to open; responds to sounds; hiccups; **viability** occurs after 23rd week with intensive care; roughly 12 inches and 2 lbs by end of this period.

Month 7 (weeks 25–28): Hearing is fully developed; responds to light; grows to 2–4 pounds; likely to survive if born.

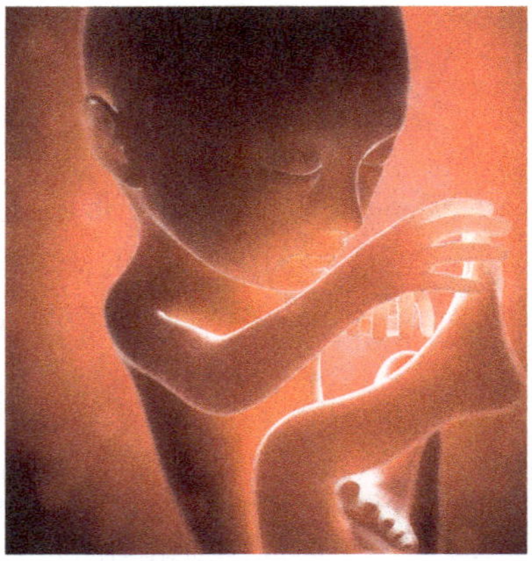

A 3-D-rendered illustration of a fetus at month 7.

Third Trimester

Month 8 (weeks 29–32): Can see and hear; lungs may still be immature.

Month 9 (weeks 33–36): Can blink, grasp, respond to sound, light, and touch.

Month 10 (weeks 37–40): Could go into labor at any time.[6]

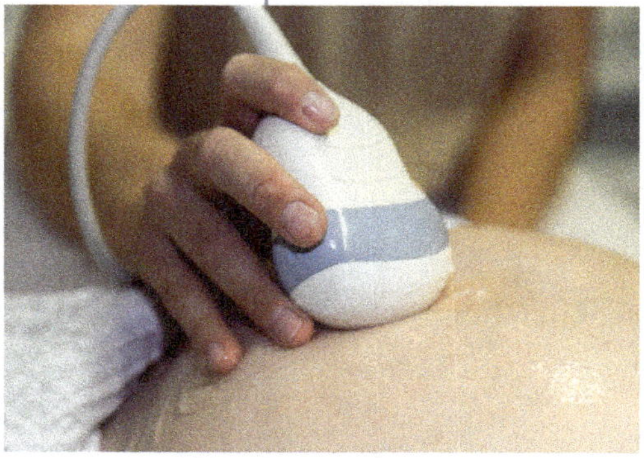

© SP-Photo/Shutterstock.com

A woman 8 months pregnant getting an ultrasound.

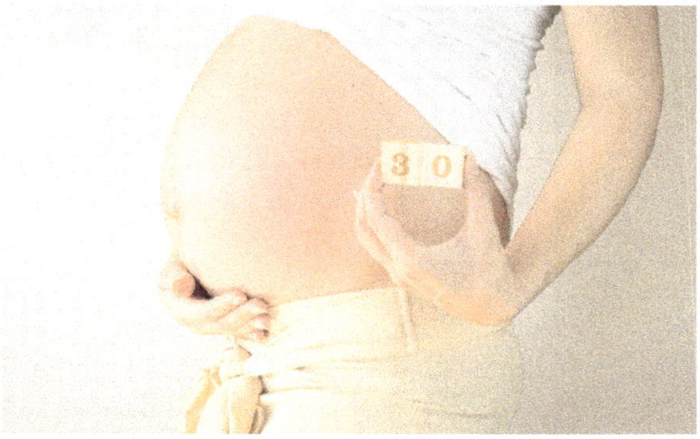

© Vivvi Smak/Shutterstock.com

A photo of a woman 30 weeks pregnant.

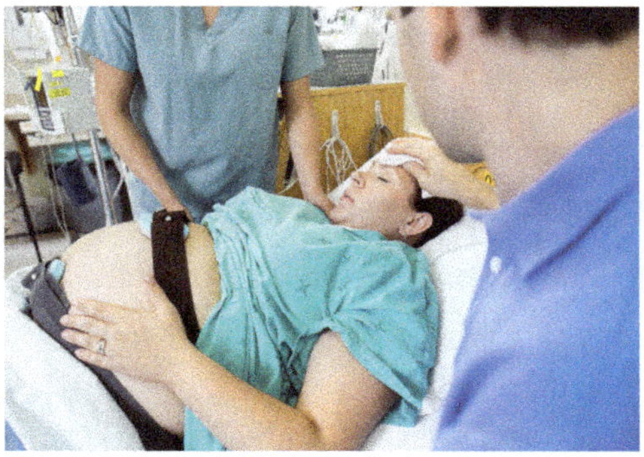

© Tyler Olson/Shutterstock.com

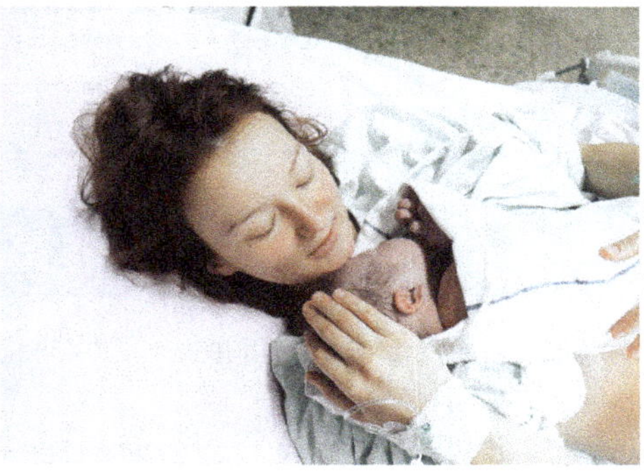

© Natalia Deriabina/Shutterstock.com

© Monkey Business Images/Shutterstock.com

5.2.2 Methods for Abortion: Brief Overview

Up to week 9	**Early medication** (non-surgical) possible; if it doesn't work, surgery may be needed.
Weeks 6–14	**Suction Curettage (Aspiration):** Cervix is dilated, tube attached to suction machine inserted into uterus, which is emptied by suction; then, tool (curette) is used to scrape wall of uterus, removing remnants of fetus and afterbirth that remain; shots given to woman, antibiotics may be ordered, other medicines may be used to reduce bleeding.
Weeks 12–24	**Dilation and Evacuation:** Most common method after 12 weeks; sponges ("luminaria") inserted into opening of cervix to cause slow opening over several hours; other methods could be used to stretch and open cervix; various anesthetizing methods may be used; "tools and suction tubes" are inserted into uterus to remove fetus; for woman: shots given, antibiotics may be ordered, other medicines may be used; very slight chance fetus will survive.
Advanced Pregnancy:	**Induction of Labor:** Usually done in hospital setting; several methods can be used to open cervix; several methods can be used to induce labor; could take 20 hours or more to deliver; chemicals injected into uterus to ensure fetus does not survive; "slight chance that the fetus could live for a short time"; for woman: shots given, antibiotics may be ordered, other medicines may be used.
Advanced Pregnancy	**Hysterotomy/Cesarean Delivery:** Uterus is cut open; has same risks as Cesarean delivery; for woman: shots given, antibiotics may be ordered, other medicines may be used.[7]

QUESTIONS FOR CONSIDERATION

a. What are your initial reactions to the descriptions of the stages of labor and the methods used for abortion?
b. How do you think a person who is pro-life would react to the term "safe abortion"? Why does it matter to consider this perspective?
c. Do you think abortion is just a women's issue? Why or why not?

5.2.3 Legal History

Because of the famous *Roe v. Wade* (1973) US Supreme Court decision, abortion is legally protected in the US under the following conditions:

- During the first trimester (conception to 12 weeks)
- Whenever the health of the mother is in danger
- *Roe v. Wade* does not prohibit abortions in other circumstances, but rather, leaves it up to states to determine. These circumstances include:
  - In the second trimester (weeks 13–28) when the health of the mother is threatened, states may *regulate* but not *ban* abortion.

- In the third trimester (weeks 29–40) when the woman's health is not threatened, states may ban abortion.

Additional US Supreme Court rulings and their implications are as follows:

- *Planned Parenthood of Southeastern Pennsylvania v. Casey* (1992): Restrictions on abortion are unconstitutional if they result in an "undue burden" on a woman's ability to obtain an abortion before the point of viability.[5]
- *Gonzales v. Carhart* (2007): Partial-Birth Abortion Ban Act (2003) upheld, which prohibited "intact dilation and evacuation."
- *Whole Woman's Health v. Hellerstedt* (2016): Struck two provisions requiring clinics to attain standards of "ambulatory surgical centres and abortion doctors to have admitting privileges at a nearby hospital."
- *June Medical Services LLC v Russo* (2020): Declared unconstitutional a law nearly identical to the one struck down in 2016.[8]

The US Supreme Court building in Washington, DC.

Notably, the US Supreme Court does not recognize the unborn as a person, though it does make an effort to protect the life of a fetus in the third trimester. Some noteworthy implications of US law on abortion are as follows:

- According to US federal law, a woman could have an abortion in week 39, right before the baby's birth, for any reason, as long as their state did not ban it.
- If the woman's health is threatened (not necessarily her life), US federal law dictates that her state must allow her to obtain an abortion even in the 39th week.
- In reality, only 1.3% of abortions in the US take place after 21 weeks.[9]
- According to the chairman of obstetrics and gynecology at Oregon Health and Science University, there are no abortions in the US at the 38th or 39th week.[10]

5. This is the point at which the unborn may survive outside the womb, perhaps with intensive care. Currently, it is the 23rd week. See "Fetal Development: Stages of Growth," Cleveland Clinic, last reviewed April 16, 2020, https://my.clevelandclinic.org/health/articles/7247-fetal-development-stages-of-growth.

- According strictly to US federal law, a woman who is raped may not be able to obtain an abortion after week 12 if her health is not in jeopardy.
- In reality, most states allow abortion in cases of rape, and studies indicate that only 1% of women seek abortion because they have been raped.[11]
- In New York State, a woman can abort in the 23rd week of pregnancy, when the fetus could survive outside the womb with intensive care, even if the mother's health is not at risk. At week 24, in New York, women can only have abortions if their life is at risk or in the case of "fetal abnormality."[12]
- In Georgia, a law signed into effect on May 7, 2019, would make it illegal for a young teen to have an abortion after 6 weeks of pregnancy, as long as her health is not at risk and a police report for rape or incest had not been filed.[13]

© Foxys Graphic/Shutterstock.com

5.2.4 Abortion Statistics in the US

5.2.4.1 2016 Data on Abortion from the CDC

- 623,471 legal abortions were reported in 2016
- There were 186 abortions for every 1,000 births
- The number of abortions fell by 2% from 2015, and by 24% since 2007[6]
- 91% took place in the first trimester (65.5% before 8 weeks), 7.7% from 14–20 weeks, and 1.2% after 21 weeks[14]
- Those under age 15 accounted for .3% of all abortions
- Age 15–19: 9.4%
- The percentage and rate of abortions among teens decreased 43% and 56% respectively since 2007
- 43.1% of abortions were for women with one or more previous induced abortions[15]

6. There is some debate about whether or not abortions decrease more when Democrats are in control of the government, as opposed to Republicans.

5.2.4.2 Reasons Given for Having an Abortion

In 2004, according to one study reported by the Guttmacher Institute[7]:

- Not prepared/bad timing: 25%
- Finances: 23%
- Done with childbearing/others depending on me: 19%
- Don't want to be single mom/have relationship problems: 8%
- Feel immature/too young to be a parent: 7%
- Would interfere with education or career: 4%
- Health problem for mother: 4%
- Health problem for unborn: 3%
- Rape: < .5%
- Husband or partner wants abortion: <.5%
- Parents want me to have the abortion: <.5%
- Don't want people to know I had sex/got pregnant: <.5%
- Other: 6%[16]

5.2.4.3 Views on Abortion According to Gallup

Statistics from 2020 Polls:

On the Legality of Abortion:

- 35% think it should be legal only in a few circumstances
- 29% think it should be legal under any circumstance
- 20% think it should be illegal under all circumstances
- 14% think it should be legal under most circumstances
- 3% have no opinion

Political Stances on Abortion:

- 48% consider themselves pro-choice
- 46% consider themselves pro-life
- 4% "Mixed/Neither"
- 2% "Don't know what terms mean"

On the Morality of Abortion:

- 47% think it is "morally wrong"
- 44% think it is "morally acceptable"
- 9% think morality depends on situation
- 1% have no opinion on the morality of abortion

Statistics from 2018 Polls:

Regarding the Stage of Pregnancy:

- 60% thought abortion should be legal in the first three months of pregnancy
- 28% thought it should be legal in the second three months
- 13% thought it should be legal in the last three months

7. This is a left-leaning institution.

Regarding Circumstances in the First Trimester:

- 83% thought it should be legal in the first trimester when the woman's life is in danger
- 56% thought it should be legal in the first trimester when the child would be born with a mental disability
- 67% thought it should be legal in the first trimester "when the child would be born with a life-threatening illness"
- 77% thought it should be legal in the first trimester if the result of rape or incest
- 45% thought it should be legal in the first trimester "when the woman does not want the child for any reason"
- 49% thought it should be legal in the first trimester when the child would have Down Syndrome[17]

QUESTIONS FOR CONSIDERATION

a. What are your initial reactions to these statistics? Was anything surprising? Why or why not?
b. What are your thoughts about the reasons given for wanting an abortion?
c. What do you think about the very last statistic reporting those who approve of abortion for fetuses with Down Syndrome?[8]

5.3 Legality and Morality

This chapter examines arguments for and against the morality of abortion through the lens of the film *Juno*, as well as scholarly work by Judith Jarvis Thomson, Don Marquis, and Lisa Cahill. It's crucial to point out here that legality does not equal, and does not imply, morality. Ancient and medieval political theorists like Aristotle and Augustine argued that government should foster virtue in those governed. However, modern theorists like John Locke and John Stuart Mill argue for less government involvement in the behavior and character formation of the people. The result of this shift in theory is that in recent democratic governments, laws are determined with regard to the protection of basic rights, rather than whether or not they cultivate ethical behavior among the citizenry. Just because something is legal, does not mean that all of the actions it permits are moral. This has always been true, but it is arguably truer now than it was before Enlightenment thinkers like Locke and Mill. In US states like New Hampshire, for instance, parents have the legal right to homeschool their children. This does not mean, however, that parents should

8. Information about what Down Syndrome is: "Down Syndrome," Mayo Clinic, accessed October 15, 2020, https://www.mayoclinic.org/diseases-conditions/down-syndrome/symptoms-causes/syc-20355977; information about quality of life with Down Syndrome: Jeanne Mancini, "People with Down syndrome are happy. Why are we trying to eliminate them?" *The Washington Post*, August 24, 2017, https://www.washingtonpost.com/news/posteverything/wp/2017/08/24/people-with-down-syndrome-are-happy-why-are-we-trying-to-eliminate-them/.

use this ability to more easily indoctrinate their children into the belief system of a cult. Someone with undiagnosed and untreated narcolepsy might be able to legally obtain a driver's license, but that doesn't mean it's ethical for that person to operate a motor vehicle. Though it's legal to eat three pounds of factory-farmed red meat each day, it's probably immoral, as Chapter Eight makes clear, as well as harmful to one's health! In conclusion, the legality of abortion does not imply its morality.

5.4 *Juno*, Thomson, and Marquis on the Morality of Abortion

5.4.1 Summary of the Film's Treatment of Abortion

In the film *Juno*, 16-year-old Juno MacGuff (Elliot Page) initiates unprotected sex with her boyfriend Paulie (Michael Cera), becomes pregnant, and decides to have an abortion just around the end of the first trimester (week 12). She ultimately decides not to go through with it, and gives the baby up for adoption instead. The film leads the viewer to sympathize with her initial decision to abort: she is still in high school, does not know how to raise a child, expresses a great deal of fear and anxiety about her pregnancy, and her friends (including her boyfriend) are very supportive of her decision. Because of *Roe v. Wade*, her abortion would have been legal throughout the US, regardless of state restrictions. Many on the pro-choice side would consider her initial decision morally permissible. However, a famous defender of abortion, Judith Thomson, provides some reasons to possibly doubt the moral permissibility of Juno's initial decision.

© Featureflash Photo Agency/Shutterstock.com

© Featureflash Photo Agency/Shutterstock.com

5.4.2 *Juno* and Judith Thomson

Thomson argues that in the early stages of the first trimester, the unborn is clearly not a person. She relies on an argument from analogy, stating that "a clump of cells" is "no more a person than an acorn is an oak tree."[18] Thomson provides an example of when the fetus *does* bear a striking resemblance to a human being, mentioning the 10-week mark.[19] Though she does not offer a detailed argument for the beginning of personhood, these considerations seem to be behind her claim that early first trimester abortions are obviously not immoral. Juno's pregnancy at the time she visits the abortion clinic is on the cusp of the second trimester. At this point of a pregnancy, Thomson argues that abortion is morally justified only under certain circumstances.

Thomson's argument hinges on several analogies, most notably, one about a person who finds themselves plugged into a famous violinist. The violinist's life depends on being connected to that person, such that if the violinist is unplugged before nine months pass, he will die. The fantastic scenario, she muses, was orchestrated by the "Society of Music Lovers,"[20] and happened to the person while they were unaware of what was going on. She applies the most common pro-life argument to this scenario, saying it would be analogous to claiming that the person must stay plugged into the violinist for as long as the violinist's life depends on that connection, even if it happened to be beyond nine months, or for life. Though the person has a right to determine what happens to their body, this right is outweighed by the violinist's right to life, since he is a person. Thomson points out that such an argument is clearly "outrageous."[21] The violinist has no right to the use of the person's kidneys, but the person does have a clear right to determine what happens to their body.[22] Thomson argues that though it might be the decent or kind thing to do, the person does not have a moral *obligation* to let the violinist use their body in this way, so if the person unplugged the violinist, it would not be unjust. On the basis of this **argument from analogy**, Thomson concludes that when a woman neither is open to the idea of pregnancy nor consents to allowing the possibility of becoming pregnant, abortion is morally permissible. Clearly then, in cases of rape, Thomson's argument states that abortion is justifiable. She, however, leaves open the possibility that carrying to term and delivering the baby may be the decent thing to do even though it is not morally obligatory.

ARGUMENT FROM ANALOGY
Uses an analogy as a key premise in its effort to prove or support the conclusion.

The moral implications of Thomson's analogy would be different if the person did something knowingly that might result in being attached to the violinist. Though that action is not the same as "inviting the violinist" to use her body, if she "unplugged" him, it nonetheless would amount to depriving the violinist of what he has a right to.[23] In this way, Thomson's argument supports the stance that if a woman consents to sex and is open to the possibility of becoming pregnant, abortion would not be morally justified.

A different analogy Thomson uses is a woman who installs bars in her windows to protect from burglars, or even hapless innocent people, because she knows such people will come through her windows otherwise, and yet someone gets in when she opens the window because of a defect in the bars. Thomson implies that it's ridiculous to say that the person who came through the window now has a right to use the woman's house because it is the only way their life can be saved.[24] This scenario is analogous to a woman having protected sex, without the intention of becoming pregnant, but being impregnated nonetheless because of a defective contraceptive. Thomson implies that if a woman in these circumstances wanted an abortion, it would not be unjust or immoral—but she adds a significant qualifier later on, as will become clear.

Thomson points out that there are likely to be circumstances, other than those above, in which the fetus does or does not have a right to use of the woman's body. One part of her essay uses yet another analogy to argue for a woman's right to abort when the pregnancy threatens her life. Regarding the violinist analogy, she argues that even if he only needed the person's body for an hour, and the person really *ought* to allow it, the violinist, strictly speaking, still does not have a *right* to the person's body. Though we could condemn the person's decision if they disconnected the violinist, it still would not be accurate to call the action unjust. Legally compelling the person to remain connected to the violinist, or for the woman with the defective bars to let the invader use her house, imposes a higher standard of morality on the person than is legally typical. Such abortion laws, Thomson argues, force women to be Good Samaritans.[25] In other words, for example, these laws would be on par with making it illegal not to help the homeless, or not to give to charity. In this way, they would legally enforce the **supererogatory**, which is discussed in Chapter Four.

SUPEREROGATORY
The name ascribed to the category of moral decisions and actions that are not strictly obligatory; those that are good or decent but that are morally optional, rather than necessary.

Thomson adds an important qualifier to the end of her argument, saying that although in some cases a woman may have the right to detach herself from the unborn, the woman does not have the right to "secure" the death of the fetus, even in the instances of rape or a threat to the mother's life.[26] The implications of this qualifier are that abortion methods would need to somehow make every effort to remove or deliver the baby safely, and then do what is legally and morally required to save the baby's life. In abortions after viability, then, Thomson implies that even if the woman's life is threatened, every effort must be made to deliver the baby without killing it. This would mean that any woman whose pregnancy is beyond the 23-week mark could not abort the fetus in a way that makes little or no effort to save its life. The expectant mother in such a scenario, then, would have to deliver her baby, since it has a chance of survival with intensive care.

QUESTIONS FOR CONSIDERATION

a. As a matter of review, under what circumstances is abortion morally permissible according to Thomson? Under what circumstances is the expectant mother morally obliged to deliver the baby as safely as possible for the both of them?
b. Is it surprising or out of line with your understanding of the pro-choice stance to learn of this famous abortion advocate's arguments about the morality and legality of abortion?
c. Do you agree with Thomson that at the early stages of the first trimester, the fetus is no more a human than an acorn is an oak tree? Do you think the acorn and oak tree analogy is accurate and useful?
d. What counts as a pregnancy that is unintentional and beyond the woman's control, besides rape and defective contraception?

e. Do you think the violinist analogy is accurate and useful? Why or why not?
f. Do you think the barred window analogy is accurate and useful? Why or why not?
g. What would Thomson think about Juno's initial decision to have an abortion?

5.4.3 *Juno* and Don Marquis

Don Marquis, a well-known opponent to abortion, argues that abortion is immoral because it deprives one of a "future like ours." He writes:

> What primarily makes killing wrong is neither its effect on the murderer nor its effect on the victim's friends and relatives, but its effect on the victim. The loss of one's life is one of the greatest losses one can suffer. The loss of one's life deprives one of all the experiences, activities, projects, and enjoyments that would otherwise have constituted one's future. Therefore, killing someone is wrong, primarily because the killing inflicts (one of) the greatest possible losses on the victim. [. . .] It would seem that what makes killing any adult human being prima facie[9] seriously wrong is the loss of his or her future.[27]

The criterion that makes it wrong to kill anyone applies to the unborn, according to Marquis, because just as an adult is deprived of their future by being killed, so is an embryo or fetus. The argument against abortion does not depend on successfully establishing the personhood of the unborn. All that matters is whether or not it has a future—specifically a "future like ours."[28] This means that Marquis's argument is not limited to humans, but would include any species who arguably has such a future.[29]

Exceptions include cases in which "the loss consequent on failing to abort would be at least as great" as aborting.[30] He also makes an exception for the very early stages of pregnancy when an individual subject (an "I" or "ego"[10]) is not clearly defined yet.[31] Experts agree that this is the case for the first two weeks, when twinning is still possible. Marquis briefly notes that he is not discussing "rare" "hard cases," like those when the woman's life is threatened, or when she has been raped. This does not mean Marquis supports abortion in those instances, but just that he is not exploring such cases in the essay at hand.[32]

QUESTIONS FOR CONSIDERATION

a. Is there anything about Marquis's pro-life stance that surprises you given your previous understanding of what it meant to be pro-life?
b. What do you think of Marquis's argument? Does he give a good reason for his claim that abortion is wrong for the same reasons that killing a newborn, a child, or an adult is wrong?
c. What do you think about the exceptions Marquis grants?
d. What would Marquis think about Juno's initial decision to abort?

9. On the face of it; at first.
10. A Kantian conception of the human person.

5.4.4 Conclusions about *Juno*, Thomson, and Marquis

Because Juno was 16, most US states would indicate that she was able to consent. Even in those states with a higher age of consent, some laws specify a necessary age difference (two to five years) between the two parties in order for statutory rape to occur.[33] So, it's technically possible but unlikely one would be able to argue convincingly that Juno was raped. Also, the viewer has no reason to think she was unaware of the possible consequences of her decision to have unprotected sex. She is portrayed as an intelligent, articulate young woman with caring parents and access to education. Her pregnancy at the time she considered aborting, furthermore, had progressed past the point at which both Thomson and Marquis argue there is not clearly a human subject present. For these reasons, it's difficult to see how a strict interpretation of Thomson would be in favor of Juno's decision to have an abortion. It's also quite clear that Marquis would be opposed to this choice, unless one can somehow argue that what Juno would lose regarding her own future outweighs the future that her fetus stood to lose.

5.4.5 Possible Problems with *Juno*'s Treatment of Abortion

It is likely that those on the extremes of the abortion debate, and possibly others, would find fault with the film. Reviewers of the film are divided about whether it leans toward a pro-life or pro-choice stance, and even some who are not on the extremes may find certain aspects of it problematic.

Some reasons why the film might lean pro-choice, and therefore might upset pro-lifers:

- The fact that Juno has the option to abort is not presented negatively.
- Other likable characters in the film support Juno's initial decision.
- Juno's parents (Allison Janney and J. K. Simmons), presented as reasonable and likable, do not indicate that they would have condemned her if she chose to have an abortion.
- Su-Chin (Valerie Tian), the young acquaintance of Juno protesting alone outside the abortion clinic is portrayed as a bit ridiculous and probably rather naïve.

Some reasons why the film might lean pro-life, and therefore upset those who are pro-choice:

- The abortion clinic is portrayed as dismal and depressing.
- Juno's decision to opt for adoption instead of abortion enables Vanessa Loring (Jennifer Garner) to become a mother. The film seems to present this in a positive fashion.
- The film portrays the process of adoption favorably. Some objectors argue that the process is more difficult and complex in reality.
- Juno's ability to conduct her academic and social life are not halted by her pregnancy, though they are challenged by it. This might not be in line with reality.

- Juno is not portrayed as facing condemnation from her peers or society more widely for being pregnant as a teenager. This might not be in line with reality.

QUESTIONS FOR CONSIDERATION

a. Do you think the film leans pro-choice? Pro-life? Neither? Why?
b. Do you think the film should have portrayed a pro-life character besides Su-Chin? Or perhaps should it have portrayed her differently? Should there have been other opponents to Juno's initial decision?
c. Do you think Juno's pregnancy is easy compared to teen pregnancies you'd consider typical?
d. Do you think the process of adoption is portrayed unrealistically in the film?
e. Do you think the film's playful tone is appropriate for its subject matter? Why or why not?
f. Are there other changes you would have liked to see in the film?
g. Why is it important to fully understand and appreciate differing perspectives on the abortion debate?

5.5 Ethical Theory and Abortion

Though it is difficult to pinpoint specific views on abortion from the most famous ethical theorists, one can nonetheless draw some conclusions about the ways in which they would think about the morality of abortion.

5.5.1 Natural Law

According to natural law, espoused by the Catholic Church, the killing of innocents is seriously immoral, as discussed in Chapter Three. Current adherents of natural law see abortion as the murder of innocent victims, and therefore conclude that it is seriously immoral. One exception for natural law theorists is when the mother's life is threatened by her pregnancy. In such a case, they argue, any measures can be taken to save her life, as long as they do not have the *intention* of killing the baby. If such measures *unintentionally* end the baby's life, they would not be immoral, according to the principle of **double effect**.

DOUBLE EFFECT
A principle stating that no harm may be done intentionally, but if harm results unintentionally, it may be morally justified under certain circumstances. For example, trying to save a woman's life by means of a procedure that may unintentionally end the life of the fetus is morally justified.

As is clear above, there are a number of different stages from conception to birth that can arguably mark where life begins. Though natural law theorists argue that life begins at conception, pro-lifers like Marquis argue that it should be very early in the first trimester. Yet others offer arguments for later stages to mark the official beginning of personhood. US law only officially recognizes one as a person after birth. Some conservative political activists and lawmakers advocate for "personhood provisions," which would establish the fetus as a person under the law. One might respond by arguing that the fertilized egg has the unique potential for human life, and that it therefore ought to be treated as such, but philosophers have cast doubt on this argument. Why is it a fertilized egg has such a unique potential? Why not a sperm and egg prior to fertilization? The possibility of a slippery slope makes this argument difficult to support.

Even if one could successfully defend the claim that life begins at conception, one could argue, as Thomson does, that certain circumstances cast doubt on the equivalence of abortion to murder. A natural law theorist might reply to Thomson by citing the infrequency of abortions performed under the circumstances Thomson describes, as well as the practical difficulties involved in performing them in the ways she argues is just.

SLIPPERY SLOPE
The logical fallacy that occurs when a chain of causes and effects is wrongfully assumed, often resulting in dubious consequences.
Example A: If I fail this test, I will fail this course, and if I fail this course, I'll never get into college, and if I don't go to college, I'll be homeless. Therefore, if I fail this test, I will become homeless. A slippery slope argument can be unfallacious if the chain of causality is reasonable.
Example B: If Russia drops a hydrogen bomb on New York City, the US will retaliate proportionately, then Russia will strike back, nuclear allies will get involved in an all-out-nuclear war, resulting in an apocalypse. Therefore, if Russia nukes New York City, the world will experience a nuclear apocalypse. There are good reasons that this chain of causes and effects could actually happen as a result of the initiating event or one like it. See the film *Fail-Safe* (1964).

5.5.2 Kantian Ethics (Deontology)

In Kant's non-consequentialist ethics,[11] rational beings are ends in themselves, and ought to be treated as such. A person may never be treated as a means to an end. If the unborn embryo or fetus is a person, a Kantian is likely to be seriously opposed to its killing for the sake of the mother's health, financial well-being, education, ability to care for others, desires for the future, and so on. This is because, in any such case, the termination of the unborn human being is a means to some end of the pregnant woman. A Kantian might make an exception for situations in which the mother's life is threatened, since the mother is also an end and ought to be treated with the proper dignity and respect. Additionally, a deontologist might heavily weigh the possible circumstance in which the unborn embryo or fetus is using the woman's body as a means to an end without the woman's consent—similar to Thomson above—as in the case of rape.

A very important factor in the deontologist's argument is the question of whether or not the unborn being is a person. The life circumstances affecting the pregnant woman would be of very minor concern to the Kantian non-consequentialist, in the vast majority of cases.

5.5.3 Utilitarianism

Though there are examples of famous utilitarians like Peter Singer who take an extremely liberal stance on abortion, this is not necessarily the case for all utilitarians.

An act utilitarian would make their decision strictly on the maximization of happiness for all parties involved. Clearly, any possible happiness of the unborn would be negated by an abortion. The mother, and even possibly the father as well as other loved ones, might benefit in overall well-being as a result of the abortion. The question here is whether or not the happiness afforded to the mother and others outweighs that deprived of the unborn. The circumstances of the pregnancy would matter a great deal here.

A rule utilitarian like John Stuart Mill cares more than an act utilitarian about the question of whether or not the unborn is a person, for reasons given in Chapter Four. For one, Mill argues that utilitarianism supports the Christian dictum that we should do unto others what we would want for ourselves. Such a utilitarian's

11. See Chapter Three on Kantian ethics.

calculation about abortion, then, would depend on their assessment of when life begins, as well as the relationship of the abortion decision to various rules pertaining to the maximization of happiness. For instance, if the arguer thinks the fetus is a human life, what is the impact on widespread happiness if any mother can kill her child whenever the mother's life might benefit from doing so? One marker a utilitarian might use to designate where life begins is the point at which the fetus is sentient. Sentience is an important criterion for moral respect when it comes to non-human animals, according to Bentham and others. This is discussed further in Chapter Eight. If the utilitarian does not consider the unborn embryo or fetus to be a human life, their question might be: "What are the implications on overall happiness if a woman must sacrifice her overall well-being for the sake of what is essentially a body part?" Another question posed by the rule utilitarian might be: "What is the impact on overall happiness if a woman must carry a rapist's offspring to term?"

QUESTIONS FOR CONSIDERATION

a. What might representatives from each of the above ethical theories think about Juno's initial decision to have an abortion? In what ways would they agree or disagree? Why?
b. What might representatives from each of the above ethical theories think about Juno's ultimate decision to carry the fetus to term and give the baby up for adoption? In what ways might they agree or disagree? Why?

5.6 Finding Common Ground: Lisa Cahill

Cahill points out that pro-lifers and pro-choicers are usually at an impasse—a stalemate—characterized by divisive claims, resulting in an inability to work together toward common ground solutions.[34] According to Cahill, most people are in favor of significant restrictions to abortion[12] and only 7 percent of abortions take place because of the "hard cases," such as "rape, incest, severe fetal defects, or a serious health risk to the mother."[35] However, many who are in favor of the legality of abortion cite such cases as a basis for their stance.[36] Also, those who are pro-life often soften their stance when it comes to those difficult cases, as Marquis does. As this chapter has shown, there are good reasons to consider the likelihood that most pro-lifers and pro-choicers are not as far apart in their views as may initially seem to be the case. Though the Catholic Church supports the natural law stance, which is opposed to abortion, Pope John Paul II advocated for a rather nuanced position about imposing judgment on women who choose to have abortions.[37] Clearly, pro-choicers would tend to agree with the idea of withholding judgment on

12. Lisa Sowle Cahill cites a 2004 Zogby poll showing that 56 percent would "accept significant restrictions" on abortion, with 60.5 percent of 18–25-year-old respondents favoring such restrictions. See Cahill, *Theological Bioethics* (Washington, DC: Georgetown University Press, 2005): 171.

such women.[13] The Vatican also takes a strong stance on "socioeconomic solidarity with the poor,"[38] which is in agreement with the stance that is characteristic of the American Left. Mario Cuomo, a pro-choice Catholic who formerly was governor of New York, called for cooperation between Left and Right on reducing abortions by decreasing the number of unplanned pregnancies and providing more resources for poor women who become pregnant so that they can give the child up for adoption. His vision, according to Cahill, ranged from "prenatal care to education and job training."[39] Angela Senander looks to social action that can give women and girls in "crisis pregnancies" more freedom to choose a course of action other than abortion as a way to "unite pro-life and pro-choice **feminists**[14] around common goals."[40] Cahill cites a Rutgers University study that links a drastic uptick in abortions with restrictive reforms to welfare programs.[41] Catholic Charities[15] and other Catholic organizations are determined advocates for programs that benefit the poor,[42] and these are clearly actions that the political Left would support. Cahill mentions an "abortion 'common ground' effort" by "a past president of Missouri Citizens for Life, and the director and a staff member from St. Louis Reproductive Health Services," whose joint action goal was to "decrease the demand for abortions." Cahill explains further: "Members banded together around better perinatal care, treatments for substance abuse, welfare reforms, day care, affordable housing, adoption, recruitment of foster parents, and job and educational opportunities and testified on measures before the state legislature."[43] There was also a "national coalition of religious, civil rights, and women's rights organizations that issued a press release in 1995 rejecting the family cap" (welfare reform). "They included the American Civil Liberties Union,[16] the National Organization for Women, Catholic Charities USA, and Feminists for Life."[44]

FEMINISTS

Broadly conceived, those who are in favor of women having equal rights to men; others conceive of feminism differently.

Cahill's writing underscores another option in the pro-life versus pro-choice debate: Instead of arguing to defeat the other side, which may be fruitless, argue for common goals. Based on the above, there are many candidates for such goals. If those across the political spectrum argue for an increase in social supports that would make it more feasible for women to carry unplanned pregnancies to term, they might protect woman's rights while also reducing abortions. There is widespread agreement that abortion is not a good thing, regardless of its morality or legality. Rather than focusing on the arguments that divide, Cahill argues that we should focus on the common goal of reducing abortions by means of giving pregnant women a better set of options for unplanned pregnancies. If motherhood is less fraught with financial hardship, and if giving a baby up for adoption is less overwhelming, fewer women with unplanned pregnancies will see abortion as the most viable option.

13. According to Cynthia Cameron, from a correspondence with me, it is certainly not the case that JPII had no moral judgment at all of women who have abortions. Rather, he was making a more nuanced statement about how women who choose abortion are not and cannot be considered evil-doers (people of vicious or evil character), simply because of that choice. Their decision to have an abortion has to be seen within the wider context of their life circumstances. However, that does not remove responsibility for a sinful act; it just puts that sinful act into context.

14. See Noelle McAfee, "Feminist Philosophy," *Stanford Encyclopedia of Philosophy*, 2018, https://plato.stanford.edu/entries/feminist-philosophy/#WhatFemi

15. https://www.catholiccharitiesusa.org/

16. https://www.aclu.org/

5.7 Philosophical Doubts about the Politics of Abortion

Well-meaning pro-lifers often see the overturning of *Roe v. Wade* and the imposition of restrictions on abortion access as the main pathways to protecting the unborn. There are reasons for which their opponents might doubt this approach:

- The American College of Obstetricians and Gynecologists (ACOG) estimates that 200,000–1.2 million induced abortions per year occurred in the US before *Roe v. Wade*.[45] As stated above, the 2016 yearly rate is 623,471, and the figure has been trending downward. So, it is questionable to conclude that overturning *Roe v. Wade* would reduce the yearly abortion rate. Also, illegal abortions were much riskier for the lives and health of pregnant women, though it is difficult to pinpoint an exact number of those who died as a result of such procedures before their legalization.

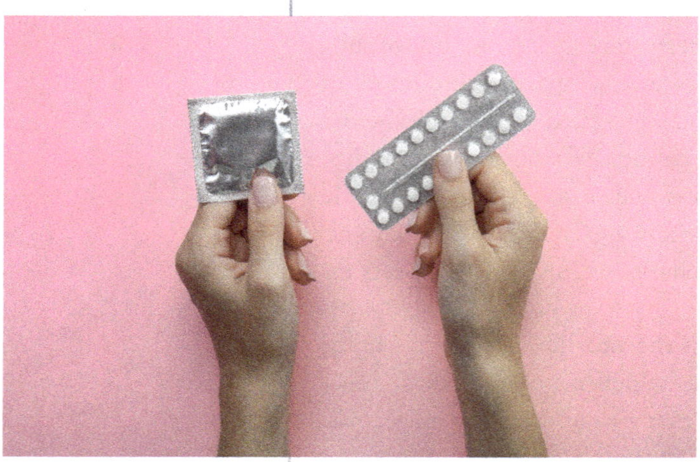

Those on the right also often argue against the use of contraceptives, largely on the basis of natural law ethics. However, non-abortifacient contraceptives reduce abortions. In this way, pro-lifers often take a contradictory stance according to their opponents.[46]

Those on the Right often use **appeals to emotion** to rouse their base, by referring to late-stage abortions that are allowed by *Roe v. Wade* but that are virtually non-existent even in liberal states. Such tactics alienate moderates and liberals who might be sympathetic to aspects of the pro-life cause, such as reducing the overall number of abortions through social supports and imposing agreeable restrictions on access.

APPEAL TO EMOTION
Synonymous with appeal to pity; see p. 73.

There are reasons for which the opponents of the pro-choice movement object to elements of the latter's stance:

- Those on the pro-choice side often mistake legality for morality, and sometimes applaud the fact that a woman can have an abortion because they see it as empowering. Many of their slogans indicate this. There are reasons to doubt such a positive view of abortion.
- Those on the Left will often say simply that "It's a woman's choice." Or "It's up to the woman." On the one hand, such statements support a woman's reasonable right to have a final say on what happens to her body. On the other, these statements indicate **moral relativism**, which risks dismissing arguments like those of Thomson and Marquis and making the whole debate subjective. When moral relativism is taken to its furthest logical extent, we might find ourselves allowing people to kill or enslave others if they think it suits them.

MORAL RELATIVISM
The notion that morals are completely individualistic or subjective; the idea that morals are not based on objective standards determined by theories or religious codes; taken to an extreme, moral relativists would not object to a person choosing to be a mass murderer if that person thinks it's right for them.

- Moderates and independents might very well claim that those on both sides often ignore or dismiss reasonable arguments from their opponents because of their tendency to stay true to party politics. The result of this tendency is to miss out on opportunities like those below to work together to make women's lives better and reduce abortions:
    - Representatives from across the political spectrum, for instance, agree that cuts to welfare will increase the number of abortions. There are substantial reasons for such a claim.[47]
    - Both pro-lifers, like Pope John Paul II, and abortion advocates, argue against stigmatizing women who are considering abortion, or who have had one.[48]
    - Pro-lifers want adoption to be a more viable choice for those with unplanned pregnancies, and pro-choicers want pregnant women to have feasible options. Across the spectrum then, many can work together to make adoption a more palatable choice.[49]

QUESTION FOR CONSIDERATION

a. Reflect on your personal abortion stance prior to seeing *Juno* and reading this chapter. Has your stance changed at all? Has it moved left or right? Is it more moderate or less? Are you less sure of your stance than you initially were?

5.8 Resources for Further Learning

5.8.1 Politically Neutral Support for Women Who Have Had Abortions

https://www.afterabortion.com/

5.8.2 On Public Opinion about Abortion

Dennis Sadowski, "Notre Dame study examines 'everyday' Americans' attitudes toward abortion," *National Catholic Reporter*, July 15, 2020, https://www.ncronline.org/news/people/notre-dame-study-examines-everyday-americans-attitudes-toward-abortion.

"Public Opinion on Abortion," Pew Research Center, August 29, 2019, https://www.pewforum.org/fact-sheet/public-opinion-on-abortion/#:~:text=As%20of%202019%2C%20public%20support%20for%20legal%20abortion,should%20be%20illegal%20in%20all%20or%20most%20cases.

5.8.3 On Contraception

"Reproductive Health," Centers for Disease Control and Prevention," last reviewed August 13, 2020, https://www.cdc.gov/reproductivehealth/contraception/index.htm.

5.8.4 On Adoption

"Adoption," Child Welfare Information Gateway," accessed October 15, 2020, https://www.childwelfare.gov/topics/adoption/.

Olga Khazan, "Why So Many Women Choose Abortion Over Adoption," *The Atlantic*, May 20, 2019, https://www.theatlantic.com/health/archive/2019/05/why-more-women-dont-choose-adoption/589759/.

5.8.5 Forum for Philosophical Arguments for and against Abortion

"Arguing Dialectically About Abortion," *Political Animal Magazine*, August 23, 2019, https://www.politicalanimalmagazine.com/2019/08/23/arguing-dialectically-about-abortion/.

5.8.6 A Philosophy Podcast Arguing "Dispassionately" about Abortion

Cynthia Gorney, "Abortion," Philosophy Talk, March 24, 2013, https://www.philosophytalk.org/shows/abortion.

Endnotes

1. See Singer, *Practical Ethics*, 3rd ed. (Cambridge: Cambridge University Press, 2011).
2. "Fetal Development: Stages of Growth," Cleveland Clinic, last reviewed April 16, 2020, https://my.clevelandclinic.org/health/articles/7247-fetal-development-stages-of-growth#:~:text=Fetal%20Development%3A%20Stages%20of%20Growth%201%20As%20the,feel%20your%20baby%20moving%20around.%20More%20items...%20.
3. Ibid.
4. Ibid.
5. Jon-Stewart Gordon, "Abortion," *Internet Encyclopedia of Philosophy*, accessed October 15, 2020, https://iep.utm.edu/abortion/.
6. "Fetal Development: Stages of Growth," Cleveland Clinic, last reviewed April 16, 2020, https://my.clevelandclinic.org/health/articles/7247-fetal-development-stages-of-growth#:~:text=Fetal%20Development%3A%20Stages%20of%20Growth%201%20As%20the,feel%20your%20baby%20moving%20around.%20More%20items...%20.
7. "Methods of Abortion," S.C. Department of Health and Environmental Control, accessed October 15, 2020, https://www.scdhec.gov/methods-abortion.
8. *Encyclopedia Britannica*, s.v. "Roe v. Wade," accessed October 15, 2020, https://www.britannica.com/event/Roe-v-Wade; "Fetal Development: Stages of Growth," Cleveland Clinic, last reviewed April 16, 2020, https://my.clevelandclinic.org/health/articles/7247-fetal-development-stages-of-growth.

9. Mona Chalabi, "The truth about late-term abortions in the US: they're very rare," *The Guardian*, March 8, 2019, https://www.theguardian.com/news/datablog/2019/mar/07/abortion-late-term-what-pregnancy-stage; Kim Painter, "Ripped from the womb? Late-term abortion explained," *USA Today*, October 21, 2016, https://www.usatoday.com/story/news/2016/10/21/doctors-trump-wrong-late-abortions/92515324/.
10. Ibid.
11. Alia E. Dastagir, "Rape and incest account for hardly any abortions. So why are they now a focus?" *USA Today*, May 24, 2019, https://www.usatoday.com/story/news/nation/2019/05/24/rape-and-incest-account-few-abortions-so-why-all-attention/1211175001/.
12. Susan Milligan, "A Guide to Abortion Laws by State," *US News & World Report*, June 27, 2019, https://www.usnews.com/news/best-states/articles/2019-06-27/a-guide-to-abortion-laws-by-state.
13. Ibid.
14. See "Reproductive Health," Centers for Disease Control and Prevention, last reviewed November 25, 2019, https://www.cdc.gov/reproductivehealth/data_stats/abortion.htm.
15. See "Morbidity and Mortality Weekly Report. Abortion Surveillance—United States, 2016," Centers for Disease Control and Prevention," November 29, 2019, https://www.cdc.gov/mmwr/volumes/68/ss/ss6811a1.htm.
16. Lawrence B. Finer, et al, "Reasons U.S. Women Have Abortions: Quantitative and Qualitative Perspectives," *Perspectives on Sexual and Reproductive Health* 37 (2005): 110–118, https://www.guttmacher.org/sites/default/files/pdfs/pubs/psrh/full/3711005.pdf.
17. "Abortion," Gallup, accessed October 15, 2020, https://news.gallup.com/poll/1576/abortion.aspx.
18. Thomson, "A Defense of Abortion," *Philosophy and Public Affairs* 1 (1971): 48.
19. Ibid. 47–48.
20. Ibid., 48–49.
21. Ibid., 49.
22. Ibid., 55.
23. Ibid., 57–58.
24. Ibid., 58–59.
25. Ibid., 62–63.
26. Ibid., 66.
27. Marquis, "Why Abortion is Immoral," *The Journal of Philosophy* 86 (1989): 189–190.
28. Ibid., 191.
29. Ibid.
30. Ibid., 194.
31. Ibid.
32. Ibid., 183.
33. *Encyclopedia Britannica*, s.v. "Statutory Rape," accessed October 15, 2020, https://www.britannica.com/topic/statutory-rape.
34. See Lisa Sowle Cahill, *Theological Bioethics* (Washington, DC: Georgetown University Press, 2005): 174–176.
35. Ibid., 171.
36. Ibid.
37. Ibid., 172.
38. Ibid., 182.
39. Ibid., 183.
40. Ibid., 185.
41. Ibid, 187–188.
42. Ibid., 188.
43. Ibid.
44. Ibid.
45. See this *Washington Post* article that fact-checks claims by the ACOG: Glenn Kessler, "Planned Parenthood's false stat: 'Thousands' of women died every year before Roe," *The Washington Post*, May 29, 2019, https://www.washingtonpost.com/politics/2019/05/29/planned-parenthoods-false-stat-thousands-women-died-every-year-before-roe/.
46. Brian Alexander, "Free birth control cuts abortion rate dramatically, study finds," *NBC News*, October 4, 2012, https://www.nbcnews.com/health/health-news/free-birth-control-cuts-abortion-rate-dramatically-study-finds-f6285986.
47. See Jacob Alex Klerman, "Welfare Reform and Abortion," in *Welfare, the Family, and Reproductive Behavior*, ed. Robert A. Moffit, (Washington, DC: National Academy Press, 1998): 98–134, https://www.ncbi.nlm.nih.gov/books/NBK230343/.

48. Christine Dehlendorf, et al., "Disparities in Abortion Rates: A Public Health Approach," *American Journal of Public Health* 103 (2013): 1772–1779, https://www.ncbi.nlm.nih.gov/pmc/articles/PMC3780732/.
49. Olga Khazan, "Why So Many Women Choose Abortion Over Adoption," *The Atlantic*, May 20, 2019, https://www.theatlantic.com/health/archive/2019/05/why-more-women-dont-choose-adoption/589759/.
50. See "Reproductive Health," Centers for Disease Control and Prevention, last reviewed November 25, 2019, https://www.cdc.gov/reproductivehealth/data_stats/abortion.htm.
51. "Pregnancy week by week," Mayo Clinic, February 24, 2018, https://www.mayoclinic.org/healthy-lifestyle/pregnancy-week-by-week/in-depth/twin-pregnancy/art-20048161.
52. Berit Brogaard, "The Timing of Twinning," *Psychology Today*, July 4, 2013, https://www.psychologytoday.com/us/blog/the-superhuman-mind/201307/the-timing-twinning.
53. Collins, s.v. "blastocyst," accessed October 15, 2020, https://www.collinsdictionary.com/dictionary/english/blastocyst.
54. Merriam-Webster, s.v. "embryo," accessed October 15, 2020, https://www.merriam-webster.com/dictionary/embryo.
55. Merriam-Webster, s.v. "fetus," accessed October 15, 2020, https://www.merriam-webster.com/dictionary/fetus.

Chapter 6

Euthanasia and Assisted Suicide

6.1 Introduction

The modern Western world tends to see death as an evil to fend off. In the medical field, death is the enemy and heroic measures are often taken to combat it. Advances in medical technology have enabled people to live longer, and further advances may allow human beings to live well beyond what seems possible today. However, Western philosophers have not always adopted such a negative attitude toward death. The notion of a good death, or a noble death, has its roots in ancient philosophy, and is present today in the debate surrounding **euthanasia** and **assisted suicide**. In fact, the word "euthanasia" literally means "good death" or "easy death."[1] Clearly there are many instances in which the lifesaving or life-prolonging measures of modern medicine are highly desirable. In this chapter, the reader will explore the perspective that allowing death to take place, and even initiating it, may be ethical in some cases, but highly unethical in others. Ethical theorists vary widely on which cases fall into either category.

EUTHANASIA
When one person takes measures to end another's life or let them die in a way intended to make their death good to a greater or lesser extent, either for the patient/victim themselves or others.

ASSISTED SUICIDE
Occurs when someone, usually a medical professional, provides a patient with a lethal dose which the patient self-administers.

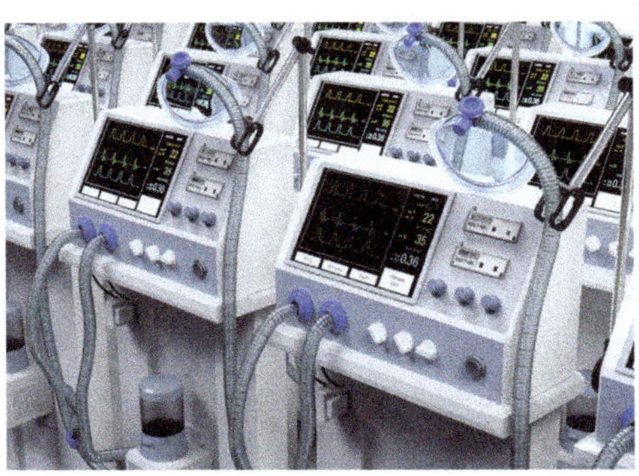

Ventilator machines.

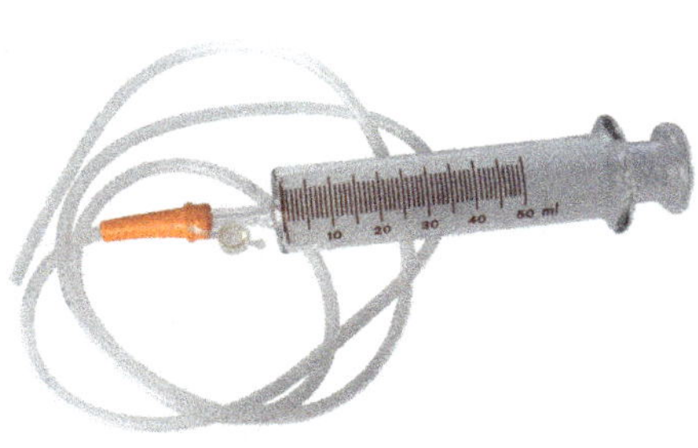

Feeding tube.

QUESTIONS FOR CONSIDERATION

a. Reflect on your own personal stance before reading further. What is it? If you watched *Million Dollar Baby* before beginning to read this, what was your stance before you watched the film? Keep that in mind as you read. Perhaps jot it down in a notebook or journal.

6.2 Ancient Perspectives on Death

6.2.1 Epicurus

HEDONIST
A pleasure-seeker.

Epicurus's[1] philosophy focuses on living the most pleasurable life possible. Happiness is pleasure, according to Epicurus, and pleasure is the good. However, he is not a crude **hedonist**—he does not advocate pursuing all pleasures indiscriminately. Rather, his work explains how to attain the most long-term or lasting pleasure, by doing things like philosophy and living a simple lifestyle unaccustomed to luxury and sensuous gratification. What follows is an excerpt about his thoughts on how to view death in order to live a pleasant life.

Excerpts from Epicurus's *Letter to Menoecus*:

> Become accustomed to the belief that death is nothing to us. For all good and evil consists in sensation, but death is deprived of sensation. And therefore a right understanding that death is nothing to us makes the mortality of life enjoyable, not because it adds to it an infinite span of time, but because it takes away the craving for immortality. For there is nothing terrible in life for the man who has truly comprehended that there is nothing terrible in not living. [. . .] For that which gives no trouble when it comes, is but an empty pain in anticipation. So death, the most terrifying of ills, is nothing to us, since so long as we exist, death is not with us; but when death comes, then we do not exist. [. . .]
>
> [. . .] The wise man neither seeks to escape life nor fears the cessation of life, for neither does life offend him nor does the absence of life seem to be any evil. [. . .][2]

QUESTIONS FOR CONSIDERATION

a. Is death good or bad according to Epicurus? Or is it neither? Or both? Why or why not?
b. What do you think Epicurus means when he says that a proper understanding of death can make life more enjoyable? Use the excerpt to formulate your answer.

6.2.2 Epictetus

Epictetus was a Stoic philosopher, and one of his central theses is that one lives the best sort of life when one attains self-control, especially with regard to one's emotions. The following are a few excerpts of a text attributed to Epictetus about having the proper perspective on death.

1. Please see the appendix for information about the philosophers discussed in this chapter.

Excerpts from Epictetus's *Encheiridion:*

> 5. [. . .] Death is nothing terrible, else it would have seemed so even to Socrates; rather it is the idea that death is terrible that is terrible. [. . .]
>
> [. . .]
>
> 11. Never say about anything that you have 'lost it,' but that you have 'given it back.' Your child has died? It has been given back. Your wife has died? She has been given back. [. . .] What concern is it of yours, through whom the gift was returned to the giver? For the time it is given to you, treat it as someone else's, as travelers do an inn.
>
> [. . .]
>
> 21. Let death and exile and all dreadful appearances be before your eyes every day, and most of all, death; and you will never deem anything trivial, nor desire anything excessively.[3]

QUESTIONS FOR CONSIDERATION

a. Why does Epictetus distinguish death from the idea of death? What emotion do you think he is trying to help his readers control?
b. What do you think about Epictetus's viewing life as a gift that is merely borrowed? What emotion do you think he's trying to help the reader overcome with such a claim?
c. Why do you think Epictetus wants us to confront death, exile, and dread on a regular basis, rather than avoid it or put it out of our minds? Use the excerpt to formulate your response. This is especially relevant given that much of this book focuses on death and tragedy!

6.2.3 Seneca

Seneca was also a Stoic, so like Epictetus, his work also focuses a great deal on attaining self-control and inner tranquility, especially with regard to one's emotions. Seneca has a great deal to say about death in his letters, so the following is but one example of many. He says some things below that might surprise the modern Western reader.

Excerpts from Seneca's Letters:

> Letter 70
>
> [. . .] We poor fools think death is a reef, but it is harbor to be reached at some time, but never to be rejected; if someone is carried there in his first years, he should no more lament than the sailor who has made his voyage expeditiously. [. . .]
>
> Think that the same thing is happening to us: life has brought some men swiftly to their destination even when they lingered, whereas it has soaked and stewed others. But, as you know, life is not always worth holding on to: since it is not good to live, but to live well. So the wise man will live as long as he ought, not as he can. He will see where he is going to live, with whom, how, and what he will be doing. He always thinks about the quality, not the length, of his life. If many distressing events occur that disturb his calm, he discharges

> himself, and he does not do this only at the last necessity, but as soon as he begins to suspect Fortune he looks around carefully to see whether should put an end to it. [. . .] It does not matter whether he dies more quickly or slowly, but it does matter whether he dies well or badly; for dying well is to escape the risk of living badly. [. . .]
>
> [. . .]
>
> [. . .] If a man lives on, knowing he will die on the third or fourth day at the whim of his enemy, he is doing another man's business.
>
> [. . .] If one death will entail torture, and the other is simple and easy, why should a man not lay hands on himself? As I would choose a ship to travel in or a house to dwell in, so I shall choose my death as I leave life. What is more, just as a longer life is not better at all costs, so dying is worse at all costs if it is prolonged. We should follow our own humor more in dying than in any other business. Let a man take his leave as his impulse seizes him;[2] whether he is looking for steel or a noose or some drug to fill his veins, let him proceed and break the chains of slavery. A man should win others' approval for his life, but his own approval for death; [. . .]
>
> [. . .] Human affairs are well placed because nobody is wretched except through his own fault. Do you like it? Then live. If you don't, then you are free to return whence you came. [. . .]
>
> [. . .] The dirtiest of deaths is to be preferred to the cleanest form of slavery.[4]

QUESTIONS FOR CONSIDERATION

a. Why is Seneca saying that it is permissible to end one's life? Under what conditions is it permissible?
b. Does Seneca see death as good or bad? Both or neither? Why?
c. What do you think are the intended effects of the words above on the reader?
d. Do you agree or disagree with Seneca about death and suicide? Why or why not?

6.3 Assisted Suicide: Overview

PHYSICIAN-ASSISTED SUICIDE (PAS)
When a person dies by means provided to them by a physician, and when such means are self-administered.

Modern-day **physician-assisted suicide (PAS)** differs from euthanasia in that the former is self-administered with the oversight of a medical professional while the latter is administered by a medical professional. PAS is self-administered, usually by the patient consuming a lethal dose prepared or ordered by the medical professional. Dr. Jack Kevorkian was a famous practitioner of assisted suicide in the 1990s, but he did so when it was illegal, so he was imprisoned. He remains a controversial figure, since proponents of PAS view him as one who brought much-needed advocacy for PAS to the forefront of American politics, while others view him as responsible for murder.[5] Advocates of PAS argue that it is morally acceptable, and should be legal for those who wish to die on their own terms. The Death with Dignity movement

2. This line is potentially confusing, because Seneca does not actually advocate committing suicide impulsively, as a result of being overcome with emotion. He's suggesting that suicide is appropriate under specific conditions. Seneca committed suicide himself, but he was forced to by Nero.

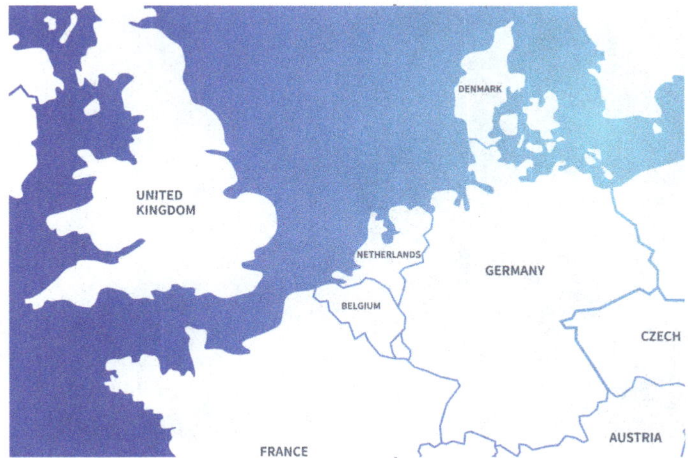

champions this view.[6] It is usually reserved for those with terminal illnesses, debilitating diseases, and persistent, extreme pain that is impossible to alleviate. As of 2020, PAS is legal in nine US states, the District of Columbia, and six countries. In the US, patients must have fewer than six months to live. In California, in 2018, 337 people died after taking their dispensed PAS medication. In Oregon, as of February 25, 2020, 1,657 people died in this manner since 1997. The number for Washington, going back to 2009, is 1,622.[7] In the Netherlands, known for very liberal PAS laws, the patient must meet certain requirements: They must be in the proper mental state, they must have been informed of their diagnosis and prognosis, their request must be voluntary, their suffering must be "lasting and unbearable and with no prospect of improvement," and an "independent second opinion" is required. Some of these determinations are fairly subjective, which is a matter of controversy.[8] In Belgium and the Netherlands, PAS is legal for children, which is also a matter of much controversy.

Modern philosophical perspectives on suicide are strikingly different from that of Seneca. John Locke argues that it is a violation of the law of nature for a person to take their own life, because human beings are God's property, and one must not take what belongs to God. Immanuel Kant takes a less theological and more strictly philosophical approach by arguing that committing suicide amounts to using one's life as a means to escape from a difficult situation. Because of the second formulation of the categorical imperative, as discussed in Chapter Three, it is clearly immoral to treat one's life as a means rather than as an end in itself.[3] Kant explicitly argues that the action of preserving one's life even when one desires not to do so is of moral worth in that it is done from duty to the categorical imperative.

6.4 Death with Dignity: Velleman and *The Elephant Man*

Specifically with regard to assisted suicide, recent scholars vary in their stances. One notable figure with a nuanced perspective is J. David Velleman. Though he argues against the "right to die," he qualifies his argument by stating that he is "very far from an all-things-considered judgment" on the matter.[9] He summarizes an opposing argument, explaining that some argue that life-preserving treatments "violate a patient's dignity," and that because of a patient's autonomy, we should "respect his competent and considered wishes, including a wish to die."[10] Velleman points out though that dignity has more than one meaning. For Kant, dignity pertains to rationality, not "the ability to walk unaided, to feed oneself, or to control one's bowels."[11] Velleman then points out that modern culture has an "obsession

3. See Chapter Three for further explanation of Locke's law of nature and Kant's categorical imperative.

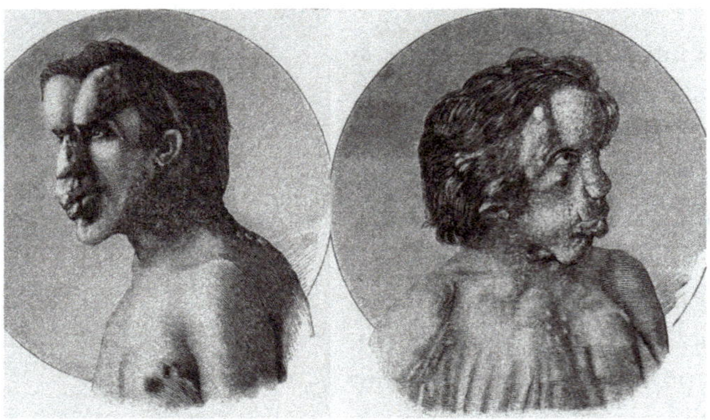

Bust portrait engravings of Joseph Merrick (1862–1890), published in the British Medical Journal, 1886.

with independence, physical strength, and youth."[12] There is much doubt about what kind of dignity ought to be valued.

In *The Elephant Man* (1980),[13] John Merrick (John Hurt) lives his tumultuous life with a partially debilitating disease caused by trauma to his mother while she was pregnant with him. He has a severe physical deformity, chronic bronchitis, lacks the use of his right arm, has difficulty walking and speaking, and must sleep sitting up.[4] Furthermore, viewers of the film learn that his condition gets progressively worse as his life goes on. Dr. Frederick Treves (Anthony Hopkins)[14] and the hospital staff provide John with **palliative care**, knowing that his condition is incurable. Upon his return to London after being kidnapped, the viewer learns that John is dying, and the film ends with John taking his own life by lying flat in his hospital bed after his cathedral model was complete. The quality of John's life is certainly affected by his disease, but the film draws one's attention to the effects of his treatment by others on his life.[5]

PALLIATIVE CARE
Care administered with the goal of improving quality of life, rather than curing; usually for those with little to no hope of recovery; focuses on pain mitigation; can occur alongside life-prolonging therapies.[35]

QUESTIONS FOR CONSIDERATION

a. In *The Elephant Man*, does John Merrick live with dignity? What constitutes dignity in his life?
b. Does he deserve to live with basic human dignity? On what basis?
c. Did John die with dignity?
d. What would Seneca think about John's death? Locke? Kant?
e. Do you think it was moral for John to take his own life? Why or why not?

6.5 Velleman: It's Worse to Have the Legal Option for Assisted Death

Velleman's main argument pertains to the legal option to die with assistance, specifically in the form of euthanasia. Drawing on Schelling and Dworkin, Velleman argues that the very option to legally die with assistance can be harmful even if it is

4. It is highly recommended to view *The Elephant Man* before reading this short section further. For one, what immediately follows contains spoilers. Also, one's reading and learning experience will benefit from having familiarity with the movie. Go to a website like https://www.justwatch.com/ for information about which streaming services have the film and whether or not it is free, for rent, or for purchase.
5. For some information about the real person, see "Joseph Merrick," Biography, updated September 15, 2020, https://www.biography.com/performer/elephant-man-joseph-merrick.

not exercised. Velleman provides an analogy of a cashier at a convenience store who is better off not knowing the combination to the safe. Having the correct combination would make him more of a target for robbers. Options can be "undesirable [. . .] because they subject one to various kinds of pressure."[15] Once one has an option besides the status quo, one "can no longer have the status quo without choosing it."[16] Just as in the case of the cashier, one's situation is changed for the worse when one has the legal option to die with assistance.[17] Velleman says, "The most important way in which the option of euthanasia may harm patients, I think, is that it will deny them the possibility of staying alive by default."[18] What Velleman means here is that one really has to choose to go on living every day when one wakes up knowing that they have the legal option to die with assistance at any time. The decision to keep living is no longer determined by default; rather, it must be constantly chosen. The task of constantly justifying one's own existence is daunting, impractical, and liable to result in poor decisions. Velleman writes, "The burden of justifying one's existence might make existence unbearable—and hence unjustifiable."[19] Also, "Forcing a patient to take responsibility for his continued existence may therefore be tantamount to confronting with the following prospect: unless he can explain, to the satisfaction of others, why he chooses to exist, his only remaining reasons for existence may vanish."[20] In sum, people may choose to die who otherwise wouldn't, simply because they have the legal option of assisted death.

QUESTIONS FOR CONSIDERATION

a. How is the cashier situation analogous to someone having the legal option to die?
b. Do you think that having the legal option for assisted death would force people to confront the value and justification of their very existence more so than is already the case just by being a human being?
c. Do you agree with Velleman's argument against the legal right to die? Why or why not?

6.6 Euthanasia

6.6.1 Overview

Euthanasia's history, legality, and morality largely depend on what form of euthanasia is under discussion. Euthanasia can be active or passive, as well as voluntary, non-voluntary, and involuntary. **Active euthanasia**, also known as **mercy killing**, involves one party performing an action that ends the life of another. **Passive euthanasia** occurs when someone is allowed to die, by withholding or withdrawing lifesaving measures. Legally, there is a significant difference between active and passive euthanasia, most notably, some forms of the latter are widely legal and approved by the medical profession. One example, allowing someone to refuse **extraordinary means of treatment**, happens regularly in medical settings, especially hospice care. **Ordinary means of treatment** are those that medical professionals are duty-bound to provide. Shannon and Kockler describe the way this distinction has been historically understood: "Ordinary therapies typically referred to medicines,

ACTIVE EUTHANASIA/MERCY KILLING
When one takes the life of another in a way intended to make their death good to a greater or lesser extent, either for the patient/victim themselves or others.

PASSIVE EUTHANASIA
When one allows another to die, in such a way that is intended to make their death good to a greater or lesser extent, either for the patient/victim themselves or others.

EXTRAORDINARY MEANS OF TREATMENT
Those that caregivers are not morally obligated to provide.

ORDINARY MEANS OF TREATMENT
Those that caregivers morally obliged to provide.

SUPEREROGATORY
That which goes beyond the merely morally obligatory.

VOLUNTARY EUTHANASIA
When one requests that another person kill them or let them die, with the intention to make their death good to a greater or lesser extent, either for themselves or others.

treatments, or operations that offered a reasonable amount of benefit to a patient without excessive pain, expense, or other inconvenience."[21] Extraordinary means of treatment are those that go beyond what is obligatory. Shannon and Kockler describe them as "Morally optional; They are supererogatory. Extraordinary therapies were those that, while offering only some or little benefit, were very costly, very painful, and exceptionally inconvenient."[22] Understood morally, the benefits of ordinary treatments are "likely to outweigh the burdens," unlike those of extraordinary treatments.[23] Ordinary treatments in some circumstances may be extraordinary in others, and vice versa. Voluntary euthanasia occurs when the patient clearly gives consent in a right frame of mind, without coercion. This can happen by advance directive, if the patient has created one in order to state their wishes in the event that they are no longer competent to make medical decisions. If a surrogate or proxy is available along with the advance directive or living will, a subjective standard is legally present. Non-voluntary euthanasia occurs when: (i) a patient is no longer capable of expressing their wishes, for example, if they are in a persistent vegetative state (PVS), (ii) an advance directive is not present, and (iii) some effort is made to do what would or might be in accord with their wishes. It may be possible to infer their desires from a proxy or surrogate who is legally or morally appropriate to make decisions on their behalf. If this is the case, US law recognizes these decisions as meeting the limited objective standard. If the patient is unrepresented and their wishes cannot be inferred, and a decision must be made purely on the basis of what is reasonable and precedential, then that decision meets the pure objective standard. Finally, involuntary euthanasia occurs *against* the patient's wishes, is widely illegal, and considered immoral.[24]

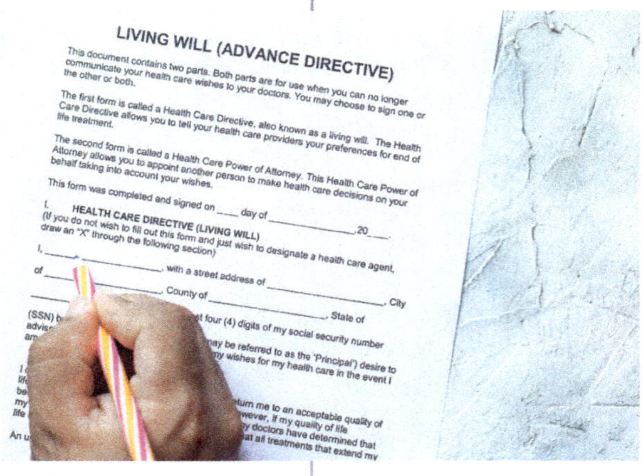

© G.Tbov/Shutterstock.com

© Marc F Gutierrez/Shutterstock.com

6.6.2 Passive Voluntary Euthanasia

ADVANCE DIRECTIVE (AD)
A living will; a document that indicates the medical care one wishes to have in the event that they are not able to provide such guidance.

SURROGATE/PROXY
One who represents a patient and makes health care decisions on their behalf.

SUBJECTIVE STANDARD
Occurs when the patient has clearly made their wishes for end-of-life care known.

Passive voluntary euthanasia occurs when lifesaving means of treatment are withheld or withdrawn. Though it is widely legal to withhold or withdraw both ordinary and extraordinary means of treatment if a patient requests it, only the latter is considered moral according to natural law ethics. Consider the fictitious examples below.

Example A: An eighty-year-old man sustains a debilitating injury and slips into a PVS, being kept alive only by medical intervention, including Assisted Nutrition and Hydration (ANH) and a ventilator. He is unlikely to regain consciousness and physicians agree that he has fewer than six months left to live. His advance directive is discovered, which indicates that he does not want his life to be prolonged by a respirator. It is removed, and the man dies.

Example B: The same accident occurs described above, except the man refuses any treatment when first responders offer it, even though such treatments would alleviate his pain and have a chance of stabilizing him. As a result, he dies at the scene of the accident.

Both of these scenarios are legally acceptable, but only Example A is considered morally acceptable according to natural law ethics.

QUESTIONS FOR CONSIDERATION

a. Do you think one or both of the examples above are moral? Immoral? Why or why not? Do you think they should both be legal? Use the ethical theories of Chapters Three and Four in your determinations, as well as the excerpts above from Epicurus, Epictetus, and Seneca.

Natural law proponents also argue that the voluntary hastening of death by pain mitigation or palliative care can be moral, unlike the withholding or removing ordinary means of treatment.

Example C: A woman in her seventies is terminally ill from cancer, her condition is getting progressively worse, and physicians agree she only has weeks left to live. She is in a great deal of pain and the doses of morphine that she needs in order for the pain to be bearable are likely to bring on her death more quickly. She requests those doses nonetheless, they are administered, and she dies within a few days.

b. This voluntary hastening of death is widely legal and accepted, including by natural law. Do you think it should be? Do you think it's moral? Why or why not? Use the ethical theories of Chapters Three and Four in your determinations, as well as the excerpts above from Epicurus, Epictetus, and Seneca.

6.6.3 Passive Non-Voluntary Euthanasia

Passive non-voluntary euthanasia is much more controversial, legally and ethically, than passive voluntary euthanasia. This is because of the lack of clear direction from the patient. Consider two famous cases:

Example A: In 1990, at age 41, Terry Schiavo suffered cardiac arrest that resulted in brain damage. She slipped into a coma, was being kept alive by ANH, and doctors concurred that she would not recover. She had no advance directive, but three surrogates were present to make a decision about whether to remove her feeding tube: her husband and her parents. Her husband believed that she would not want to be kept alive by machines, and so, five years after she slipped into a PVS, he advocated for the removal of ANH. Her parents doubted her husband and wanted her feeding tube to remain in place, hoping for her miraculous recovery. The Catholic Church, the governor of Florida, and the president of the United States took her parents' stance, but the law did not. After a drawn out, much publicized legal battle, her feeding tube

NON-VOLUNTARY EUTHANASIA
When one person takes action to kill someone or let them die without knowing the patient's exact wishes, but with some knowledge of what those wishes might be if the patient were able to state them.

PERSISTENT VEGETATIVE STATE (PVS)
A long-lasting unconscious state resulting from brain damage.[36]

LIMITED OBJECTIVE STANDARD
Occurs when there is some degree of reliable knowledge about how to act in accord with a patient's wishes when the patient is not able to state them and there is no AD.

PURE OBJECTIVE STANDARD
Occurs when there is no reliable knowledge about what a patient's end-of-life care wishes would be if they were able to state them.

INVOLUNTARY EUTHANASIA
Killing someone or letting them die against their wishes.

ASSISTED NUTRITION AND HYDRATION (ANH)
Medical means used to hydrate someone and/or feed them; for example, a feeding tube.

was removed and she died shortly thereafter. An autopsy confirmed that "her brain was severely atrophied, weighing less than half of what it should have." It was and still is impossible to reverse that kind of brain damage.[25]

QUESTIONS FOR CONSIDERATION

a. Which of the following standards were available for making the decision about whether to remove Mrs. Schiavo's feeding tube: The subjective standard, the limited objective standard, or the pure objective standard?
b. Which category of treatment do you think was in question: Ordinary or extraordinary means? Do you think such a question could ever be difficult or impossible to answer clearly?
c. Do you think the courts made the right decision in her case? Why or why not? Use the ethical theories of Chapters Three and Four in your determinations.

Example B: Karen Ann Quinlan, at age 21, came home from a party and slipped into a PVS as a result of consuming tranquilizers and alcohol.[26] She was being kept alive only by a ventilator for several months with no signs of improvement. No advance directive was present. Based on suppositions about her possible wishes, her parents asked for her life support to be withdrawn, while the hospital refused. After legal battles, a New Jersey court allowed her breathing support to be removed[27] because they did not think there was a "reasonable possibility" she would recover. She died a surprising ten years later.[28]

d. What standard was present in the decision made on Miss Quinlan's behalf: A subjective standard, a limited objective standard, or a pure objective standard? Why?
e. Do you think the courts ultimately made the right decision? Use the ethical theories of Chapters Three and Four in your determinations.

6.6.4 Rachels on Passive versus Active Euthanasia

Though legal and moral standards typically make a sharp distinction between passive and active euthanasia, James Rachels provides some reasons to question that distinction.

First, Rachels points out that it may take longer for a patient to die, and involve more pain and suffering, in the case of withholding or removing treatment. He reasons that if this will be the case, active euthanasia ought to be preferred.

Second, he brings up the example of babies born with Down Syndrome[6] who also have "intestinal obstructions" for which a fairly uncomplicated surgery is needed to save their lives. Parents typically serve as the proxy for the child, and in

6. For information about what Down Syndrome is, see: "Down Syndrome," Mayo Clinic, March 8, 2018, https://www.mayoclinic.org/diseases-conditions/down-syndrome/symptoms-causes/syc-20355977. Chris Burke is one of the most famous people with Down Syndrome. He is best known for playing Charles "Corky" Thatcher on the show *Life Goes On*. See https://www.imdb.com/title/tt0096635/.

some cases, parents ask that the operation not take place, preferring to let the baby die. Since anyone can legally refuse any kind of treatment and since parents are usually considered reliable surrogates, US law allows this to happen. Watching these babies die from dehydration and infection for hours or possibly days is excruciating for hospital staff. Rachels points out that it would clearly be more humane to end the babies' lives swiftly and without pain by means of an injection. But this is not his main point. He argues that in such cases, parents are making their decision based on the fact that the child has Down Syndrome, not that the baby has an intestinal blockage. Such grounds are not relevant for deciding life or death, says Rachels. In this way, the accepted and widely practiced distinction between passive and active euthanasia is seriously flawed.

Rachels's third example involves two invented scenarios. In the first one, "Smith" will inherit a sizable fortune upon the death of his cousin, who is age six. When the child is taking a bath, Smith drowns him and makes it look like an accident. The second scenario involves "Jones," who will also benefit if his six-year-old cousin dies. Jones was planning on drowning the boy when he was in the bath, but as he's about to do it, he notices the boy slip, smack his head, and fall with his face down in the water. Jones simply then watches the boy die. Rachels then points out that there is hardly any difference between the actions of the boy's two cousins, thus casting a great deal of doubt on the active/passive distinction.[29]

QUESTIONS FOR CONSIDERATION

a. Do you find any of Rachels's arguments persuasive? Why or why not?

6.6.5 Active Voluntary Euthanasia

In active voluntary euthanasia, someone takes measures to end the life of another upon their request. There is much debate about the legality and morality of this. It is legal in many of the same places assisted suicide is legal,[30] and many of the same arguments for assisted suicide are used to justify active voluntary euthanasia. Legal entities clearly are concerned with the voluntariness of the decision, rather than the agent who implements it. Active voluntary euthanasia is discussed so much more frequently than other kinds, that it is often referred to simply as "euthanasia."

Don Marquis, whose pro-life stance is discussed in Chapter Five, argues against abortion on the basis of the value of a human being's future, which it is wrong to take away from someone. He writes the following about active voluntary euthanasia:

> The claim that the loss of one's future is the wrong-making feature of one's being killed does not entail, as sanctity of human life theories do, that active euthanasia is wrong. Persons who are severely and incurably ill, who face a future of pain and despair, and who wish to die will not have suffered a loss if they are killed. It is, strictly speaking, the value of a human's future which makes killing wrong in this theory. This being so, killing does not necessarily wrong some persons who are sick and dying.[31]

QUESTIONS FOR CONSIDERATION

a. Do you think Marquis is correct to argue that it is not wrong to deprive those who request active euthanasia of their future, as long as they meet certain criteria? Why or why not? Is it possible that a "future like ours" always has a value worth preserving—that is, without exceptions? Use the ethical theories of Chapters Three and Four in your determinations, as well as the excerpts above from Epicurus, Epictetus, and Seneca.

6.6.5.1 *The Walking Dead* and *Million Dollar Baby*

In the post-apocalyptic world of *The Walking Dead,*[32] examples abound of active voluntary euthanasia.[7] Someone has been bitten or scratched by a "walker" (a zombie), and requests implicitly or explicitly to be shot or stabbed in the head so that they don't "turn" and threaten everyone else. In these cases, it is abundantly clear that there is no hope for recovery, that pain and suffering will only increase, that there is not a great deal of time between infection, death, and re-animation, and that walkers "live" to bite and scratch others, thereby infecting them. There are a few exceptional characters, like Hershel (Scott Wilson) initially (Season 2, 2011), who think there might be a cure, or that the walkers really are not dead. However, these hopers represent a small minority, and they quickly change their views after having more experience with the walking dead. Those who carry out the mercy killings hardly have an easy time doing so—for the most part—but the death that the recipient experiences is certainly easier and better than if they had been left to suffer, die, and "turn."

In *Million Dollar Baby,* Maggie Fitzgerald (Hilary Swank) is a poor waitress who hopes to become a professional boxer.[8] She seeks out the expert training of Frankie Dunn (Clint Eastwood), who initially rejects her several times because of her gender and age (31). After she diligently proves her grit and persistence to him, he agrees to train her and she becomes a highly successful athlete. In the latter half of the film, Maggie sustains an injury that leaves her paralyzed from the neck down. Doctors express no hope for recovery, and her condition worsens over time, especially when her leg is amputated, though it is unclear how long she may have lived. She eventually asks Frankie to secretly end her life for her, and he complies in the end, by removing her breathing tube and giving her a high dose of morphine followed by adrenaline. In the film, it is unclear which substance actually kills her. Though the adrenaline was supposed to, viewers are left wondering if the morphine may have done the job on its own. Ultimately, withdrawal of the breathing tube would have resulted in her death if the other two measures did not.

---

7. It is recommended, but not necessary, to view Seasons One and Two, at least, before reading further. What follows does not contain spoilers. Go to a website like https://www.justwatch.com/ for information about which streaming services have the show and whether or not it is free, for rent, or for purchase.

8. It is highly recommended to view the film before reading the rest of this paragraph. What follows contains significant spoilers. Also, one's reading and learning experience will benefit from having familiarity with the movie. Go to a website like https://www.justwatch.com/ for information about which streaming services have *Million Dollar Baby,* and whether or not it is free, for rent, or for purchase.

© Stokkete/Shutterstock.com

© Evgeny Apin/Shutterstock.com

© Rommel Canlas/Shutterstock.com

QUESTIONS FOR CONSIDERATION

a. What ethically crucial differences are there between the euthanasia of *The Walking Dead* versus that of *Million Dollar Baby*?
b. Watch one or both closely, looking for information critical to your ethical determinations, then choose the ethical theory or theories that you agree with most and apply it/them to one or both depictions of euthanasia. What are the results? Do you think active euthanasia was practiced ethically? Why or why not?

6.6.6 Non-Voluntary and Involuntary Euthanasia: *Breaking Bad*[9] and *COVID-19*

Whether active or passive, non-voluntary and involuntary euthanasia are widely frowned upon and usually considered criminal as well as immoral. In some cases, these species of euthanasia clearly constitute murder—especially active involuntary euthanasia.

Breaking Bad (2008–2013),[33] heartbreakingly depicts an incident of passive involuntary euthanasia (Season 2, ep. 12–13) when Walter (Bryan Cranston) finds

9. It is highly recommended to view at least episodes 12–13 of *Breaking Bad*, Season Two before reading the second paragraph and questions for consideration in this section, which both discuss details of that show. Of course, watching all of the episodes up to and including those mentioned would be best. The parts of this section previously mentioned contain spoilers. Also, one's reading and learning experience will benefit from having familiarity with the show. Go to a website like https://www.justwatch.com/ for information about which streaming services have *Breaking Bad*, and whether or not it is free, for rent, or for purchase.

Jesse (Aaron Paul) and his girlfriend Jane (Krysten Ritter) passed out from heroin. Walter notices Jane choking on her own vomit, but he does nothing to help her, and she dies. Jesse and Jane's father (John de Lancie) are devastated, which has drastic consequences. One surmises that Walt's motivation was to gain more control over Jesse. Though it seems clear that Jane did not *intend* to die, because of her decision to resume using heroin, one must ask whether she was actually open to, willing, or hoping for death, thus raising the prospect that her death was non-voluntary rather than involuntary.

Other instances of passive non-voluntary or involuntary euthanasia may occur when medical caregivers must quickly triage the injured in times of great emergency. This happened during the COVID-19 pandemic throughout the world, but perhaps most notably in Italy, when doctors and nurses in overwhelmed hospitals decided to let some patients die so that others could live. In some cases, the wishes of the suffering could only be assessed through surrogates, or could not be reliably determined at all, thus constituting *non-voluntary* passive euthanasia. In other cases, patients who wanted to live were allowed to die, which constitutes *involuntary* passive euthanasia. Those who were most likely to survive and with the "longest remaining life" were prioritized, along with front-line health care workers. The goal was to "maximize the number of lives saved."[34]

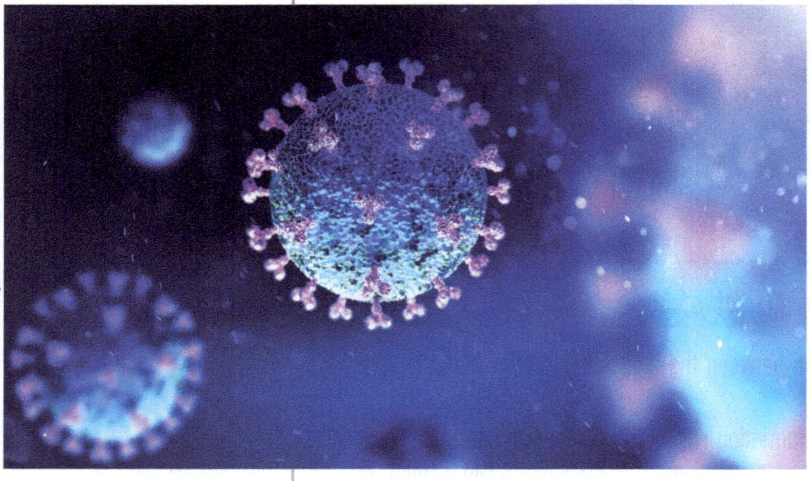

QUESTIONS FOR CONSIDERATION

a. What are the ethically relevant differences between the examples of euthanasia from *Breaking Bad* and COVID-19?
b. Watch the episode and read the article cited (see endnotes) about euthanasia and the coronavirus. Are there other ethically significant differences between the two examples?
c. Do you think Jane's death was non-voluntary or involuntary?
d. Do you agree with the medical profession's use of utilitarianism to make decisions about whom to treat and whom to let die?
e. Do you agree with the criteria used to determine who would receive care and who wouldn't? Why or why not?

6.7 Resources for Further Investigation and Learning

6.7.1 Articles about Euthanasia and the 2020 Coronavirus

Hamid Dabashi, "Coronavirus and the prospect of mass involuntary euthanasia," *AlJazeera*, April 17, 2020, https://www.aljazeera.com/indepth/opinion/coronavirus-prospect-mass-involuntary-euthanasia-200515122939558.html.

Karen Weise and Mike Baker, "'Chilling' Plans: Who Gets Care as Washington State Hospitals Fill Up?," *The New York Times*, March 20, 2020, https://www.nytimes.com/2020/03/20/us/coronavirus-in-seattle-washington-state.html.

6.7.2 Statistics on Assisted Suicide and Euthanasia

Megan Brenan, "Americans' Strong Support for Euthanasia Persists," *Gallup*, May 31, 2018, https://news.gallup.com/poll/235145/americans-strong-support-euthanasia-persists.aspx.

Michael Lipka, "Americans of all ages divided over doctor-assisted suicide laws," *FactTank*, October 22, 2014, https://www.pewresearch.org/fact-tank/2014/10/22/americans-of-all-ages-divided-over-doctor-assisted-suicide-laws/.

Michael Lipka, "5 facts about Americans' views on life-and-death issues," *FactTank*, January 7, 2014, https://www.pewresearch.org/fact-tank/2014/01/07/5-facts-about-americans-views-on-life-and-death-issues/.

6.7.3 Articles on *Million Dollar Baby* and Euthanasia

Arthur Caplan, "Movie asks the 'Million Dollar' question," *NBC News*, February 17, 2005, http://www.nbcnews.com/id/6970787/ns/health-health_care/t/movie-asks-million-dollar-question/#.Xz_l6YhKipo.

Christopher Orr, "The Movie Review: 'Million Dollar Baby,'" *The Atlantic*, July 12, 2005, https://www.theatlantic.com/entertainment/archive/2005/07/the-movie-review-million-dollar-baby/69445/.

"Why 'Million Dollar Baby' infuriates the disabled," *Chicago Tribune*, February 2, 2005, https://www.chicagotribune.com/news/ct-xpm-2005-02-02-0502020017-story.html.

6.7.4 Books Related to *The Elephant Man*

A biography of Joseph Merrick:

Michael Howell and Peter Ford, *The True History of the Elephant Man* (London: Allison & Busby, 1980, 1983, 1992), https://www.amazon.com/True-History-Elephant-Man/.

The book that inspired the film:

Ashley Montagu and Trent Angers, *The Elephant Man: A Study in Human Dignity* (Acadian House Publishing, 1971, 2001), https://www.goodreads.com/book/show/156379.The_Elephant_Man.

Sir Frederick Treves's book:

Sir Frederick Treves, *The Elephant Man and Other Reminiscences* (London: Cassell and Company, LTD, 1923), https://www.amazon.com/Elephant-Man-Other-Reminiscences/.

6.7.5 Resources on Human Dignity

Internet Encyclopedia of Philosophy, s.v. "Human Dignity," accessed October 13, 2020, https://iep.utm.edu/hum-dign/.

"Life and Dignity of the Human Person," United States Conference of Catholic Bishops, 2020, https://www.usccb.org/beliefs-and-teachings/what-we-believe/catholic-social-teaching/life-and-dignity-of-the-human-person.

Endnotes

1. *Merriam-Webster*, s.v. "euthanasia," accessed October 13, 2020, https://www.merriam-webster.com/dictionary/euthanasia.
2. *The Extant Remains*, trans. Cyril Bailey (Oxford: Oxford University Press, 1926).
3. Epictetus, *Encheiridion*, trans. Wallace I. Matson in *Classics of Philosophy*, ed. Louis P. Pojman and Lewis Vaughn (Oxford: Oxford University Press, 2011): 352–354.
4. Seneca, *Selected Letters*, trans. Elaine Fantham (Oxford: Oxford University Press, 2010): 110–113.
5. "Jack Kevorkian: How he made controversial history," BBC, June 3, 2011, https://www.bbc.com/news/world-us-canada-13649381.
6. https://www.deathwithdignity.org/
7. "Physician-Assisted Suicide Fast Facts," CNN, June 11, 2020, https://www.cnn.com/2014/11/26/us/physician-assisted-suicide-fast-facts/index.html.
8. Preston, 2018, 150.
9. J. David Velleman, "Against the Right to Die," in *Death in the Clinic*, ed. Lynn A. Jansen (Lanham: Rowman & Littlefield Publishers, Inc., 2006), 49.
10. Ibid., 50.
11. Ibid.
12. Ibid.
13. All information about films' production dates, creators, and actors in this chapter is from IMDb. See https://www.imdb.com/.
14. "The Elephant Man," IMDb, accessed October 13, 2020, https://www.imdb.com/title/tt0080678/.

15. Velleman, 54.
16. Ibid.
17. Ibid., 55.
18. Ibid., 56.
19. Ibid., 57.
20. Ibid.
21. Thomas A. Shannon and Nicholas J. Kockler, *An Introduction to Bioethics*, Fourth ed. (New York: Paulist Press, 2009), 145.
22. Ibid., 146.
23. Ibid.
24. Ibid. and Lewis Vaughn, *Doing Ethics*, Fifth ed. (New York: W.W. Norton & Company, Inc., 2019).
25. Arthur Caplan, "Ten Years After Terri Schiavo, Death Debates Still Divide Us: Bioethicist," *NBC News*, March 31, 2015, https://www.nbcnews.com/health/health-news/bioethicist-tk-n333536.
26. Robert D. McFadden, "Karen Ann Quinlan, 31, Dies; Focus of '76 Right to Die Case," *The New York Times*, June 12, 1985, https://www.nytimes.com/1985/06/12/nyregion/karen-ann-quinlan-31-dies-focus-of-76-right-to-die-case.html.
27. "The Karen Ann Quinlan Case," Centers for Disease Control and Prevention, accessed October 13, 2020, https://www.cdc.gov/training/ACP/page33994.html.
28. McFadden, "Karen Ann Quinlan, . . ."
29. James Rachels, "Active and Passive Euthanasia," *The New England Journal of Medicine* 292 (1975): 78–79.
30. Penney Lewis, "Assisted dying: What does the law in different countries say?" *BBC News*, October 6, 2015, https://www.bbc.com/news/world-34445715.
31. Marquis, 191.
32. *The Walking Dead*, created by Frank Darabont and Angela Kang, 2010–2020, https://www.imdb.com/title/tt1520211/?ref_=ttfc_fc_tt.
33. *Breaking Bad*, created by Vince Gilligan, 2008–2013, https://www.imdb.com/title/tt0903747/?ref_=ttfc_fc_tt.
34. Austin Frakt, "Who Should Be Saved First? Experts Offer Ethical Guidance," *The New York Times*, March 29, 2020, https://www.nytimes.com/2020/03/24/upshot/coronavirus-rationing-decisions-ethicists.html?referringSource=articleShare.
35. "WHO Definition of Palliative Care," World Health Organization, 2020, https://www.who.int/cancer/palliative/definition/en/#:~:text=Palliative%20care%20is%20an%20approach%20that%20improves%20the,pain%20and%20other%20problems%2C%20physical%2C%20psychosocial%20and%20spiritual.
36. *Merriam Webster*, s.v. "Persistent Vegetative State," accessed October 13, 2020, https://www.merriam-webster.com/dictionary/persistent%20vegetative%20state.

Chapter 7

Environmental Ethics: Dominion and Harmony

Co-Authored with Mark Sentesy

7.1 Introduction

Every human community lives in a relationship with the natural world. We are connected to nature through the air we breathe, the plants and animals that clean our water and grow our food, the material of the things we buy, our energy sources, and the infrastructure of our civilization, as well as our practices, experiences, concepts, identities, and goals. There are two forms of inheritance: internal (e.g., DNA and our living bodies with all their features), and external (e.g., values, skills, social practices, and the surrounding world—the **environment** that shapes us and makes our lives possible). Human communities have adopted many forms of relationship with our surrounding world, which ultimately affect both forms of inheritance.

Most of the harm humans have done to nature and our descendants has been done by societies that have represented nature as a resource we are supposed to exploit. The ideological roots of the idea that human beings have dominion over nature include the Book of Genesis, and the work of Francis Bacon, Rene Descartes, and John Locke.[1] This idea helped give rise to the **Industrial Revolution**, which led human beings to assume mastery of the natural world on an unprecedented scale—dominion became domination and destruction, which was never intended by the Judeo-Christian tradition and its followers. Human beings are shaping the biology and chemistry of the oceans, land, and atmosphere to such an extent that geologists have proposed naming our current epoch the **Anthropocene**.

Avatar (2009) portrays industrial civilization's consumption of nature as a military operation, showing the violence of its impacts on a world in which people

ENVIRONMENT
The dynamic systems surrounding an individual or a community on which they depend and with which they engage in order to breathe, eat, drink, clothe themselves, or build homes and everything else humans make. The environment shapes people, and people shape the environment.

INDUSTRIAL REVOLUTION
The massive societal change that resulted from the increased use of steam and coal-powered machines, as well as electricity, to produce mankind's goods. Please see the appendix for further information.

ANTHROPOCENE
The time period in Earth's history defined by mankind's effects on it.

1. Please see the appendix for important background information about each philosopher and time period discussed in this chapter.

live in harmony with nature. *An Inconvenient Truth* (2006) and *An Inconvenient Sequel* (2017)[1] explain the reality of human-caused global heating, and by projecting its impacts—life-threatening heat waves, intensified storms and floods, more frequent and more severe droughts, fires, famine, migration, and political conflict—the film enjoins its viewers to reconstruct industrial society to stop heating the planet. The films present these solutions as building a better world by drawing on human vision, ingenuity, collaboration, and commitment. *Cooked: Survival by Zip Code* (2018) examines how disasters like hurricanes and heatwaves are entangled with socially-created environments, such as the slow disaster of poverty-creation, the isolation of elders, and the history of racism, by looking at how and why the 1995 Chicago heatwave killed a disproportionate number of black citizens.

> Though all of the films discussed in this chapter are highly recommended, it is not strictly necessary to watch all of them in order to attain a basic grasp of the chapter's content. One exception is *Avatar*, which one must view in order to understand section 7.4.3.2. That section treats the relationship of the film to the work of Aldo Leopold, and it contains spoilers.

7.2 A Brief History of Dominion: Man's Proper Relationship with the Natural World According to the Bible and Enlightenment Thinkers

7.2.1 The Bible: Genesis Book One, Chapter One

Chapter One of the Book of Genesis reads, "Then God said: 'Let us make man in our own image, after our likeness. Let them have dominion over the fish of the sea, the birds of the air, and the cattle, and over all the wild animals and all the creatures that crawl on the ground.'"[2] One verse later, the text says:

> God blessed them, saying: 'Be fertile and multiply; fill the earth and subdue it. Have dominion over the fish of the sea, the birds of the air, and all the living things that move on the earth.' God also said: 'See, I give you every seed-bearing plant all over the earth and every tree that has seed-bearing fruit on it to be your food; and to all the animals of the land, all the birds of the air, and all the living creatures that crawl on the ground, I give all the green plants for food.'[3]

These verses have been extremely familiar to Jews, Christians, and many others around the world for over two millennia. They emphasize the notion that God wants humankind to dominate the natural world, by using its resources, especially for food. This account of creation suggests that it is inherent in human nature to use natural resources for nourishment and for the propagation of the human race. The verses above do not suggest destruction. Neither dominion nor subduing is synonymous with depletion or death. Rather, Genesis paints a picture of humans flourishing from nature. Such flourishing obviously would not be possible if nature were depleted or ruined.

7.2.2 Bacon, *New Organon*

Francis Bacon was the thinker who inaugurated the modern scientific-technological method. He saw the mastery of nature it offered as the way to restore our dominion over and therefore harmony with the natural world, which humankind lost in our sinful fall out of Eden. He writes:

> Whence there cannot but follow an improvement in man's estate, and an enlargement of his power over nature. For man by the fall fell at the same time from his state of innocency and from his dominion over creation. Both of these losses however can even in this life be in some part repaired; the former by religion and faith the latter by arts and sciences.[4]

A key part of Bacon's new method was the view that controlling nature is both the way to discover its truths, and the way to establish order in it. He and his followers presented this method of experimentation variously as binding nature (e.g., in the form of the Greek god Proteus) using violent force to control its behavior, and torturing it on the rack to force it to reveal its secrets.

> For you have but to follow and as it were hound nature in her wanderings, and you will be able when you like to lead and drive her afterward to the same place again.[5]

In 1700, Jean Baptiste du Hamel, secretary of the Paris Academy of Sciences, wrote of this method that "We discover the mysteries of nature much more easily when she is tortured [*torqueatur*] by fire or some other aids of art than when she proceeds along her own road." Against this, the Romantic thinker Johann Wolfgang von Goethe argued that "nature falls silent on the rack." "Phenomena must once and for all be removed from their gloomy empirical-mechanical-dogmatic torture chamber."[6]

7.2.3 Descartes's *Discourse on Method*

The seventeenth-century philosopher Rene Descartes discusses man's mastery of nature in a similar way to Bacon when he discusses his knowledge of physics and the possibility "of discovering a practical philosophy" that could replace "speculative philosophy" as that taught in schools. He writes:

> Through this philosophy we could know the power and action of fire, water, air, the stars, the heavens and all the other bodies in our environment, as distinctly as we know the crafts of our artisans; and we could use this knowledge—as the artisans use theirs—for all the purposes for which it is appropriate, and thus make ourselves, as it were, the lords and masters of nature. This is desirable not only for the invention of innumerable devices which would facilitate our enjoyment of the fruits of the earth and all the goods we find there, but also, and most importantly, for the maintenance of health, which is undoubtedly the chief good and the foundation of all the other goods in this life. . .[7]

Descartes expresses optimism about the mastery of nature and the future of technology, focusing on the good it would bring to mankind. Though his vision of the future of medicine is prescient, he does not acknowledge the many dangers inherent in technological progress. Key among these dangers is something completely neglected in the technological utopian vision: the ever-increasing detruitus, the garbage and pollution of technological and industrial processes that poison our land, choke our sea life, and heat the planet more rapidly than at any time in its history. Because of the dangers of such technology, including the threat of nuclear annihilation, the twentieth-century philosopher Hans Jonas argues that humanity should prioritize responsibility in its advancement of technology.[8]

QUESTIONS FOR CONSIDERATION

a. Do you think of the method of experimentation as ethical, like Bacon, or unethical, like Goethe? Explain why.
b. What forms of knowledge can you think of that we cannot get through technological control? How do we come to know those things?
c. Do you share Descartes's high level of optimism about the potential for science and technology to make life better for humankind?
d. What are the potential environmental drawbacks of Descartes's statements about the mastery of nature?

7.2.4 Locke's Theory of Property: Annotated Excerpts from the *Second Treatise of Government*

Another seventeenth-century philosopher, John Locke, echoes the Biblical teaching above and puts it in the context of modern democracy in his *Second Treatise of Government*, when he explains his now famous theory of private property:

> Sect. 25. Whether we consider natural reason, which tells us, that men, being once born, have a right to their preservation, and consequently to meat and drink, and such other things as nature affords for their subsistence: or revelation, which gives us an account of those grants God made of the world to Adam, and to Noah, and his sons, it is very clear that God, as king David says, Psal. Cxv. 16. has given the earth to the children of men; given it to mankind in common. . .

This is a Biblical reference, to the Book of Psalms.

Note here that Locke distinguishes "natural reason" from "revelation." By the latter, he means the content in the Bible that is based on faith, or the belief in the divine. From both perspectives—reason and faith—the natural world is meant for mankind to use as it sees fit, according to Locke.

Sect. 26. God, who hath given the world to men in common, hath also given them reason to make use of it to the best advantage of life, and convenience. The earth, and all that is therein, is given to men for the support and comfort of their being . . .

Sect. 27. Though the earth, and all inferior creatures, be common to all men, yet every man has a property in his own person: this no body has any right to but himself. The labour of his body, and the work of his hands, we may say, are properly his. Whatsoever then he removes out of the state that nature hath provided, and left it in, he hath mixed his labour with, and joined to it something that is his own, and thereby makes it his property. It being by him removed from the common state nature hath placed it in, it hath by this labour something annexed to it, that excludes the common right of other men: for this labour being the unquestionable property of the labourer, no man but he can have a right to what that is once joined to, at least where there is enough, and as good, left in common for others.

This is the crux of Locke's theory of private property. Just as our bodies belong to us, so does anything in nature to which we apply our physical labor. Locke adds important conditions here though: The natural resources we claim must first be in a "common state," meaning that they cannot already have been claimed by a person or other entity. Also, when we make something ours, we must ensure that those resources are not in short supply. We cannot deplete a resource in such a way that our use of it makes it unavailable to others as a result.

[. . .]

Sect. 31. It will perhaps be objected to this, that if gathering the acorns, or other fruits of the earth, &c. makes a right to them, then any one may ingross as much as he will. To which I answer, Not so. The same law of nature, that does by this means give us property, does also bound that property too. God has given us all things richly [. . .]. But how far has he given it us? To enjoy. As much as any one can make use of to any advantage of life before it spoils, so much he may by his labour fix a property in: whatever is beyond this, is more than his share, and belongs to others. Nothing was made by God for man to spoil or destroy. And thus, considering the plenty of natural provisions there was a long time in the world, and the few spenders; and to how small a part of that provision the industry of one man could extend itself, and ingross it to the prejudice of others; especially keeping within the bounds, set by reason, of what might serve for his use; there could be then little room for quarrels or contentions about property so established.

Here, Locke affirms the qualifiers or conditions of his theory of property. One must not consume a natural resource in a limitless or completely uninhibited way. In addition to the two conditions above, Locke adds here that one must not lay claim to anything that will spoil or go unused. These boundaries on man's use of nature are based on reason as well as Locke's interpretation of the Bible (revelation).

[. . .]

Sect. 36. The measure of property nature has well set by the extent of men's labour and the conveniences of life: no man's labour could subdue, or appropriate all; nor could his enjoyment consume more than a small part; so that it was impossible for any man, this way, to intrench upon the right of another [. . .]. This measure did confine every man's possession to a very moderate proportion, and such as he might appropriate to himself, without injury to any body, in the first ages of the world [. . .]. And the same measure may be allowed still without prejudice to any body, as full as the world seems [. . .]. Nay, the extent of ground is of so little value, without labour, that I have heard it affirmed, that in Spain itself a man may be permitted to plough, sow and reap, without being disturbed, upon land he has no other title to, but only his making use of it. [. . .] But be this as it will, which I lay no stress on; this I dare boldly affirm, that the same rule of propriety, (viz.) that every man should have as much as he could make use of, would hold still in the world, without straitening any body; since there is land enough in the world to suffice double the inhabitants, had not the invention of money, and the tacit agreement of men to put a value on it, introduced (by consent) larger possessions, and a right to them [. . .].

> Locke thinks there are enough natural resources in existence that if everyone abides by his theory of property acquisition, everyone will always have the resources they need. The main problem in the practical application of this theory is that "the invention of money" has enabled people to lay claim to more property than they need.

Sect. 37. [. . .] . . .He who appropriates land to himself by his labour, does not lessen, but increase the common stock of mankind: for the provisions serving to the support of human life, produced by one acre of inclosed and cultivated land, are (to speak much within compass) ten times more than those which are yielded by an acre of land of an equal richness lying waste in common. [. . .]

> Locke thinks that people add value to nature when they cultivate land, as opposed to letting it exist in its natural state, unclaimed and unused by humans.

Before the appropriation of land, he who gathered as much of the wild fruit, killed, caught, or tamed, as many of the beasts, as he could; he that so imployed his pains about any of the spontaneous products of nature, as any way to alter them from the state which nature put them in, by placing any of his labour on them, did thereby acquire a propriety in them: but if they perished, in his possession, without their due use; if the fruits rotted, or the venison putrified, before he could spend it, he offended against the common law of nature, and was liable to be punished; he invaded his neighbour's share, for he had no right, farther than his use called for any of them, and they might serve to afford him conveniences of life.[9]

> Try to create your own interpretation box here by explaining in a sentence or two what this last paragraph means.

QUESTIONS FOR CONSIDERATION

a. Does Locke's theory of private property accurately reflect the Biblical teaching of the Book of Genesis about man's relationship with nature? Does Locke add anything of his own?
b. Do you agree with Locke's theory about the acquisition of private property? Do you think it ought to be put into practice? Is that even possible?
c. Do you agree with Locke that as long as each person only takes from nature what they will use, there will always be sufficient natural resources for everyone? In 1690, the world's population was just over half a billion. As of July 2020, the world's population is 7.6 billion.[10]
d. What do you think about the limits that Locke puts on a person's use of natural resources? Are they too severe? Or should further limits be added?

7.3 Using the Energies of Nature

Human dominion over the natural world grew exponentially during the Industrial Revolution. This revolution replaced the skill and strength of living bodies with the machine of the factory and energy released through combustion.[2] This shift in energy produced modern industrial civilization. It was only possible because living things "store" energy in solid objects in the form of carbon compounds. All sources of energy that power our civilization, except nuclear energy, are derived from sunlight. Through photosynthesis plants store sun energy in molecules made of CO_2 from the air and H_2O from the soil. When animals eat plants, they use this energy to grow and move. Combustion does the same thing, using energy stored in biomass such as wood, or the concentrated ancient biomass of coal, oil, and gas. Both respiration and burning release CO_2 back into the air. It was not until Eunice Foote's discovery of the **greenhouse effect** in 1856 that scientists realized that pumping ancient carbon rapidly back into the air by burning fossil fuels could raise the temperature of the whole planet.[11]

GREENHOUSE EFFECT
The rise in temperatures that results from the excessive levels of certain gases, like carbon dioxide and methane, building up in the atmosphere and trapping the sun's heat.

Two further innovations now define the possibilities of technological civilization: the technology of electricity, and renewable technologies that harness solar energy directly from sunlight, wind, and water without needing to burn the remains of living things.

The technological innovations brought about by these energy revolutions have included, but are not limited to: the complete transformation of travel and transportation, once propelled only by muscles and wind, but then also by steam trains, combustion engines, cargo ships, airplanes, and electric motors; the revolution in materials production on a massive scale, through the extraction, refinement, and shaping of metals and plastic into skyscrapers, syringes, tanks, couches, and earphones; new ways to heat and cool our buildings; electric technology like light bulbs, telephones, radio, television, computers; industrial agricultural machinery and the rise of the global food industry, allowing people in the developed world to consume plants and animals

2. Combustion engines are those fueled by burning.

brought to them from thousands of miles away, which are themselves fertilized and fed by nutrients from hundreds or thousands of miles away.

7.3.1 *An Inconvenient Truth*

ECOSYSTEMS
Intricate, complex networks of interrelated and often interdependent biological creatures, from simple microscopic organisms to large predators.

CLIMATE CHANGE
As opposed to weather, gradual changes in trends and patterns; global warming is an example, but despite the fact that global temperatures generally rise, other changes include regional cooling; for instance in Europe, if the Gulf stream is "shut off" due to warming.

The most severe negative effects of the implementation of the inventions above are well-known, including, but not limited to: the pollution of **ecosystems** and degradation of soil, the endangerment or extinction of many plant and animal species, and the increasing damages caused by man-made global heating (**climate change**). The widely known statistic is that 97 percent of climate scientists in 2020 agree that humans are causing global warming, but the actual number is much closer to 100 percent.[3]

An Inconvenient Truth explains how global warming is happening, in layman's terms. Greenhouse gases like carbon dioxide act like a blanket: they let sunlight warm the earth, but trap this heat, preventing it from radiating back out into space. Ice core drills, championed by Lonnie Thomson, reveal that carbon dioxide levels in the twenty-first century are higher than they've ever been in the past 650,000 years.[12] Scientists have since shown that they are now higher than at any time in the last 3 million years, when the warmer climate meant sea levels were as much as sixty-five feet higher, and Antarctica was covered in trees.[13] The film highlights trends in rising global temperatures by noting that recent years are the hottest on record. Corroborating one claim by the 2006 film: As of 2019, the eight hottest years have all occurred since 2010. Ocean temperatures in the past sixty years are trending upward, raising sea levels and producing stronger hurricanes and much more flooding, as we saw with the sixty inches of rain Hurricane Harvey dropped on Houston. Warming leads to more evaporation, which increases humidity, strengthening storms and hurricanes, and intensifying rainfall and flooding. It also causes more soil evaporation, which causes more drought. These hydrological extremes can damage agriculture, buildings, and energy and transportation infrastructure.[14] *An Inconvenient Sequel* explains that the Syrian civil war and refugee crisis resulted at least in part from the millions of people displaced there by the 1998–2012 drought. This is one reason the Pentagon describes climate change as a threat multiplier.[15] *An Inconvenient Truth* explains that a one-degree rise in temperature at the equator is a twelve-degree rise at the poles. The polar ice caps diminished by 40 percent in the thirty years prior to the 2006 film, and the Greenland ice sheet had begun to disappear. Scientists now estimate that the Arctic could be ice-free in the summer as soon as 2035, accelerating heating in the region.[16] This melting threatens animals like polar bears, and sea

3. "Do scientists agree on climate change?" NASA, accessed October 14, 2020, https://climate.nasa.gov/faq/17/do-scientists-agree-on-climate-change/. For more information about those who deny anthropogenic climate change, see "COVIDeniers: Anti-Science Coronavirus Denial Overlaps with Climate Denial," Desmog blog, accessed October 14, 2020, https://www.desmogblog.com/covideniers-anti-science-covid-19-denial-overlaps-climate-denial. There are reasons to think that all climate scientists now assert that human beings are the cause of current warming: Fermin Koop, "No room for denialists: 100% consensus on anthropogenic global warming," ZME Science, November 27, 2019, https://www.zmescience.com/science/denialists-100-consensus-anthropogenic-global-warming/. An analysis of the handful of papers that contest the evidence for anthropogenic climate change found each of them makes critical errors. See Katherine Ellen Foley, "Those 3% of scientific papers that deny climate change? A review found them all flawed," Quartz, September 5, 2017, https://qz.com/1069298/the-3-of-scientific-papers-that-deny-climate-change-are-all-flawed/.

level rise threatens coastal cities like Miami, San Francisco, New York, Beijing, New Orleans, Shanghai, and Calcutta. It also threatens the Atlantic Ocean current that keeps Europe's climate relatively mild. If that conveyor stopped, Europe would enter an ice age within a few decades, and it could last for a millennium.[17] The most significant causes of greenhouse gas emissions, according to the film, are deforestation and the reliance on coal, oil, and gas as opposed to solar and wind power.

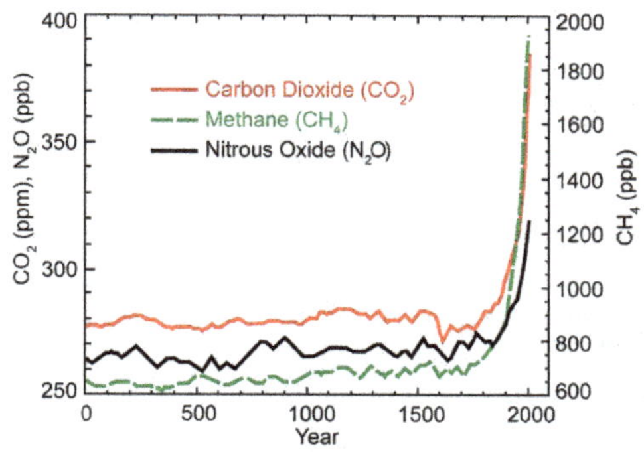

Source: U.S. National Climate Assessment (2014).[4]

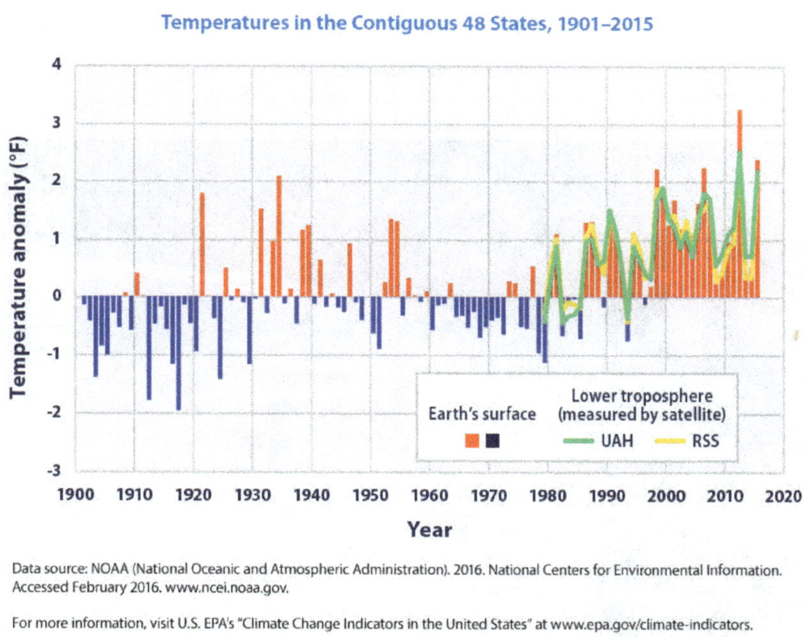

Data source: NOAA, 2016[5]

4. According to the Environmental Protection Agency, "This graph shows the increase in greenhouse gas (GHG) concentrations in the atmosphere over the last 2,000 years. Increases in concentrations of these gases since 1750 are due to human activities in the industrial era. Concentration units are parts per million (ppm) or parts per billion (ppb), indicating the number of molecules of the greenhouse gas per million or billion molecules of air." See "Causes of Climate Change," United States Environmental Protection Agency, last updated December 27, 2016, https://19january2017snapshot.epa.gov/climate-change-science/causes-climate-change_.html.

5. According to the EPA, "This figure shows how annual average temperatures in the contiguous 48 states have changed since 1901. Surface data come from land-based weather stations. Satellite measurements cover the lower troposphere, which is the lowest level of the Earth's atmosphere. 'UAH' and 'RSS' represent two different methods of analyzing the original satellite measurements. This graph uses the 1901–2000 average as a baseline for depicting change. Choosing a different baseline period would not change the shape of the data over time. Data source: NOAA, 2016." See "Climate Change Indicators: US and Global Temperature," United States Environmental Protection Agency, last updated December 17, 2016, https://19january2017snapshot.epa.gov/climate-indicators/climate-change-indicators-us-and-global-temperature_.html.

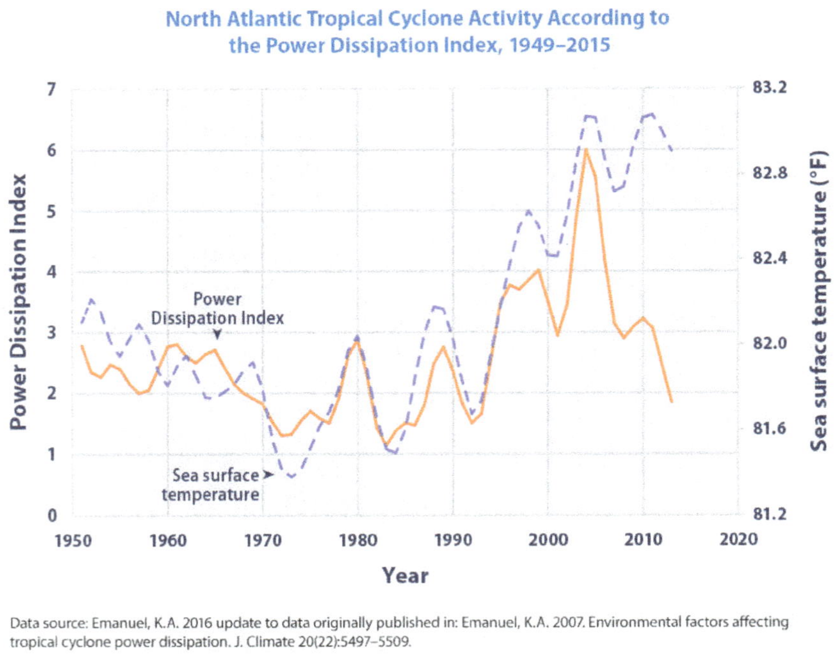

Data source: Emanuel, 2016[6]

6. According to the EPA, "This figure presents annual values of the Power Dissipation Index (PDI), which accounts for cyclone strength, duration, and frequency. Tropical North Atlantic sea surface temperature trends are provided for reference. Note that sea surface temperature is measured in different units, but the values have been plotted alongside the PDI to show how they compare. The lines have been smoothed using a five-year weighted average, plotted at the middle year. The most recent average (2011–2015) is plotted at 2013. Data source: Emanuel, 2016." See: "Climate Change Indicators: Tropical Cyclone Activity," United States Environmental Protection Agency, last updated December 17, 2016, https://19january2017snapshot.epa.gov/climate-indicators/climate-change-indicators-tropical-cyclone-activity_.html.

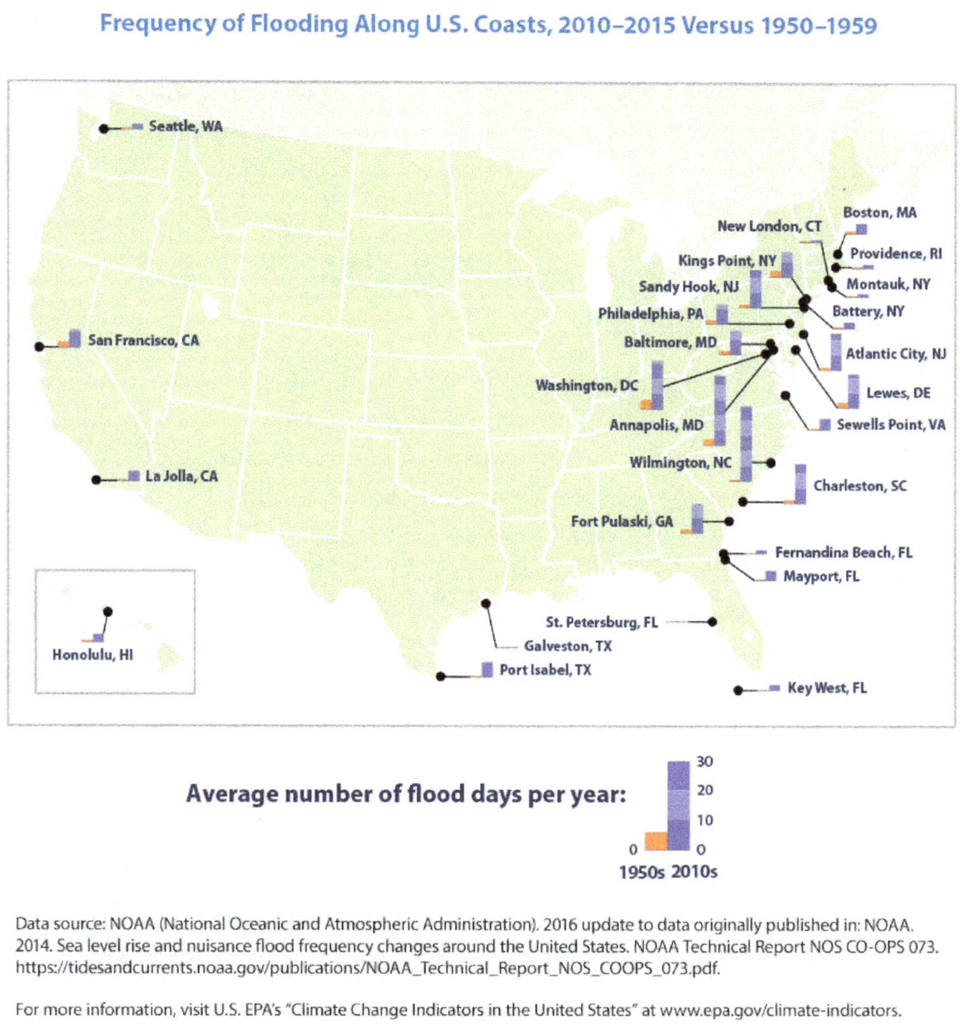

Data source: NOAA, 2016[7]

7.3.2 An Inconvenient Sequel: Truth to Power

An Inconvenient Sequel (2017) notes that the burning of coal is the main contributor of carbon dioxide. The film highlights renewable energy sources as the main solution to the problem of climate change. It also focuses on the relationship between higher temperatures and increases in infectious diseases. The film gives the viewer a close-up of the 2015 Paris Climate Agreement, according to which every country in the world agrees to reduce net greenhouse gas emissions to zero in the next few decades to keep global heating as far as possible below 2°C. The film also highlights the status of the United States as the top historical contributor of greenhouse gas emissions, and its pending withdrawal from the Paris agreement at the order of

7. According to the EPA, "This map shows the average number of days per year in which coastal waters rose above the local threshold for minor flooding at 27 sites along U.S. coasts. Each small bar graph compares the first decade of widespread measurements (the 1950s in orange) with the most recent decade (the 2010s in purple). Data source: NOAA, 2016." See "Climate Change Indicators: Coastal Flooding," United States Environmental Protection Agency, last updated on December 17, 2016, https://19january2017snapshot.epa.gov/climate-indicators/climate-change-indicators-coastal-flooding_.html.

President Trump. The film highlights the nonpartisan nature of climate solutions by telling the story of how Georgetown, Texas, one of the most conservative cities in the United States, went 100 percent renewable. The mayor points out that renewable energy is both cheaper and its costs are less volatile than fossil fuels, and that we do not need science to know that it is better not to pollute the air.

7.3.3 Further Explanation of the Causes and Effects of Greenhouse Gas Emission

Carbon circulates through the atmosphere, land, ocean, and life in short- and long-term cycles. Plants turn CO_2 into sugars, storing energy in carbon molecules. Animals and bacteria use this energy to grow and move, releasing CO_2. Fossil fuels are the sun's energy in the form of organic carbon, buried and condensed over millions of years. Burning them rapidly releases carbon from long-term storage in the Earth. Earth radiates heat energy as infrared light.[18] CO_2, water vapor, and similar gases trap this energy, warming the Earth. Ordinarily, this keeps Earth at a livable 15°C, on average, instead of −18°C. But burning fossil fuels is thickening this blanket, heating the planet over 1°C in the last eighty years.[19] CO_2 is accumulating in the air because we are pouring it into the air faster than it is getting drawn down or sequestered by plants and by mixing with water.[20]

Humans are by far the largest contributor to global warming since 1950.[21] Other factors such as solar activity and volcanic carbon emissions barely changed the climate during this time.[22] By extrapolating from current carbon reduction pledges, by 2100 we will heat Earth by up to 3.7°C (6.6°F), though heating will continue for centuries after that.[23] Temperature increases on land are roughly double the global average, and much greater at the poles than at the equator. Minor temperature differences have major effects. A 4°C (7°F) lower temperature puts a mile of ice over Canada.

7.3.4 The Effects of Fossil Fuel Emissions on Infectious Disease

Fossil fuel pollution makes lung infections like influenza and COVID-19 more likely and more deadly.8 [24] Fossil fuel pollution causes neurological damage and lung disease through lung-damaging particulate emissions (PM2.5), airborne toxins (including mercury and lead from coal), and spills. But fossil fuel air pollution has pandemic-scale damages all its own. Most particulate emissions (PM2.5) come from fossil fuels.[25] The replacement of 330 US coal-fired power plants with gas plants saved an estimated 26,610 lives between 2005 and 2016 (and increased nearby crop yields).[26] On its own fossil fuel air pollution causes 3.6 million deaths per year, which is two-thirds of all human air pollution deaths; up to 52 thousand of those happen in the US.[27] This is more than die from infectious disease, smoking, or violence. Energy deathprints from emissions vary by type of fuel.[28]

Warming-driven wildfires, like those that engulfed the Australia and the West coast of the US in 2020, also cause lung disease and morbidity. Pollution from Australia's 2020 bushfires killed 417 people, and put 4,456 more in the hospital.[29] On a hotter planet there are more wildfires. Warming made Australian wildfires in 2019 at least 30 percent more likely, and it has raised California's temperature by 3°F since 1980, while reducing rainfall by 30 percent, leading to a 500 percent increase in burn area.[30]

About 233 million years of life are lost to air pollution per year, disproportionately from marginalized and poor communities.

Deforestation and habitat loss, which also drive climate change, increasingly force insects and animals to live in contact with human beings, which contributes to disease transmission, possibly including the 2014 Ebola outbreak.[31] As insects and animals move into new regions, the rising temperature is spreading diseases.[32] There is also evidence that ancient pathogens frozen in permafrost are re-emerging.[33] In 2016, anthrax released from melting permafrost sickened and killed reindeer and at least one boy in Siberia.[34] Fracking waste can be radioactive, and can leak into rivers used for drinking water.[35]

The United Nations reports that "the destruction of nature by humans and the growing demand for meat" are the root causes of the rise in zoonotic epidemics like Ebola, West Nile virus, Rift Valley fever, and perhaps most notably SARS (including COVID-19).[36] *The Guardian* reports that even before the 2020 pandemic, 2 million people died because of zoonotic diseases yearly.[37]

7.3.5 The Social Cost of Carbon

The Social Cost of Carbon adds costs (healthcare, lost productivity, damages to property, climate damages) that are not yet included in the price of fossil fuels. When we include these along with direct subsidies to the fossil fuel industry,9 the

8. See this collation of studies: Robert Roy Britt, "A Surprise Surge in Air Pollution May Be Causing More Coronavirus Complications," Medium, published July 20, 2020, https://elemental.medium.com/a-surprise-surge-in-air-pollution-may-be-causing-more-coronavirus-complications-c444e82a659e.

9. Governmental payments to companies in the industry.

IMF[10] estimates, fossil fuel subsidies add up to 6.5 percent of global GDP[11] ($5.2T), $649B in the US ($50B more than the military budget).[38] Removing fossil fuel subsidies, the IMF argues, would reduce air pollution fatalities by over 45 percent (and free up 4 percent of global GDP to help the vulnerable).[39] Some argue that the economic costs of sickness and loss of life caused by fossil fuels would on their own pay for a transition to renewable energy.[12]

CLIMATE JUSTICE
The effort or movement that seeks the rectification or avoidance of inequalities that result from climate change.

7.3.6 Climate Justice: Effects on Vulnerable Populations

> In studying the relationship between climate change and its effects, work hard to foreground marginalized groups. It is important to identify how exactly impacts worsen the lives of marginalized people and how they worsen inequality. Always ask the questions:
>
> - What harms are being caused? Who is going to suffer them? How is this suffering distributed?
> - Who is more responsible for these impacts, and who is less so? Who benefits from causing them?
> - Who determines who has access to a clean environment, and how do institutions make these decisions?
> - What resources do vulnerable people have to prevent or respond to climate impacts? What systematic obstacles stand in their way?
> - How can these impacts be avoided or justly distributed? What policies could bring this about?

ETHICS
The study of the good, and specifically, the good life; The study of how we ought to behave in order to live well.

ENVIRONMENTAL JUSTICE
Is concerned with the unjust distribution of climate change impacts, as well as the systematic and contingent factors that produce—and that may also solve—this inequality.

SOCIAL JUSTICE
The effort or movement to bring about equality among entire communities, as opposed to just individual people; involves considering ways to mitigate or reverse, for instance, the poverty inflicted on one community, perhaps unintentionally, by another.

Climate change is an ethical, social, political, economic, and environmental problem at the same time. **Ethics** studies how we can and should care for one another's needs, and how we should prevent and respond to harms. **Environmental justice** is concerned with unjust distribution of impacts, the systematic and contingent factors that produce this inequality, and solutions. Climate impacts reflect a broader pattern of environmental injustice, affecting women, low-income communities, people of color, and developing countries the most, although they are the least responsible for causing it.

Women suffer more from climate impacts due to their social roles. Often caring for family means they deal with water and food shortages and sickness, are less mobile than men, have fewer economic options, and face abuse in times of family stress and dislocation.[40] Most disaster deaths are women, as are 80 percent of climate refugees, who often then face unsanitary conditions and sexual violence.[41]

Black and Indigenous people of color are subjected to disproportionate amounts of pollution and other health stresses, both because black neighborhoods have been segregated by redlining, and because of systemic political marginalization.[13] The

10. International Monetary Fund.
11. Gross Domestic Product.
12. David Roberts, "Air pollution is much worse than we thought," Vox, published August 12, 2020, https://www.vox.com/energy-and-environment/2020/8/12/21361498/climate-change-air-pollution-us-india-china-deaths.
13. See Nina Lakhani, "Killer heat: US racial injustices will worsen as climate crisis escalates," *The Guardian*, published July 28, 2020, https://www.theguardian.com/us-news/2020/jul/28/us-racial-injustices-will-worsen-climate-crisis-escalates. Brad Plumer and Nadja Popovich, "How Decades of Racist Housing Policy Left Neighborhoods Sweltering," *The New York Times*, published August 24, 2020, https://www.nytimes.com/interactive/2020/08/24/climate/racism-redlining-cities-global-warming.html.

documentary *Cooked: Survival by Zip Code* explores the relationships between the slow disasters of climate, racism, and poverty, drawing on a seminal analysis of the 1995 Chicago heatwave.[42]

Race is the number one indicator for the placement of toxic facilities in the United States.[43] For example, Delaware County, PA, is 80.32 percent white. But in the county's Chester city, 75 percent are African American, where the largest waste facilities are located.[44] Only 1.6 percent of the trash comes from there. Burning it emits nitrogen and sulfur dioxides.[45] Of the children in Chester, 38.5 percent have asthma, which is five times higher than the national average. Chester residents also develop cancer at a higher rate than anywhere else in their county.[46]

7.3.7 The Effects of Climate Change on Shortages in Food and Water, and Resulting Conflict

Too much heat leads to plant stress, and less crop yield. Warming has already reduced global wheat yields by 0.9 percent per year.[47] For each +1°C above the optimum, people lose 10 percent of the cereal crop (possibly up to 17 percent).[48] This matters because most of the breadbaskets of the world are already at peak growing temperature. Climate change increases people's vulnerability, and is already increasing migration. Over 16 million people a year are displaced by wars, violence, and persecution, but 21.5 million are displaced annually by climate-related disasters, such as floods, storms, wildfires, and extreme weather.[49] By 2050, estimates are that there will be 200–500 million climate refugees, usually the most vulnerable people. People fleeing environmental disasters are not currently considered refugees under international law. According to a 2020 study published by the National Academy of Sciences, 3.5 billion people in the next fifty years could be living in temperatures so high that they are inhospitable to human life, as a result of climate change. Many of these people live in India, Nigeria, Niger, and Sudan. This could result in the migration of hundreds of millions of people, most of whom are among the many who do not bear the responsibility for the climate crisis.[50]

Drought and food scarcity can lead to conflict, which the Pentagon says multiplied the risk of the Syrian Civil War.[51] So climate change is a national and global security threat.[52]

QUESTIONS FOR CONSIDERATION

The effects of man-made climate change raise the following questions:

a. The Universal Declaration of Human Rights includes a safe and clean environment as a fundamental human right. Brainstorm ways our environment could be dangerous due to climate or climate-related pollution.
b. How might environmental impacts strain or violate other human rights? What ways can action on climate secure and preserve human rights at the same time?
c. In what way are human beings in fact masters and possessors of nature, and in what way are we not? Why? Does solving climate change require our civilization to seek an alternative to this project? Do other ecological crises require this?

7.4 Solutions to the Threat of Climate Change

PROXIMATE CAUSES
Those that contribute to an effect, but are themselves effects of yet other causes; they are not the first or foundational cause, but rather, are one in a series that results from the first.

ULTIMATE CAUSES
The most underlying or foundational factors responsible for a series of effects.

ANTHROPOCENTRISM
The view that human beings are the central source of value; outlook in which value is placed solely or mainly on human beings, as opposed to other living or non-living things.

NON-ANTHROPOCENTRISM
The view that an outlook in which things besides humans have ethical value and are therefore deserving of moral respect.

SPECIESISM
The perspective that ascribes a privileged status to certain species over others; this usually involves the assumption that human beings are more deserving of moral respect and consideration than all other living species, including non-human animals.

BIOCENTRISTS
Those who argue that many or all living things are sources of value because each of them is alive.

ECOCENTRISTS
Those who take a still larger view than biocentrists, arguing that living things only exist because they dwell in a web of relationships with other living and non-living things; what is good for each individual derives from what is good for the whole ecosystem.

Possible solutions to the crisis of global warming can be grouped according to the ethical basis for action, and the strategic targets of action. Systems of ethical values can be anthropocentric, biocentric, and ecocentric. Actions can address **proximate causes** or **ultimate causes**. Since environmental problems usually have collective causes, the solutions must often be collective before they are individual.

Anthropocentrism takes human life to be the basis or center of value. If people want to save plants, animals, and ecosystems, we do not do so for the sake of those things, the argument goes, but only because they are useful and pleasurable to human beings. In principle, anthropocentrism is compatible with a spaceship-ecology vision of the future, in which the only remaining forms of life are human beings, the things we eat, and things we enjoy. Non-anthropocentrists argue that animals, plants, and even the land itself have an ethical status that deserves respect for their own sake. This is why, although Kant privileged human life over other forms, and therefore was a **speciesist**, non-anthropocentrists often use elements of his duty-oriented non-consequentialist ethics to advocate for non-human life forms.[53] **Biocentrists** argue that many or all living things are sources of value because each of them is alive (*bios* in Greek): cats enjoy the sunlight, worms wriggle to avoid harm, plants thrive in certain mineral soils, but perish in others. Because each is intrinsically a source of value, we have a duty to respect them. **Ecocentrists** take a still larger view, that living things only exist because they dwell (the *eco-* in *ecology* and *economy* comes from the Greek word for "home" or "abode") in a web of relationships with other living and non-living things. For example, if pollinators die off, plants cannot make seeds and they dwindle, so animals starve. What is good for each individual derives from what is good for the whole ecosystem.

Some people with chronic but preventable health conditions prefer to address proximate causes, making efforts to deal with the symptoms without addressing the ultimate causes, for example taking painkillers or applying bandages. Similarly, many farmers spray special fertilizer on their fields instead of adopting farming practices that enrich the soil instead of depleting it. Adaptation to increasing climate disruption of human communities addresses proximate causes like sea-level rise, flooding and drought, without necessarily reducing the amount of warming we are causing. Adaptation to environmental damages and eliminating the causes of these damages are not mutually exclusive. Indeed, the less mitigation we do, the more costly and less successful our adaptation will be.

7.4.1 High-Impact Solutions That Address Proximate Causes

7.4.1.1 *Cowspiracy* and Veganism

Cowspiracy (2014) argues that the most significant emitter of greenhouse gas is livestock, especially cattle. It also makes the case that major environmental organizations avoid highlighting this fact because of the threat of lawsuits from the beef industry and others. The film explains not only the problematic emission of greenhouse gases that results from raising animals for food, but also the staggering amount of plant matter and land needed to raise livestock. It also briefly covers the unsustainability of the fishing industry. Through interviews and expert testimony, *Cowspiracy* pre-sents the argument that anyone who is a true environmentalist ought to commit to **veganism**. Its argument incorporates anthropocentric and non-anthropocentric perspectives by focusing on the cost of meat-eating to humans, as well as the harm to and suffering of animals themselves.

VEGANISM
The avoidance of all animal products in one's way of life, especially one's diet.

VEGETARIANISM
The avoidance of meat-eating, but not necessarily the shunning of all animal products.

7.4.1.2 Renewable Energy

The way to stop heating the globe is simple: stop emitting greenhouse gases. But these gases come from our primary energy source, and energy drives almost everything human beings do. The climate transition involves producing all electricity from renewable sources, electrifying transit, heating, and industry, increasing efficiency, and focusing agriculture and forest management on maximizing carbon absorption. The climate transition is already happening. Policies can help it or hurt it.[54] From an anthropocentric perspective, every aspect of human life will be affected by the climate transition in some way, sometimes invisibly: From farming and transit to water purification and the internet, from making shoes to home heating and cooling, from refining metals to making paper.

According to an analysis of the 2019 US Dept. of Energy report, clean jobs outnumber fossil fuels jobs nearly three to one (3.26M to 1.17M).[55] These jobs are in several sectors: renewable energy installation, building efficiency, clean vehicles, and energy storage. Solar alone employs more than twice the number of coal workers. There are more clean energy employees than schoolteachers.

Renewable energy is now cheaper in most cases than energy produced by fossil fuels. It is cheaper to build new solar than it is to continue to run 75 percent of existing coal plants, according to Lazard's Levelized Cost of Energy.[56] Battery storage is independently profitable because it is much cheaper than running peaker plants.[57] Electric cars are cheaper to run and maintain, costing less than any combustion car after their first five years. According to the Rocky Mountain Institute and others, coal is no longer an economically viable source of electricity.[58]

Many analyses of the transition to clean energy show that it would be an economic boon.[14] According to the most comprehensive analysis of US energy usage, "Mobilizing for a Zero-Carbon America," it is possible to put the country on track to stay under 1.5°C of warming if it electrifies everything, making every new piece of technology electric: "This is fairly simple to imagine: when someone's car reaches retirement age, it is replaced with an electric vehicle. When a natural gas plant is retired, it is replaced with nuclear or renewables."[15] This rapid and total decarbonization of the US economy would create 25 million jobs by 2035, replace nearly every fuel-burning machine with an electric one, massively build out solar power, and improve the efficiency of most buildings. Once the new system is in place, each household would be saving $1,000–$2,000 per year because renewable energy is cheaper and electricity is much more efficient.

14. See Marc Jacobson, "100% Clean, Renewable Energy and Storage for Everything," Stanford University, accessed October 13, 2020, https://web.stanford.edu/group/efmh/jacobson/WWSBook/WWSBook.html for another prominent example.
15. Rewiring America, "Home," accessed October 13, 2020, https://www.rewiringamerica.org.

Financial institutions are beginning to take action on climate issues as well. To respond to climate risks, institutions that have committed to divesting from some form of fossil fuel now control 26 percent of the stock market ($7 Trillion BlackRock, $1.5T Goldman Sachs, $2.7T JP Morgan Chase, $1.5T Barclays, $11T other).[59] The University of California's Board of Trustees wrote, "We believe hanging on to fossil fuel assets is a financial risk. That's why we will have made our $13.4-billion endowment 'fossil free' as of the end of this month, and why our $70-billion pension will soon be that way as well."[60] Corporate Knights showed that divesting ten years earlier would have saved them $19B.[61] BlackRock, the largest fund manager in the world, echoed this assessment, saying that sustainability is the top investor issue.16 [62] Even oil majors are planning for carbon neutrality, acknowledging the reality of the energy transition and aiming to reduce their risk. Shell, Repsol, Eni, and Total plan to reduce their emissions to keep below +2°C.[63] Their plans often include end-use emissions: gas burned in cars and trucks.[64] BP, too, is planning for carbon neutrality by 2050, cutting its fossil fuel output 40 percent in the next ten years.17 BP's CEO said, "The world's carbon budget is finite and running out fast; we need a rapid transition to net zero. It will require nothing short of reimagining energy as we know it. This will certainly be a challenge, but also a tremendous opportunity."[65]

7.4.2 Medium- and Low-Impact Solutions That Address Proximate Causes

7.4.2.1 Scrubbers

Devices known as "scrubbers," which eliminate greenhouse gas emissions from the air, vary in type and effectiveness.18

7.4.2.2 "Fast Fashion"

The clothing sector contributes to about 3 percent of the world's global production of CO_2, mostly because of the use of energy to produce attire. The hectic pace of **fast fashion** contributes to this figure as clothes are discarded or quickly fall apart.

---

16. See also this interview with the CEO of BlackRock: Sam Meredith, "BlackRock CEO says the climate crisis is about to trigger 'a fundamental reshaping of finance,'" CNBC, last updated January 14, 2020, https://www.cnbc.com/2020/01/14/blackrock-ceo-larry-fink-says-climate-change-will-soon-reshape-markets.html.

17. Shadia Nasralla and Ron Bousso, "BP to cut fossil fuels output by 40% by 2030," Reuters, August 4, 2020, https://mobile.reuters.com/article/amp/idUSKCN2500NH.

18. The following are a few helpful resources for learning about this technology:
Jennifer Horton, "How CO2 Scrubbing Works," How Stuff Works, July 28, 2008, https://science.howstuffworks.com/environmental/green-science/co2-scrubbing.htm.
Houston Space Center, "Apollo 13 Infographic: How did they make that CO2 scrubber?" April 10, 2019, https://spacecenter.org/apollo-13-infographic-how-did-they-make-that-co2-scrubber/.
Wil Crisp, "Thousands of ships fitted with 'cheat devices' to divert poisonous pollution into sea," *Independent*, October 25, 2019, https://www.independent.co.uk/environment/shipping-pollution-sea-open-loop-scrubber-carbon-dioxide-environment-a9123181.html.
Mark Spalding, "Science: Mangrove Forests as Incredible Carbon Stores," Cool Green Science (blog), *Nature*, October 11, 2013, https://blog.nature.org/science/2013/10/11/new-science-mangrove-forests-carbon-store-map/.

One helpful measure is hang-drying one's clothes when possible, and using dryer balls when it's not.

FAST FASHION
The production, selling, and buying of quickly-produced, low-cost clothing often used and discarded within a relatively short time frame.

7.4.2.3 Palm Oil and *Years of Living Dangerously*

According to episodes one and two of the show *Years of Living Dangerously* (2014), palm oil is an ingredient in a staggering number of food products, but its production contributes to rapid deforestation and dangerous greenhouse gas production. According to the show, effective actions include avoiding products that use palm oil, and pressuring corporations to ensure their products are rainforest-friendly.

7.4.2.4 Minimalism

MINIMALISM
The practice of maintaining only the possessions one truly needs, as well as a relatively small selection of those one wants; may include living in a "tiny home," using public transportation or a bicycle instead of owning a car, and/or maintaining a sparse, simple wardrobe intended to be re-used with greater frequency and duration than is customary.

By owning fewer things, minimalists argue, one gains freedom. True wealth, according to the minimalist, is not being burdened by material possessions. By owning less, living in smaller dwellings, and driving smaller vehicles, we make a significant step toward the reduction of greenhouse gas emission.[19]

People often think that solving environmental issues requires us to give up comfortable lifestyles or advanced technologies. One of the reasons for this is that we tend to interpret environmental damage as a form of sinfulness that requires penance to be discharged.

QUESTIONS FOR CONSIDERATION

a. Causes can have more than one effect, and more than one cause can produce a single effect. What are points of intersection between the impacts of climate change and other forms of physical, social, economic, and political vulnerability? Imagine you are a marginalized person experiencing two or more of these impacts, and describe the challenges they present in your day-to-day life and the ways they shape your hopes for the future.
b. What forms of privilege and precariousness do you and your loved ones have that affect your vulnerability to or protection from climate-related issues?
c. Among the benefits of action on environmental issues discussed in this chapter, what do you think are the most important, and why?
d. Values are things you want and choose most of all (e.g., family, equality, happiness, purity, loyalty, opportunity, fairness, health). What values connect you to climate change issues, and how exactly do they connect you with it?
e. The solutions to climate change might not only avoid negative impacts, but make our lives better. How could solving climate change help you live your deepest values? Imagine a climate-solved world answering and embodying your most cherished ethical values. What

19. Sources about minimalism:
Abundantly Minimal, "How Minimalism Helps the Planet | Environmental Benefits of Minimalism," YouTube video, September 26, 2017, 13:23, https://www.youtube.com/watch?v=JZlZ6gWG-Fw.
Joshua Fields Millburn and Ryan Nicodemus, "What Is Minimalism?" The Minimalists, accessed October 14, 2020, https://www.theminimalists.com/minimalism/.
Joshua Becker, "What Is Minimalism?" Becoming Minimalist, last updated November 13, 2019, https://www.becomingminimalist.com/what-is-minimalism/.
Matt D'Avella, "What minimalism really looks like," YouTube video, December 3, 2018, 8:31, https://www.youtube.com/watch?v=jrf_dMnatW0.

would be different about the way you and your society go about life? What things are different, surprising, or wonderful (e.g., no-car days, festivals funded by selling energy from solar panels, buildings that produce more energy than they use, food grown on bus stops)?

7.4.3 Solutions That Address the Ultimate Cause: Leopold's "The Land Ethic" and James Cameron's *Avatar*

Humanity's relationship with nature is the ultimate cause of modern-day environmental problems. This is especially true of Western society, perhaps most prominently exemplified in the United States of America. Dominion over nature does not need to entail destruction or depletion, nor should it, as the Bible and Locke convey. If humanity cannot flourish without nature, we must use its resources in a sustainable way. Ultimately, this means living in harmony with nature. Dominion and harmony need not be mutually exclusive. The United Nations champions a "one health" approach that treats human, animal, and environmental health in a united way.[66] Two other examples that show the possible path forward are the film *Avatar* and "The Land Ethic," by Aldo Leopold. Leopold is largely responsible for creating the first Wilderness Area in the US (1922) and laying the foundation for the discipline of wildlife management (1924). "The Land Ethic" is the final essay in *A Sand County Almanac*, and it argues for expanding ethical considerations beyond human beings, to animals, plants, waters, and even the soil itself.[67]

7.4.3.1 Excerpts from "The Land Ethic"

The Community Concept

All ethics so far evolved rest upon a single premise: that the individual is a member of a community of interdependent parts. His instincts prompt him to compete for his place in the community, but his ethics prompt him also to co-operate (perhaps in order that there may be a place to compete for).

The land ethic simply enlarges the boundaries of the community to include soils, waters, plants, and animals, or collectively: the land.

> Note here the very specific, and very broad, meaning of "the land," according to Leopold.

[. . .]

In short, a land ethic changes the role of Homo sapiens from conqueror of the land-community to plain member and citizen of it. It implies respect for his fellow-members, and also respect for the community as such.

In human history, we have learned (I hope) that the conqueror role is eventually self-defeating. Why? Because it is implicit in such a role that the conqueror knows, *ex cathedra*,[20] just what makes the community clock tick, and just what

20. Meaning "with full authority."

and who is valuable, and what and who is worthless, in community life. It always turns out that he knows neither, and this is why his conquests eventually defeat themselves.

[. . .]

The ordinary citizen today assumes that science knows what makes the community clock tick; the scientist is equally sure that he does not. He knows that the biotic mechanism is so complex that its workings may never be fully understood.

[. . .]

The Land Pyramid

[. . .]

Plants absorb energy from the sun. This energy flows through a circuit called the biota, which may be represented by a pyramid consisting of layers. The bottom layer is the soil. A plant layer rests on the soil, an insect layer on the plants, a bird and rodent layer on the insects, and so on up through various animal groups to the apex layer, which consists of the larger carnivores.

[. . .]

The lines of dependency for food and other services are called food chains. Thus soil-oak-deer-Indian is a chain that has now been largely converted to soil-corn-cow-farmer. Each species, including ourselves, is a link in many chains. The deer eats a hundred plants other than oak, and the cow a hundred plants other than corn. Both, then, are links in a hundred chains. The pyramid is a tangle of chains so complex as to seem disorderly, yet the stability of the system proves it to be a highly organized structure. Its functioning depends on the co-operation and competition of its diverse parts.

In the beginning, the pyramid of life was low and squat; the food chains short and simple. Evolution has added layer after layer, link after link. Man is one of thousands of accretions to the height and complexity of the pyramid. Science has given us many doubts, but it has given us at least one certainty: the trend of evolution is to elaborate and diversify the biota.

Land, then, is not merely soil; it is a fountain of energy flowing through a circuit of soils, plants, and animals. Food chains are the living channels which conduct energy upward; death and decay return it to the soil. The circuit is not closed; some energy is dissipated in decay, some is added by absorption from the air, some is stored in soils, peats, and long-lived forests; but it is a sustained circuit, like a slowly augmented revolving fund of life. There is always a net loss by downhill wash, but this is normally small and offset by the decay of rocks. It is deposited in the ocean and, in the course of geological time, raised to form new lands and new pyramids.

[. . .]

The Outlook

It is inconceivable to me that an ethical relation to land can exist without love, respect, and admiration for land, and a high regard for its value. By value, I of course mean something far broader than economic value; I mean value in the philosophical sense.

> [. . .]
>
> [. . .] A thing is right when it tends to preserve the integrity, stability, and beauty of the biotic community. It is wrong when it tends otherwise.
>
> It of course goes without saying that economic feasibility limits the tether of what can or cannot be done for land. It always has and it always will. The fallacy the economic determinists[21] have tied around our collective neck, and which we now need to cast off, is the belief that economics determines *all* land use. This is simply not true. An innumerable host of actions and attitudes, comprising perhaps the bulk of all land relations, is determined by the land-users' tastes and predilections, rather than by his purse. The bulk of all land relations hinges on investments of time, forethought, skill, and faith rather than on investments of cash. [. . .][68]

7.4.3.2 *Avatar* and "The Land Ethic"

James Cameron's *Avatar* (2009), with striking similarity to "The Land Ethic," portrays the land of "Pandora" as a highly complex web of connections, from the ground and tree roots, to the massive birds that fly overhead. The film describes the living community of Pandora as a "network of energy that flows through all living things." All living beings in Pandora are worthy of serious ethical consideration, according to the planet's natives (the Na'vi). The people mourn over the death of trees and animals, just as they do over the deaths of people. In these ways, the film vividly portrays significant elements of "The Land Ethic." Additionally, just as Leopold explains that scientists may never fully understand the complexity of nature, the Na'vi acknowledge the mystery of their natural surroundings in their spiritual relationship with Eywa. The Na'vi subdue nature, but they do not conquer, dominate, destroy, or deplete it. They hunt for food, but place a high value on a "clean kill," which is swift and humane, and which they follow with words of respect toward the animal whose life they took. The Omaticaya exclaim in agreement with Jake Sully (Sam Worthington), when he says, "This is our land," but they do not exercise private possession of their resources in the way that Western society does. For the Omaticaya, people pick fruit and hunt animals, which become theirs, and each warrior has a banshee that is theirs for life, but "all energy is borrowed and one day you have to give it back," they say. "Pandora" means "all gifts." The Na'vi see their planet as a gift, a gift that they owe back. It is not a gift to use and destroy. Their relationship with nature is so profound that it is a way of seeing the world, including one another, exemplified in the repeated greeting, "I see you." Those who do not see in this way, like Jake initially, and like most humans from Earth, are portrayed as insane, ignorant, and destructive. Also, they are essentially enslaved by their own limited perspective. Their settlement on Pandora looks like a prison, and they have doomed themselves by destroying "their mother": Earth. The "sky people" are out of touch with reality.[22] Their way of life is incompatible with the natural rhythms and harmony of Pandora. Their attempts to dominate and conquer are foiled, resulting in death and imprisonment. Recall Leopold's words about the doomed fate of attempts to conquer nature.

21. For further consideration of determinism, see Chapter Nine.
22. The next two sentences contain a spoiler about the film.

Extrapolating from *Avatar* and Leopold, the ultimate cure for the symptoms of humanity's problematic relationship with nature is to see nature differently. The land is never fully ours to possess, and its full value is greater than even great minds can comprehend. Those who extract and manipulate natural resources must do so with an attitude of respect and docility, and with the understanding that a long chain of unforeseen consequences will result. When one takes from nature or manipulates nature, therefore, one must make every effort to return the land to its original state or compensate for any negative consequences. When a person thinks they know exactly what they are doing to the natural world, and exactly what the consequences will be, Leopold and Cameron provide an impetus to realize the flawed arrogance in their thinking.

QUESTIONS FOR CONSIDERATION

a. If you've seen the film, what correspondence do you see between *Avatar* and Leopold, beyond that explained above?
b. Do you think the words of the Bible and John Locke, about the dominion of man over nature, are compatible with Leopold's "The Land Ethic"? With *Avatar*?
c. Is solving the problem of climate change as simple as changing our attitude, such that all solutions that address proximate causes are unnecessary?
d. How can your knowledge of proximate and ultimate causes, as well as the corresponding solutions, come together in your understanding of the environment and your interactions with it?

QUESTIONS FOR ENVIRONMENTAL SELF-REFLECTION

a. News organizations often do not cover environmental issues because they think they are too slow-paced and complicated for people to care about. How often do I share how much I care about environmental issues? Do my friends and the people I vote for know my beliefs? In what ways do I support and/or undermine collective political action about environmental issues?
b. If I choose to eat animal products, do I know if the animals have been raised sustainably? Do I know if they've been killed humanely? What ways do I know of to support local farmers, and farmers who use methods to absorb carbon?
c. Can I do without a car? If I drive a car, van, or truck, have I researched the different electric vehicles that are available, or made enough effort to find the most fuel-efficient car I can afford? Do I drive it more than I need to? Can I cut down on trips or carpool? Do I fly more often than necessary?
d. Do I make every effort to limit my home energy use? Renewable energy costs are competitive with electricity from fossil fuels. If you pay your own electric bill, it's likely that you can sign up for 100 percent renewable energy.
e. If I adopt an animal as a pet, or if I raise animals for food, how will I offset the greenhouse gases released by my actions? How will I ensure that the resources I use on animals are being used sustainably?

f. Do I exercise enough self-reflection about my possessions, including my clothing? Do I really need all of the material goods I surround myself with? Can I downsize? Can I sell, donate, or recycle my unwanted things rather than discarding them? Can I repair what is no longer useable, or replace it with something that will last for a long time?
g. Am I fully aware of my carbon footprint? Find out what makes up the biggest part of your carbon footprint with an emissions calculator at https://coolclimate.berkeley.edu/calculator.[69]
h. What community organizations am I part of or do I know of that engage environmental issues? How do they work to promote environmental justice?

Endnotes

1. All film production details in this chapter, including actor information, is from IMDb: https://www.imdb.com/.
2. Genesis 1:26; *The New American Bible* (Iowa Falls: World Bible Publishers, Inc., 1991), 9.
3. Genesis 1: 28–30; Ibid.
4. Bacon, *New Organon*, Works IV, 247–248.
5. Bacon, *De Dignitate et Augmentis Scientiarum* (Table 1, col. 2).
6. See Carolyn Merchant, "The Scientific Revolution and The Death of Nature" *Isis*, 2006, 97: 513–533, https://nature.berkeley.edu/departments/espm/env-hist/articles/84.pdf. See also Carolyn Merchant, *The Death of Nature: Women, Ecology, and the Scientific Revolution* (San Francisco: HarperCollins, 1990).
7. Descartes, *Discourse on the Method*, CSM 61–62. See John Cottingham, Robert Stoothoff, and Dugald Murdoch, *The Philosophical Writings of Descartes*, vol. 1 (Cambridge: Cambridge University Press, 1985).
8. See Hans Jonas, *The Imperative of Responsibility* (Chicago: The University of Chicago Press, 1984).
9. Locke, *Second Treatise of Government*, Chapter 5, Sections 25–27, 31, 36–37. See Project Gutenberg: https://www.gutenberg.org/files/7370/7370-h/7370-h.htm.
10. See "U.S. and World Population Clock," United States Census Bureau, accessed October 15, 2020, https://www.census.gov/popclock/world.
11. For the story of Eunice Foote, see Ian Steadman, "The Forgotten Woman Who Unlocked the Greenhouse Effect," How We Get to Next, March 15, 2019, https://howwegettonext.com/the-forgotten-woman-who-discovered-the-greenhouse-effect-ad954a6ea7d9. To learn more about the history of climate science, see Meg Rosenburg, "The Not-So-Brief History of Climate Change Science," True Anomalies, March 23, 2015, https://www.trueanomalies.com/the-not-so-brief-history-of-climate-change-science/ and John Mason, "The History of Climate Science," Skeptical Science, June 5, 2020, https://skepticalscience.com/history-climate-science.html.
12. For more about Thompson and ice core drilling, see Maria, "Ice Core Climate Records of the World Prof. Lonnie Thompson, TUC Radio, accessed October 14, 2020, https://tucradio.org/catalog/environmental-climate-change/ice-core-climate-records-world-prof-lonnie-thompson/.
13. See Doyle Rice, "Earth's carbon dioxide levels highest in 3 million years, study says," *USA Today*, last updated April 4, 2019, https://www.usatoday.com/story/news/nation/2019/04/04/global-warming-earths-carbon-dioxide-levels-highest-3-million-years/3367027002/.
14. Myles R. Allen et al., "Summary for Policymakers," in *Special Report. Global Warming of 1.5°C*, ed. V. Masson-Delmotte et al. (IPCC, 2018), https://www.ipcc.ch/sr15/chapter/spm/.
15. Drought helped push many Syrians into cities before the war, worsening tensions and leading to rising discontent (Colin P. Kelley et al., "Climate change in the Fertile Crescent and implications of the recent Syrian dought," Proceedings of the National Academy of Sciences 112 (2015): 3241–3246, https://www.pnas.org/content/early/2015/02/23/1421533112.abstract); crop losses led to unemployment that stoked Arab Spring uprisings in Egypt and Libya (Caitlin E. Werrell, Francesco Femia, and Anne-Marie Slaughter, "The Arab Spring and Climate Change," Center for American Progress, February 28, 2013, https://www.americanprogress.org/issues/security/reports/2013/02/28/54579/the-arab-spring-and-climate-change/.)

16. See "Arctic summer sea ice could disappear as early as 2035," *National Geographic*, last updated August 13, 2020, https://www.nationalgeographic.com/science/2020/08/arctic-summer-sea-ice-could-be-gone-by-2035/. See also "Interactive: When will the Arctic see its first ice-free summer?" Carbon Brief, last updated December 12, 2019, https://interactive.carbonbrief.org/when-will-the-arctic-see-its-first-ice-free-summer/.
17. For updated information about the threat to ocean currents, see Denise Chow, "Climate change models predicted ocean currents would speed up—but not this soon," *NBC News*, February 11, 2020, https://www.nbcnews.com/science/environment/climate-change-models-predicted-ocean-currents-would-speed-not-soon-n1135176.
18. "How do we know more CO2 is causing warming?" Skeptical Science, last updated October 15, 2016, https://skepticalscience.com/empirical-evidence-for-co2-enhanced-greenhouse-effect-intermediate.htm.
19. Myles R. Allen et al., *Special Report. Global Warming of 1.5° C*, ed. V. Masson-Delmotte et al. (IPCC, 2018), https://www.ipcc.ch/sr15/.
20. "Causes of Climate Change," United States Environmental Protection Agency, last updated December 27, 2016, https://19january2017snapshot.epa.gov/climate-change-science/causes-climate-change_.html; "How climate change alters ocean chemistry," in *World Ocean Report*, ed. Tim Schroeder (Hamburg: Maribus gGmbH, 2010), 27–54, https://worldoceanreview.com/en/wor-1/ocean-chemistry/co2-reservoir/.
21. Rajendra K. Pachaurl et al., *Climate Change 2014 Synthesis Report*, (IPCC, 2015), https://ar5-syr.ipcc.ch/topic_observedchanges.php.
22. Pachaurl et al., *Climate Change 2014*.
23. Ottmar Ebenhofer et al., "Summary for Policymakers" in *Climate Change 2014: Mitigation of Climate Change*, ed. Ottmar Ebonhofer et al., (IPCC, 2014), https://www.ipcc.ch/site/assets/uploads/2018/02/ipcc_wg3_ar5_summary-for-policymakers.pdf.
24. Jamie Smith Hopkins, "A Likely but Hidden Coronavirus Risk Factor: Pollution," The Center for Public Integrity, March 7, 2020, https://publicintegrity.org/health/coronavirus-and-inequality/a-likely-but-hidden-coronavirus-risk-factor-pollution/. Allison Insero, "Air Pollution Linked to Lung Infections, Especially in Young Children," AJMC, May 6, 2018, https://www.ajmc.com/view/air-pollution-linked-to-lung-infections-especially-in-young-children. Joseph Vempilly et al., "The synergetic effect of ambient PM2.5 exposure and rhinovirus infection in airway dysfunction in asthma: A pilot observational study from the Central Valley of California," *Experimental Lung Research* 39 (2013): 434–440, https://pubmed.ncbi.nlm.nih.gov/24245976/. Karen Clay, Joshua Lewis, and Edson Severnini, "Pollution, Infectious Disease, and Mortality: Evidence from the 1918 Spanish Influenza Pandemic," *The Journal of Economic History* 78 (2018): 1179–1209, https://www.cambridge.org/core/journals/journal-of-economic-history/article/pollution-infectious-disease-and-mortality-evidence-from-the-1918-spanish-influenza-pandemic/8A69CC00A169F36B11A49113404C93B0. Karen Clay, Joshua Lewis, and Edson Severini, "What explains cross-city variation in mortality during the 1918 influenza pandemic? Evidence from 438 U.S. cities," *Economics and Human Biology* 35 (2019): 42–50, https://www.sciencedirect.com/science/article/pii/S1570677X18302909. Chris Mooney, "The coronavirus is deadly enough. But some experts suspect bad air makes it worse," *The Washington Post*, March 15, 2020, https://www.washingtonpost.com/climate-environment/2020/03/15/smoking-air-pollution-coronavirus/.
25. Xiao Wu et al., "Air pollution and COVID-19 mortality in the United States: Strengths and limitations of an ecological regression analysis," Harvard University, last updated September 18, 2020, https://projects.iq.harvard.edu/covid-pm. Hiroko Tabuchi, "In the Shadows of America's Smokestacks, Virus Is One More Deadly Risk," *New York Times*, last updated May 19, 2020, https://www.nytimes.com/2020/05/17/climate/pollution-poverty-coronavirus.html. Katherine Hayhoe, "The Pandemic's Effects on Climate Change | Special Episode," Global Weirdling with Katherine Hayhoe, YouTube video, March 25, 2020, 5:55, https://www.youtube.com/watch?v=62IzyebP1_o.
26. Jennifer A. Burney, "The downstream air pollution impacts of the transition from coal to natural gas in the United States," *Nature Sustainability* 3 (2020): 152–160, https://www.nature.com/articles/s41893-019-0453-5#citeas.
27. Jos Lelieveld et al., "Effects of fossil fuel and total anthropogenic emission removal on public health and climate," *Proceedings of the National Academy of Sciences* 116 (2019): 7192–7197, https://www.pnas.org/content/116/15/7192. Jos Lelieveld et al., "Loss of life expectancy from air pollution compared to other risk factors: A worldwide perspective," *Cardiovascular Research* 116 (2020): 1910–1917, https://academic.oup.com/cardiovascres/article/116/11/1910/5770885. Jay Apt, "The Other Reason to Shift away from Coal: Air Pollution That Kills Thousands Every Year," *Scientific American*, republished June 7, 2020, https://www.scientificamerican.com/article/the-other-reason-to-shift-away-from-coal-air-pollution-that-kills-thousands-every-year/. Fabio Caiazzo et al., "Air pollution and early deaths in the United States. Part I: Quantifying the impact of major sectors in 2005," *Atmospheric Environment* 79 (2013): 198–208, https://www.sciencedirect.com/science/article/abs/pii/S1352231013004548.

28. James Conca, "Natural Gas and the New Deathprint for Energy," *Forbes*, January 25, 2018, https://www.forbes.com/sites/jamesconca/2018/01/25/natural-gas-and-the-new-deathprint-for-energy/#66d570505e19.
29. Nicolas Borchers Arriagada et al., "Unprecedented smoke-related health burden associated with the 2019–20 bushfires in eastern Australia," *The Medical Journal of Australia* 213 (2020): 282–283, https://onlinelibrary.wiley.com/doi/full/10.5694/mja2.50545.
30. Flora Graham, "Daily briefing: Climate change made Australian fires at least 30% more likely," *Nature*, March 4, 2020, https://www.nature.com/articles/d41586-020-00665-6.
31. Renee Cho, "How Climate Change Is Exacerbating the Spread of Disease," State of the Planet (blog), Earth Institute at Columbia University, September 4, 2014, https://blogs.ei.columbia.edu/2014/09/04/how-climate-change-is-exacerbating-the-spread-of-disease/.
32. Catherine Hayhoe, "Climate Change and Coronavirus | Special Episode," Global Weirding with Catherine Hayhoe, YouTube video, March 25, 2020, 9:40, https://www.youtube.com/watch?v=ruOl1R5cpnw. Rob Jordan, "How does climate change affect disease," Stanford Earth, March 15, 2020, https://earth.stanford.edu/news/how-does-climate-change-affect-disease#gs.innie9. "Climate change and human health risks and responses. Summary," World Health Organization, 2003, https://www.who.int/globalchange/summary/en/index5.html.
33. Sara Goudarzi, "As the Earth Warms, the Diseases that May Lie within Permafrost Become a Bigger Worry," *Scientific American*, November 1, 2016, https://www.scientificamerican.com/article/as-earth-warms-the-diseases-that-may-lie-within-permafrost-become-a-bigger-worry/. Rosie McCall, "Melting Glaciers and Thawing Permafrost Could Release Ancient Viruses Locked Away for Thousands of Years," *Newsweek*, February 6, 2020, https://www.newsweek.com/melting-glaciers-thawing-permafrost-ancient-viruses-1486037.
34. Alec Luhn, "Thawing Siberian permafrost soil risks rise of anthrax and prehistoric diseases," *The Telegraph*, April 14, 2019, https://www.telegraph.co.uk/global-health/climate-and-people/thawing-siberian-permafrost-soil-risks-rise-anthrax-prehistoric/. Melody Schreiber, "The Next Pandemic Could Be Hiding in the Arctic Permafrost," *The New Republic*, April 2, 2020, https://newrepublic.com/article/157129/next-pandemic-hiding-arctic-permafrost.
35. Joshua B. Pribanic and Talia Wiener, "Pennsylvania is Discharging Radioactive Fracking Waste Into Rivers As Landfill Leachate, Impacting The Chesapeake Bay & Ohio River Watersheds," ed. Melissa Troutman, *Public Herald*, August 7, 2019, https://publicherald.org/pennsylvania-is-discharging-radioactive-fracking-waste-into-rivers-as-landfill-leachate-impacting-the-chesapeake-bay-ohio-river-watersheds/.
36. Damian Carrington, "Coronavirus: World treating symptoms, not cause of pandemics, says UN," *The Guardian*, July 6, 2020, https://www.theguardian.com/world/2020/jul/06/coronavirus-world-treating-symptoms-not-cause-pandemics-un-report.
37. Carrington, "Coronavirus: world treating symptoms."
38. David Coad et al., "Global Fossil Fuel Subsidies Remain Large: An Update Based on Country-Level Estimates," IMF, May 2, 2019, https://www.imf.org/en/Publications/WP/Issues/2019/05/02/Global-Fossil-Fuel-Subsidies-Remain-Large-An-Update-Based-on-Country-Level-Estimates-46509.
39. Coad et al., "Global Fossil Fuel Subsidies Remain Large: An Update."
40. Patricia Scotland, "Women shouldering the burden of climate crisis need action, not speeches," *The Guardian*, March 13, 2020, https://www.theguardian.com/global-development/2020/mar/13/women-shouldering-the-burden-of-climate-crisis-need-action-not-speeches. Verania Chao and Carolina Rivera, "Gender Data and Analysis: Gateway for Inclusive National Climate Action," UNDP, April 20, 2019, https://www.ndcs.undp.org/content/ndc-support-programme/en/home/impact-and-learning/ideas-and-insights/20190/gender-data-and-analysis–gateway-for-inclusive-national-climate.html. Fiona Harvey, "Climate breakdown 'Is increasing violence against women'," *The Guardian*, January 29, 2020, https://www.theguardian.com/environment/2020/jan/29/climate-breakdown-is-increasing-violence-against-women.
41. John Aglionby, "Four times as many women died in tsunami," *The Guardian*, March 26, 2005, https://www.theguardian.com/society/2005/mar/26/internationalaidanddevelopment.indianoceantsunamidecember2004.
42. Eric Klinenberg, "Denaturalizing Disaster: A social autopsy of the 1995 Chicago heat wave," *Theory and Society* 28 (1999): 239–295, https://doi.org/10.1023/A:1006995507723.
43. Chloe Reichel, "Toxic waste sites and environmental justice: Research roundup," Journalist's Resource, September 24, 2018, https://journalistsresource.org/studies/environment/superfund-toxic-waste-race-research/. Ihab Mikati et al., "Disparities in Distribution of Particulate Matter Emission Sources by Race and Poverty Status," *American Journal of Public Health* 108 (2018), https://ajph.aphapublications.org/doi/abs/10.2105/AJPH.2017.304297?journalCode=ajph&.
44. Will Sullivan, "Too Much Pollution for One Place," PBS, August 23, 2017, https://www.pbs.org/wgbh/nova/article/too-much-pollution/.

45. For more about the relationship between women, people of color, and environmentalism, see Jasmine C. Leyva, "Why the Climate Movement Is Failing Us: From A Black Woman Who Doesn't Trust Science," Sentient Media, April 23, 2020, https://sentientmedia.org/why-the-climate-movement-is-failing-us-from-a-black-woman-who-doesnt-trust-science/?utm_source=Sentient+Today&utm_campaign=56763752b6-EMAIL_CAMPAIGN_2020_04_23_09_16&utm_medium=email&utm_term=0_5b050108b9-56763752b6-69088294.
46. Dr. Reverend Horace Strand, "Chester," Center of Excellence in Environmental Toxicology, University of Pennsylvania, accessed October 13, 2020, http://ceet.upenn.edu/target-communities/chester/.
47. Deepak Ray, "Climate change is affecting crop yields and reducing global food supplies," *The Conversation*, July 9, 2019, https://theconversation.com/climate-change-is-affecting-crop-yields-and-reducing-global-food-supplies-118897.
48. David S. Battisti and Rosamond L. Naylor, "Historical Warnings of Future Food Insecurity with Unprecedented Seasonal Heat," *Science* 323 (2009): 240–244, https://science.sciencemag.org/content/323/5911/240.
49. "Global Trends: Forced Displacement in 2017," UNHCR, June 25, 2018, https://www.unhcr.org/globaltrends2017/.
50. See Joe Purtell, "Billions could face temperatures inhospitable to life in the next 50 years, study finds," *NBC News*, May 6, 2020, https://www.nbcnews.com/news/world/billions-could-face-temperatures-inhospitable-life-next-50-years-study-n1201471.
51. "Climate Change, The Arab Spring and Food Prices," American Security Project, November 1, 2012, https://www.americansecurityproject.org/climate-change-the-arab-spring-and-food-prices/. David Biello, "Can Climate Change Cause Conflict? Recent History Suggests So," *Scientific American*, November 23, 2009, https://www.scientificamerican.com/article/can-climate-change-cause-conflict/. Thomas L. Friedman, "Without Water, Revolution," *The New York Times*, May 19, 2013, https://www.nytimes.com/2013/05/19/opinion/sunday/friedman-without-water-revolution.html. Caitlin Werrell and Francesco Femia, "Air Force Chief of Staff: Military Often Has to Respond to the Effects of Climate," The Center for Climate and Security, April 5, 2019, https://climateandsecurity.org/2019/04/air-force-chief-of-staff-military-often-has-to-respond-to-the-effects-of-climate-change/. Link TV, "Climate and National Security," YouTube video, August 5, 2014, 4:45, https://www.youtube.com/watch?v=RyBYQMUCE3U.
52. Nafeez Ahmed, "U.S. Military Could Collapse Within 20 Years Due to Climate Change, Report Commissioned By Pentagon Says," *Vice*, October 24, 2019, https://www.vice.com/en/article/mbmkz8/us-military-could-collapse-within-20-years-due-to-climate-change-report-commissioned-by-pentagon-says. Daniel R. Coats, "World Threat Assessment of the US Intelligence Community," Office of the Direct of National Intelligence, January 29, 2019, https://www.dni.gov/files/ODNI/documents/2019-ATA-SFR--SSCI.pdf. Bruce Lieberman, "A brief introduction to climate change and national security," Yale Climate Connections, July 23, 2019, https://yaleclimateconnections.org/2019/07/a-brief-introduction-to-climate-change-and-national-security/.
53. The work of Mark Sagoff presents an excellent example of a Kantian system of environmental ethics.
54. "Top Policies," Energy Policy Solutions, accessed October 13, 2020, https://www.energypolicy.solutions/policies/. "Energy Policy Design," Energy Policy Solutions, accessed October 13, 2020, https://www.energypolicy.solutions/energy-policy-design/. Vox, "Watch the US stall on climate change for 12 years," YouTube video, October 10, 2018, 12:05, https://www.youtube.com/watch?v=yzDjjUAt3zc&t=115s.
55. "Clean Jobs America 2019," E2, March 13, 2019, https://e2.org/reports/clean-jobs-america-2019/.
56. "Levelized Cost of Energy and Levelized Cost of Storage 2019," Lazard, November 7, 2019, https://www.lazard.com/perspective/lcoe2019.
57. Charles Newberry, "Energy Storage Poses a Growing Threat to Peaker Plants," Transform, October 1, 2018, https://www.ge.com/power/transform/article.transform.articles.2018.oct.storage-threat-to-peaker-plants.
58. Agence France-Presse, "New Analysis Says Coal's Hit a 'Tipping Point' And No Longer Makes Financial Sense," *Science Alert*, July 1, 2020, https://www.sciencealert.com/scientists-think-coal-had-reached-a-financial-tipping-point-making-it-uncompetitive-with-renewables/amp.

59. Sam Meredith, "BlackRock CEO says the climate crisis is about to trigger 'A fundamental reshaping of finance,'" CNBC, last updated January 14, 2020, https://www.cnbc.com/2020/01/14/blackrock-ceo-larry-fink-says-climate-change-will-soon-reshape-markets.html. "Sustainable Finance," Goldman Sachs, accessed October 14, 2020, https://www.goldmansachs.com/what-we-do/sustainable-finance/. "Understanding Our Climate-Related Risks and Opportunities," JP Morgan Chase, May 2019, original URL https://www.jpmorganchase.com/corporate/Corporate-Responsibility/document/jpmc-cr-climate-report-2019.pdf, Internet Archive, accessed October 14, 2020, https://web.archive.org/web/20200425162444/https://www.jpmorganchase.com/corporate/Corporate-Responsibility/document/jpmc-cr-climate-report-2019.pdf. Reuters, "Barclays sets 2050 'net zero' carbon goal after investor pressure," Thomson Reuters Foundation News, March 30, 2020, https://news.trust.org/item/20200330125756-pf1vb/. Yossi Cadan, Ahmed Mokgopo, Clara Vondrich, "$11 Trillion and Counting," 350, September 8, 2019, https://financingthefuture.platform350.org/wp-content/uploads/sites/60/2019/09/FF_11Trillion-WEB.pdf.
60. Jagdeep Singh Bachher and Richard Sherman, "Opinion: UC investments are going fossil free. But not exactly for the reasons you may think," *Los Angeles Times*, September 17, 2019, https://www.latimes.com/opinion/story/2019-09-16/divestment-fossil-fuel-university-of-california-climate-change.
61. Toby A. A. Heaps, "Divestment would have made NY pension fund $22B richer," Corporate Knights, October 4, 2018, https://www.corporateknights.com/channels/climate-and-carbon/divestment-made-ny-pension-fund-22b-richer-15386364/.
62. Larry Fink, "A Fundamental Reshaping of Finance," BlackRock, accessed October 14, 2020, https://www.blackrock.com/corporate/investor-relations/larry-fink-ceo-letter.
63. "Shell's ambition to be a net-zero emissions energy business," Shell, accessed October 14, 2020, https://www.shell.com/energy-and-innovation/the-energy-future/shells-ambition-to-be-a-net-zero-emissions-energy-business.html#iframe=L3dlYmFwcHMvY2xpbWF0ZV9hbWJpdGlvbi8. Repsol, "Repsol will be a net zero emissions company by 2050," press release, December 2, 2019, https://www.repsol.com/en/press-room/press-releases/2019/repsol-will-be-a-net-zero-emissions-company-by-2050.cshtml. Mike Scott, "Europe's Oil Majors Start To Embrace Alternative Energy And Climate Targets," *Forbes*, May 14, 2020, https://www.forbes.com/sites/mikescott/2020/05/14/europes-oil-majors-start-to-embrace-alternative-energy-and-climate-targets/amp/.
64. "Shell's Net Carbon Footprint ambition: Frequently asked questions," Shell, accessed October 14, 2020, https://www.shell.com/energy-and-innovation/the-energy-future/what-is-shells-net-carbon-footprint-ambition/faq.html.
65. BP, "BP sets ambition for net zero by 2050, fundamentally changing organisation to deliver," press release, February 12, 2020, https://www.bp.com/en/global/corporate/news-and-insights/press-releases/bernard-looney-announces-new-ambition-for-bp.html.
66. Carrington, "Coronavirus: world treating symptoms."
67. See The Aldo Leopold Foundation, *A Discussion Guide for A Sand County Almanac* (Baraboo: The Aldo Leopold Foundation, n.d.), https://ethz.ch/content/dam/ethz/special-interest/usys/ites/ecosystem-management-dam/documents/EducationDOC/Readings_DOC/SandCountyAlmanacDiscussionGuide.pdf.
68. Originally published as "The Land Ethic," in *A Sand County Almanac*, 2nd ed., 201–226. (Oxford: Oxford University Press, 1949, 1977).
69. "Household Calculator," CoolClimate Network, accessed October 14, 2020, https://coolclimate.berkeley.edu/calculator.

Chapter 8

Animal Ethics

Co-Authored with Lucille Thibodeau

Preface

QUESTIONS FOR INITIAL CONSIDERATION

a. Before reading this chapter and watching any of the films discussed, take note of your position on whether or not nonhuman animals deserve any degree of moral respect. Should they get the same ethical treatment as human beings? What are the reasons for your viewpoint?
b. Also consider your own relationship with nonhuman animals. Do you have pets? If so, how do you treat them? How much effort do you put into caring for them and ensuring their quality of life? Do you eat meat? If so, do you select the source of your meat with care? What are the standards your food has to meet? Are you aware of the relationship between meat-eating and climate change? Do you hunt? If so, why? Do you kill animals humanely and treat them with respect? Why or why not?
c. Do you have an open mind about what you're about to read? Why or why not?
d. After jotting down these initial thoughts, reflect on them and note any changes after reading the chapter and watching the films discussed.

8.1 Introduction

Contagion (2011), written by Scott Z. Burns and directed by Steven Soderbergh,[1] is a prophetic portrayal of a global pandemic, replete with social distancing, conspiracies, school and business closures, self-isolation, and strict quarantines. It is a stark reminder that many experts knew a pandemic like that of 2020 was going to happen. Its cast includes Gwyneth Paltrow, Matt Damon, Laurence Fishburne, Jude Law, Marion Cotillard, Kate Winslet, and Bryan Cranston, among others. The film focuses on the role of humanity's relationship with nonhuman animals[2] in its portrayal of the cause of the pandemic as well as the rapid search for treatments and a vaccine. Several scenes, especially the closing montage, show viewers the cause, underscoring an **anthropocentric** argument about the treatment of animals: Forcing some animals away from their natural habitats and raising other animals for food in problematic conditions, put humankind at great risk for the spread of infectious disease. In its portrayal of the solution to the pandemic—extensive medical testing on rhesus monkeys—the film highlights the reality that animals will endure great suffering during the many experiments needed to find a vaccine. This portrayal raises the **nonanthropocentric** argument that animals deserve ethical consideration—moral respect—and therefore should not have to endure unnecessary suffering. The philosophical foundations of this argument, as well as arguments about what kind of suffering is reprehensible and what is tolerable, are worthy of serious consideration for ethicists and anyone whose life impacts animals—which is each one of us.

ANTHROPOCENTRIC
Focusing on humankind as the most important element of existence.

NONANTHROPOCENTRIC
Focusing on nonhuman creatures as deserving of moral consideration and respect.

8.2 Nonanthropocentric Arguments about Nonhuman Animals' Rights

8.2.1 Animals Do Not Have a Moral Status: Descartes and Kant

Animal ethics developed recently as a subfield of ethics, which is, in turn, a subfield of philosophy. Philosophers before the founding of this subdiscipline largely argued that animals are not deserving of any **moral status**.[3] Two notable proponents of this view are Descartes and Kant.[4]

MORAL STATUS
Synonymous with "ethical status"; the degree of beneficial consideration something merits.

Rene Descartes, a father figure of modern philosophy, claims that animals are merely part of the deterministic machine that is the physical world. Influenced by Newtonian physics, and understandably unaware of the unpredictability modern

1. The following paragraph contains spoilers about the film. Though the films in this chapter are highly recommended, viewing them is not a prerequisite for understanding the content of the chapter. While viewing *Contagion,* take note of the role of nonhuman animals in the film. Locate each film on a site like justwatch.com, which lists their availability on all streaming services. All information about the production, cast, and crew of each film in this chapter is from IMDb.com.
2. Throughout the chapter, they are sometimes referred to simply as "animals" purely for the sake of simplicity.
3. It should be noted that many of these thinkers also argued that animals ought not to be treated cruelly, because such treatment could make humans treat each other similarly.
4. Please see the appendix of biographies for important background information on the philosophers discussed in this chapter.

scientists now acknowledge about the physical world, Descartes theorized that all of nature functions like the gears of a clock. The activities of the natural world are all the inevitable results of previous actions.[1] The physical world is highly predictable and unspontaneous, including nonhuman animals, who function almost like robots in Descartes's theory. They cannot experience pain, let alone reason, and therefore, are not worthy of moral respect.[2]

© FERNANDO BLANCO CALZADA/ Shutterstock.com

Immanuel Kant, another Enlightenment thinker, also sees the natural world in the deterministic way that Descartes does, at least according to Section Three of the *Grounding for the Metaphysics of Morals*. As Chapter Three explains, the foundation of Kant's ethics is human reason. It is reason that generates the **categorical imperative**, including its second formulation, and it is the human ability to reason that makes it necessary to treat all people as ends in themselves, and never as means.[3] Creatures that lack reason, then, including nonhuman animals, may be treated as means according to Kant.

CATEGORICAL IMPERATIVE
The supreme commandment or central moral principle of Kant's deontological ethics; see Chapter Three.

8.2.2 Nonhuman Animals Have a Moral Status and Are Deserving of Respect: Bentham and Others

Jeremy Bentham, as discussed in Chapter Four, founded modern **utilitarianism**. He is also a father figure to animal ethics. This is mainly because of his argument that the question of whether or not animals can reason is not the key concern in determining their moral status, but rather, the crucial question is whether or not they are sentient, whether they can *suffer*. The affirmative answer to this question implies that animals are worthy of moral consideration in themselves, and not just in how they affect or relate to human beings. **Sentience**, the ability to experience pain and pleasure, is the morally significant factor for Bentham and his followers like Peter Singer.[4]

UTILITARIANISM
The ethical theory whose goal is maximizing overall happiness; see Chapter Four.

SENTIENCE
The ability to feel things such as pain, comfort, suffering.

Other notable philosophers who argue for animal rights include Theodor Adorno, Jacques Derrida, and Elie Wiesel.[5] Though Kant is opposed to animal rights, not all Kantians have followed suit. Tom Regan is a notable example.[6]

8.2.3 Implications of Nonanthropocentric Arguments about Animal Rights: Factory Farming in the United States and Food, Inc.

8.2.3.1 What Is Factory Farming?

Food, Inc. (2008), written and directed by Robert Kenner, explains the transition from traditional farming to factory farming, which took place in the twentieth century.[7] Passers-by used to be able to see animals being raised for food in pleasant rustic settings, but beginning in the middle of the twentieth century, most animals

© Official/Shutterstock.com

© David Tadevosian/Shutterstock.com

© Mark Agnor/Shutterstock.com

being raised for human consumption spent their lives in tightly-packed quarters out of view to the public. Despite this transition, the film explains, the pleasant farm-related imagery from earlier days is used to market the animals raised on factory farms. When the film was made, the top four beef suppliers controlled 80 percent of the market, and the data was similar for pork and chickens.

Today, more animals suffer at human hands than at any other time in history. It is therefore not surprising that an intense and controversial debate is taking place over the status of the sixty-plus billion animals raised and slaughtered for food worldwide every year. To keep up with the high demand for meat, industrialized nations employ modern processes generally referred to as "factory farming." This chapter focuses on factory farming in the United States because the United States inaugurated this approach to farming, because factory farming is more highly sophisticated there than elsewhere, and because the government agency overseeing it, the Department of Agriculture (USDA), publishes abundant readily available statistics that reveal the astonishing scale of factory farming in this country.[5]

Contemporary scientific evidence—supplementing what most people have understood, with plain common sense, since pre-history—proves that mammals and birds, among other species, do possess sentience and self-awareness.[6] It must

5. "Upwards of 99 percent of all animals eaten in this country come from 'factory farms.'" Jonathan Safran Foer, *Eating Animals* (New York: Little, Brown, 2009), 12. Factory farms are also called CAFOs ("confined animal feeding operations") and factory farming is sometimes referred to as "industrialized farm animal production" (IFAP).

6. "The Cambridge Declaration on Consciousness," proclaimed on July 7, 2012, presents the conclusions of a prominent international group of neuroscientists, and validates the findings of numerous prior scientific studies. The declaration, as well as several of the seventeen talks and presentations of the Francis Crick Memorial conference, can be found at http://www.fcmconference.org. On animal sentience, self-awareness, emotion, and suffering, see also Marc Bekoff, *The Emotional Lives of Animals: A Leading Scientist Explores Animal Joy, Sorrow, and Empathy—And Why They Matter* (Novato, CA: New World Library, 2007); Andrew Linzey, *Why Animal Suffering Matters: Philosophy, Theology, and Practical Ethics* (Oxford: Oxford University Press, 2009); Carl Safina, Beyond Words: What Animals Think and Feel (New York: Henry Holt, 2015); Frans de Waal, *Are We Smart Enough to Know How Smart Animals Are?* (New York: W.W. Norton, 2016); and Jennifer Ackerman, *The Genius of Birds* (New York: Penguin Press, 2016).

be said that since we cannot know some things with absolute certainty, we cannot claim knowledge of those things. So, because we cannot know with absolute certainty that some animals are sentient and aware of themselves, we cannot claim to know that some, or any, of them are not. The arguments of Bentham, Singer, and Linzey, among others, are supported by a 2008 report published jointly by the Pew Charitable Trusts and the Johns Hopkins Bloomberg School of Public Health. In "Putting Meat on the Table: Industrial Farm Animal Production in America," the Commission found that "the present system of producing food animals in the United States is not sustainable and presents an unacceptable level of risk to public health and damage to the environment, as well as unnecessary harm to the animals we raise for food."[7] The Commission recommends the total phase-out of intensive confinement practices and asserts unequivocally that "the most intensive confinement systems . . . constitute inhumane treatment" and thus fall short of current ethical and societal standards.[8]

Sixty-plus years ago, the American countryside was studded with thousands of small, family-owned farms where one crop was grown and several species of livestock were raised. The growing demand for meat by a booming post-World-War-II population led to the gradual replacement of these small farms by large facilities housing 2,000 animals or more. These operations were supported (and still are) by huge government subsidies for certain crops—corn especially—that were found to be cost-effective in feeding large numbers of farm animals. The aim of these large operations was to grow more animals more quickly in less space by using cost-effective food and by replacing human labor with technology as much as possible. The industry devised a series of discrete production processes connected down to the minutest detail by economic transactions.[9] When the economic logarithms kicked in, farmers and consumers found themselves at the extreme ends of the spectrum of animal "production." 'The factory farm . . . succeeded by divorcing people from their food, eliminating farmers, and ruling agriculture by corporate fiat.'[10]

8.2.3.2 The Treatment of Factory-Raised Chickens

Chickens are complex creatures who are intelligent, have emotions, and feel pain and distress. For example, chickens can distinguish between more than one hundred faces of their own species, even after months of separation, and many faces of the human species as well. They form complex social structures ("pecking orders"), and every chicken knows its place on the social ladder. They have full-color vision. They experience rapid eye movement (REM) sleep, which means they dream just

7. "Putting Meat on the Table: Industrial Farm Animal Production in America," a report of the Pew Commission on Industrial Farm Animal Production, viii. The Pew Charitable Trusts. Accessed October 24, 2020. http://www.pewtrusts.org/.

8. Ibid., 38. The positions of Pythagoras, Plutarch, the Hebrew Bible, the New Testament, the hagiographical literature of medieval monasticism, Thomas Aquinas, the Catechism of the Catholic Church, and Pope Francis are briefly highlighted. The positions of many other philosophers, religious figures, and activists receive extensive treatment in Norm Phelps, *The Longest Struggle: Animal Advocacy from Pythagoras to PETA* (New York: Lantern Books, 2007).

9. In the industry these processes are called "vertical integration." Matthew Scully, *Dominion: The Power of Man, the Suffering of Animals, and the Call to Mercy* (New York: St. Martin's Press, 2002), 250. Scully points out that "As in all forms of tyranny, management intensifies as knowledge [of], interest in, or even curiosity about the subjects passes away," 272.

10. Foer, *Eating Animals*, 237.

like we do. They have pain receptors, enabling them to feel pain and distress. Hens defend their young from predators, and have more than thirty types of vocalizations to distinguish between threats. Like human mothers, they talk to their babies in the womb; a mother hen begins teaching calls to her chicks before they hatch.[11] Adult chickens have at least thirty different categories of conversation, pertaining to mating, eating, nesting, rearing, and warning.[12]

Using footage and interviews from a grower for a large company, *Food, Inc.* portrays the unsanitary and overcrowded conditions in which factory-farmed chickens are raised. According to the filmmakers, the chickens have been designed to be overweight, which limits their ability to move, and they are violently thrown into drawers and cages when picked up for transport to processing facilities.

When motivated mainly by profits and efficiency, ethical standards are likely to fall short. How they fall short leads us to ask: "What happens to animals in such a system?" Are they able to express behaviors natural to them? Are they given food that their digestive systems are designed to metabolize? Are they subjected to physical

---

11. See "10 Surprising Facts About Chickens," People for Ethical Treatment of Animals, April 24, 2020, https://www.peta.org/action/10-surprising-facts-chickens/ for all of the above examples.

12. See Unferth, Deb Olin, "[Report]: Cage Wars, Deb Olin Unferth," *Harper's Magazine,* May 15, 2015, https://harpers.org/archive/2014/11/cage-wars/. For more information about chickens (and other animals), see the recent best-selling book *Animalkind* by Ingrid Newkirk. For detailed recent scientific data about the cognition and emotional lives of chickens, see Lori Marino, "Thinking Chickens: A Review of Cognition, Emotion, and Behavior in the Domestic Chicken," *Springer Berlin Heidelberg,* January 2, 2017, https://ncbi.nlm.nih.gov/pmc/articles/PMC5306232.

alterations in the interest of their not harming one another or the humans who handle them? In other words, what is it like to be an animal living in such a system?[13]

On factory farms, 98 percent of the nine billion chickens (up from 1.6 billion in 1960) raised and slaughtered in a year in the US are egg-laying hens, the vast majority of whom live out their entire two-year lives in battery cages—tiny wire cages in which several hens are packed together, each one allotted the industry standard (set by United Egg Producers) of sixty-seven spare inches of space—less than a standard sheet of 8½ × 11″ paper. Such limited space interferes with a hen's ability to express behaviors natural to her such as stretching her wings, taking short flights, and pecking on the ground or in the grass for food.[14] Furthermore, as a tiny chick, she will have her beak cut off without benefit of anesthetic by a specially designed machine so that as she grows, she will not peck at or cannibalize the other hens in the cage. According to Deb Olin Unferth, "During beak trimming, workers . . . place each chick's beak into a hot-iron guillotine-type machine, and when it snaps the tip [the front third to front half] of the beak off, the chick's face smokes and the chick struggles."[15] Because a hen's laying cycle is linked to light, egg barns are kept dark most of the time. The hens never experience sunlight, except on the day they are put into crates and trucked to the slaughterhouse. Moreover, by taking away light and food for as long as fourteen days, producers trigger year-round unnatural but lucrative laying cycles. Artificially forced to produce at this rate, and kept relatively disease-free by antibiotics in her unsanitary, crowded cage until her immune system fails her, a hen will lay over 300 eggs a year, whereas the norm before factory farming was about one-third of that.

What about the male chickens? According to the most recent USDA statistics, every year over 250 million male chicks are "rendered" on egg farms the day they are born because they are of no use. Deemed unfit to be fed because they lay no eggs and their flesh is of poor quality, the chicks are macerated alive in high-speed grinders, the slurry of their carcasses disposed of as trash or fed to other chickens and farm animals.[16] Chickens selectively bred as "broilers" on other farms, especially for breast meat, are fed growth hormones so as to get up as quickly as possible to a market weight of five pounds in seven weeks or less. (Pre-factory-farm chickens

13. Jacques Derrida is one of the few contemporary philosophers who has taken on these questions. He writes: ". . . no one can today deny . . . the *unprecedented* proportions of this subjection of the animal. Such a subjection . . . can be called violence in the most morally neutral sense of the term . . . . No one can deny seriously anymore, or for very long, that men do all they can to dissimulate this cruelty or to hide it from themselves; in order to organize on a global scale the forgetting or misunderstanding of this violence, which some would compare to the worst cases of genocide . . . ." The *Animal That Therefore I am*, ed. Marie-Louise Mallet, trans. David Wills (New York: Fordham University Press, 2008), 25–26.

14. An adult chicken needs a minimum of 197 square inches to turn around, 138 square inches to stretch, 290 square inches to flap wings, and 172 square inches to preen—all basic biological activities. Karen David, *Prisoned Chickens, Poisoned Eggs: An Inside Look at the Modern Poultry Industry* (Summertown, TN: Book Publishing Company, 1997), 100.

15. Unferth, "Cage Wars: A Visit to the Egg Farm," *Harper's Magazine* (November 2014), 48. Research based on observation of their behaviors has shown that hens suffer chronic acute pain all their lives because of this procedure.

16. "United Egg Producers—the industry group that represents hatcheries that produce 95 percent of all eggs produced in the United States—announced Thursday that it would end this 'culling' of millions of chicks by 2020, or as soon as it's 'economically feasible' and an alternative is 'commercially available' . . . . In a country that's hardly famous for humane animal farming practices, this is a big deal." Karin Brulliard, "Egg Producers Pledge to Stop Grinding Newborn Male Chickens to Death," *Washington Post,* June 10, 2016, https://www.washingtonpost.com/news/animalia/wp/2016/06/10/egg-producers.

took twice as long to grow up to three pounds.) These chickens become too heavy to stand; their legs break under their weight, and they topple over onto their chests ("flip-over syndrome"). Some of them starve when they can no longer stand up to reach food or water. Or their organs shut down and their hearts stop beating, unable to cope with their body's unnaturally rapid growth. For them, it's about thirty-five days from birth to death. For the industry, the equation is simple: if the extra weight on birds who make it to slaughter brings in a greater profit than the loss in dead birds, then it's good for business. The same equation applies to laying hens: increased total egg output outweighs the number of hens who die due to crowding, stress, and illness. A massive production rate pre-supposes, and factors in, a high attrition rate.[17]

QUESTIONS FOR CONSIDERATION

a. Do you think that chickens' lack of reason is a good justification for treating them in the previously-described manner? Why or why not? Consider Descartes, Kantian ethics, and utilitarianism.
b. Why do you think workers at facilities like those described above choose to occupy and remain in such roles? Why do you think some of them seem inured[18] to treating chickens violently?[19]

8.2.3.3 Pigs

The scientific research on pigs indicates that they have excellent long-term memories, understand symbolic language, anticipate future events, and are adept at navigating mazes and other spatial tasks. They also play creatively while living in complex social communities where they easily distinguish others: both pigs and humans. Pigs

© paul prescott/Shutterstock.com

© SOMRERK WITTHAYANANT/Shutterstock.com

17. For detailed information on what happens to broilers and egg-laying hens as well as pigs, calves, and cows in the factory farm system, see Peter Singer, *Animal Liberation*, 95–157.
18. Accustomed to accepting something problematic or undesirable.
19. For information about cage-free and organic eggs, as well as farmers' markets and raising one's own chickens, see: Kristin Kirkpatrick, "Should You Pay More for Cage-Free or Organic Eggs?" *Health Essentials from Cleveland Clinic*, March 18, 2016, https://health.clevelandclinic.org/should-you-pay-extra-for-cage-free-or-organic-eggs/.

have the ability to use deception, are emotional, and are able to manipulate joysticks and use mirrors to find food.[20]

On factory farms, for 124 days (her gestation period), a sow is confined in a "gestation crate" in which she cannot turn around or roll over or lie down comfortably.[21] After she gives birth in a "farrowing crate," her piglets are taken away from her just a few days later instead of the natural few weeks. She is then artificially re-inseminated and the cycle repeats itself as many as eight times until she dies or is sent to slaughter.[22] Female piglets, when grown, are put into gestation crates in which, like their mothers, they will live out their two-year lifespan completely immobilized. If they die in their crates before slaughter, they are buried in a "dead hole," a mass grave of thousands of sows, each one in an airtight bag, or "rendered"—ground into feed for other sows.[8] When artificially grown to industry standards (about 250 pounds, half their adult weight), male pigs are slaughtered. According to Eisnitz, "Since uniform size is so important to packers, piglets who don't grow quite fast enough . . . are quickly weeded out. Picked up by their hind legs, thousands are swung and then bashed headfirst onto the concrete floor. This standard practice used by mega-farm workers is called 'thumping.'"[9] Then their intestines are ground up and fed to their mothers.

8.2.3.4 Factory Farm Animals in Relation to Pets (Companion Animals): Legal Differences

Those who own house pets typically treat them with a great deal of care, often like another member of the family. In the US, there are laws in place to protect such nonhuman animals from abuse and neglect. Most people can call to mind a high-profile local or national story about the abuse or neglect of cats or dogs and the legal punishment that ensued. However, factory-farmed animals do not have the same protections as other nonhuman animals.[10]

QUESTIONS FOR CONSIDERATION

a. Do you own a pet? If not, you probably know someone who does. Consider the possible scenario of that pet being treated like the chickens or pigs described above. Are there differences that justify the treatment of the chickens or pigs, but not the house pet? If so, does that give one license to treat the chickens or pigs in the ways described above? If not, what are the implications for factory farming and the food you choose to eat?[23]

20. "THINKING PIGS: Cognition, Emotion, and Personality," The Someone Project, accessed October 24, 2020, https://www.farmsanctuary.org/content/uploads/2016/06/TSP_PIGS_WhitePaper_vF.pdf. The above-mentioned cognitive, social, and emotional capacities are listed on pp. 19–20, quoted verbatim. For more information about pigs, see: Lori Marino and Christina M. Colvin, "Thinking Pigs: Cognition, Emotion, and Personality" *Mammalogy* 1: (2016): http://animalstudiesrepository.org/mammal.

21. "The pregnant pigs . . . must lie or step in their excrement to force it through the slatted floor. . . . The system makes good welfare practices more difficult because lame and diseased animals are almost impossible to identify when no animals are allowed to move." Foer, *Eating Animals,* 184, and note for page 184 on page 316. Sows suffer from "sores, tumors, ulcers, pus pockets, lesions, cysts, bruises, torn ears, swollen legs." Scully, *Dominion,* 267.

22. Over 90 percent of large hog farms use artificial insemination. See Foer, *Eating Animals,* 157.

23. A resource about ethical meat: Abigail Curtis, "You Want to Eat Meat That's Been Ethically Raised. But How Can You Know for Sure?" *Bangor Daily News,* January 15, 2018, https://bangordailynews.com/2018/01/12/homestead/you-want-to-eat-meat-thats-been-ethically-raised-but-how-can-you-know-for-sure/.

8.2.3.5 Cows

Cows are highly sentient and display distinct personalities. As in the case of chickens and pigs, there is relatively little attention paid to the study of cow intelligence, personality, and sociality at a basic level. But as a matter of fact, cows display "long-term memory," the ability to learn a variety of tasks with remarkable efficiency, the ability to determine the location of a hidden moving object, differentiate complex stimuli, and "discriminate humans from one another." According to Bekoff's interpretation of Marino and Allen's extensive work, cows "show learned fear responses to humans who have previously treated them badly." Cows experience a variety of emotions. For example, their eyes and ears are clear indicators of fear and anxiety. Like humans, "they too show pronounced stress responses, such as decreased feeding and increased cortisol release. Mothers and calves also show extreme distress when separated," writes Bekoff. Cows like to play, as do countless other nonhuman animals, and they "display a full range of personalities including boldness, shyness, sociability, gregariousness, and being temperamental." They exhibit complexity in their social relations, and their hierarchies and bonds demonstrate highly complex social interactions. Bekoff concludes: "All in all, the cognitive and emotional lives of cows are not all that different from many other non-food animals, including the companions with whom we share our homes." Unfortunately, when it comes to cows and other factory-farmed animals like chickens and pigs, we still do not acknowledge the complexity of their emotions and intelligence as we do for our companion animals.[24]

Food, Inc. highlights a few of the issues factory-farmed cows face. Despite the fact that they've evolved to eat grass, and not corn, they're forced to eat the latter because of its cost-effectiveness and easy availability. Also, the film focuses on the inhumane causes and treatment of "downer cows."

What is life like for cows on factory farms? Dairy cows are kept tethered to a stall and artificially inseminated on what the industry calls a "rape rack" in order that the cow will continue to lactate and provide milk that will be denied to her calf, who will be taken away from her two hours after birth. The milk denied the calf is sold to us humans who don't need to drink cow's milk. The calf, who does need its mother's milk, gets "milk replacer," a cheap, inferior nutrition. If the calf is female, like her mother she too will be forcibly impregnated and injected with synthetic bovine growth hormone to increase her milk production. She will give birth to four or five calves in a four-to-five-year period, will develop udder infections, and if she hasn't been literally milked to death, will become a "chopper cow," slaughtered at a fraction of her natural life span. On the kill floor, she will be stunned into

24. A major review essay published in the journal *Animal Behavior and Cognition* by Lori Marino and Kristin Allen entitled "The Psychology of Cows" (free online here: http://www.kimmela.org/wp-content/uploads/2017/12/The-Psychology-of-Cows.pdf) is briefly summarized by Marc Bekoff in his *Psychology Today* blog. The quoted passages in the above paragraph are taken from Bekoff's summary. See Marc Bekoff, "Cows: Science Shows They're Bright and Emotional Individuals," *Psychology Today,* November 2, 2017, https://www.psychologytoday.com/us/blog/animal-emotions/201711/cows-science-shows-theyre-bright-and-emotional-individuals.

© yngerman/Shutterstock.com

© Yana Vasileva/Shutterstock.com

© Yana Vasileva/Shutterstock.com

unconsciousness by a captive bolt gun[25] and hoisted upside down by one leg over rapidly moving conveyor belt lines where, within roughly forty-five minutes, she will be bled, skinned, dismembered, and eviscerated until what was a large living animal is "processed" into several shrink-wrapped packages of hamburger. If her calf is male, he will either be killed on the spot if he is sickly, or chained by the neck and confined for life (about fifteen weeks) in a wooden crate in which he is unable to turn around. He will be fed an iron-deficient diet to make him anemic and turn his flesh pale because consumers prefer the taste and color of "veal" that comes from anemic calves.[26]

QUESTIONS FOR CONSIDERATION

a. What are your thoughts in response to the above about the treatment of cows on factory farms?
b. Eight percent of American young adults in 2018 indicated that they were vegetarians, but only 2 percent of Americans over fifty-five did.[11] Does this difference strike you as accurate based on your own experience? What do you think might account for the disparity?[27]

---

25. Animals in US slaughterhouses are routinely beaten, skinned, dismembered, and scalded while fully conscious. See Gail A. Eisnitz, *Slaughterhouse: The Shocking Story of Greed, Neglect, and Inhumane Treatment Inside the U.S. Meat Industry* (Amherst, NY: Prometheus Books, 2007), 300. Eisnitz has interviewed individuals who, having spent a combined total of more than two million hours on kill floors, speak publicly about what's really taking place behind the closed doors of America's slaughterhouses.
26. A word like "veal" helps us forget what we are eating. The words "pork" and "beef" do the same thing. "Even the wooden stalls and neck chains are part of the plan, as these restrictions keep the calf from licking his own urine and feces to satisfy his craving for iron." Jim Mason and Mary Finelli, "Brave New Farm?" *In Defense of Animals: The Second Wave*, ed. Peter Singer (Oxford: Blackwell, 2006), 110.
27. Resources about grass-fed, certified angus, organic beef: Nancy Matsumoto, "Is Grass-Fed Beef Really Better For The Planet? Here's The Science," *NPR*, August 13, 2019, https://www.npr.org/sections/thesalt/2019/08/13/746576239/is-grass-fed-beef-really-better-for-the-planet-heres-the-science.

8.3 Anthropocentric Arguments about the Treatment of Nonhuman Animals

8.3.1 Cows and Climate Change: *Cowspiracy*

Written and directed by Kip Anderson and Keegan Kuhn, *Cowspiracy: The Sustainability Secret* (2014), is a documentary focused on the claim that factory farmed animals are the leading contributor of greenhouse gas emissions. It also argues that raising animals for food is unsustainable at its current pace, in part because of the land and plant matter it requires. One additional argument is that the current practices of the fishing industry are unsustainable. The film's conclusion, then, is that **veganism** is the most ethically responsible way to eat if we wish to change the current course of global warming.

The data about the greenhouse gas emissions of animal agriculture are in dispute, with some sources claiming that factory farming contributes to 14.5 percent of anthropogenic global greenhouse gas emissions, and others claiming that its contribution is closer to 51 percent. Regardless of the figure, there is widespread agreement that cattle are the top emitters by far, with pigs coming in second. Other sources confirm *Cowspiracy*'s claim about the unsustainability of land use by animal agriculture, pointing to deforestation, land degradation, pollution, and decreases in biodiversity. The Worldwatch Institute, which argues for the 51 percent figure, also presents data in support of the argument that the fishing industry is unsustainable because of fish farms that produce unsustainable amounts of sewage, which leads to nitrogen emissions and the reduction of biodiversity.[12]

VEGANISM
The practice of avoiding all animal products in one's diet and way of life; As opposed to vegetarianism, which consists in the elimination of meat, but not fish and other animal products.

QUESTIONS FOR CONSIDERATION

a. After seeing the film, do you find *Cowspiracy* persuasive? Are some claims more convincing than others?
b. Are you considering changing any of your eating habits as a result of seeing the film?[28]

8.3.2 Humans' Treatment of Animals and the Threat of Infectious Disease

8.3.2.1 Cows and E. Coli According to *Food, Inc.*

According to *Food, Inc.*, the extremely high demand for beef in the US is met by its capacity for corn production, which factory farms use instead of grass to feed cows

28. For information on veganism and vegetarianism, see: "Vegetarian Starter Guide," ChooseVeg, July 14, 2020, https://chooseveg.com/vsg/.

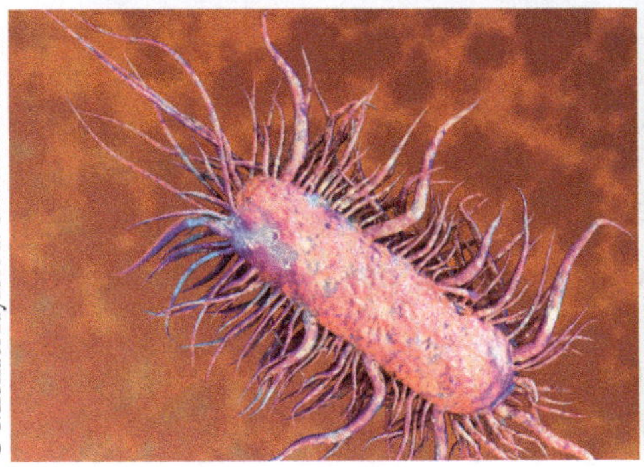

E. coli.

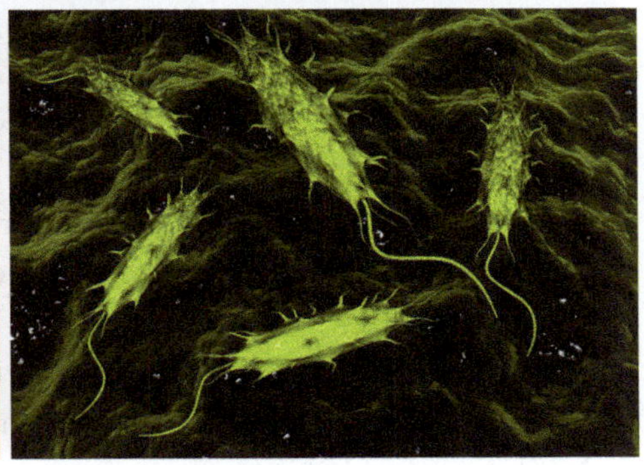

A 3-D rendering of E. coli.

because of the low cost and bountiful supply of corn. The film explains that cows evolved to eat grass, which sheds *Escherichia coli*, unlike corn. The result of using corn to feed cattle, then, raises the risk of E. coli poisoning in the population. The industry responds to this threat by using ammonia to kill the E. coli, but this presents its own set of problems.[13] Through interviews, the film highlights the relative safety of grass-fed beef, as well as the reduction of emissions that results from not having to transport corn.

QUESTIONS FOR CONSIDERATION

a. After seeing the film, do you find *Food, Inc.* persuasive? Are some claims more convincing than others?
b. Are you considering changing any of your eating habits as a result of seeing the film?

8.3.2.2 *Contagion* (2011) and the 2020 Coronavirus Pandemic

Contagion tells the harrowing story of a novel virus spread from a bat to a pig, which makes its way into Beth Emhoff's (Gwyneth Paltrow) food at a casino in Hong Kong while she's on a business trip.[29] She is unknowingly infected, transmits the virus to others in Hong Kong, and initiates its spread in the US by traveling on a plane to Minneapolis via Chicago. The film depicts the various people to whom Beth transmits the virus, as well as the ways in which they spread it to others. The CDC attempts to get the epidemic under control with school and business closures, social distancing, travel restrictions, and the development of a vaccine, but the epi-

29. This paragraph also contains spoilers.

demic quickly becomes a global pandemic that kills thousands (including Beth and her young son) before being halted by a vaccine. Problems that officials encounter along the way include those who resist halting business-as-usual as well as those who foster conspiracy theories. As it turns out, it was Beth's own company that bulldozed the bats' habitat and forced them to migrate into close proximity with domestic pigs.

In December 2020, a novel coronavirus, SARS-CoV-2, emerged in Wuhan, China. Within several weeks the virus had spread throughout China and caused outbreaks in neighboring countries, eventually leading to a worldwide pandemic. With varying degrees of success, countries mitigated the virus's effects by encouraging and enforcing social distancing, mask-wearing, increased sanitizing, travel restrictions, restrictions on social gatherings, school and business closures, contact tracing, and the development of medications. As of October 27, 2020, there were over 43.6 million cases worldwide, including over 1.1 million deaths,[14] with the *possibility* of a vaccine still several months away, which was not expected to be available to most people until well into 2021. The US accounted for just over 8.7 million cases and 225,692 deaths.[15] Conspiracy theorists and deniers made the efforts of the CDC, WHO[30] and those of other organizations and scientists less effective. Virologists suspect the SARS-CoV-2 virus is a zoonotic pathogen that evolved from a virus affecting an animal host (the viral reservoir). Researchers believe the most likely animal reservoir is the horseshoe bat and the virus was initially transmitted from the horseshoe bat to an intermediate host (possibly the pangolin) and then transmitted to humans.[16]

A wet market in Kunming, China.

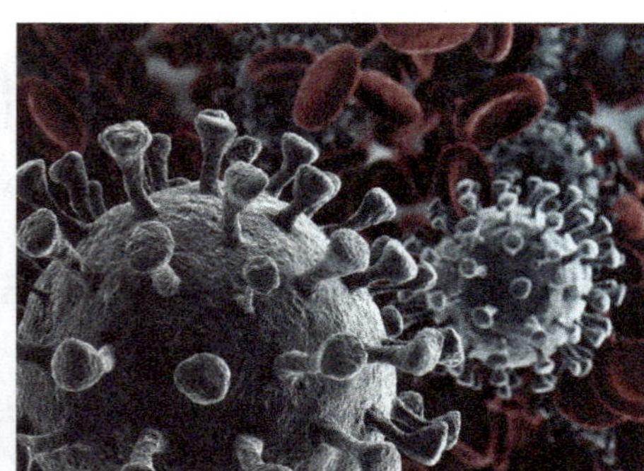

A 3-D rendering of the 2019 novel coronavirus.

30. The Centers for Disease Control and the World Health Organization.

8.3.2.3 How and Why Human Treatment of Nonhuman Animals Causes Infectious Disease and Pandemics

In its portrayal of the effort to find patient zero and the ultimate source of the virus, *Contagion* explores other possibilities of disease transmission from animals to humans, including mercury poisoning from fish, bird flu, and the various risks that factory-farmed livestock pose. In fact, the possibilities of epidemics and pandemics caused by such **zoonoses** abound, with four significant drivers: deforestation, factory farming, the wildlife trade, and decreases in biodiversity.[17] It should be noted here that there is overlap among these factors, especially the effects of deforestation and factory farming on decreases in biodiversity.[31]

ZOONOSES
Diseases originating from animals that spread to humans, mediated by human action in most cases; they have caused nearly every pandemic in human history.

8.3.2.3.1 Deforestation

Deforestation brings wildlife into closer proximity with human communities than they otherwise would be, increasing the probability of zoonotic disease outbreaks.[18] From 1997–1998, man-made forest fires in Southeast Asia destroyed many species of bats' natural habitats inducing them to migrate to orchards bordering the forests in the search for food. Fragments of fruit saturated with bat saliva are likely to have fallen into pigsties, which the pigs then consumed.[32] The bats were carrying the Nipah virus, which farmers contracted through the bat-infected pigs. This scenario inspired the final scenes of *Contagion*.[19]

Beef, soy, palm oil, and wood products are the main drivers of tropical deforestation and the resulting decrease in biodiversity. When animal habitats decrease in size, wildlife contact with humans increases, making zoonoses in humans more likely. Yellow fever, malaria, Venezuelan equine encephalitis, hantavirus, and Ebola have all been linked to deforestation.[20]

8.3.2.3.2 Factory Farming

Since 1980, tens of thousands of cows have suffered from bovine spongiform encephalopathy (BSE), or "mad cow" disease. Hundreds of people have died from the disease, which is termed Creutzfeldt-Jakob disease in humans.[21]

In spring 2009, a novel virus, H1N1 influenza, also known as "swine flu" entered North America from factory-farmed pigs in Mexico transported between continents. It triggered a global pandemic that killed between 151,700 and 575,400 people.[22] The 1918 Spanish Flu, the most lethal flu epidemic ever (at least 50 million deaths worldwide), may have evolved in poultry farms, according to genetic analysis.[23]

The widespread use of antibiotics in factory farming primes the human population for the spread of deadly superbugs resistant to antimicrobial treatment.[24] U.K.-appointed experts estimate that such microbes will lead to 10 million deaths per year by 2050.[25]

---

31. It is difficult to say whether these four are the *primary causes.*
32. Other Nipah virus outbreaks to consider include one in Bangladesh associated with drinking palm sap, as well as a Malaysia outbreak in pig farms after clear-cutting land for the Kuala Lumpur airport.

8.3.2.3.3 The Wildlife Trade and Wet Markets

Wet markets can have an allure to them because of the fresh produce on sale there. The wet markets that slaughter live animals on their premises are more problematic, especially when they are in close proximity to other animals and humans, because pathogens can be spread easily in such an environment. Another problematic condition of a wet market arises when animals are stacked on top of one another in cages, spreading disease to one another easily through bodily fluids. Such conditions have been linked to the COVID-19 pandemic.[26] The 2003 SARS outbreak was traced to a wet market in China (Guangdong province).[27] Wet markets have also been linked to some outbreaks of avian influenza.[28] Anthony Fauci, director of the National Institute of Allergy and Infectious Diseases (NIAID), recommended shutting down all live markets, including those in the US.[29]

A trader in Indonesia who sells several types of animals in the animal market.

The World Wildlife Fund distinguishes wildlife markets from wet markets. The latter is a broader term for those that sell a wide variety of perishable products. Wildlife markets are unique in that they sell live and dead wild animals, including species that are legal to trade, those that are illegal to trade because they are legally protected, and "domestic animals." Such wildlife markets support the wildlife trade, which is in turn fueled by the fur industry, traditional Chinese medicine, zoos, pets, research, and food. Historically, local governments have protected the wildlife trade because poor farmers rely on it.[30]

8.3.2.3.4 Other Factors Decreasing Biodiversity

When humans reduce the diversity of "biological basins" that usually keep contagions under control, they increase the risk of epidemics caused by zoonoses.[31] A highly biodiverse environment helps keep animal populations in balance that could contribute to zoonotic infections. For example, a biodiverse woodland habitat supporting medium- and large-sized predators helps keep populations of white-footed mice in check that contribute to Lyme disease. Highly urbanized environments reduce biodiversity, which some scientists link with the 1999 West Nile Virus epidemic in New York City. Bird species that are unsuitable hosts normally keep the virus in check in areas with diverse bird communities. But in regions lacking diversity, robins may flourish, and they are very efficient at spreading West Nile Virus.[32]

The United Nations warns that more zoonotic pathogens like SARS-CoV-2 are likely to emerge as a result of the wildlife trade, factory farming, and climate change.[33]

QUESTIONS FOR CONSIDERATION

a. Adopt the perspective of a natural law theorist and consider the ethical implications of deforestation, factory farming, and the wildlife trade. Do the same for Kantianism and utilitarianism. Compare and contrast your findings.
b. How does income inequality factor into the problem of zoonoses?
c. What thoughts do you have about actions people around the globe need to take in order to prevent future pandemics? What should the leaders of nations do? What about average citizens?

8.4 Resources for Further Learning

8.4.1 The Oxford Centre for Animal Ethics

https://www.oxfordanimalethics.com/home/

8.4.2 *Eating Animals* (2017)

Written and directed by Christopher Dillon Quinn. Book written by Jonathan Safran Foer.

8.4.3 Articles and Book Chapters

Tom Regan, "The Case for Animal Rights" in *In Defense of Animals*, ed. Peter Singer (Oxford: Basil Blackwell, 1985): 13–26.

Peter Singer, "All Animals are Equal," *Philosophic Exchange* 1 (1974).

Lucille Claire Thibodeau, "'All Creation Groans': The Lives of Factory Farmed Animals in the United States," in *Ethical Vegetarianism and Veganism*, ed. Andrew Linzey and Clair Linzey (New York: Routledge, 2019), 140–51.

8.4.4 Books

Jacques Derrida, *The Animal That Therefore I Am*, Translated by David Wills (New York: Fordham University Press, 2008).

Christine M. Korsgaard, *Fellow Creatures* (Oxford: Oxford University Press, 2020).

Peter Singer, *Animal Liberation* (New York: HarperCollins, updated edition, 2009).

Endnotes

1. See Descartes's Sixth Meditation, in *Meditations on First Philosophy*, AT 84–85, 86–89. (CSM 58-61). Also, Part Five of the *Discourse on the Method*, AT 41–45 (CSM 131–134).
2. See Part Five of Descartes's *Discourse on the Method*, AT 45–60 (CSM 133–141).
3. See Sections One and Two of the *Grounding for the Metaphysics of Morals*.
4. See Bentham, *An Introduction to the Principles of Morals and Legislation* (Mineola, NY: Dover Publications, 2007), 311. Also Singer, *Animal Liberation* (New York: HarperCollins, 2009).
5. On Adorno and Wiesel, see Thibodeau, 8. On Derrida, see *The Animal That Therefore I Am*.
6. See Regan, "The Case for Animal Rights," in *In Defense of Animals*, ed. Singer (Oxford: Basil Blackwell, 1985): 13–26. For a concise take on Regan and animal rights, see Lewis Vaughn, *Doing Ethics*, 5th ed. (New York: Norton, 2019): 376–377.
7. All information about the production and personnel involved in each film is from IMDb. See https://www.imdb.com/.
8. Scully, *Dominion*, 261 and 266.
9. Gail A. Eisnitz, *Slaughterhouse: The Shocking Story of Greed, Neglect, and Inhumane Treatment Inside the U.S. Meat Industry* (Amherst, NY: Prometheus Books, 2007), 220.
10. "Laws That Protect Animals," Animal Legal Defense Fund, August 4, 2020, https://aldf.org/article/laws-that-protect-animals/.
11. Nicholas Kristof, "The Mistakes That Will Haunt Our Legacy," *The New York Times*, July 11, 2020, https://www.nytimes.com/2020/07/11/opinion/sunday/animal-rights-cruelty.html.
12. See Nicholas Carter, "The Climate Crisis Secret," *Sentient Media*. September 10, 2019, https://sentientmedia.org/the-climate-crisis-secret/. In addition to data from The Worldwatch Institute, the author uses data from the U.N., *Science*, and the NIH.
13. See A. N. Hristov, M. Hanigan, A. Cole, R. Todd, T. A. McAllister, P. M. Ndegwa, and A. Rotz, "Ammonia Emissions from Dairy Farms and Beef Feedlots," Department of Dairy and Animal Science, Pennsylvania State University, October 1, 2010, https://naldc.nal.usda.gov/download/48762/PDF.
14. "Covid World Map: Tracking the Global Outbreak," *The New York Times*, October 27, 2020, https://www.nytimes.com/interactive/2020/world/coronavirus-maps.html.
15. "Covid in the U.S.: Latest Map and Case Count," *The New York Times*, October 27, 2020, https://www.nytimes.com/interactive/2020/us/coronavirus-us-cases.html.
16. See Hannah Bugga, "What Do Wet Markets and Factory Farms Have in Common?" Mercy For Animals, April 20, 2020, https://mercyforanimals.org/what-do-wet-markets-and-factory-farms-have; also see David Benatar's *New York Times* opinion piece: Benatar, "Our Cruel Treatment of Animals Led to the Coronavirus," *The New York Times*, April 13, 2020, https://www.nytimes.com/2020/04/13/opinion/animal-cruelty-coronavirus.html. Additionally, see Charles Camosy, "Nonhuman Animals and the COVID-19 Pandemic," *National Catholic Reporter*, May 12, 2020, https://www.ncronline.org/news/earthbeat/nonhuman-animals-and-covid-19-pandemic. A very in-depth explanation of the transmission of Covid-19 from bats to humans is in: Ferris Jabr, "How Humanity Unleashed a Flood of New Diseases," *The New York Times*, June 17, 2020, https://www.nytimes.com/2020/06/17/magazine/animal-disease-covid.html.
17. Damian Carrington, "Coronavirus: World Treating Symptoms, Not Cause of Pandemics, Says UN," *Guardian News and Media*, July 6, 2020, https://www.theguardian.com/world/2020/jul/06/coronavirus-world-treating-symptoms-not-cause-pandemics-un-report.
18. Jabr, "How Humanity Unleashed a Flood of New Diseases."
19. Kaw Bing Chua, Beng Hui Chua, and Chew Wen Wang, "Anthropogenic Deforestation, El Niiio and the Emergence of Nipah Virus in Malaysia." Departments of Medical Microbiology and Biochemistry, Faculty of Medicine, University of Malaya, 2002, http://www.mjpath.org.my/past_issue/MJP2002.1/anthropogenic-deforestation.pdf., Jabr, "How Humanity Unleashed a Flood of New Diseases."
20. Amy Y. Vittor, Gabriel Zorello Laporta, and Maria Anice Mureb Sallum, "Analysis: How Deforestation Helps Deadly Viruses Jump from Animals to Humans," *Public Broadcasting Service*, June 25, 2020, https://www.pbs.org/newshour/science/analysis-how-deforestation-helps-deadly-viruses-jump-from-animals-to-humans., The PBS Article Cites Amy Y. Vittor, William Pan, Robert H Gilman, James Tielsch, Gregory Glass, Tim Shields, Wagner Sánchez-Lozano, et al. "Linking Deforestation to Malaria in the Amazon: Characterization of the Breeding Habitat of the Principal Malaria Vector, Anopheles Darlingi," *The American Journal of Tropical Medicine and Hygiene*, July 2009, https://www.ncbi.nlm.nih.gov/pmc/articles/PMC3757555/. , Ilacqua, Roberto Cardoso, Leonardo Suveges Moreira Chaves, Eduardo Sterlino Bergo, Jan E Conn, Maria Anice Mubeb Sallum, and Gabriel Zorello Laporta, "A Method for Estimating the Deforestation Timeline in Rural Settlements in a Scenario of Malaria Transmission in Frontier Expansion in the Amazon Region," *SciELO*, July 23, 2018, https://www.scielo.br/scielo.php?Script=sci_arttext., B. E.

Barber, T. William, C. Daneshvar, B. Singh, A. J. Henry, C. L. Moyes, J. Cox-Singh, J. Cox-Singh, S B. Millar, B. Singh, P. C. S. Divis, R. Culleton, J. Cox-Singh, et al. "Predicting the Geographical Distributions of the Macaque Hosts and Mosquito Vectors of Plasmodium Knowlesi Malaria in Forested and Non-Forested Areas," BioMed Central, January 1, 1970, https://parasitesandvectors.biomedcentral.com/articles/10.1186/s13071-016-1527-0., Jesús Olivero, John E. Fa, Raimundo Real, Ana L. Márquez, Miguel A. Farfán, J. Mario Vargas, David Gaveau, et al. "Recent Loss of Closed Forests Is Associated with Ebola Virus Disease Outbreaks," *Nature Publishing Group*, October 30, 2017, https://www.nature.com/articles/s41598-017-14727-9.

21. See "Facts about Variant Creutzfeldt-Jakob Disease," European Centre for Disease Prevention and Control, June 26, 2017, https://www.ecdc.europa.eu/en/vcjd/facts, "'Mad Cow Disease': What Is BSE?" *BBC News*, October 18, 2018, https://www.bbc.com/news/uk-45906585., Bugga, "What Do Wet Markets and Factory Farms Have in Common?", and Benatar, "Our Cruel Treatment of Animals Led to the Coronavirus."
22. See "The Burden of the Influenza A H1N1pdm09 Virus since the 2009 Pandemic," Centers for Disease Control and Prevention, June 10, 2019, https://www.cdc.gov/flu/pandemic-resources/burden-of-h1n1.html., "First Global Estimates of 2009 H1N1 Pandemic Mortality Released by CDC-Led Collaboration," Centers for Disease Control and Prevention, June 25, 2012, https://www.cdc.gov/flu/spotlights/pandemic-global-estimates.htm., Bugga, "What Do Wet Markets and Factory Farms Have in Common?", and Macken Murphy, "Coronavirus Should Make You Reconsider Eating Meat," *Sentient Media*, March 18, 2020, https://sentientmedia.org/coronavirus-should-make-you-reconsider-eating-meat/.
23. Michael Worobey, Guan-Zhu Han, and Andrew Rambaut, "A Synchronized Global Sweep of the Internal Genes of Modern Avian Influenza Virus," *Nature Publishing Group*, February 16, 2014, https://www.nature.com/articles/nature13016., Murphy, "Coronavirus Should Make You Reconsider Eating Meat," "1918 Pandemic (H1N1 Virus)," Centers for Disease Control and Prevention, March 20, 2019, https://www.cdc.gov/flu/pandemic-resources/1918-pandemic-h1n1.html.
24. Fiona Harvey, "Jane Goodall: Humanity Is Finished If It Fails to Adapt after Covid-19," *Guardian News and Media*, June 3, 2020, https://www.theguardian.com/science/2020/jun/03/jane-goodall-humanity-is-finished-if-it-fails-to-adapt-after-covid-19., Harvey, "Antibiotic Resistance as Big a Threat as Climate Change—Chief Medic." *Guardian News and Media*, April 29, 2019, https://www.theguardian.com/society/2019/apr/29/antibiotic-resistance-as-big-threat-climate-change-chief-medic-sally-davies.
25. Murphy, "Coronavirus Should Make You Reconsider Eating Meat," Jim O'Neill, "Antimicrobial Resistance: Tackling a Crisis for the Health and Wealth of Nations," Review on Antimicrobial Resistance, accessed December 2014, https://amr-review.org/sites/default/files/AMR%20Review%20Paper%20-%20Tackling%20a%20crisis%20for%20the%20health%20and%20wealth%20of%20nations_1.pdf., O'Neill, "Antimicrobials In Agriculture and the Environment: Reducing Unnecessary Use and Waste," Review on Antimicrobial Resistance, December 2015, https://amr-review.org/sites/default/files/Antimicrobials%20in%20agriculture%20and%20the%20environment%20-%20Reducing%20unnecessary%20use%20and%20waste.pdf.
26. Amy Vittor, Gabriel Zorello Laporta, and Maria Anice Mureb Sallum, "Analysis: How Deforestation Helps Deadly Viruses Jump from Animals to Humans," PBS, June 25, 2020, https://www.pbs.org/newshour/science/analysis-how-deforestation-helps-deadly-viruses-jump-from-animals-to-humans, Manuela Sironi, Seyed E. Hasnain, Benjamin Rosenthal, Tung Phan, Fabio Luciani, Marie-Anne Shaw, M. Anice Sallum, Marzieh Ezzaty Mirhashemi, Serge Morand, and Fernando González-Candelas, "SARS-CoV-2 and COVID-19: A Genetic, Epidemiological, and Evolutionary Perspective," *Infection, Genetics and Evolution* 84 (2020), https://doi.org/10.1016/j.meegid.2020.104384, Linda Givetash, Dawn Liu, and Leou Chen, "After the Coronavirus, China Moves to Kick Its Exotic Meat Habit," *NBC News*, July 6, 2020, https://www.nbcnews.com/news/world/after-coronavirus-china-moves-kick-its-exotic-meat-habit-n1232935, Denise Chow, "Where Did the Coronavirus Come from? Past Outbreaks Provide Hints," *NBC News*, May 6, 2020, https://www.nbcnews.com/science/science-news/where-did-new-coronavirus-come-past-outbreaks-provide-hints-n1144521.
27. See Bugga, "What Do Wet Markets and Factory Farms Have in Common?", and Dina Fine Maron, "'Wet Markets' Likely Launched the Coronavirus. Here's What You Need to Know," *National Geographic*, July 20, 2020, https://www.nationalgeographic.com/animals/2020/04/coronavirus-linked-to-chinese-wet-markets/; also see Aylin Woodward, "Both the new coronavirus and SARS outbreaks likely started in Chinese 'wet market.' Historic photos show what the markets looked like," *Business Insider*, February 26, 2020, https://www.businessinsider.com/wuhan-coronavirus-chinese-wet-market-photos-2020-1. Benatar, "Our Cruel Treatment of Animals Led to the Coronavirus," and Y. Guan, B. J. Zheng, Y. Q. He, X. L. Liu, Z. X. Zhuang, C. L. Cheung, S. W. Luo, et al. "Isolation and Characterization of Viruses Related to the SARS Coronavirus from Animals in Southern China," *American Association for the Advancement of Science*, October 10,

2003, https://science.sciencemag.org/content/302/5643/276., and Matthew Scully, "China's Wet Markets, America's Factory Farming," *National Review*, September 25, 2020, https://www.nationalreview.com/2020/04/chinas-wet-markets-americas-factory-farming-both-violate-moral-common-sense/, Charles C. Camosy, "Nonhuman Animals and the COVID-19 Pandemic," Harvey, "Jane Goodall: Humanity Is Finished If It Fails to Adapt after Covid-19."

28. See Benatar, "Our Cruel Treatment of Animals Led to the Coronavirus," and Patrick Cy Woo, Susanna Kp Lau, and Kwok-Yung Yuen, "Infectious Diseases Emerging from Chinese Wet-Markets: Zoonotic Origins of Severe Respiratory Viral Infections," *Current Opinion in Infectious Diseases* 19 (2006): 401–7, https://doi.org/10.1097/01.qco.0000244043.08264.fc.
29. See Scully, "China's Wet Markets, America's Factory Farming," Scott Neuman, "U.S. Pressures China To Close Wet Markets Thought To Be Source Of COVID-19," *NPR*, April 23, 2020, https://www.npr.org/sections/coronavirus-live-updates/2020/04/23/842178010/u-s-pressures-china-to-close-wet-markets-thought-to-be-source-of-covid-19.
30. Linda Givetash, Dawn Liu, and Leou Chen, "After the Coronavirus, China Moves to Kick Its Exotic Meat Habit," *NBC News*, July 6, 2020, https://www.nbcnews.com/news/world/after-coronavirus-china-moves-kick-its-exotic-meat-habit-n1232935.
31. Jabr, "How Humanity Unleashed a Flood of New Diseases."
32. Caren Chancey, Andriyan Grinev, Evgeniya Volkova, and Maria Rios, "The Global Ecology and Epidemiology of West Nile Virus," Hindawi Publishing Corporation, August 10, 2014, http://downloads.hindawi.com/journals/bmri/2015/376230.pdf., B.F. Allan, et al. "Ecological Correlates of Risk and Incidence of West Nile Virus in the United States," *Oecologia. U.S. National Library of Medicine*, accessed October 23, 2020, https://pubmed.ncbi.nlm.nih.gov/18941794/., Jabr, "How Humanity Unleashed a Flood of New Diseases."
33. "Coronavirus: Fear over Rise in Animal-to-Human Diseases," BBC News, July 6, 2020, https://www.bbc.com/news/health-53314432., Scott Neuman, "U.N. Predicts Rise In Diseases That Jump From Animals To Humans Due To Habitat Loss," *NPR*, July 7, 2020, https://www.npr.org/sections/coronavirus-live-updates/2020/07/06/888077232/u-n-predicts-rise-in-diseases-that-jump-from-animals-to-humans., "Preventing the next Pandemic - Zoonotic Diseases and How to Break the Chain of Transmission," July 6, 2020, https://www.unenvironment.org/resources/report/preventing-future-zoonotic-disease-outbreaks-protecting-environment-animals-and.

UNIT 3

Ethics and Politics

Chapter 9

Dangerous Ideologies

9.1 Overview

As early as the ancient period, there's evidence of numerous ethically disastrous events resulting from the influence of various ways of thinking on political leadership. As discussed in Chapter Ten, the Romans waged numerous wars because of their belief in the glory of conquest. According to Biblical accounts, based on beliefs about the application of religious teachings, the Jews were to stone women accused of extramarital sex.[1] Because of their beliefs about blasphemy, Jewish leaders convinced the Romans to execute a man who many now believe was either God on earth, a prophet, or simply an exemplar of a life well-lived.[2] The Catholic Church implemented the Inquisition fueled by teachings about the evils of non-belief.[1]

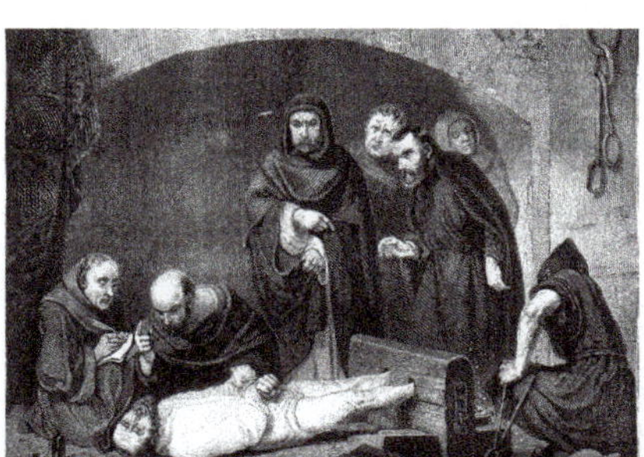

© Morphart Creation/ Shutterstock.com

Engraved illustration of Inquisition torture; Magasin Pittoresque 1841.

© roman tohtohunov/ Shutterstock.com

Tools of the Inquisition; Torture iron masks.

© Sergio Foto/Shutterstock.com

Medieval Inquisition torture device.

1. The Spanish Inquisition of the fifteenth and sixteenth centuries is probably the most horrendous example, though it is only one chapter in the history of Christian inquisitions. See "A Brief History of the Inquisition," University of Notre Dame Hesburgh Libraries Rare Books and Special Collections, accessed October 22, 2020, https://inquisition.library.nd.edu/brief_history.RBSC-INQ:COLLECTION.

Slavery based on firmly-rooted ideas about the racial inferiority of Africans was legally instituted in the American colonies, and later, in the United States of America.[2] Even after its abolition, Jim Crow laws were instituted throughout the country based on theories about inherent differences between races, including long-held notions about the superiority of the white race.[3] Eugenics programs throughout the world violated the rights of people of color and people with disabilities because of assumptions about their inferiority.[4] All of these horrors resulted from dangerous ideas and beliefs, but not all of the examples resulted from ideologies in the sense that Hannah Arendt uses the term below. An **ideology** is a set of beliefs with specific characteristics.

IDEOLOGY
Generally, a systematic or thorough adherence to a set of ideals or principles; in Arendt and perhaps in political philosophy more widely, single-minded or close-minded adherence to a narrow set of ideals, beliefs, or principles, which, despite their narrowness, "can explain everything and every occurrence."[43]

Vintage engraved illustration of Africans taken into slavery; Journal des Voyage 1880–1881.

Nineteenth-century engraving of African slaves yoked together.

Five generations of an African American family, all slaves, all born on the plantation of J. J. Smith in Beaufort, South Carolina.

2. For an account of the psychological origins of racism in the US, See Winthrop D. Jordan, *The White Man's Burden* (New York: Oxford University Press, 1974). For an interactive timeline of slavery in the US, see "A History of Slavery in the United States," *National Geographic*, accessed October 22, 2020, https://www.nationalgeographic.org/interactive/slavery-united-states/.

3. For examples of specific Jim Crow laws, see "Jim Crow Laws," National Park Service, last updated April 17, 2018, https://www.nps.gov/malu/learn/education/jim_crow_laws.htm.

4. For an interactive overview, see Lisa Ko, "Unwanted Sterilization and Eugenics Programs in the United States," PBS Independent Lens, January 29, 2016, https://www.pbs.org/independentlens/blog/unwanted-sterilization-and-eugenics-programs-in-the-united-states/.

Terrorism, based on radical ideologies, has plagued the world since at least the Enlightenment.[5]

Newspaper (German Bild) front page from March 23, 2017; terror incident in London at Westminster Bridge.

November 14, 2015, at the French embassy in Kiev, Ukraine, in memory of victims of Paris terror attacks the day before.

Aerial view of 9/11 Memorial in New York City.

The most gruesome examples of crimes against humanity seem to have emerged in the twentieth century with the rise of totalitarianism. Hitler's ideology about the superiority of the Aryan race and the inherent inferiority of other peoples, especially the Jewish people, resulted in the murder of at least six million Jews during the Holocaust.[6] The implementation of Marx's philosophy in Communist Russia resulted in the rise to power of Stalin's ideology and murderous regime, which may

Hitler on August 19, 1934, when he became Leader and Chancellor of Nazi Germany.

Statue of Joseph Stalin by Zurab Tsereteli at the Livadia Palace, Crimea, where the Yalta Conference was held in 1945.

Chinese propaganda art in Shanghai, China, depicting Mao Zedong; photo taken on February 12, 2013.

5. For prominent examples and brief explanations, see Jeffrey W. Lewis, "Ten Terrorist Attacks in History," *Origins*, March 7, 2016, http://origins.osu.edu/connecting-history/top-ten-origins-terrorist-attacks.
6. For resources about the Holocaust, see the United States Holocaust Memorial Museum website: https://www.ushmm.org/learn.

have claimed more lives than Hitler's.[3] Similar atrocities, on an even larger scale, occurred in Communist China with Mao's ideology and coming to power.[4] 7

POLITICAL PHILOSOPHY
The branch or subdivision of philosophy that focuses on exploring questions such as: What is the common good? What is the best form of government? What constitutes a good leader? This branch of philosophy has been closely intertwined with ethics since Plato.

Read in its own historical context, without the backdrop of the Communist totalitarianism that followed, Marx's **political philosophy** is a comprehensive and systematic attempt to respond to the evils of capitalism, which had reached odious proportions during the Industrial Revolution.8 Many professional scholars today study Marxism as a legitimate philosophy that still has merit, despite the aforementioned atrocious attempts to implement it.9 The political philosophy of Plato's *Republic*, discussed in Chapter One, has had similarly divided interpretations. Some see it as a seriously-proposed political theory with some notably negative features. Karl Popper stands out as a prominent intellectual who took the political proposals of the *Republic* seriously and placed part of the blame on them for the totalitarian regimes in the twentieth century.[5] Many others have seen Plato's political philosophy in the *Republic* as something not to be interpreted at face value, but rather, in a non-literal way.10 An extreme example is Stanley Rosen, who sees the political project of the *Republic* as a work of satire, meant to serve as a warning about the dangers of mixing philosophy and politics.[6]

Like all political philosophies, those of Plato and Marx require careful study and a nuanced approach to understand well. Without such an approach, those who

---

7. Nicole Loring explained in a correspondence with me: The estimates for the death toll in China under Mao are extremely spotty, but it seems as though those from the Great Leap Forward range from 18–45 million. Jonathan Spence does an excellent job describing the crisis of overreporting grain crops and the overcommitment of the CCP to the Soviets, which ultimately led to the famine.

Loring quotes the following from Spence: "As China's investment in industry rose to an amazing 43.4 percent of national income in 1959, grain exports to the Soviet Union were also increased to pay for more heavy machinery. The average amount of grain available to each person in China's countryside, which had been 205 kilos in 1957 and 201 kilos in 1958, dropped to a disastrous 183 kilos in 1959, and a catastrophic 156 kilos in 1960. In 1961 it fell again—to 154 kilos. The result was famine on a gigantic scale, a famine which claimed 20 million lives or more between 1959 and 1962. Many others died shortly thereafter from the effects of the Great Leap—especially children, weakened by years of progressive malnutrition. In the China of 1957, before the Great Leap began, the median age of those dying was 17.6 years; in 1963 it was down to 9.7. Half of those dying in China that year, in other words, were under ten years old. The Great Leap Forward, launched in the name of strengthening the nation by summoning all the people's energies, had turned back on itself and ended by devouring its young." See Spence, *The Search for Modern China*, 3rd ed. (New York: Norton, 2013), 522–523.

Loring explains further: "What's important about this event is that the Great Chinese Famine was not a genocide in the intentional sense of the word, wherein an ethnic/racial/religious in-group actively targets an ethnic/racial/religious out-group for extermination. Instead, this was a series of unintended consequences following strict quota requirements for grain production that were untenable. Local cadres' positions of power within the Chinese Communist Party relied on their local area meeting grain production goals, and so when their farmers failed to do so (often because the farmers had to follow procedures developed by CCP administrators that were not always the most efficient ways to farm), the local leaders simply lied and claimed that they *had*, in fact, met their goal. Years of this overreporting of the grain crops from local officials meant that the central committee in the CCP did not have an accurate understanding of how much grain stores were actually available, and so they oversold grain to the Soviets when it was really needed to feed the people of China."

8. The best known and most widely read example is *The Communist Manifesto*, which Marx co-authored with Friedrich Engels. For a freely available translation, see http://www.gutenberg.org/ebooks/61.

9. See the appendix for background information about the philosophers, time periods, and major historical movements discussed in this chapter.

10. Ancient interpreters of Plato were the first to read the work of Plato figuratively or allegorically. The following contemporary Plato scholars are just a few of many who stand by a symbolic or non-literal interpretation of parts or all of Plato's *Republic*: Eva Brann, *The Music of the Republic* (Philadelphia: Paul Dry Books, 2004); Martin Heidegger, "Plato's Doctrine of Truth," in *Pathmarks*, ed. William McNeill (Cambridge: Cambridge University Press, 1998); Eric Voegelin, *Plato* (Columbia, MO: University of Missouri Press, 1957).

implement those theories are more liable to succumb to radical ideologies, which despite having ostensibly good intentions, may commit serious injustices.

Many of the horrors above resulted from ways of thinking that are more obviously flawed in hindsight, like the theories about the superiority of certain races, or the demand for a religion to legally punish nonbelievers.

QUESTIONS FOR CONSIDERATION

a. How, then, are we to interpret political philosophies today, without letting our ideas about them lead to ideological extremism and the crimes against humanity like those described above that result from flaws in such extremism?
b. Why did so many people not see those flaws when these gross offenses were committed?
c. Are we liable to similar errors, and thus, to further crimes against humanity in our own time?
d. How can we avoid falling into unethical beliefs and actions in the political realm?

This chapter provides a basis for answering such questions, through the lens of *Schindler's List* (1993) and two works by major thinkers of the twentieth century: Emmanuel Levinas and Hannah Arendt.[7]

"Reflections on the Philosophy of Hitlerism" is an essay Emmanuel Levinas wrote just as Hitler was coming to power. It provides profound insight into the ideological roots of Nazism, and proposes three antidotes to help humanity avoid such a dangerous way of thinking. Hannah Arendt[11] wrote a massive treatise on the methods Hitler, Stalin, and Mao used to create their totalitarian systems. This book, *The Origins of Totalitarianism*, contains many insights about political practices that one needs to view with a great deal of caution if one wishes to avoid the resurgence of a government like that of Hitler.[12] Alongside these two works, this chapter focuses on the film *Schindler's List*, which portrays not only the suffering of the victims and survivors

Plaque in front of what was Oskar Schindler's enamel factory, Krakow, Poland.

11. See the appendix of biographies to learn about who these thinkers were.
12. I am grateful for the late Peter Sampo who played a significant role in my learning about Arendt's *Origins of Totalitarianism*.

Railway entrance to Auschwitz Birkenau concentration camp in Oswiecim, Poland, as of February 2018.

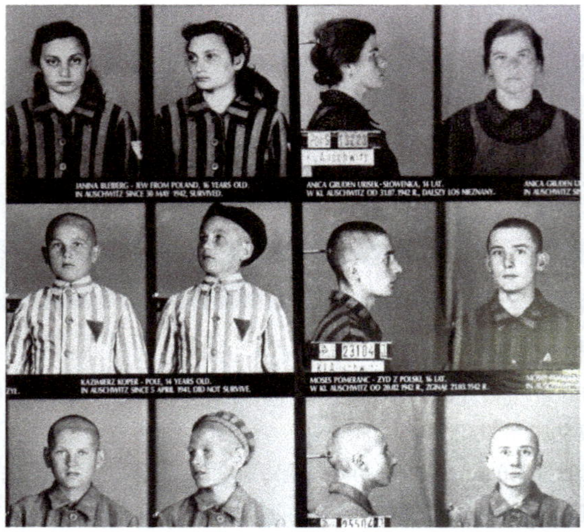

Concentration camp victims photos; Auschwitz Birkenau.

Monument at the former site of the Plaszow concentration camp in Krakow, Poland; memorial to the victims.

of the Holocaust, but the dangerous ways of thinking adopted by its perpetrators. These are but two of the means by which this film brings the work of Levinas and Arendt into relief.

9.2 *Schindler's List* Overview[13]

Directed by Steven Spielberg, and written by Thomas Keneally and Steven Zaillian, *Schindler's List* portrays the character arc of the wealthy entrepreneur Oskar Schindler (Liam Neeson), from a Nazi party member and an exploiter of Jewish labor, to a dissident who saved over a thousand people. Alongside the story of Schindler's life, the film portrays the initial raids on Jewish people's homes in Krakow, Poland, to their internment in ghettos, to their dismal existence in concentration camps, with a focus on Plaszow and Auschwitz.

The film uses strategically-placed details to call the viewer's attention to particular themes. Some examples include the scene of Nazi soldiers playing Mozart while raiding a Jewish home, the little girl in red, the depictions of Jewish material possessions, including the shot of the gold teeth, and the portrayal of water in various significant contexts.[14] The film's focus on Amon Goeth (Ralph Fiennes), administrator of the Plaszow camp,[15] draws out the Nazi obsession with power, with the destruction of Jewish civilization, and with the extinguishing of civilization itself. Itzak Stern (Ben Kingsley) is the film's moral compass, and the chief representative of Judaism. *Schindler's List* portrays in vivid, highly emotional detail, the reduction of humanity, crude materialism, primitiveness, and thirst for blood and

13. Though it is not absolutely necessary to watch the film before reading further, it is strongly recommended. What follows will make much more sense after doing so, including a number of questions for consideration that involve the film.
14. In literature, the symbolism of water includes but is not limited to purification, sadness, and redemption.
15. The film *Hitler's Children* (2011) portrays Goeth as well as the plight of his descendants.

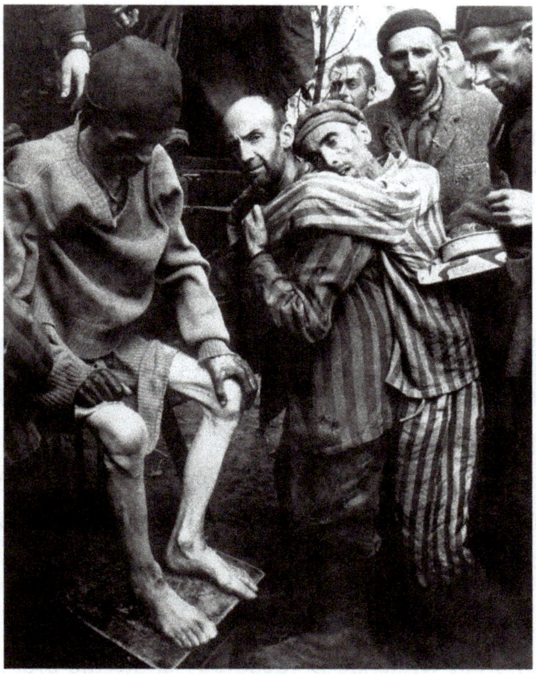

© Everett Collection/Shutterstock.com

Liberated prisoners of Wobbelin Concentration Camp, May 4, 1945.

domination that characterized the executioners of Nazi ideology. It also conveys the redemptive power of forgiveness and mercy, and the contrasting assessments of the value of human life by the Nazis on the one hand, by their Jewish victims on the other, and by Schindler's moral ambiguity. The work of Levinas below conveys a deeply insightful assessment of the inhumanity of Nazi ideology ("Hitlerism"), which Levinas contrasts with not only Judaism, but Christianity and **liberalism**.

9.3 Annotated Excerpts from Levinas's "Reflections on the Philosophy of Hitlerism"

Levinas philosophically draws out the particular nature of the evil that characterized Hitlerism—its **materialism**, **reductionism**, and its **determinism**—in contrast to the redemptive and freeing power of Christianity, Judaism, and liberalism. The following is an article originally written in French for a Catholic journal in 1934, when Levinas was a young man—well before the bulk of his scholarship, and also prior to his family being murdered in the Holocaust.

© AntonGu/Shutterstock.com

© Ilookmah/Shutterstock.com

LIBERALISM
In the classical sense, the tradition associated with attainment of freedom through intellectual activity and consent of those being ruled.

MATERIALISM
In everyday English, the attraction to or obsession with material possessions, such as clothing, furniture, and jewelry; in philosophy, the belief that only the physical really exists; everything in existence is only physical.

REDUCTIONISM
Simplification; sometimes controversial, as in philosophy that reduces the essence of a human being to a brain, or philosophy that reduces personhood to race and religion.

DETERMINISM
Typically opposed to free will; purports that everything that happens is the inevitable result of a strict cause and effect process, which when applied to humans, can rule out the possibility of deviation from such a process by free choice.

9.3.1 The Text: Excerpts from Levinas's Prefatory Note

[. . .]

The article stems from the conviction that the source of the bloody barbarism of National Socialism[16] lies not in some contingent anomaly within human reasoning, nor in some accidental ideological misunderstanding. This article expresses the conviction that this source stems from the essential possibility of *elemental Evil* into which we can be led by logic and against which Western philosophy had not sufficiently insured itself.[8]

QUESTIONS FOR CONSIDERATION

a. Based on the quotation, does Levinas think Hitlerism was a one-time occurrence due to unique misunderstandings or does he think its causes are more pervasive?
b. What role did Western philosophy play in the rise of Hitlerism according to this excerpt?

[. . .]

The philosophy of Hitler is simplistic [. . .]. But the primitive powers that burn within it burst open its wretched phraseology under the pressure of an elementary force. They awaken the secret nostalgia within the German soul. Hitlerism is more than a contagion or a madness; it is an awakening of elementary feelings.

c. Is Levinas saying that Hitlerism was uniquely German?

But from this point on, this frighteningly dangerous phenomenon becomes philosophically interesting. For these elementary feelings harbor a philosophy.

They express a soul's principle attitude towards the whole of reality and its own destiny. They predetermine or prefigure the meaning of the adventure that the soul will face in the world.

Can "feelings harbor a philosophy"? Feelings certainly cannot be the equivalent of a philosophy, and they definitely can motivate, inspire, or support one, but can they "harbor" one?

Recall that Nazism completely determines the value of someone's humanity, and their future, by their racial, religious, and cultural heritage. The Jews in *Schindler's List* were forced to wear a Star of David signifying all that anyone needed to know about their self-worth and their destiny, according to the Nazis.

The philosophy of Hitlerism therefore goes beyond the philosophy of Hitlerians. It questions the very principles of a civilization.[9]

[. . .]

16. Nazism.

d. In your own words, what is Levinas saying in the prefatory note about Hitler's philosophy? Try to be thorough and complete in your response.

9.3.2 Excerpts from Part One of Levinas's Essay

[. . .] True freedom, the true beginning would require a true present, which, always at the peak of a destiny, forever recommences that destiny.

> Levinas focuses on the present, a beginning, and a recommencement of destiny as requirements of freedom, in contrast to ways of thinking that place people into boxes—that restrict people—on the basis of their past.

Judaism bears this magnificent message. Remorse—the painful expression of a radical powerlessness to redeem the irreparable—heralds the repentance that generates the pardon that redeems. Man finds something in the present with which he can modify or efface the past. Time loses its very irreversibility. It collapses at the feet of man like a wounded beast. And he frees it.

> Levinas *may* have in mind certain Jewish holidays that focus on sorrowful events in their past. On these days, Jews remember those events and bring them into the present with specific rituals and/or customs.

QUESTIONS FOR CONSIDERATION

a. How does Judaism relate to the past in a way that frees man, according to Levinas?

[. . .]

[. . .] Christianity proclaims freedom and makes such freedom fully possible.

Not only is the choice of destiny a free one. Once the choice is made, it does not form a chain. Man retains the possibility—a supernatural possibility, certainly, but also a concrete and graspable one—of terminating the contract into which he freely entered.

At any moment he can regain the nudity he had during the first days of creation.[10]

> In Christianity, forgiveness is central. For Roman Catholics, if one confesses their sins, expresses remorse, and does penance, one can be forgiven.

b. Why do you think Levinas uses the notion of a "contract" here? Is it a metaphor?

c. Why do you think Levinas uses the metaphor of "nudity" here?

d. In your own words, what is Levinas saying about the "possibility" that "man retains" in Christianity?
e. How does *Schindler's List* portray forgiveness?

[. . .]

[. . .] The equal dignity of each and every soul, which is independent of the material or social conditions of people,

[. . .]. It is due to the power given to the soul to free itself from *what has been*, from everything that linked it to something or engaged it with something [. . .], so it can regain its first virginity.

> According to Levinas, human dignity does not depend on factors like material possessions, physical traits, and social customs.

The Creation of Eve by Gustave Dore, 1866.

f. Why do you think Levinas uses the metaphor of "virginity"?
g. How is human dignity related to freedom, according to this excerpt?
h. How does Levinas's view of human dignity contrast with Hitler's philosophy?

[. . .]

In the world of liberalism, man is not weighed down by a history in choosing his destiny. He does not experience the possibilities open to him as a series of restless powers that seethe within him and already push him down a determined path. For him, they are only logical possibilities that present themselves to a dispassionate reason that makes choices while forever keeping its distance.[11]

i. What do you think Levinas might mean by "possibilities" here?
j. How does Levinas contrast liberalism to Hitlerism in this excerpt?

MARXISM
The philosophy associated with Karl Marx, which argues for rule by the workers, or proletariat, instead of the wealthy, or bourgeoisie; the workers are to own and control the means of production (capital) rather than the rich. Marx established this philosophy largely in response to the abuse of workers by their employers, who were essentially members of an elite class that owned factories, plants, farms, etc. In its abolition of private property, it can be characterized as Communism (all property is owned communally). Marx was a materialist, meaning that he did not believe in an incorporeal soul or other spiritual entities.

9.3.3 An Excerpt from Section Two

Marxism was the first doctrine in Western history to contest this view of man.

Marxism no longer sees the human spirit as pure freedom, or a soul floating above any attachment. The spirit is no longer a pure reason that partakes in a realm of ends. It is prey to material needs. [. . .][12]

QUESTION FOR CONSIDERATION

a. What is Levinas saying here about the relationship between Marxist materialism and freedom?

[. . .]

9.3.4 Excerpts from Section Three

[. . .]

[. . .] For such people (popular materialists), the whole of the spirit's essence lies in the fact that it is chained to the body.[13]

> Here, Levinas seems to be discussing the materialism that has taken hold in the adherents of racist ideologies, specifically Hitlerism. He is not necessarily characterizing Marx or Marxists.

[. . .] The biological, with the notion of inevitability it entails, becomes more than an object of spiritual life. It becomes its heart. The mysterious urgings of the blood, the appeals of heredity and the past for which the body serves as an enigmatic vehicle, lose the character of being problems that are subject to a solution put forward by a sovereignly free Self. Not only does the Self bring in the unknown elements of these problems in order to resolve them; the Self is also constituted by these elements. Man's essence no longer lies in freedom, but in a kind of bondage [. . .]. To be truly oneself does not mean taking flight once more above contingent events that always remain foreign to the Self's freedom; on the contrary, it means becoming aware of the ineluctable[17] original chain that is unique to our bodies, and above all accepting this chaining.[14]

[. . .]

[. . .] Man no longer finds himself confronted by a world of ideas in which he can choose his own truth on the basis of a sovereign decision made by his free reason. He is already linked to a certain number of these ideas, just as he is linked by birth to all those who are of his blood.[15]

QUESTIONS FOR CONSIDERATION

a. How does materialism lead to the claim that our identity is pre-determined by our ancestry?
b. Why is materialism dangerous, based on Levinas's thoughts above?
c. Does *Schindler's List* portray materialism? How? What do you think the film is conveying about the relationship between Judaism and materialism? Between Nazism and materialism?

17. Unavoidable; inescapable.

Nazi book-burning, 1933.

The Gedaechtnis Kirche in Berlin, a church partially destroyed in WWII, left standing as a stark reminder of the destruction wreaked on Germany by the Nazis.

[. . .]

> [. . .] Perhaps we have succeeded in showing that racism is not just opposed to such and such a particular point in Christian and liberal culture. It is not a particular **dogma** concerning **democracy**, **parliamentary government**, **dictatorial regime**, or religious politics that is in question. It is the very humanity of man.[16]

d. Why is racism a threat to all of humanity, based on Levinas's thoughts above?
e. How does *Schindler's List* portray the Nazis reveling in the destruction of civilization?

DOGMA
A belief, idea, teaching, or principle that is accepted and/or asserted unquestioningly and uncritically, or assumed to be true without the need for proof, evidence, or argument; in Catholicism, it includes core beliefs that are accepted by faith because of divinely revealed truths recorded in Scripture; such core beliefs accepted by faith are nonetheless explained by reason in Catholicism.

DEMOCRACY
In Plato and Aristotle, a system of government in which the poor (who are the majority) rule over the rich (the minority); in modernity, a system of government based on majority rule.

PARLIAMENTARY GOVERNMENT
A form of government in which a group of representatives of the people make and revise laws.

DICTATORSHIP
System of government in which all laws and practices are determined by a single person, without checks on their power such as a congress, parliament, or judiciary.

9.4 Levinas and *Schindler's List*

According to Levinas, National Socialism is not just an anomaly; it's not something that happens just because of a unique series of events; it was not an accident; it was not just an ideological misunderstanding. It came from an elemental evil into which human beings can perennially be led by logic and not just through a lack of rationality.[18] It's fundamental or foundational in that it lies deep within human beings and can be called forth or suppressed. Levinas thinks that Western philosophy had not yet insured itself well enough against the ability for people to be led into such an evil. He clearly thinks that philosophy, by using reason to examine features of Judaism, Christianity, and liberalism, can provide protection against the surfacing of such primitive, primordial evil.

The Christian notion of the dignity of the soul involves the idea that the soul can be freed and can have a second chance. It can be freed from its history. The idea that the soul can be freed from its history is not something that Hitlerism allows for. In National Socialist ideology, people are inextricably linked to their

18. Intellectual elites—people reputed to be highly rational—such as Martin Heidegger, were among those who fell prey to the fallacious logic of Nazism.

racial and cultural past in a deterministic way. One's ancestry and physical makeup determines everything that anyone needs to know about a person. Someone with features deemed inferior is condemned at the outset. There's nothing one can do to redeem or free themselves in this twisted philosophy. For Levinas, not just in Judaism and Christianity, but in liberalism, a human being's destiny is not solely determined by its history. One's history, ancestry, cultural past, religion, and physical features just present logical possibilities from among which we can make choices using reason. One can decide if one is going to follow the religion into which one has been raised, if one will continue the cultural practices of one's family, or if one will use one's physical abilities for this or that.

For a certain kind of materialist, the self is only the body, and one is linked to the physical in such a way that everything one does is utterly and completely determined by one's physicality. There is no possibility for spontaneity, or for reason to introduce an unexpected or unpredictable course of action. Freedom from the cold, hard physical facts does not exist. Not all Marxists are such materialists, and not all materialists are determinists. In fact, not all determinists are completely opposed to acknowledging some freedom of the will. The Nazi, however, is a materialist in the dangerously deterministic sense, according to Levinas.[19] Since this racist ideology is something all human beings are vulnerable to, racism is not just a political issue that's isolated to certain circumstances. It's not just about democracy. It's not an issue of the Left or just of the Right. It's an issue that lies at the heart of the very humanity of man. It's not just opposed to Judaism, Christianity, and liberalism. It's opposed to humanity; to civilization itself. It undermines our freedom, our dignity, and our spiritual identity.

In *Schindler's List*, one sees that the materialism of the Nazis was so severe that even the hair and the gold teeth of the Jews was put to use in ruthless fashion. In fact, the Jews' particular material attributes were valued more than their lives. Their shoes were worth saving, but not their dignity or their lives.

Schindler's List offers examples of how the National Socialist regime embraced 'German culture' but rejected the concept of culture itself. The Nazis are clearing out the homes of the Jews fairly early in the film, and the viewer can observe the juxtaposition between one of the officers playing Mozart while gunfire is strikingly audible in the background. That shooting is presumably killing Jews who were hiding. Another soldier walks in the room and asks if the music is Bach, after which yet another soldier identifies the music as Mozart. The scene suggests the divide between German civilization, art, and culture on the one hand, and the Nazi way of thinking on the other hand.[20] Artistic expression is a mere amusement or distraction for the Nazi soldiers, and it is something they don't really comprehend. The film uses Mozart here to show that one cannot simply equate Nazism with

19. In a correspondence with me, Martin Menke wrote: "And yet, the Nazis promoted the 'Triumph of the Will' as a concept, not just a documentary. The choice in Nazism is whether or not one chooses to fulfill one's pre-determined destiny. Hitler blamed defeat on a lack of will among the Germans."

20. Menke recommends Ralf Dahrendorf's *Society and Democracy in Germany*. In it, Dahrendorf explores the German distinction between culture and civilization. He argues that Germans perceived themselves as a "*Kulturvolk*," something more profound and elemental than a civilization, something more like a form for the substance of culture, but often dissonant from actual culture. See Dahrendorf, *Society and Culture in Germany* (New York: Norton, 1979).

German culture. Rather, Nazism simultaneously rejects the richness of German culture and civilization as a whole. The latter is evident in the scene where Goeth is setting up the Plaskow concentration camp and he and his crew are rejoicing at the destruction of centuries of Jewish civilization, including education, art, and literature. He mentions that the Jews in that area of Poland came there after the plague, had been there for 600 years or so, and they came there with nothing. He specifically says that they did really well in education and other areas, and announces that it's all over. He sees that as a good thing. He and his comrades rejoice at that destruction of civilization. It seems likely that the SS wanted to eliminate Jewish culture in order to deny its existence and value.

Another physical attribute that the Nazis value in the film is technical craftsmanship. There are a few scenes in which people who are musicians or teachers try to get work in the factory so that they could be saved, and they have to lie and say that they are metal workers. The skills they need, and that the Nazis value, are perhaps not even as significant as genuine craftsmanship. People just need to have a knack with metalworking in order for their lives to have any value. The only reason they are worth keeping alive is for the possibility of simple labor. Artistic skill, literary knowledge, the ability to teach, or to be a great musician did not matter at all to Nazi ideology. The film focuses on metal more than is necessary for historical accuracy. Wood, in contrast to metal, has a flexibility or capacity for forgiveness, if you will. Perhaps the continued emphasis on metal reflects the harsh, unforgiving, and even unnatural tendencies of the Nazis.

There's also something clearly primitive about the Nazis portrayed in *Schindler's List*. Goeth best exemplifies the taste for blood and obsession with domination that characterize many of the soldiers and officers in the film. At first, he shoots people who are taking a break, but then he becomes even more indiscriminate. At one point, Schindler convinces him for a short time that power is about having every justification to kill and then not killing. But Goeth has this primitive urge that he can't, or won't, suppress. The rational Schindler introduces a dose of reason that a beast like Goeth cannot stomach.

At the end of the film, Schindler is forgiven by the Jews he saved. He was a Nazi—a full-fledged member of the party. He admits it, and he admits that he initially profited off of Jewish slave labor. The unpredictability and spontaneity of his freely made choice to change his ways is accompanied by the decision of the many freed Jews not to kill him or turn him in once they were able to. He realizes that to the Nazis, the fancy car he held onto was worth two more lives—two more innocent people who could have been saved. He realizes that a piece of gold is worth another human life to them. He falls to his knees and weeps. It almost seems as if he fully realizes at that moment the injustice of what the Nazis were doing, when they reduced human life to material possessions and attributes. He grasps the value of human life when he realizes that it's worth everything he has. He realizes that human life is worth sacrificing his wealth, comfort, and even his security. The question remains about whether or not he forgives himself. As a result of his epiphany, and the catharsis that accompanies it, he carries a great deal of guilt, evidenced by his expressions of pain and his wife trying to console him. Perhaps his remorse is freeing or purifying. Perhaps it is a sign of the punishment that accompanies the evil of Nazism. Goeth is hung, and Schindler is tormented internally despite his conversion from evil to good.

Like Levinas, Hannah Arendt sees philosophy as a possible source of protection against such evil. Her approach examines the political foundations of dangerous ideologies, and through her work, one can develop further resistance to their simplistic appeal.

9.5 Annotated Excerpts from Hannah Arendt's *The Origins of Totalitarianism*

9.5.1 From the Preface to Part Three: Totalitarianism

9.5.1.1 Preface

The original manuscript of *The Origins of Totalitarianism* was finished in autumn 1949, more than four years after the defeat of Hitler Germany, less than four years before Stalin's death. The first edition of the book appeared in 1951. In retrospect, the years I spent writing it, from 1945 onwards, appear like the first period of relative calm after decades of turmoil, confusion, and plain horror—the revolutions after the First World War,[21] the rise of **totalitarian** movements and the undermining of parliamentary government, followed by all sorts of new **tyrannies**, **Fascist** and semi-fascist, one-party and military dictatorships, finally the seemingly firm establishment of totalitarian governments resting on mass support: in Russia in 1929, the year of what is now often called the "second revolution," and in Nazi Germany in 1933.[17]

[. . .]

[. . .] Decisive in our context is that totalitarian government is different from dictatorships and tyrannies; the ability to distinguish between them is by no means an academic issue which could be safely left to the 'theoreticians,' for total domination is the only form of government with which coexistence is not possible. Hence, we have every reason to use the word "totalitarian" sparingly[22] and prudently.[18]

[. . .]

This is a significant statement about political philosophy, and about the limitations of pure theory. According to Arendt, in order to really gain knowledge of the forms of government she discusses, one needs more than theory—one must examine the facts—the data. This is exactly what she does, combing carefully and methodically through the accounts of Hitler's Germany, Stalin's Russia, and Mao's China that were available to her.

TOTALITARIANISM
Arendt distinguishes this system of government from fascism, dictatorship, and tyranny, though it is often associated with those; according to Arendt, it is essentially the all-encompassing, all-inclusive, complete domination of a mass of people by one person or regime; all beliefs, artistic expressions, cultural practices, publications, and even formal and informal public discourse, must completely conform to the will of the ruler and/or regime; Arendt writes, "Totalitarian movements are mass organizations of atomized, isolated individuals. Compared with all other parties and movements, their most conspicuous external characteristic is their demand for total, unrestricted, unconditional, and unalterable loyalty of the individual member."[44]

TYRANNY
A form of government by a leader who has no care or regard for the well-being of those being ruled; such a leader only does what he considers good or pleasing for himself, and is typically seen as evil by everyone else.

FASCISM
Authoritarian, autocratic movement or system of government; declarations of such fascist leaders may be arbitrary in that they are not based on reasoned judgment or established rule of law; such leaders are typically not challenged or criticized, and their declarations are carried out unquestioningly; often associated with nationalism.

21. World War I, or the "Great War," which took place mostly in Europe from 1914–1918.
22. Martin Menke wrote in a correspondence with me: "This is important. Some scholars have discounted totalitarianism as a viable concept just because of this. I would argue that some regimes have totalitarian aspirations but historically this seems impossible to achieve."

9.5.1.2 Stalin, Propaganda,[23] and Control of the Press

> [. . .] The Stalin regime was ruthlessly consistent: all facts that did not agree, or were likely to disagree, with the official fiction—data on crop-yields, criminality, true incidences of 'counter-revolutionary' activities as distinguished from the later conspiracy fictions—were treated as non-facts. [. . .]

QUESTIONS FOR CONSIDERATION

a. Why is such control over the press problematic?
b. Can you think of any recent leaders, governments, or corporate entities that have acted similarly to Stalin in this regard?

[. . .]

9.5.1.3 What Held Totalitarian Regimes Together

> [. . .] We always suspected, but we now know that the regime was never 'monolithic' but 'consciously constructed around overlapping, duplicating, and parallel functions,' and that this grotesquely amorphous structure was kept together by the same Fuehrer-principle—the so-called 'personality cult'—we find in Nazi Germany.[19] [. . .]

[. . .]

Woman weeping in the Sudetenland while saluting the victorious Hitler in 1938.

A large crowd saluting Hitler upon his arrival at the opening of the 1936 Olympic Games in Berlin, Germany. The stadium still stands in Berlin and its street, once bearing Hitler's name, was renamed after Jesse Owens, an African American athlete who defied Hitler's Aryan philosophy by winning four gold medals in the 1936 Olympics. See clips of Owens here: Team USA, "Jesse Owens Makes History at the 1936 Olympic Games. . .", June 14, 2018, YouTube video, 0:24, https://www.youtube.com/watch?time_continue=2&v=aHGM8GyzXn0&feature=emb_logo.

23. Propaganda includes media of any form designed to influence the beliefs of its recipients, and that tends to distort or ignore the truth for the sake of that influence.

c. What do you think Arendt means by "personality cult"?
d. How did it affect the totalitarian governments of Stalin and Hitler?
e. Can you think of a modern example of a cult of personality?

9.5.1.4 A Method of Control Over the Masses: Conspiracy-Fueled Ideology

> The most dramatic new element in this last purge (of 1952), which Stalin planned in the last years of his life, was a decisive shift in ideology, the introduction of a Jewish world conspiracy. [. . .] It now became startlingly clear how deep an impression this mainstay of Nazi ideology must have made on Stalin—the first indications of this had been in evidence ever since the Hitler-Stalin pact[24]—partly, to be sure, because of its obvious propaganda value in Russia as in all of the satellite countries, where anti-Jewish feeling was widespread and anti-Jewish propaganda had always enjoyed great popularity, but partly also because this type of a fictitious world conspiracy provided an ideologically more suitable background for totalitarian claims to world rule than Wall Street, capitalism, and imperialism.[25] [. . .][20]

f. Why would a conspiracy about a certain group of people help a totalitarian dictator, or any leader, exert control over the masses?
g. What are the dangers of such a conspiracy?
h. What evidence of Hitler's perceived Jewish conspiracy against Germany or the world did you observe in *Schindler's List*?
i. Can you think of a recent example of a similar conspiracy theory?

Monument in Elista, Russia, to the Kalmyk victims of Stalin.

24. The agreement between Hitler and Stalin that they would not attack each other; Stalin trusted Hitler and was quite surprised, shocked, and concerned when Hitler violated the pact.
25. Menke wrote in a correspondence with me that he'd "argue the USSR did not need National Socialist antisemitism to augment historical Russian antisemitism."

9.5.2 Excerpts from Chapter Ten: A Classless Society

[. . .] Hitler [. . .] during his lifetime exercised a fascination to which allegedly no one was immune [. . .] Fascination is a social phenomenon, and the fascination Hitler exercised over his environment must be understood in terms of the particular company he kept. Society is always prone to accept a person offhand for what he pretends to be, so that a crackpot posing as a genius always has a certain chance to be believed. In modern society, with its characteristic lack of discerning judgment, this tendency is strengthened, so that someone who not only holds opinions but who also presents them in a tone of unshakeable conviction will not so easily forfeit his prestige, no matter how many times he has been demonstrably wrong.[21] [. . .]

DEMAGOGUE
A person who uses rhetoric to influence, persuade, and possibly control groups of people; in Book Eight of Plato's *Republic*, the demagogue comes to be in the anarchic stage of democracy, and when he takes power, he becomes a tyrant.

QUESTIONS FOR CONSIDERATION

a. Does *Schindler's List* portray any of the "fascination" with Hitler (or other Nazi leaders) that Arendt mentions above?
b. What is Arendt saying here about society's reception of Hitler?
c. Do you think our society now is just as vulnerable to the effects of such a demagogue?
d. What can we do to protect ourselves from such an influence according to Levinas?

[. . .]

[. . .] Hitler's rise to power was legal in terms of majority rule and neither he nor Stalin could have maintained the leadership of large populations, survived many interior and exterior crises, and braved the numerous dangers of relentless intra-party struggles if they had not had the confidence of the masses. [. . .] The widespread belief that Hitler was simply an agent of German industrialists and that Stalin was victorious in the succession struggle after Lenin's death only through a sinister conspiracy are both legends which can be refuted by many facts but above all by the leaders' indisputable popularity. [. . .] Experience has proved time and again that the propaganda value of evil deeds and general contempt for moral standards is independent of mere self-interest, supposedly the most powerful psychological factor in politics.

e. Arendt is expressing a claim above that is similar to one of Levinas's core claims. What is it?
f. What does Arendt mean in the last sentence of the above excerpt? Do you agree? Why or why not?
g. Is "contempt for moral standards" a powerful influence on Nazis in *Schindler's List*?
h. What possible solution to such a "psychological factor" does Levinas present?

IDEALISM
In everyday English, the tendency to value principles or ideals highly, in a way that may be impractical; usually opposed to realism; in philosophy, it can denote the belief that only the nonphysical or spiritual really exists; in philosophy, it can also denote Kant's philosophy and its followers, in that things-in-themselves cannot be truly experienced or known.

The attraction of evil and crime for the mob mentality is nothing new. [. . .] The fanaticism of totalitarian movements, contrary to all forms of **idealism**, breaks down the moment the movement leaves its fanaticized followers in the lurch, killing in them any remaining conviction that might have survived the collapse of the movement itself. But within the organizational framework of the movement, so long as it holds together, the fanaticized members can be reached by neither experience nor argument; identification with the movement and total conformism seem to have destroyed the very capacity for experience, even if it be as extreme as torture or the fear of death.[22]

[. . .]

Totalitarian movements are possible wherever there are masses who for one reason or another have acquired the appetite for political organization. Masses are not held together by a consciousness of common interest and they lack that specific class articulateness which is expressed in determined, limited, and obtainable goals. The term masses applies only where we deal with people who either because of sheer numbers, or indifference, or a combination of both, cannot be integrated into any organization based on common interest, into political parties or municipal governments or professional unions or trade unions. Potentially, they exist in every country and form the majority of those large numbers of neutral, politically indifferent people who never join a party and hardly ever go to the polls.

People saluting Hitler on October 9, 1935, at a meeting in the Kroll Opera in Berlin.

It was characteristic of the rise of the Nazi movement in Germany and of the Communist movements in Europe after 1930 that they recruited their members from this mass of apparently indifferent people whom all other parties had given up as too apathetic or too stupid for their attention. The result was that the majority of their membership consisted of people who never before had appeared on the political scene. This permitted the introduction of entirely new methods into political propaganda, and indifference to the arguments of political opponents [. . .][23]

i. In the three preceding excerpts, what is Arendt saying about the people who supported Stalin and Hitler?
j. Why were Hitler and Stalin able to manipulate such people?
k. Do you think your own society includes a population that fits some (or possibly all) of Arendt's description? Why or why not?
l. What could a government and its citizens do to ensure that such a population does not form?
m. What do you think is the most productive way for governments and their citizens to interact with people who seem to resemble the population Arendt describes?

[. . .]

What is more disturbing to our peace of mind than the unconditional loyalty of members of totalitarian movements, and the popular support of totalitarian regimes, is the unquestionable attraction these movements exert on the elite, and not only on the mob elements in society. It would be rash indeed to discount, because of artistic vagaries or scholarly naivete, the terrifying roster of distinguished men whom totalitarianism can count among its sympathizers, fellow-travelers, and inscribed party members.[24]

n. How does *Schindler's List* portray the attraction of "elite" members of German society to Nazism?
o. Do you know of elites in any modern nation who are attracted to the regime of a dictator?

[. . .]

The pronounced activism of the totalitarian movements, their preference for terrorism over all other forms of political activity, attracted the intellectual elite and the mob alike. [. . .] What proved so attractive was that terrorism had become a kind of philosophy through which to express frustration, resentment, and blind hatred [. . .][25]

[. . .]

[. . .] Totalitarianism in power invariably replaces all first-rate talents, regardless of their sympathies, with those crackpots and fools whose lack of intelligence and creativity is still the best guarantee of their loyalty.[26]

p. Does *Schindler's List* portray anyone who could be described as a "crackpot" or a "fool" and who was nonetheless in a position of leadership?
q. Do you know of any recent governments or corporations in the world that gave power and responsibility to people just because of their loyalty, and not their abilities?

9.5.3 Excerpts from Arendt, Chapter Eleven: The Totalitarian Movement

[. . .] The chief qualification of a mass leader has become unending infallibility; he can never admit an error. [. . .][27]

QUESTIONS FOR CONSIDERATION

a. Is it the mark of a good leader to admit fallibility? Why or why not? If so, to what extent?

[. . .]

[. . .] Before mass leaders seize the power to fit reality to their lies, their propaganda is marked by its extreme contempt for facts as such, for in their opinion fact depends entirely on the power of man who can fabricate it.[28] [. . .]

RELATIVISM
Typically opposed to objectivity; purports individual or subjective determination, differing on a case-by-case basis, rather than universal or objective determination; in morality, when taken to an extreme, indicates that each person decides what is right for themselves, in such a way that can vary wildly from others, from convention, from religious doctrines, or from ethical theories; when taken to an extreme, would agree with the idea that someone can rightfully be a Nazi if they think it's right for them.

b. Recall previous discussions in this textbook about **relativism**. What is Arendt saying here about relativism?
c. What would a Kantian think about a leader who lies? Why?

[. . .]

The most efficient fiction of Nazi propaganda was the story of a Jewish world conspiracy. Concentration on anti-Semitic propaganda had been a common device of demagogues ever since the end of the nineteenth century, and was widespread in the Germany and Austria of the twenties. [. . .]

[. . .] Exaggerated notions of Jewish world power [. . .] can be traced back to the end of the eighteenth century, when the intimate connection between Jewish business and nation-states had become visible. The representation of the Jew as the incarnation of evil is usually blamed on remnants and superstitious memories from the Middle Ages, but is actually more closely connected with the more ambiguous role which Jews played in European society since their emancipation. One thing was undeniable: in the postwar period Jews had become more prominent than ever before.[29]

d. How does *Schindler's List* portray anti-Semitic ideas?
e. How does *Schindler's List* portray the prominence of Jewish people in Germany whom Arendt describes?

9.5.4 Excerpts from Chapter Twelve: Totalitarianism in Power

[. . .]

Total domination, which strives to organize the infinite plurality and differentiation of human beings as if all humanity were just one individual, is possible only if each and every person can be reduced to a never-changing identity of reactions, so that each of these bundles of reactions can be exchanged at random for any other. The problem is to fabricate something that does not exist, namely, a kind of human species resembling other animal species [. . .]

[. . .]

The camps are meant not only to exterminate people and degrade human beings, but also serve the ghastly experiment of eliminating, under scientifically controlled conditions, spontaneity itself as an expression of human behavior and of transforming the human personality into a mere thing, into something that even animals are not [. . .].[30]

[. . .]

[. . .] Hell in the most literal sense was embodied by those types of camp perfected by the Nazis, in which the whole of life was thoroughly and systematically organized with a view to the greatest possible torment. [. . .][31]

[. . .]

The real horror began, however, when the SS[26] took over the administration of the camps. The old spontaneous bestiality gave way to an absolutely cold and systematic destruction of human bodies, calculated to destroy human dignity; death was avoided or postponed indefinitely. The camps were no longer amusement parks for beasts in human form, that is, for men who really belonged in mental institutions, and prisons; the reverse became

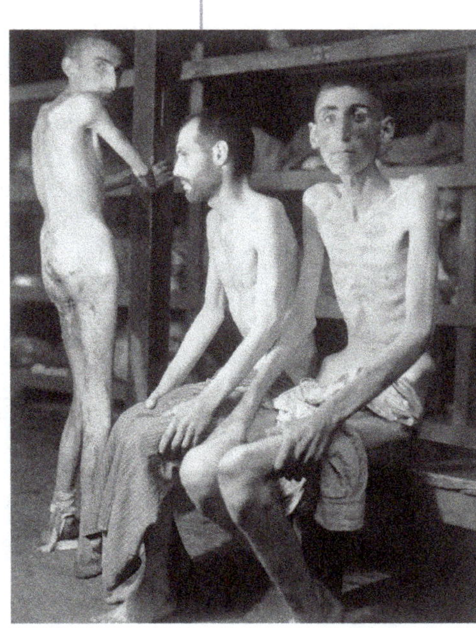

© Everett Collection/Shutterstock.com

Slave laborers at Buchenwald concentration camp on April 16, 1945.

© Militarist/Shutterstock.com

SS insignia.

26. *Schutzstaffel*; Nazi special police that included the Gestapo; included Hitler's bodyguards and the administrators of concentration camps.

true: they were turned into 'drill grounds,' on which perfectly normal men were trained to be full-fledged members of the SS.[32]

QUESTIONS FOR CONSIDERATION

a. How does *Schindler's List* portray the aspects of concentration camps that are similar to Arendt's description above?
b. Do you think that the concentration camp administrators and guards portrayed in *Schindler's List* resemble "beasts in human form" or "normal men who were trained to be full-fledged members of the SS"? Did some resemble the former and did others resemble the latter?
c. How is Arendt's description of the effects of the camps on people similar to Levinas's characterization of the way Hitlerism reduces people's humanity?

[. . .]

[. . .] It is more significant that those individually condemned to death very seldom attempted to take one of their executioners with them, that there were scarcely any serious revolts, and that even in the moment of liberation there were very few spontaneous massacres of SS men. For to destroy individuality is to destroy spontaneity, man's power to begin something new out of his own resources, something that cannot be explained on the basis of reactions to environment and events. Nothing then remains but ghastly marionettes with human faces, which all behave like the dog in Pavlov's experiments,[27] which all react with perfect reliability even when going to their own death, and which do nothing but react.[33]

Roll call at Buchenwald concentration camp (ca. 1938–1941); notice two prisoners in foreground supporting a man, and perhaps saving him from being killed.

27. Famous experiments using rewards and punishments to train dogs into consistent, highly predictable behavior.

d. What is Arendt's explanation for the low number of revolts in WWII concentration camps?

[. . .]

It is chiefly [. . .] for the sake of complete consistency, that it is necessary for totalitarianism to destroy every trace of what we call human dignity. For respect for human dignity implies the recognition of my fellow men or our fellow-nations as subjects, as builders of worlds or co-builders of a common world. No ideology which aims at the explanation of all historical events of the past and at mapping out the course of all events in the future can bear the unpredictability which springs from the fact that men are creative, that they can bring forward something so new that nobody ever foresaw it.[34]

[. . .]

e. What does it mean to "respect" "human dignity" according to Arendt?
f. In what way does totalitarian ideology attempt to snuff out human dignity according to the above excerpt?
g. How does *Schindler's List* portray the value of human life?
h. What dignifies human beings according to *Schindler's List*? Material possessions? Forgiveness? Authenticity? Integrity? Power? Remorse?
i. How does natural law respect human dignity? How does deontological ethics do so? Utilitarianism?

9.5.5 Excerpts from Chapter Thirteen: Ideology and Terror: A Novel Form of Government

[. . .]

If it is true that the elements of totalitarianism can be found by retracing the history and analyzing the political implications of what we usually call the crisis of our century, then the conclusion is unavoidable that this crisis is no mere threat from the outside, no mere result of some aggressive foreign policy of either Germany or Russia, and that it will no more disappear with the death of Stalin than it disappeared with the fall of Nazi Germany. It may even be that the true predicaments of our time will assume their authentic form—though not necessarily the cruelest—only when totalitarianism has become a thing of the past.[35]

QUESTIONS FOR CONSIDERATION

a. What is Arendt saying about the way in which totalitarianism came to be in Germany and Russia? Is this similar to Levinas's explanation of the causes of the rise of Hitlerism?

[. . .]

[. . .] The ideal subject of totalitarian rule is not the convinced Nazi or the convinced Communist, but people for whom the distinction between fact and fiction (i.e., the reality of experience) and the distinction between true and false (i.e., the standards of thought) no longer exist.[36]

b. Why do you think Arendt makes the claim above about the "ideal" subjects of totalitarianism? Do you agree or disagree?
c. What are the implications of her claim, if it is true, on current societal conditions?

[. . .]

Loneliness, the common ground for terror, the essence of totalitarian government, and for ideology or logicality, the preparation of its executioners and victims, is closely connected with uprootedness and superfluousness[28] which have been the curse of modern masses since the beginning of the industrial revolution and have become acute with the rise of imperialism at the end of the last century and the break-down of political institutions and social traditions in our own time. To be uprooted means to have no place in the world, recognized and guaranteed by others; to be superfluous means not to belong to the world at all. Uprootedness can be the preliminary condition for superfluousness, just as isolation can (but must not) be the preliminary condition for loneliness.[37]

[. . .]

Loneliness is not solitude. Solitude requires being alone whereas loneliness shows itself most sharply in company with others. [. . .] In solitude [. . .] I am 'by myself,' 'together with my self, and therefore two-in-one, whereas in loneliness I am actually one, deserted by all others.[38]

[. . .]

What makes loneliness so unbearable is the loss of one's own self which can be realized in solitude, but confirmed in its identity only by the trusting and untrustworthy company of my equals. In this situation, man loses trust in himself as the partner of his thoughts and that elementary confidence in the world which is necessary to make experiences at all.[39]

d. What is the difference between loneliness and solitude according to Arendt?
e. What can cause the loneliness she describes?
f. Why is loneliness so problematic according to Arendt?
g. What do you think modern societies can do to prevent the loneliness Arendt describes?

9.6 Hannah Arendt and *Schindler's List*

The shots of the young girl taunting the recently uprooted Jews provides a window into the mentality of the masses who supported Hitler. Perhaps the fact that she is a child represents the primitive, irrational nature of Nazi ideology, and the ignorant simple-mindedness of those who supported it. As a child, the ability to distinguish fact from fiction makes her the perfect candidate for supporting totalitarianism. Scenes of Jewish people, including children, trying to escape discovery by Nazi soldiers, occur several times during the film in different contexts. Such scenes illustrate

28. Extra, dispensable, unnecessary.

the all-encompassing nature of totalitarian rule, and the difficulty of escaping its ruthless attempt to spread its control everywhere and over everyone. Shots of Jews' personal possessions, even down to gold teeth and shoes, evoke the totality of their domination by Nazism. Human dignity is snuffed out in the camps, portrayed in many ways, including but not limited to prisoners being made to run around naked and malnourished for selection, being forced to live in filthy conditions, having their corpses discarded like garbage, and being killed arbitrarily on the whims of power-crazed officers. The hellish nature of the camps, to use Arendt's phrasing, comes into relief in *Schindler's List*, but by no means into full relief. As a mainstream film, the very worst horrors of the Holocaust could not be included. One must turn to other sources, including documentaries, for a fuller picture, and even then, the full horror probably still remains incomprehensible. Rather than foisting unremittent horror and anguish on viewers, the film directs us to the possibility of conversion, repentance, cleansing, forgiveness, and hope with its water-related imagery and the story of Schindler and the many he saved.[29]

9.7 Fallacies and Cognitive Errors That Contribute to Racist Ideologies

- **Hasty generalization**: The logical fallacy that makes a claim about an entire population based on an inadequate sample; proper sampling requires fulfilling many statistical criteria, but we have a tendency to make blanket statements about populations based on data that are skewed, incomplete, one-sided, or problematic in other ways. Sometimes, racism occurs based on highly individualized anecdotal evidence, which deviates even further from a proper survey.
- **Appeal to the people**: The logical fallacy that relies on the incorrect assumption that because many people do something or think something, it must be right; this is utilized as a manipulative technique in advertising and political rallies especially. When it occurs in the latter, it is often heightened by the emotion stirred up by one's surroundings. Large groups of people often do things, say things, and believe things for poor reasons, or for no reason. The mere assent to something by a group, then, is not a good reason to accept something as right or true. Some exceptions include situations in which crowdsourcing is called for. Perhaps the practice of checking online reviews for a restaurant or product can be an exception if certain cautions are observed.
- **The Dunning-Kruger Effect**: The cognitive error stemming from not being aware of one's ignorance or inability; double delusion; ignorance of ignorance; see Chapter One and the "Allegory of the Cave" for Plato's take on such ignorance and delusion. As Loring explains: Dunning-Kruger is even more than being unaware of one's ignorance—it's that the more

29. Some find this relatively upbeat ending to be problematic. Another issue, according to Menke (in a correspondence with me), is that the film did not portray the rarity of rescuers like Schindler.

ignorant you are, the more likely you are to THINK you know a lot or performed well. This also means that people who do know a lot tend to underestimate their own knowledge or performance. For instance, students who performed badly on a midterm exam are more likely to expect high scores, while students who performed very well on the midterm exam expect much lower scores than they actually got.[30]

9.8 For Further Study

9.8.1 Books

Man's Search for Meaning, by Viktor Frankl: An autobiographical account of life in Auschwitz about finding hope and motivation in meaning[40]

Night, by Elie Wiesel: Autobiographical account of life in Auschwitz and Buchenwald concentration camps[41]

The Communist Manifesto, by Marx and Engels. For a freely available translation, see Project Gutenberg: http://www.gutenberg.org/ebooks/61.

The Drowned and the Saved, by Primo Levi, Auschwitz survivor. See especially Chapter Two: "The Gray Zone."[42]

9.8.2 Online Sources

National Geographic, "The Last Voices of World War II": https://www.nationalgeographic.co.uk/the-last-voices-world-war-ii.

For resources about the Holocaust, see https://www.ushmm.org/learn.

9.8.3 Websites for Information about Experiential Learning

Index of Holocaust memorials and museums in the US: https://www.jewishvirtuallibrary.org/u-s-holocaust-museums-memorials

List of World War II memorials throughout the world: https://en.wikipedia.org/wiki/Category:World_War_II_memorials_by_country

Oskar Schindler's enamel factory, Krakow, Poland: https://www.muzeum-krakowa.pl/branches/oskar-schindlers-factory

Auschwitz Birkenau concentration camp in Oswiecim, Poland: http://auschwitz.org/en/

Monument at the former site of the Plaszow concentration camp in Krakow, Poland: https://www.atlasobscura.com/places/krakow-plaszow-concentration-camp

The Gedaechtnis Kirche in Berlin: https://www.berlin.de/en/museums/3110106-3104050-kaiser-wilhelm-gedaechtnis-kirche.en.html

30. For more about the Dunning-Kruger effect, see: "The Dunning-Kruger Effect," *Psychology Today*, accessed October 22, 2020, https://www.psychologytoday.com/us/basics/dunning-kruger-effect. For details about more cognitive biases, see: "Bias," *Psychology Today*, accessed October 22, 2020, https://www.psychologytoday.com/us/basics/bias.

Site of the 1936 Olympic Games in Berlin, Germany: https://olympiastadion.berlin/en/sightseeing/

Memorial to the Murdered Jews in Europe, in Berlin, Germany (adjacent to Hannah Arendt Street): https://www.berlin.de/en/attractions-and-sights/3560249-3104052-memorial-to-the-murdered-jews-of-europe.en.html

Monument in Elista, Russia to the Kalmyk victims of Stalin: http://www.kalmykia.net/sights/monument-exodus-and-return/#more-2016

Endnotes

1. See Deuteronomy 23:20–21 and John 8:1–11.
2. See Matthew 26:57–68; Mark 14:53–65; Luke 22:66–71; 23:1–25; and John 18:28–40.
3. See Arendt, *Origins of Totalitarianism* (New York: Harcourt, 1968), xxix.
4. Ibid., xxvi.
5. See Popper, *The Open Society and Its Enemies* Vol. 1 (Princeton: Princeton University Press, 1945).
6. Stanley Rosen, *Plato's Republic: A Study* (New Haven: Yale University Press, 2008).
7. All details about the production of films discussed in this chapter, as well as the actors who starred in those films, is from IMDb. See https://www.imdb.com/.
8. Emmanuel Levinas, "Reflections on the Philosophy of Hitlerism," trans. Sean Hand, *Critical Inquiry* 17 (1990): 63.
9. Ibid., 64.
10. Ibid., 65.
11. Ibid., 66.
12. Ibid., 67.
13. Ibid., 68.
14. Ibid., 69.
15. Ibid., 70.
16. Ibid., 71.
17. Arendt, xxiii.
18. Ibid., xxvii–xxviii.
19. She is quoting Merle Fainsod, *How Russia is Ruled* (Cambridge: Cambridge University Press, 1959), 71, 93. Arendt, xxxii.
20. Ibid., xxxix–xl.
21. Ibid., 305.
22. Ibid., 306–308.
23. Ibid., 311–312.
24. Ibid., 326.
25. Ibid., 331–332.
26. Ibid., 339.
27. Ibid., 348–349.
28. Ibid., 350. Recall relativism.
29. Ibid., 354.
30. Ibid., 438.
31. Ibid., 445.
32. Ibid., 454. The quoted phrase is of Eugen Kogon.
33. Ibid., 455.
34. Ibid., 458.
35. Ibid., 460.
36. Ibid., 474.
37. Ibid., 475.
38. Ibid., 476.
39. Ibid., 477.
40. Frankl, *Man's Search for Meaning* (Cutchogue, NY: Buccaneer Books, 1959, 1962, 1984, 1992).
41. Wiesel, *Night* (New York: Hill and Wang, 1972, 1985).
42. Levi, *The Drowned and the Saved* (New York: Simon and Schuster, 1986, 1988).
43. Arendt, 468.
44. Ibid., 323.

Chapter 10

Just War Theory

10.1 *The Vietnam War* Documentary Mini-Series

The Vietnam War (2017) ten-part mini-series by Burns and Novick spans the entire Vietnam War, from its nineteenth- and early twentieth-century roots, to the collapse of the South Vietnamese government in Saigon (now Ho Chi Minh City) on April 30, 1975. It even briefly treats the subsequent American involvement in the country.[1] Each installment combines firsthand accounts of soldiers, government officials, activists, and journalists with photos and videos composed of real footage rather than reenactments. Burns and Novick include the testimony not only of Americans who experienced the war, but that of Vietnamese people. Former North Vietnamese Army and Viet Cong soldiers are among the interviewees. This series highlights many ethical issues of the war and focuses intently on some that are central to Just War Theory.

1. Note to the reader: It is recommended, but not necessary, to watch some or all of this film series, in order to clearly understand this chapter up to section 10.5.2, after which point the chapter will not make much sense to a reader who has not watched at least a few installments of the docu-series. Before watching, jot down the basic tenets of modern Just War Theory, which are listed in 10.5.2. Keep these in mind while viewing each installment. The best reading experience can be achieved by watching all ten installments attentively. One can locate the platforms on which the series is available by looking it up on a website like justwatch.com. In the event that it is not freely available anywhere, which was the case for part of 2020, the reader will either need to purchase a copy or obtain it from a local or university library. See *The Vietnam War*, directed by Ken Burns and Lynn Novick (Florentine Films, 2017), https://www.imdb.com/title/tt1877514/?ref_=ttco_co_tt.

Aerial view of modern-day Ho Chi Minh City.

Bui Vien Street, Ho Chi Minh City, 2018.

10.2 Assessing the Justice of War

The Vietnam War remains among the costliest in several measures, especially lives lost.[2] Charles Hirschman, Samuel Preston, and Vu Manh Loi use modern demography to estimate the number of Vietnamese killed to be one million, which they say is a lower estimate than the other notable ones to which they compared theirs.[1] Vietnam officially estimates the number of civilian deaths as potentially as many as two million.[2] The goal of the war was to stop the spread of communism to Vietnam, which was not achieved.[3] According to Gallup, since 1968, more Americans have viewed the Vietnam War as a mistake than those who have approved of US involvement. As of 2000, 69 percent of Americans see US fighting in Vietnam as a mistake.[3]

---

2. 47, 434 US solders are among the dead from the Vietnam War, according to The Department of Veterans' Affairs. See "America's Wars," Department of Veterans Affairs, November 2019, https://www.va.gov/opa/publications/factsheets/fs_americas_wars.pdf.

3. See the appendix for context about the philosophical origins of Communism in Marx's philosophy as well as the spread of Communism throughout the world. Consider Chapter Nine for context about why many people throughout the world considered the spread of Communism to be highly detrimental to humankind.

Despite these figures, the US has waged a number of other foreign interventions since Vietnam, most notably the Iraq War and the War in Afghanistan.[4] Though American military deaths from the latter two wars number much lower than Vietnam,[5] utilitarian cost versus benefit analyses of those wars indicate a mixed assessment of their rectitude. *The Washington Post* estimates that over half a million Iraqis were killed from 2003 to 2018,[4] and "Iraq Body Count," a source recommended by that newspaper, places the documented civilian death toll between 185,084 to 208,029 as of June 2020.[5] The goal of deposing Saddam Hussein clearly was achieved. It is very difficult, however, to assess how many lives were saved by destroying his regime as well as by killing or capturing terrorists in the course of the war. Pew surveys indicate a rise in American disapproval of the Iraq War from 20 percent in 2003 to 54 percent in 2007.[6] The Watson Institute of International and Public Affairs at Brown University reports that as of January 2020, about 157,000 people have been killed in the Afghanistan war since 2001, including over 43,000 civilians.[6] The war was waged in response to the September 11, 2001, terror attacks, which killed 2,977 American civilians.[7] Just as is the case with the Iraq War, it is very difficult to assess the number of lives saved from terror attacks as a result of terrorists killed or captured in the war.[7] Another major goal of the war was the destruction of the Taliban, and although they suffered severe losses in their ranks and their territory, as of June 2020, they still remained in Afghanistan and still controlled some territory. As of 2019, according to Gallup, 52 percent of Americans thought US fighting in Afghanistan was not a mistake, versus 43 percent who thought it was.[8]

TABLE 10.1

	Civilian Deaths	US Military Deaths	Early Disapproval	Later Disapproval
Vietnam War	<2,000,000	47,434	24% (1965)	69% (2000)
Iraq War	185,084–208,029	4,418	22% (2003)	54% (2007)
War in Afghanistan	>43,000	2,219	44% (2013)	43% (2019)[9]

4. For an overview of the US war in Iraq, see Edward Wong, "Overview: The Iraq War," *The New York Times*, February 15, 2008, https://archive.nytimes.com/www.nytimes.com/ref/timestopics/topics_iraq.html. For an overview of the US war in Afghanistan, see "Why is there a war in Afghanistan? The short, medium, and long story," BBC News, February 29, 2020, https://www.bbc.com/news/world-asia-49192495.

5. As of June 1, 2020, the U.S. Department of Defense reports 4,418 total American military deaths in Operation Iraqi Freedom, including 3,481 killed in action. It also reports 2,219 U.S. military deaths in Afghanistan, including 1,833 killed in action, from Operation Enduring Freedom. See "Casualty Status," U.S. Department of Defense, June 1, 2020, https://www.defense.gov/casualty.pdf.

6. Tom Rosentiel, "Iraq and Vietnam: A Crucial Difference in Opinion," Pew Research Center, March 22, 2007, https://www.pewresearch.org/2007/03/22/iraq-and-vietnam-a-crucial-difference-in-opinion/. Gallup reports a 53 percent disapproval rating as of March 18, 2013, the tenth anniversary of the Iraq war.

7. In 2016, the *Los Angeles Times* published a list of prominent terror leaders killed in Afghanistan: See Razzan Nakhlawi, "The kill list: Islamic State leaders taken off the battlefield," *Los Angeles Times*, June 29, 2016, https://www.latimes.com/world/middleeast/la-fg-targeted-killings-drone-snap-htmlstory.html.

New York City skyline featuring the Twin Towers of the World Trade Center, destroyed September 11, 2001.

New York City panorama featuring One World Trade Center, built after the destruction of the Twin Towers.

POST-TRAUMATIC STRESS DISORDER (PTSD)
A mental health condition that results from the experience of a traumatic event; can involve anxiety, flashbacks, nightmares, and depression; interferes with daily life; can result in physical harm to self or others; see "Post-traumatic stress disorder (PTSD)," Mayo Clinic, accessed October 23, 2020, https://www.mayoclinic.org/diseases-conditions/post-traumatic-stress-disorder/symptoms-causes/syc-20355967.

Assessing the loss of civilian life in the figures above for which the US specifically bears responsibility is complex and difficult. It requires determining the number of deaths that specifically resulted from US military action, distinguished from those caused by the actions of US enemies. Assessing the overall cost of war is even more complex than the daunting challenge of calculating lives lost, both military and civilian, versus lives saved. An act utilitarian[8] might ask: What were all of the goals of the war? Were they achieved and at what cost? Other costs to consider are the numbers of wounded, captured, and/or affected by **Post-Traumatic Stress Disorder (PTSD)**.[9] How many people were displaced from their homes? What were the effects on the societies involved? What was the financial cost? How has the war affected the general reputation of the United States around the world?

QUESTION FOR CONSIDERATION

a. How do you think a rule utilitarian would assess the ethics of US foreign wars? Perhaps the ethics of pre-emptive strikes or unilateral action would be involved, or outcomes such as the Geneva Accords.

8. See Chapter Four for explanation of this ethical theory.
9. Burns and Novick give an in-depth portrayal of the causes and effects of PTSD. See specifically Episode Two.

© Saeschie Wagner/Shutterstock.com

The Kawergosk Refugee Camp in Iraq, 2017.

Such assessments are so complex that they are well beyond the scope of this book, and beyond the capabilities of even thoughtful citizens who have an important say in whether or not their leaders wage other wars. How, then, are citizens to decide whether to support a war and the politicians who wish to engage in them? Just War Theory is a resource established by some of humanity's greatest minds to assess whether a war should be waged. In contrast to the calculations above, it is clear and concise, and it remains a useful tool for citizens and political leaders alike. Its roots go back to late antiquity in the work of Augustine of Hippo,[10] and modern scholars are still honing and developing it today. The following excerpts lay out highlights of its development, and in so doing, occur in chronological order.

LATE ANTIQUITY
Spans the late ancient period and the early medieval period; roughly the second century CE to eighth century; see Peter Brown, *The World of Late Antiquity: AD 150–750* (New York: Norton, 1989).

10.3 Augustine of Hippo on the Justice of War: Annotated Excerpts from *The City of God Against the Pagans*

The excerpts below are from *The City of God Against the Pagans*, a massive volume originally written in Latin in the early fifth century CE. In what follows, Augustine discusses the morality of warfare waged by Rome, which was already in decline while this text was being written.

10. Please see the appendix for more information about ancient Rome and Augustine.

Sculpture of a Roman soldier in Vienna, Austria.

10.3.1 Excerpts from *The City of God*, Book Three, Chapter Ten

Whether it was desirable that the Roman empire should be increased by such a furious succession of wars, when it might have been quiet and safe by following in the peaceful ways of Numa.

Do they reply that the Roman empire could never have been so widely extended, nor so glorious, save by constant and unintermitting wars? A fit argument, truly! Why must a kingdom be distracted in order to be great? In this little world of man's body, is it not better to have a moderate stature, and health with it, than to attain the huge dimensions of a giant by unnatural torments, and when you attain it to find no rest, but to be pained the more in proportion to the size of your members? [. . .]

But obviously the Romans have a plausible defence for undertaking and carrying on such disastrous wars,—to wit, that the pressure of their enemies forced them to resist, so that they were compelled to fight, not by any greed of human applause, but by the necessity of protecting life and liberty. [. . .] This was to build up Rome's greatness by honourable means. But, in Numa's reign,[11] I would know whether the long peace was maintained in spite of the

11. According to Plutarch, after Romulus disappeared, Rome was in a state of commotion about who should be the next king. After some time and deliberation, it was decided that Numa Pompilius should reign. He was considered virtuous, and was begged to rule. He was supposedly born on the day when Romulus founded Rome, April 21, and it was difficult to persuade him to rule, since he preferred to live in peace and quiet. Once he agreed to rule, he took measures to make Rome less warlike. See Plutarch, *The Parallel Lives*, "The Life of Numa" 1–8: http://penelope.uchicago.edu/Thayer/E/Roman/Texts/Plutarch/Lives/Numa*.html. Though some details of Plutarch's account seem embellished and historically doubtful, and much about Numa is shrouded in mystery, the legendary Numa is said to have lived from the 700s–600s BCE, was Rome's second king, and thus ruled very early in Rome's history, when it was a republic—well before it became an empire. Many considered him to be one of Rome's greatest rulers.

Sculpture of Janus.

incursions of wicked neighbours, or if these incursions were discontinued that the peace might be maintained? For if even then Rome was harassed by wars, and yet did not meet force with force, the same means she then used to quiet her enemies without conquering them in war, or terrifying them with the onset of battle, she might have used always, and have reigned in peace with the gates of Janus[12] shut. [. . .]

QUESTIONS FOR CONSIDERATION

a. What is Augustine saying in the first few lines above about the creation of a large empire?
b. What conditions justify the use of "honourable" violence, according to the above?
c. Does Augustine think that provocations by enemies always necessitate war?
d. Would it have been better for Rome to reign "in peace" through nonviolent foreign relations, rather than through the conquering of enemies, according to Augustine?

10.3.2 Excerpts from *The City of God*, Book Four, Chapter Three

Whether the great extent of the empire, which has been acquired only by wars, is to be reckoned among the good things either of the wise or the happy.

Now, therefore, let us see how it is that they dare to ascribe the very great extent and duration of the Roman empire to those gods whom they contend that they worship honourably, even by the obsequies[13] of vile games and the ministry of vile men: although I should like to first inquire for a little what reason, what prudence, there is in wishing to glory in the greatness and extent of

12. Doors that were closed during times of peace and open in times of war. Janus was god of gates, doors, and passages, among other things. See *Encyclopedia Britannica*, s.v., "Janus," accessed October 23, 2020, https://www.britannica.com/topic/Janus-Roman-god.
13. Funeral or burial rites.

© Ollyy/Shutterstock.com

the empire, when you cannot point out the happiness of men who are always rolling, with dark fear and cruel lust, in warlike slaughters and in blood, which, whether shed in civil or foreign war, is still human blood; so that their joy may be compared to glass in its fragile splendour, of which one is horribly afraid lest it should be suddenly broken in pieces. [. . .] But let us suppose a case of two men; for each individual man, like one letter in a language, is as it were the element of a city or kingdom, however far-spreading in its occupation of the earth. Of these two men let us suppose that one is poor, or rather of middling circumstances; the other very rich. But the rich man is anxious with fears, pining with discontent, burning with covetousness, never secure, always uneasy, panting from the perpetual strife of his enemies, adding to his patrimony[14] indeed by these miseries to an immense degree, and by these additions also heaping up most bitter cares. But that other man of moderate wealth is contented with a small and compact estate, most dear to his own family, enjoying the sweetest peace with his kindred neighbours and friends, in piety religious, benignant in mind, healthy in body, in life frugal, in manners chaste, in conscience secure. I know not whether any one can be such a fool, that he dare hesitate which to prefer. As, therefore, in the case of these two men, so in two families, in two nations, in two kingdoms, this test of tranquility holds good; and if we apply it vigilantly and without prejudice, we shall quite easily see where the mere show of happiness dwells, and where real felicity.[15] [. . .]

QUESTIONS FOR CONSIDERATION

a. According to Augustine, are violent and warlike men happy? Why or why not?
b. What about rich men, in comparison to those of moderate means? Who is happier and why?
c. What do Augustine's thoughts in this chapter imply about the nature and size of a political entity like a republic?

14. Inheritance.
15. Happiness.

© Vadym Sh/Shutterstock.com

© Vuk Kostic/Shutterstock.com

10.3.3 An Excerpt from *The City of God*, Book Five, Chapter Seventeen

To what profit the Romans carried on wars and how much they contributed to the well-being of those whom they conquered.

[. . .] For I do not see what it makes for the safety, good morals, and certainly not for the dignity, of men, that some have conquered and others have been conquered, except that it yields them that most insane pomp of human glory, in which 'they have received their reward,' who burned with excessive desire of it, and carried on most eager wars. [. . .][10]

QUESTIONS FOR CONSIDERATION

a. Is it reasonable to wage war for the sake of conquering, and the glory that goes with it, according to Augustine? Why or why not?

10.4 Thomas Aquinas[16] on the Justice of War: Annotated Excerpts from the *Summa Theologica*

Centuries after Augustine, Aquinas builds on the extensive groundwork that the former laid on the ethics of war. Both thinkers approach this issue from the perspective of virtue ethics, which is discussed extensively in Chapters One to Three. Similar to the Aquinas excerpts of Chapter Three, the following are from his well-known, highly-regarded *Summa Theologica*.

16. Please see the appendix for more information about the Middle Ages and the life and work of Aquinas.

10.4.1 Excerpts from *Summa Theologica* II-II, Question 40, Article One

Whether it is always sinful to wage war?

[. . .]

Objection 2:

Further, whatever is contrary to a Divine precept is a sin. But war is contrary to a Divine precept, for it is written (Mat. 5:39): 'But I say to you not to resist evil'; and (Rom. 12:19):

'Not revenging yourselves, my dearly beloved, but give place unto wrath.' Therefore war is always sinful.

Objection 3: Further, nothing, except sin, is contrary to an act of virtue. But war is contrary to peace. Therefore war is always a sin.

Objection 4: Further, the exercise of a lawful thing is itself lawful, as is evident in scientific exercises. But warlike exercises which take place in tournaments are forbidden by the Church, since those who are slain in these trials are deprived of ecclesiastical[17] burial. Therefore it seems that war is a sin in itself.

Recall from Chapter Three, that Aquinas's *Summa Theologica* is divided into four volumes, which are further subdivided into questions and articles, as opposed to books or chapters. This question is from the third volume, also known as "The Second Part of the Second Part."

Aquinas starts each article by laying out notable objections—*views that differ from his own*. After concisely and fairly laying out those views of his opponents, he goes into his main argument, after which he replies to each objection one by one. This format stems from the style of the medieval disputation, which was a common form of public discourse then, as opposed to traditional lectures. This is explained further in the appendix.

The two references here are to the Bible: the books of Matthew and Romans. The chapter number is written first, followed by the verse number.

© St. Nick/Shutterstock.com

© Jopics/Shutterstock.com

17. Meaning a burial in accord with Church rites.

[. . .]

I answer that, In order for a war to be just, three things are necessary. First, the authority of the sovereign[18] by whose command the war is to be waged. For it is not the business of a private individual to declare war, because he can seek for redress of his rights from the tribunal of his superior. Moreover, it is not the business of a private individual to summon together the people, which has to be done in wartime. And as the care of the common weal[19] is committed to those who are in authority, it is their business to watch over the common weal of the city, kingdom or province subject to them. And just as it is lawful for them to have recourse to the sword in defending that common weal against internal disturbances, when they punish evil-doers, according to the words of the Apostle (Rom. 13.4):

> This the point in the article at which Aquinas begins to lay out his own argument.

'He beareth not the sword in vain: for he is God's minister, an avenger to execute wrath upon him that doth evil'; so too, it is their business to have recourse to the sword of war in defending the common weal against external enemies. Hence it is said to those who are in authority (Ps. 81:4)[20]: 'Rescue the poor: and deliver the needy out of the hand of the sinner"; and for this reason Augustine says (Contra Faust. Xxii, 75):[21] 'The natural order conducive to peace among mortals demands that the power to declare and counsel war should be in the hands of those who hold the supreme authority.'

> Once again, Aquinas is quoting the Book of Romans, of which Paul the Apostle is the author. Aquinas refers to him simply as "The Apostle."

Statue of Charles IV, in Prague.

Statue of Charlemagne in Aachen, in Germany.

---

18. Ruler.
19. The "common weal" is synonymous with the common good, or the well-being of the people.
20. The Book of Psalms.
21. The full name of this work of Augustine is *Contra Faustum Manichaeum,* or *Against Faustus the Manichaean.* It is a series of arguments against Faustus and the doctrine of Manichaeism. See https://www.bl.uk/collection-items/bnf-st-augustine-contra-faustum-manichaeum. For Augustine's autobiographical account of his relationship with Faustus and the Manichees, see *Confessions,* Books Three through Seven. The translations by Ryan or Sheed are highly recommended.

Secondly, a just cause is required, namely that those who are attacked, should be attacked because they deserve it on account of some fault. Wherefore Augustine says (QQ. In Hept.,[11] qu. X, super Jos.): 'A just war is wont to be described as one that avenges wrongs, when a nation or state has to be punished, for refusing to make amends for the wrongs inflicted by its subjects, or to restore what it has seized unjustly.'

Thirdly, it is necessary that the belligerents should have a rightful intention, so that they intend the advancement of good, or the avoidance of evil. Hence Augustine says (De Verb. Dom. [. . .]): 'True religion looks upon as peaceful those wars that are waged not for motives of aggrandizement, or cruelty, but with the object of securing peace, of punishing evil-doers, and of uplifting the good.' For it may happen that the war is declared by the legitimate authority and for a just cause, and yet to be rendered unlawful through a wicked intention. Hence Augustine says (Contra Faust. Xxii, 74): 'The passion for inflicting harm, the cruel thirst for vengeance, an unpacific[22] and relentless spirit, the fever of revolt, the lust of power, and such like things, all these are rightly condemned in war.'

[. . .]

Reply to Objection 2: Such like precepts, as Augustine observes (De Serm. Dom. In Monte[12] I, 19), should always be borne in readiness of mind, so that we be ready to obey them, and if necessary, to refrain from resistance or self-defense. Nevertheless it is necessary sometimes for a man to act otherwise for the common good, or for the good of those with whom he is fighting. Hence Augustine says (Ep. Ad Marcellin.[23] Cxxxviii): 'Those whom we have to punish with a kindly severity, it is necessary to handle in many ways against their will.

> These are Aquinas' replies to the specific objections above.

22. Warlike; not peaceful.
23. One of Augustine's published letters.

For when we are stripping a man of the lawlessness of sin, it is good for him to be vanquished, since nothing is more hopeless than the happiness of sinners, whence arises a guilty impunity, and an evil will, like an internal enemy.'

Reply to Objection 3: Those who wage war justly aim at peace, and so they are not opposed to peace, except to the evil peace, which Our Lord 'came not to send upon earth' (Mat. 10:34). Hence Augustine says (Ep. ad Bonif.[24] Clxxxix): 'We do not seek peace in order to be at war, but we go to war that we may have peace. Be peaceful, therefore, in warring, so that you may vanquish those whom you war against, and bring them to the prosperity of peace.'

Reply to Objection 4: Manly exercises in warlike feats of arms are not all forbidden, but those which are inordinate and perilous, and end in slaying or plundering. [. . .][13]

10.4.2 Excerpts from *Summa Theologica* II-II, Question 64, Article Six

Whether it is lawful to kill the innocent?

Objection 1: It would seem that in some cases it is lawful to kill the innocent. The fear of God is never manifested by sin, since on the contrary 'the fear of the Lord driveth out sin' (Ecclus.[25] 1:27). Now Abraham was commended in that he feared the Lord, since he was willing to slay his innocent son.

Therefore one may, without sin, kill an innocent person.

[. . .]

> Aquinas is referring here to the story of Abraham and Isaac, in which God tested Abraham's faith by commanding him to kill his son Isaac. Abraham was about to go through with it when a messenger of God stopped him. See the Book of Genesis, Chapter 22.

> Here Aquinas considers the argument that the Bible seems to indicate that it is permissible to kill the innocent. He will argue against this position.

Nineteenth-century painting depicting Abraham and Isaac in St. Jacobs Church, Brugge, Beligum, by Jan van de Kerkove.

1713 portrayal of the sacrifice of Isaac by G. B. Pittoni in the church of San Francesco della Vigna.

24. Another published letter of Augustine.
25. The Book of Ecclesiasticus.

Mosaic of Abraham, Isaac, and God's messenger in the Church of the Holy Sepulchre in Jersualem, Israel.

Vienna, Austria: Grisaille's 1490 depiction of Abraham and Isaac.

On the contrary, It is written (Ex.[26] 23:7): 'The innocent and just person thou shalt not put to death.'

I answer that, An individual man may be considered in two ways: first, in himself; secondly, in relation to something else. If we consider a man in himself, it is unlawful to kill any man, since in every man though he be sinful, we ought to love the nature which God has made, and which is destroyed by slaying him. Nevertheless, as stated above the slaying of a sinner becomes lawful in relation to the common good, which is corrupted by sin. On the other hand the life of righteous men preserves and forwards the common good, since they are the chief part of the community. Therefore it is in no way lawful to slay the innocent.

> Aquinas outlines the argument that could be made to justify killing evil people, for the sake of the common good, but a similar argument does not hold for the innocent, since the righteous contribute to the common good. It is clear, furthermore, based on Chapter Three, that because of natural law Aquinas would oppose the killing of innocents.

Reply to Objection 1: God is Lord of death and life, for by His decree both the sinful and the righteous die. Hence he who at God's command kills an innocent man does not sin, as neither does God Whose behest[27] he executes: indeed his obedience to God's commands is a proof that he fears Him.

> Aquinas is saying here that it is morally permissible to kill the innocent if God commands it.

26. The Book of Exodus.
27. Command.

[. . .]

Late seventeenth-century fresco of God the Father by Ludovico Gimignani in Rome, Italy.

Fresco by Enrico Reffo of God the Father in Turin, Italy.

QUESTIONS FOR CONSIDERATION

a. What is Aquinas's core argument in this article? What are the reasons he gives for his main claim?
b. Can you think of any possibly problematic implications of Aquinas's Reply to Objection One? Would Aquinas excuse the killing of innocents in the form of collateral damage if it resulted from military action supposedly decreed by God?

10.4.3 Excerpts from *Summa Theologica* II-II, Question 64, Article Seven

Whether it is lawful to kill a man in self-defense?

[. . .]

Objection 4: Further, murder is a more grievous sin than fornication or adultery. Now nobody may lawfully commit simple fornication or adultery or any other mortal sin[28] in order to save his own life; since the spiritual life is to be preferred to the life of the body. Therefore no man may lawfully take another's life in self-defense in order to save his own life.[29]

[. . .]

On the contrary, It is written (Ex. 22:2): 'If a thief be found breaking into a house or undermining it, and be wounded so as to die; he that slew him shall not be guilty of blood.' Now it is much more lawful to defend one's life than

28. According to Catholics, this is a type of evil act that seriously damages one's relationship with God, as opposed to a venial sin, which is less severe.

29. One could call to mind Christian martyrs who allowed themselves to be killed rather than renounce their faith by committing fornication (sex outside of marriage) or adultery (a married person having sexual intercourse with someone other than their spouse). St. Maria Goretti is a modern example of someone martyred for not committing fornication. See "St. Maria Goretti," Catholic Online, accessed October 23, 2020, https://www.catholic.org/saints/saint.php?saint_id=78. If such martyrs chose the best course of action by allowing themselves to be killed, then shouldn't any good Christian do the same when their life is threatened, rather than killing someone out of self-defense? Aquinas argues against this opposing argument below.

one's house. Therefore neither is a man guilty of murder if he kill another in defense of his own life.

> This initial, brief argument, uses Biblical authority to support Aquinas's main claim that killing in self-defense is permissible.

I answer that, Nothing hinders one act from having two effects, only one of which is intended, while the other is beside the intention. Now moral acts take their species according to what is intended, and not according to what is beside the intention, since this is accidental as explained above (Q[43], A[3][30]; FS, Q[12], A[1]). Accordingly the act of self-defense may have two effects, one is the saving of one's life, the other is the slaying of the aggressor. Therefore this act, since one's intention is to save one's own life, is not unlawful, seeing that it is natural to everything to keep itself in 'being,' as far as possible. And yet, though proceeding from a good intention, an act may be rendered unlawful, if it be out of proportion to the end. Wherefore if a man, in self-defense, uses more than necessary violence, it will be unlawful: whereas if he repel force with moderation his defense will be lawful [. . .].

> So if one's intention is to save oneself, and that action has the unintended consequence of killing the offender, the action is morally permissible. On the other hand, if one intends not only to save oneself, but also to kill the offender by using more than necessary violence, such an action would be impermissible.

Nor is it necessary for salvation[31] that a man omit the act of moderate self-defense in order to avoid killing the other man, since one is bound to take more care of one's own life than of another's. But as it is unlawful to take a man's life, except for the public authority acting for the common good, as stated above (A[3]), it is not lawful for a man to intend killing a man in self-defense, except for such as have public authority, who while intending to kill a man in self-defense, refer this to the public good, as in the case of a soldier fighting against the foe, and in the minister of the judge struggling with robbers, although even these sin if they be moved by private animosity.

[. . .]

Reply to Objection 4: The act of fornication or adultery is not necessarily directed to the preservation of one's own life, as is the act whence sometimes results the taking of a man's life.

> Aquinas's argument against the initial objection is that when one kills in self-defense, one's necessary intention is to save oneself. On the other hand, committing fornication to save oneself is not an action necessarily aimed at self-preservation directly. Essentially, he argues that the initial objection is based on a faulty analogy.

30. Question 43, Article Three.

31. The saving of one's soul; going to heaven.

[. . .]

QUESTIONS FOR CONSIDERATION

a. What is the lawful, or morally permissible effect of using force against an aggressor in self-defense? What is the morally wrong possible effect of using such force?
b. What are the implications of Aquinas's argument about the use of force against aggressors? How might such an argument translate into military action? To actions by police or other law enforcement? To "Stand your ground laws"[32]?

10.5 Modern Just War Theory, Augustine, Aquinas, and the Vietnam War

10.5.1 Overview

Well-known contemporary thinkers who have contributed to Just War Theory scholarship include but are not limited to G. E. M. Anscombe, Thomas Nagel, and Michael Walzer.[14] Vincent Ferraro provides a clear and concise overview of the modern tenets of Just War Theory, as follows:

> [1] A just war can only be waged as a last resort. All non-violent options must be exhausted before the use of force can be justified.
>
> [2] A war is just only if it is waged by a legitimate authority. Even just causes cannot be served by actions taken by individuals or groups who do not constitute an authority sanctioned by whatever the society and outsiders to the society deem legitimate.
>
> [3] A just war can only be fought to redress a wrong suffered. For example, self-defense against an armed attack is always considered to be a just cause (although the justice of the cause is not sufficient—see point #4). Further, a just war can only be fought with "right" intentions: the only permissible objective of a just war is to redress the injury.
>
> [4] A war can only be just if it is fought with a reasonable chance of success. Deaths and injury incurred in a hopeless cause are not morally justifiable.
>
> [5] The ultimate goal of a just war is to re-establish peace. More specifically, the peace established after the war must be preferable to the peace that would have prevailed if the war had not been fought.[33]
>
> [6] The violence used in the war must be proportional to the injury suffered. States are prohibited from using force not necessary to attain the limited objective of addressing the injury suffered.

JUSTICE OF WAR (*JUS AD BELLUM*)
The moral considerations involved in the decision to go to war; takes into account a comprehensive view of the war; see Seth Lazar, "War," *Stanford Encyclopedia of Philosophy*, first published May 3, 2016, https://plato.stanford.edu/entries/war/#JusAdBell.

JUSTICE IN WAR (*JUS IN BELLO*)
The moral considerations involved in the means used to conduct the war, especially as they relate to noncombatants; see Lazar, "War," https://plato.stanford.edu/entries/war/#JusBell.

32. See Sean Sullivan, "Everything you need to know about 'stand your ground' laws," *The Washington Post*, July 15, 2013, https://www.washingtonpost.com/news/the-fix/wp/2013/07/15/everything-you-need-to-know-about-stand-your-ground-laws/.
33. These first five tenets pertain to the "justice of war" (*jus ad bellum*), or the morality of going to war in the first place. The last two tenets pertain to the "justice in war" (*jus in bello*), or the moral rules that must be followed while at war.

QUESTION FOR CONSIDERATION

How would this tenet, and perhaps tenet #3, pertain to pre-emptive war?

[7] The weapons used in war must discriminate between combatants and non-combatants. Civilians are never permissible targets of war, and every effort must be taken to avoid killing civilians. The deaths of civilians are justified only if they are unavoidable victims of a deliberate attack on a military target.[15]

10.5.2 The Tenets of Modern Just War Theory in Relation to Augustine, Aquinas, and *The Vietnam War* Documentary

Using the content of this chapter, and the chart below as a guide, proceed through the questions for consideration that follow. The chart identifies aspects of Burns and Novick's series that are relevant to each tenet, without specifying whether or not those details support the US cause or not. Starting at Episode 6, fewer details are included for a few reasons, including episodes' emphasis on coverage of domestic issues, and their relative lack of relevance to justice *of* war tenets (which is most of JWT). They are nonetheless highly relevant to justice *in* war: the last two tenets.

The first tenet, that the use of force must be a "last resort," and that "all non-violent options must be exhausted," is reminiscent of Augustine's praise of Numa, under whom Rome supposedly flourished despite hostile external entities, without going to war.[16]

QUESTIONS FOR CONSIDERATION: THE FIRST TENET AND THE DOCU-SERIES

a. Based on the docu-series, did Kennedy engage in war with North Vietnam as a last resort? Were all diplomatic options exhausted?
b. Was Kennedy wrong to initiate secretive military operations in Vietnam?
c. Did the governments of Vietnam satisfy this criterion? Did they engage in any unnecessary violence in the lead-up to the war?
d. Were there factors that made diplomacy difficult or impossible on either side?

The second tenet, requiring a "legitimate authority," clearly echoes Aquinas's articulation of the criteria necessary for war to be just. On the US side, the Kennedy and Johnson administrations came to power through constitutional processes. However, the election meddling of Richard Nixon and the South Vietnamese government raises questions about the legitimacy of the authorities waging the war.

QUESTIONS FOR CONSIDERATION: THE SECOND TENET AND THE DOCU-SERIES

a. Was Diem a legitimate authority? What about Le Duan?
b. Did the American backing of certain leaders in the South undermine their legitimacy?
c. Were the North Vietnamese Army and the Viet Cong both legitimate authorities? Why or why not?
d. According to the docu-series, how did Nixon interfere in the election process? Did this undermine the legitimacy of his administration?
e. What about US allies? Did American alliances in the war effort bolster or undermine the legitimacy of American authority?

Statue of Ho Chi Minh in front of City Hall, Ho Chi Minh City, Vietnam.

TABLE 10.2

	JWT Tenet 1: Last Resort	Tenet 2: Legitimate Authority	Tenet 3: Redress/Right Intentions
Episode 1: 1858–1961	Violence of both Diem and Viet Minh	1955 "election" of Diem; shifting of power from Ho Chi Minh to Le Duan	French rule in Vietnam; Japanese rule during WWII; Ho Chi Minh's life and mission; expansion of USSR after WWII; killing of Dewey; Viet Minh killings; Korean War; JFK's position on Vietnam and its independence; containment; Communist oppression of religious populations; authoritarian leadership of Diem
Episode 2: 1961–1963	Pressure on JFK; slippery slope from covert ops	Diem's relationship with democracy and freedom; Diem's brother No Ding Nhu; generals' leadership in S. Viet. after Diem; shifting of power from Ho Chi Minh to Le Duan	JFK's position on dictators; Communist oppression in East Germany; Viet Cong brutality; violation of Buddhist civil rights
Episode 3: Jan. 1964– Dec. 1965	Naval battle off coast of N. Vietnam; LBJ's hesitancy; Tonkin Res.; UN and UK diplomatic efforts that US opposed; 1965 Christmas halt	Coups in S. Viet.	McNaughton on US aims in 1965 (51 min. mark)
Episode 4: Jan. 1966–June 1967		PM Ky	Kennan's assessment; Body count = success; US aid, rapport built by caring US soldiers; profile of VC
Episode 5: July 1967–Dec 1967			
Episode 6: Jan. 1968–July 1968		S. Viet. POW execution	
Episode 7: June 1968–May 1969		Nixon elected	Corruption in S. Viet; N. Viet. suppression of freedoms
Episode 8: April 1969–May 1970			
Episode 9: May 1970–March 1973		Nixon re-election; Thieu's election; Watergate	
Episode 10: March 1973–Onward		Thieu's repression and corruption; Watergate	

Continued

TABLE 10.2 Continued

	Tenet 4: Chance of Success	Tenet 5: Goal is Peace	Tenet 6: Proportionate Means	Tenet 7: Avoid Non-Combatants
Episode 1: 1858–1961	Korean War; French military engagement in Vietnam, esp Dien Bien Phu; Eisenhower's assessment	French rule in Vietnam; Japanese WWII rule; Goals of Ho Chi Minh; Korean War		
Episode 2: 1961–1963	New military technology, esp. helicopters and APC's; Vann's critical assessment; negative effects of ARVN tactics; Viet Cong gathering arms; ARVN hesitancy; Gen. Harkins: Goal is killing; JFK: Can't stay but need re-election	Diem's repression of liberty; corruption of Soviet gov't and military; lack of clear and strong leadership in S. Vietnam		
Episode 3: Jan. 1964– Dec. 1965	Binh Gia; George Ball's 1965 negative assessment; la Drang and mixed blessing of air and artillery; McNamara's 1965 negative assessment	Lack of clear and strong leadership in S. Vietnam	Rolling Thunder; destruction of villages, homes, schools; Cam Ne	Destruction of villages, homes, schools; Cam Ne
Episode 4: Jan. 1966–June 1967	Fulbright and Kennan: illusions about invincibility; profile of VC; Hamlet evaluation system; Dissidents and rebellion in S. Viet.; Westmoreland's "crossover point"; McNamara and morale strategy; repair efforts in North; request for more troops	US aid, rapport and care by many US soldiers	Large-scale search and destroy; bombing of Laos, Ho Chi Minh trail; defoliants; Rolling Thunder	Rolling Thunder; effects of body count strategy on noncombatants; sweeps through villages
Episode 5: July 1967–Dec 1967	PR campaign; McNamara memo		Bien Tre	Bien Tre; Anti-Asian rhetoric, objectification (esp. 17 min. mark); Tiger Force; Song Ve; Free-Fire Zones
Episode 6: Jan. 1968–July 1968	Tet; US errors; ARVN strength; LBJ counsels pulling out, doesn't run for re-election	S. Viet. POW execution		S. Viet. POW execution; Hue; VC and NVA executions outside Hue
Episode 7: June 1968–May 1969	Corruption in S. Viet.	Corruption in S. Viet.; N. Viet. suppression of freedoms	Free-fire zones; misuse of air power	Free-fire zones; refugees in the South
Episode 8: April 1969–May 1970			My Lai; incursion into Cambodia	My Lai
Episode 9: May 1970–March 1973	Easter Offensive	US withdrawal, Kissinger's negotiations	Operation Linebacker; resumed bombing in North; Christmas bombing; Trang Bang	Resumed bombing in North; Christmas bombing
Episode 10: March 1973–Onward		US withdrawal/peace agreement		Civilian deaths during and after full US withdrawal

HUMANITARIAN INTERVENTION
Military involvement in a foreign nation as a result of grave threats to human life in that nation by its own rulers; see Robert Hoag, "Armed Humanitarian Intervention," *Internet Encyclopedia of Philosophy*, accessed October 23, 2020, https://www.iep.utm.edu/hum-mili/.

SLIPPERY SLOPE ARGUMENT
Claims that the cause of one effect will lead to a series of other effects; for example: If the US struck Moscow with a nuclear weapon, this would cause Russia to retaliate, which would cause subsequent retaliation and eventually all-out nuclear war between the two nations and their allies, causing the destruction of most of civilization. This example is probably not fallacious (logically flawed). However, the following example is: If you fail your sophomore chemistry mid-term in high school, you will fail chemistry, which means you won't get into a good college, which means that you will never get a job, and therefore, you will end up homeless. This slippery slope argument contains errors in the assumptions it makes about causal relationships. Though the failure of the chemistry exam will probably lead to undesirable consequences, the likelihood of those effects including not getting into a good college, not getting a good job, and/or being homeless is *extremely* low.

The third tenet, stating the necessity of "right intentions" and a "just cause" closely resembles the words of Aquinas. War must be a response to some wrong that was suffered. According to modern just war theory, self-defense is a justified cause.

QUESTIONS FOR CONSIDERATION: THE THIRD TENET AND THE DOCU-SERIES

a. The United States and the Communist regimes around the globe were clearly enemies before and during the Vietnam War. The question remains though: Was the United States harmed by North Vietnam, or by "international Communism"?
b. Was South Vietnam harmed by the Communist North? If so, was US involvement a justified humanitarian intervention?
c. Was the policy of "containment"[34] a just cause?
d. Was the North Vietnamese effort to cast off foreign control a just cause?
e. Was the North sufficiently wronged to justify its military action?
f. Were any of the regimes involved in the war acting out of self-defense?
g. Was the US military engagement in Vietnam a just cause?

The fourth tenet, specifying the necessity for a chance of success, comes up many times through the docu-series. Burns and Novick quote Eisenhower, McNamara, and several other notable figures about their assessment of the American prospects for success. They also treat this criterion by covering the controversial standard for success, championed by Westmoreland, which focused on the number of combatants killed rather than territory gained.

© Oliver Denker/Shutterstock.com

© Prachaya Roekdeethaweesab/Shutterstock.com

34. The strategy to prevent Communism from spreading, based on the slippery slope argument that when a country becomes Communist, it leads to other countries, especially its neighbors, becoming Communist.

© Photography-by-Stretch/Shutterstock.com

© Keith Tarrier/Shutterstock.com

QUESTIONS FOR CONSIDERATION: THE FOURTH TENET AND THE DOCU-SERIES

a. According to the docu-series, did the US have a reasonable chance of success at the outset of the war? During the Johnson period? During Nixon's time in office?
b. Would their chances of success have been different if military strategy had been otherwise?
c. Did the NVA and Viet Cong have a reasonable hope for success?

© rook76/Shutterstock.com

The fifth tenet, that the goal of war is peace—specifically a better sense of peace than before the war—echoes the sentiment of Augustine's *City of God* when he discusses the restlessness and torment of a political community at war. Aquinas clearly states that the ultimate goal must be peace.

It's important when considering this criterion to keep in mind that the US waged war as a response against the spread of Communism. The perception of Communism in the 1960s and '70s was largely associated with Stalin's reign over the Soviet Union and Mao's China. Hannah Arendt explains in great detail, drawing on substantial evidence, the many injustices inflicted on people by Stalin that came to light in the 1950s and '60s. She briefly treats China and Mao Tse-tung as well, where "the first years of dictatorship" resulted in an estimated fifteen million lives lost. She estimates that this amounted to approximately 3 percent of the population in 1949.[17]

© bissig/Shutterstock.com

© Hung Chung Chih/Shutterstock.com

QUESTIONS FOR CONSIDERATION: THE FIFTH TENET OF JWT AND THE VIETNAM WAR DOCUMENTARY FILM SERIES

a. Was peace the goal of the Vietnam War, according to Kennedy? To Johnson? To Nixon? To US military leaders? To the South Vietnamese government? To Ho Chi Minh? To Le Duan?
b. Was there peace in Vietnam before the American war? What effect does your answer to this have on your assessment of whether or not the US met this criterion?

© Mr Fox/Shutterstock.com

© PhotoStockImage/Shutterstock.com

The sixth tenet, stating that those waging war must use means that are in proportion to the wrong suffered, clearly reminds one of Aquinas's explanation of self-defense, where the goal must be the preservation of one's life and not the taking of another's. Burns and Novick cover the means, or instruments, of the Vietnam War in great detail, in every installment of the series.

QUESTIONS FOR CONSIDERATION: THE SIXTH TENET AND THE DOCU-SERIES

a. Did the US use means that were proportionate to the injuries it suffered? Of perhaps more appropriately, to those that South Vietnam suffered?
b. If not, which tools of war do you think were excessive, and therefore unnecessary?
c. If so, why do you think each instrument of war that the US used was proportionate, and therefore, justly employed?

© Jindowin/Shutterstock.com

American bombs on display in Vietnam.

The seventh and final tenet, specifying the need for discrimination between combatants and civilians, and the imperative to avoid intentionally killing noncombatants, clearly echoes Aquinas's claim that one cannot kill the innocent. Burns and Novick portray the deaths of Vietnamese noncombatants throughout their docu-series, from those killed in airstrikes, to those who lost their lives in the crossfire, to those who died in the raiding of villages.

© TZIDO SUN/Shutterstock.com

© Berry Phan/Shutterstock.com

QUESTIONS FOR CONSIDERATION: THE SEVENTH TENET AND THE DOCU-SERIES

a. Did the US military distinguish between combatants and civilians? If so, was it consistent in this effort? If not, why not?
b. Were there factors that made it difficult to distinguish between noncombatants and combatants? What are the implications of these factors on the fulfillment of this criterion of Just War Theory?

OTHER QUESTIONS FOR CONSIDERATION

a. What is the influence of Augustine on Aquinas's explanation of the criteria for a just war?
b. What aspects of modern Just War Theory do not appear in the work of Augustine or Aquinas above?
c. Is Just War Theory practical? If not, why not? Does this mean it should be neglected altogether? If so, why? How should it be used?

REALISTS
Do not think morality applies to entities engaged in war in the way that moral rules apply to individuals. Nicole Loring, a political scientist, adds: From an International Relations perspective, realists believe that states can and should do anything to achieve their goals, and that the main goal of a state is to be secure. Therefore, to realists, going to war in order to make one's country (and people) safer is morally justifiable. This understanding of realism may be different from a philosophical point of view, but in political science it's not that the morals don't apply, it's that the state security is valued over everything else.[35]

PACIFISTS
Completely opposed to war.

Henry Kissinger, who figured prominently in the docu-series, is a famous **realist** with regard to war. This means that he does not think that the rules of moral systems apply to governments and militaries waging war as they do to individuals.

d. Is just war theory not sufficiently tailored to the political and military entities who ultimately make the decision to go to war?
e. Should those entities have a different set of moral rules from those that apply to individuals?

Many anti-war activists are **pacifists**, meaning that they are opposed to war, including wars that may be ethical in the eyes of just war theorists.

f. Given the knowledge you've gained from the docu-series and this chapter, is it possible that there are merits to favoring pacifism over just war theory or realism?

Clearly, just war theory has strong roots in the natural law ethics of Augustine and Aquinas.

g. Would a Kantian have any reason to disagree with any of the tenets of Just War Theory? What about a rule utilitarian? Would an act utilitarian agree with all of the principles of Just War Theory?

10.6 For Further Reading

10.6.1 Recommended Print Resources

Arendt, Hannah. *The Origins of Totalitarianism* (New York: Harcourt, 1968).
Augustine. *Political Writings*, trans. Michael W. Tkacz and Douglas Kries (Indianapolis: Hackett, 1994).
Augustine. *The City of God Against the Pagans*, trans. R.W. Dyson (Cambridge: Cambridge University Press, 1998).

10.6.2 Freely Available Online Resources

Facts about America's wars:
https://www.defense.gov/casualty.pdf
https://www.va.gov/opa/publications/factsheets/fs_americas_wars.pdf
https://www.iraqbodycount.org/
https://watson.brown.edu

Opinion polls about many topics, including wars:
https://www.pewresearch.org
https://news.gallup.com

35. This is from a correspondence with me.

A wide-ranging source on JWT recommended by scholars: http://justwar-theory.com/

Free version of Aquinas's *Summa Theologica*: https://www.ccel.org/ccel/aquinas/summa/summa.SS_Q40.html

Free version of Augustine's *City of God:* http://www.gutenberg.org/ebooks/45304

Free version of Plutarch's Lives: http://penelope.uchicago.edu/Thayer/E/Roman/Texts/Plutarch/Lives

Vincent Ferraro's work on JWT: https://www.mtholyoke.edu/acad/intrel/pol116/justwar.htm

Media Coverage of the Docu-Series:

https://www.indiewire.com/2017/09/the-vietnam-war-my-lai-massacre-lynn-novick-pbs-1201880212/

The Washington Post published interviews with Burns and Novick after the airing of the episodes. Two links to those articles are below:

https://www.washingtonpost.com/news/act-four/wp/2017/09/26/the-american-war-how-the-vietnam-war-revealed-the-fragility-of-human-decency/

https://www.washingtonpost.com/news/act-four/wp/2017/09/27/the-american-war-kent-state-was-originally-a-footnote-in-ken-burnss-documentary-then-he-visited-the-campus/

10.6.3 For Experiential Learning

The Vietnam Veterans Memorial in Washington, DC: https://www.nps.gov/vive/index.htm

The Son My memorial in Vietnam, dedicated to the 1968 My Lai Massacre: https://www.cnn.com/travel/article/my-lai-massacre-vietnam-memorial-intl-hnk/index.html

Index of Vietnam Veterans Memorials: http://www.vietvet.org/vietmems.htm

Babylift Memorial: http://www.vietnambabylift.org/Memorial.html

© dinosmichail/Shutterstock.com

© christianthiel.net/Shutterstock.com

© dinosmichail/Shutterstock.com

Endnotes

1. Hirschman, Preston, and Loi, "Vietnamese Casualties During the American War: A New Estimate," *Population and Development Review* 21 (1995): 807.
2. Encyclopedia Britannica, s.v., "Vietnam War," accessed October 23, 2020, https://www.britannica.com/event/Vietnam-War.
3. See Tim Rosentiel, "Polling Wars: Hawks vs. Doves," *Pew Research Center*, November 23, 2009, https://www.pewresearch.org/2009/11/23/polling-wars-hawks-vs-doves/.
4. Philip Bump, "15 years after the Iraq War began, the death toll is still murky," *The Washington Post*, March 20, 2018, https://www.washingtonpost.com/news/politics/wp/2018/03/20/15-years-after-it-began-the-death-toll-from-the-iraq-war-is-still-murky/.
5. https://www.iraqbodycount.org/.
6. "Costs of War," Watson Institute. International and Public Affairs. Brown University, updated January 2020, https://watson.brown.edu/costsofwar/costs/human/civilians/afghan.
7. "September 11 Terror Attacks Fast Facts," CNN, updated September 18, 2020, https://www.cnn.com/2013/07/27/us/september-11-anniversary-fast-facts/index.html.
8. R. J. Reinhart, "U.S. Views Mixed on War in Afghanistan," *Gallup*, September 11, 2019, https://news.gallup.com/poll/266546/views-mixed-war-afghanistan.aspx.
9. This table was generated from the sources cited above.
10. All Augustine excerpts are from the translation of *City of God* by Rev. Marcus Dods, retrieved from Project Gutenberg: https://www.gutenberg.org/files/45304/45304-h/45304-h.htm#Page_177.
11. *Questions on the Heptateuch*; see Mark Vessey, ed. *A Companion to Augustine* (West Sussex: Wiley, 2012), xxxii.
12. *On the Lord's Sermon on the Mount*; see Ibid., xxxiv.
13. Source: *Summa Theologica*, by St. Thomas Aquinas. Translated by The Fathers of the English Dominican Province. Benziger Brothers: 1947.
14. G. E. M. Anscombe, "War and Murder," in *Nuclear Weapons: A Catholic Response*, ed. Walter Stein (New York: Sheed and Ward, 1961), 45–62; Thomas Nagel, "War and Massacre," *Philosophy and Public Affairs* 1 (1972): 123–144; Michael Walzer, *Just and Unjust Wars: A Moral Argument with Historical Illustrations*, 2nd ed. (New York: Basic Books, 1992).
15. See "Principles of the Just War," Mt. Holyoke College, accessed October 23, 2020, https://www.mtholyoke.edu/acad/intrel/pol116/justwar.htm.
16. See Augustine, *City of God*, Book Three, Chapter Ten.
17. See Arendt, *Origins of Totalitarianism* (New York: Harcourt, 1968), xxvi.

Chapter 11

Capital Punishment

Prefatory Note

The reader is encouraged to watch *Dead Man Walking* (1995) and *Making a Murderer* (2015, 2018) before reading further.[1] The chapter contains spoilers, including some in the first section below. Much of the chapter will not make sense without first seeing *Dead Man Walking* at the very least. Also, having familiarity with the cinematic content will greatly enhance one's reading experience. Before your viewing and reading, consider the following questions:

QUESTIONS FOR CONSIDERATION

a. Reflect on your own personal stance about the death penalty before reading further. What is it? If you watched the film or the show before beginning to read this, what was your stance before your viewing experience? Keep that in mind as you read. Perhaps jot it down in a notebook or journal.

1. Go to a website like https://www.justwatch.com/ for information about which streaming services have each, and whether or not it is free, for rent, or for purchase. All details about the production and actors in the films and shows of this chapter are from IMDb. See https://www.imdb.com/.

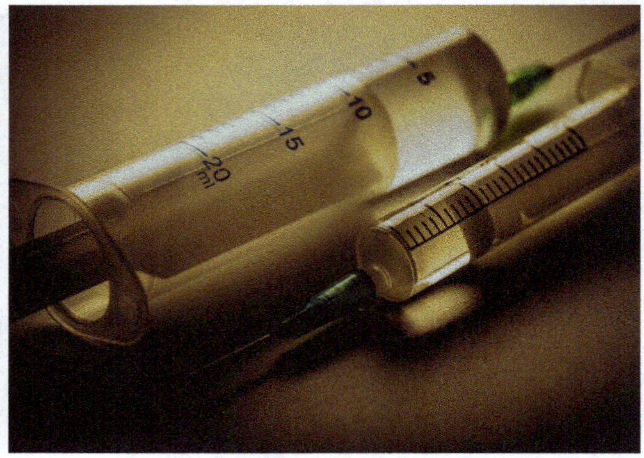

11.1 Introduction and Overview

A convicted rapist and murderer who admits to his crimes and resists expressing regret or remorse is killed by the punishment of lethal injection. The man's punishment would not strike many people as unjust or inappropriate. But this exact scenario plays out in *Dead Man Walking*, and the film nonetheless raises serious questions and doubts about the justice of the death penalty.[1]

CAPITAL PUNISHMENT
Considered synonymous with the death penalty; the most serious consequence, reserved for the most serious crimes.

RETENTIONISTS
Those in favor of maintaining the death penalty.

DETERRENCE
Prevention; the effect of compelling someone not to do something.

RETRIBUTION
Payback; responding to a wrong by inflicting harm; an eye for an eye.

LEX TALIONIS
Synonymous with "an eye for an eye"; associated with retributive justice.

Philosophers who have argued in favor of **capital punishment** (**retentionists**) include many notables, such as Aquinas, Locke, Kant, Mill, and Hegel. Aquinas, Locke, and Mill[2] focus in large part on the **deterrence** effect of such a punishment, in that it prevents heinous crime by deterring would-be offenders. Ernest van den Haag is a notable recent philosopher who uses this argument.[2] Kant heavily relies on the claim that the death penalty is the most fitting and just **retribution** for the most serious crimes, especially murder.[3] The core concept in this argument is that of "an eye for an eye," also known by the Latin phrase "***lex talionis***."[3] A notable recent thinker who addresses this argument is Igor Primoratz.[4] A third argument that some use to justify the death penalty is the satisfaction it brings to victims and their loved ones.

One notable philosopher who argues against the death penalty is the twentieth-century French thinker, Albert Camus.[5] The ancient Stoic, Seneca, also raises doubts about capital punishment.[6] Additionally, the Catholic Church has been opposed to the death penalty since 1995, and Pope Francis recently stated that opposition more strongly.[7] Those opposed

2. Recall from Chapters Three and Four that they represent the natural law, social contract, and utilitarian ethical theories, respectively. See the appendix of biographies for more information about them.
3. Recall from Chapter Three that Kant's ethics, also known as "deontological ethics," is non-consequentialist. Kant's argument for the death penalty is similarly non-consequentialist.

© bakdc/Shutterstock.com

© icedmocha/Shutterstock.com

to capital punishment are **abolitionists**.[4] Arguments against the death penalty include (1) a questioning of the deterrence effect, in some cases using statistics to show that capital punishment does not effectively deter offenders. Hugo Adam Bedau is a notable recent philosopher who makes this argument.[8] (2) The retentionist argument that relies on the notion of an "eye for an eye" also comes into question by abolitionists, most notably Jeffrey Reiman, who undermines this argument by taking it to its furthest logical extent, asking whether we should rape rapists if we justify murdering murderers.[9] Primoratz also entertains doubts about this argument, though he ultimately undermines those objections.[10] (3) Another highly significant abolitionist argument is that despite the best efforts of the legal system, the possibility always remains that the person being executed is actually innocent. The justice system is man-made, and therefore inevitably imperfect, these arguers say. Also, as the documentary series *Making a Murderer*[11] illustrates, confessions can be coerced and false. (4) An additional argument against capital punishment relies on the notion of the value and dignity of human life, which proponents say any form of murder undermines—even when the most heinous criminals are executed. Using natural law, the Catholic Church advances this argument. Bedau advances it as well.[12] (5) Yet another anti-death penalty claim is that it has a brutalizing effect on those who execute it, as well as society. Seneca suggests this and Reiman is a noteworthy recent thinker who articulates it.[13] (6) Finally, the argument that capital punishment in any form amounts to "cruel and unusual punishment" effectively eliminated it in the US from 1972 to 1976. The Supreme Court's ruling in *Furman v. Georgia* relied on this argument.[5] [14]

ABOLITIONISTS
Often used to describe those opposed to slavery; also refers to those opposed to the death penalty.

4. Plato's dialogues convey views both in favor of and against the death penalty. In the *Laws*, for instance, there are at least a few arguments emphatically in support of the death penalty. However, in more than one dialogue, Plato has Socrates argue that it is better to suffer injustice than to do it, and that the just are never harmed. If it is possible to mistakenly convict someone to death, as in the case of the real Socrates, then these teachings may imply that it is better not to sentence anyone to death. Because this line of thinking might imply an opposition to imprisonment as well, it is questionable to go down this path though.

5. In a correspondence with me, Eric Gentes provided the following helpful clarity on this topic: In Furman, the Court did not find that the death penalty was inherently cruel and unusual. Rather, they found that *the way it was carried out* in the US amounted to cruel and unusual punishment because it was so arbitrary. A good one-page summary is at: https://www.oyez.org/cases/1971/69-5030.

11.2 Deterrence

11.2.1 Excerpts from John Locke's *Second Treatise of Government:* Chapters Two and Three

POLITICAL POWER
In Locke, the ability to punish offenses, including imposing the penalty of death; distinct from paternal or maternal power, in which it is unjust to impose such an extreme penalty.

LAW OF NATURE
In Locke, the law that applies to all of mankind, that no one should harm another in their life, liberty, or property; see Chapter Three of this textbook.

STATE OF NATURE
In Locke, the state in which all humans exist when not part of a civil society with a justly agreed upon government; the law of nature still applies there and must be enforced by everyone in this state, since there is no rightful representative authority.

In Locke's *Second Treatise of Government*, he argues that those with **political power** ought to punish offenders against the **law of nature** as severely as needed in order to deter against future offenses and provide just retribution. He includes death as a justified punishment for the most severe crimes, including but not limited to murder. He discusses this largely within the context of the **state of nature**, which is what people exist in when they don't have a government.[6] The following is from Chapters Two and Three of the *Second Treatise of Government*:

Chapter Two.

Section Seven

And that all men may be restrained from invading others' rights, and from doing hurt to one another, and the law of nature be observed, which willeth the peace and preservation of all mankind, the execution of the law of nature is, in that state, put into every man's hands, whereby every one has a right to punish the transgressors of that law to such a degree, as may hinder its violation.

> By 'state,' he means the state of nature.

> This is a crucial point. The purpose of punishment is to prevent violations of the law of nature.

[. . .]

ABSOLUTE ARBITRARY POWER
Despotic or absolute power over everything and everyone with no rule of law or other guiding principles; such power is illegitimate in Locke and forces everyone into the State of Nature where they must fend for themselves and each other, including possibly overthrowing the entity with absolute power.

REPARATION
That which is given to those from whom something was unjustly taken; if their horse was stolen, the just reparation would be something equal to or greater than the value of the horse; the term is often used today to describe payments made to the descendants of former slaves.

Section Eight

And thus, in the state of nature, one man comes by a power over another; but yet no **absolute or arbitrary power**, to use a criminal, when he has got him in his hands, according to the passionate heats, or boundless extravagancy of his own will; but only to retribute to him, so far as calm reason and conscience dictate, what is proportionate to his transgression, which is so much as may serve for **reparation** and restraint: for these two are the only reasons, why one man may lawfully do harm to another, which is what we call punishment.

6. See Chapter Three of this textbook for a more detailed treatment of these concepts.

The only justifications for punishment, then, are restoring to a victim what they've lost, and preventing future crime. Note that he does not mention mere retribution, or an "eye for an eye."

In transgressing the law of nature, the offender declares himself to live by another rule than that of reason and common equity, which is that measure God has set to the actions of men, for their mutual security; and so he becomes dangerous to mankind, the tye,[7] which is to secure them from injury and violence, being slighted and broken by him. Which being a trespass against the whole species, and the peace and safety of it, provided for by the law of nature, every man upon this score, by the right he hath to preserve mankind in general, may restrain, or where it is necessary, destroy things noxious to them, and so may bring such evil on any one, who hath transgressed that law, as may make him repent the doing of it, and thereby deter him, and by his example others, from doing the like mischief. . .

Someone who is a threat can be restrained, or if needed, destroyed, for the purpose of making him and others like him not commit future crime.

Section Eleven

[. . .] By right of self-preservation, as every man has a power to punish the crime, to prevent its being committed again, by the right he has of preserving all mankind, and doing all reasonable things he can in order to that end: and thus it is, that every man, in the state of nature, has a power to kill a murderer, both to deter others from doing the like injury, which no reparation can compensate, by the example of the punishment that attends it from everybody, and also to secure men from the attempts of a criminal, who having renounced reason, the common rule and measure God hath given to mankind, hath, by the unjust violence and slaughter he hath committed upon one, declared war against all mankind, and therefore may be destroyed as a lion or tiger, one of those wild savage beasts, with whom men can have no society nor security: and upon this is grounded that great law of nature, Whoso sheddeth man's blood, by man shall his blood be shed.

In other crimes, like robbery, reparation can restore what was lost. The victim can have what was stolen returned to them, or can be remunerated for their loss.

By using this wording, Locke makes it sound as though he is for mere retribution for its own sake. However, as one can see above, he is only for *lex talionis* in order to prevent future crime. His argument for retribution is really based on deterrence.

7. Just as in modern English, British spellings often differ from American ones, there are spelling differences between seventeenth-century English and modern English.

And Cain was so fully convinced, that everyone had a right to destroy such a criminal, that after the murder of his brother, he cries out, Every one that findeth me, shall slay me; so plain was it writ in the hearts of all mankind.

> Locke is referring here to the story of Cain and Abel from the Book of Genesis.

Section Twelve

By the same reason may a man in the state of nature punish the lesser breaches of that law. It will perhaps be demanded, with death? I answer, each transgression may be punished to that degree, and with so much severity, as will suffice it to make it an ill bargain to the offender, give him cause to repent, and terrify others from doing the like. [. . .]

> Locke is focusing on deterrence here again, and he also wants the death penalty to provoke repentance in the perpetrator.

[. . .]

Chapter Three

Section Sixteen

STATE OF WAR
The state that exists when one violates the law of nature; the offender puts himself into this state, allowing anyone to harm or even execute him.

THE **state of war** is a state of enmity and destruction: and therefore declaring by word or action, not a passionate and hasty, but a sedate settled design upon another man's life, puts him in a state of war with him against whom he has declared such an intention, and so has exposed his life to the other's power to be taken away by him, or any one that joins with him in his defence, and espouses his quarrel; it being reasonable and just, I should have a right to destroy that which threatens me with destruction: for, by the fundamental law of nature, man being to be preserved as much as possible, when all cannot be preserved, the safety of the innocent is to be preferred: and one may destroy a man who makes war upon him, or has discovered an enmity to his being, for the same reason that he may kill a wolf or a lion; because such men are not under the ties of the common law of reason, have no other rule, but that of force and violence, and so may be treated as beasts of prey, those dangerous and noxious creatures, that will be sure to destroy him whenever he falls into their power.

© Erni/Shutterstock.com

> Here Locke is defending killing out of self-defense. This is another scenario in which punishing someone by killing them may be justified: if it must be done to protect one's life or others' lives.

Section Seventeen

And hence it is, that he who attempts to get another man into his absolute power, does thereby put himself into a state of war with him; it being to be understood as a declaration of a design upon his life: for I have reason to conclude, that he who would get me into his power without my consent, would use me as he pleased when he had got me there, and destroy me too when he had a fancy to it; for no body can desire to have me in his absolute power, unless it be to compel me by force to that which is against the right of my freedom, i.e., make me a slave. To be free from such a force is the only security of my preservation; and reason bids me look on him, as an enemy to my preservation, who would take away that freedom which is the fence to it; so that he who makes an attempt to enslave me, thereby puts himself into a state of war with me. He that, in the state of nature, would take away the freedom that belongs to any one in that state, must necessarily be supposed to have a design to take away everything else, that freedom being the foundation of all the rest; as he that, in the state of society, would take away the freedom belonging to those of that society or commonwealth, must be supposed to design to take away from them everything else, and so be looked on as in a state of war.

> By mentioning civil government here, Locke is implying that the justification for killing those who initiate a state of war extends from the state of nature to civil society.

> Not only is a person justified in killing someone who threatens their life, but also someone who threatens their liberty.

Section Eighteen

This makes it lawful for a man to kill a thief, who has not in the least hurt him, nor declared any design upon his life, any farther than, by the use of force, so to get him in his power, as to take away his money, or what he pleases, from him; because using force, where he has no right, to get me into his power, let his pretence be what it will, I have no reason to suppose, that he, who would take away my liberty, would not, when he had me in his power, take away everything else. And therefore it is lawful for me to treat him as one who has put himself into a state of war with me, i.e., kill him if I can; for to that hazard does he justly expose himself, whoever introduces a state of war, and is aggressor in it.

> One may kill a thief as well, because one who threatens property is likely to threaten life as well. Just as one who threatens liberty, we must assume, would also threaten life. Recall that the law of nature protects life, liberty, and property.

[. . .]

Section Twenty

But when the actual force is over, the state of war ceases between those that are in society, and are equally on both sides subjected to fair determination of the law; because then there lies open the remedy of appeal for the past injury, and to prevent future harm. . .[15]

> These last lines are very important qualifiers of Locke's claims about the justified killing of those who threaten life, liberty, or property. One can only kill in self-defense when there is no possibility of recourse to the law and its enforcers in civil society. So Locke is not attempting to justify the legality of the death penalty in cases of theft that occur within the bounds of civil society where one has recourse to the protection of law enforcement.

QUESTIONS FOR CONSIDERATION

a. Do you think Locke is correct in arguing that the punishment of death may be needed in order to prevent serious crimes? Could there be important differences between his time and ours in this regard?
b. Do you agree that if a thief or kidnapper breaks into your home, you must assume they are willing to kill you, and if you are not able to wait for law enforcement, you are justified in killing the intruder? Does a threat to liberty or property imply a threat to life as well?
c. Do you agree that there is no possibility of just reparation for murder, meaning that the penalty of death is called for when such a crime is committed?
d. Were the families of Poncelet's victims able to receive reparation for their losses in ways other than Poncelet (played by Sean Penn) receiving the death penalty?

11.2.2 Deterrence: Mill and Van den Haag, Including Annotated Excerpts from Mill's 1868 Address to the House of Commons

In an address to the House of Commons[8] from April 21, 1868, about a bill regarding capital punishment in prisons, John Stuart Mill argues that the penalty of death is an effective deterrent, in that it compels would-be criminals not to commit serious crimes.[16] Mill said:

8. The branch of the British parliament with the most law-making power.

When there has been brought home to any one, by conclusive evidence, the greatest crime known to the law; and when the attendant circumstances suggest no palliation of the guilt,[9] no hope that the culprit may even yet not be unworthy to live among mankind, nothing to make it probable that the crime was an exception to his general character rather than a consequence of it, then I confess it appears to me that to deprive the criminal of the life of which he has proved himself to be unworthy—solemnly to blot him out from the fellowship of mankind and from the catalogue of the living—is the most appropriate, as it is certainly the most impressive, mode in which society can attach to so great a crime the penal consequences which for the security of life it is indispensable to annex to it. I defend this penalty, when confined to atrocious cases, on the very ground on which it is commonly attacked—on that of humanity to the criminal; as beyond comparison the least cruel mode in which it is possible adequately to deter from the crime. If, in our horror of inflicting death, we endeavor to devise some punishment for the living criminal which shall act on the human mind with a deterrent force at all comparable to that of death, we are driven to inflictions less severe indeed in appearance, and therefore less efficacious, but far more cruel in reality.

> This part of his argument for the death penalty essentially claims that if governments attempted, without resorting to the death penalty, to properly deter offenders from committing the most heinous crimes, such punishments would be much harsher and crueler while also being less effective.

Few, I think, would venture to propose, as a punishment for aggravated murder, less than imprisonment with hard labour for life; that is the fate to which a murderer would be consigned by the mercy which shrinks from putting him to death. [. . .] What comparison can there really be, in point of severity, between consigning a man to the short pang of a rapid death, and immuring him in a living tomb, there to linger out what may be a long life in the hardest and most monotonous toil, without any of its alleviations or rewards—debarred from all pleasant sights and sounds, and cut off from all earthly hope, except a slight mitigation of bodily restraint, or a small improvement of diet? Yet even such a lot as this, because there is no one moment at which the suffering is of terrifying intensity, and, above all, because it does not contain the element, so imposing to the imagination, of the unknown, is universally reputed a milder punishment than death—stands in all codes as a mitigation of the capital penalty, and is thankfully accepted as such. [. . .] There is not, I should think, any human infliction which makes an impression on the imagination so entirely out of proportion to its real severity as the punishment of death. [. . .] As my honourable Friend the Member for Northampton (Mr. Gilpin) has himself remarked, the most that human laws can do to anyone in the matter of death is to hasten it; the man would have died at any rate; not so very much later, and on the average, I fear, with a considerably greater amount of bodily suffering. Society is asked, then, to denude itself of an instrument of punishment which, in the grave cases to which alone it is

> He is comparing living in prison for life to living in a tomb.

9. Meaning no lack of guilt.

suitable, effects its purpose at a less cost of human suffering than any other; which, while it inspires more terror, is less cruel in actual fact than any punishment that we should think of substituting for it.

Note the contrast between the perception of the death penalty and its reality, according to Mill. Also, he repeats here the notion that capital punishment is actually rather humane in his view.

[. . .] Those whose habitual way of life keeps them, so to speak, at all times within sight of the gallows, do grow to care less about it; as, to compare good things with bad, an old soldier is not much affected by the chance of dying in battle. I can afford to admit all that is often said about the indifference of professional criminals to the gallows. Though of that indifference one-third is probably bravado and another third confidence that they shall have the luck to escape, it is quite probable that the remaining third is real. [. . .] Much has been said of the sanctity of human life, and the absurdity of supposing that we can teach respect for life by ourselves destroying it.

He's addressing the objection that criminals are hardened and indifferent to the prospect of capital punishment, which was then carried out by hanging on the gallows.

He's addressing the objection here that imposing the penalty of death commits an offense against the sanctity of life.

But I am surprised at the employment of the argument, for it is one which might be brought against any punishment whatever. It is not human life only, not human life as such, that ought to be sacred to us, but human feelings. The human capacity of suffering is what we should cause to be respected, not the mere capacity of existing.[10] And we may imagine somebody asking how we can teach people not to inflict suffering by ourselves inflicting it? But to this I should answer—all of us would answer—that to deter by suffering from inflicting suffering is not only possible, but the very purpose of penal justice. . .

10. Recall Bentham's argument for respecting the lives of animals, according to Chapter Eight. He argues that the possibility of suffering implies sentience, which is deserving of moral respect. Mill was highly influenced by Bentham, which may explain the wording of his remarks here.

© Labusova Olga/Shutterstock.com

Mill then goes on to address the objection that sometimes the innocent are executed, which he thinks is very rare in Britain because judges and juries are extremely careful in meting out justice in murder cases. His overall argument may have had its intended effect, since the amendment against which Mill was arguing was indeed defeated.[17]

QUESTIONS FOR CONSIDERATION

a. Do you agree with Mill that the death penalty is less cruel than other punishments we could devise in order to deter criminals from committing the worst crimes? Is it less cruel than life imprisonment, as Mill suggests? Recall Seneca on death from Chapter Six.
b. Do you agree with Mill that capital punishment inspires more terror than any other penalty, therefore making it the most effective deterrent?
c. Do you agree with Mill that even if the penalty of death deters a fraction of murderers from killing, it is worth implementing as a punishment in such cases?
d. What do you think about Mill's argument that wrongly executing the innocent is so rare that it is not an objection worthy of serious weight?
e. How is Mill's utilitarianism evident in the argument above?
f. Do you think the prospect of being hung would have deterred Poncelet from committing the crimes for which he is guilty?

Van den Haag, in 1986, famously argued in favor of the death penalty. He acknowledges that capital punishment may not in fact be an effective deterrent. However, given the mere *possibility* that lives may be spared by the deterrence of murder, van den Haag favors retention over abolition. He argues that most abolitionists would remain opposed to the death penalty even if it were more certainly an effective deterrent. This is tantamount to valuing the lives of murderers over victims, according to van den Haag. He thinks we should value the lives of victims more, and in so doing, be in favor of capital punishment even just as a possible deterrent.[18] He argues that the lives of murderers have "negative value"[19] and that even if it deters only one murder in a year, the penalty of death is still warranted.

g. Recall *Dead Man Walking's* treatment of the value of Poncelet's life. Does the film seem to be in agreement with van den Haag that murderers' lives have "negative value"?
h. Do you agree with van den Haag on this point? Why or why not?
i. Do you think van den Haag's argument is persuasive? Does it prompt you to reconsider your views on the death penalty?

11.3 *Lex Talionis*: Kant and Bedau: Including an Excerpt from Kant's *Philosophy of Law*

Kant is perhaps the most famous example of one who argues for the death penalty primarily on the basis of retribution, or an "eye for an eye." Some relevant excerpts from his 1796 *Philosophy of Law* are as follows:

> . . . The undeserved evil which any one commits on another, is to be regarded as perpetrated on himself. Hence it may be said: 'If you slander another, you slander yourself; if you steal from another, you steal from yourself; if you strike another, you strike yourself; if you kill another, you kill yourself.' This is the Right of Retaliation ***(jus talionis)***; and properly understood, it is the only Principle which in regulating a Public Court, as distinguished from mere private judgment, can definitely assign both the quality and quantity of a just penalty. All other standards are wavering and uncertain[11] . . . [20] . . . Whoever steals anything makes the property of all insecure; he therefore robs himself of all security in property, according to the Right of Retaliation. Such a one has nothing, and can acquire nothing, but he has the Will to live; and this is only possible by others supporting him. But as the State should not do this gratuitously, he must for this purpose yield his powers to the State to be used in penal labour; and thus he falls for a time, or it may be for life, into a condition of slavery.

He's talking about imprisonment with hard labor here.

11. This language of certitude should remind us of Chapter Three and the foundations for Kant's ethics, which he says must be based on a priori reason in order to be pure and certain.

> –But whoever has committed Murder, must ***die***. There is, in this case, no juridical[12] substitute or surrogate, that can be given or taken for the satisfaction of Justice. There is no Likeness or proportion between Life, however painful, and Death; and therefore there is no Equality between the crime of Murder and the retaliation of it but what is judicially accomplished by the execution of the Criminal.[21] [. . .]

As Chapter Three makes clear, Kant values human life highly, and the above is consistent with that. Because life is so precious, the only adequate and proportionate response to murder is having the murderer's life taken. It is possible to object to this argument using Kant's own ethical theory though. If a human life is an end in itself and must be treated accordingly, eliminating a person from existence in order to right a wrong and/or prevent future harm uses their life as a means to an end.

In a 1993 essay, Hugo Adam Bedau writes about the difficulties involved in putting Kant's stance into practice. He explains that in the eighteenth century, first- and second-degree murder were distinguished, in part to assess who deserves the death penalty. Bedau adds that those killed as a result of manslaughter are nonetheless dead, just like those killed in gruesome murders. The result here, he argues, is that it is very difficult to determine who really deserves capital punishment. Another complicating factor is whether or not a legally-administered death could ever really be proportionate to the most grisly murders. Bedau draws on Camus for this argument.[22]

QUESTIONS FOR CONSIDERATION

a. Did Poncelet really receive a punishment that was proportionate to his crimes?
b. Which argument more properly acknowledges Poncelet's basic human dignity: Kant's argument for the death penalty or the possible Kantian argument against it?

11.4 *Making a Murderer* and the Possibility of Innocence

The docu-series *Making a Murderer* chronicles the life of Steven Avery, who was convicted of murder and had his sentence overturned, only to become convicted of murder once again. The series does not attempt to make a case either for his innocence or guilt; however, it presents compelling evidence about the many factors that can lead to false convictions, including corruption in the judicial system, the difficulty of finding adequate legal representation for those who are economically disadvantaged, the difficulty of establishing and maintaining an unbiased jury in the face of media coverage and public opinion, and the reality of coerced false confessions.

12. Related to the law or judicial proceedings.

Van den Haag presents data from Bedau and Radelet indicating that out of 7,000 people executed in the US between 1900 and 1985, twenty-five were innocent.[23] The lawyer featured in Season Two of *Making a Murderer,* Kathleen Zellner, has overturned nineteen convictions in twenty-three years (1997–2020) with her firm alone.[24] *USA Today* reported in 2019 that there were over sixty organizations in the country attempting to overturn wrongful convictions through DNA testing,[13] and the *Innocence Project* reported that 356 people had been proven innocent as a result.[25] The *Innocence Project* reports that 130 exonerees were wrongfully convicted for murder and that 60 percent of its total exonerees (375 from 1989 to August 2020) were African American.[26]

In a 1989 essay, Igor Primoratz primarily addresses the *lex talionis*, or retributive justice, argument for the death penalty. He argues for it, on grounds similar to Kant; however, he also suggests reform. Given the fact that there are some cases in which there is "no room whatever for reasonable doubt as to the guilt and full responsibility of the accused," the death penalty could be retained just for such cases.[27] The implication is that if there is any doubt whatsoever, the death penalty must not be applied. Doing away with capital punishment because of the possibility of innocence, he argues, would give murderers an advantage over other offenders in that they alone would not receive punishments proportionate to their crimes.[28]

QUESTIONS FOR CONSIDERATION

a. Does any of the data presented above surprise you in any way? Why or why not? How does it compare to Mill's statements about false convictions, and the data from Bedau and Radelet?
b. Though DNA evidence has overturned dozens of murder convictions in the US, it also presents a new highly reliable way of ensuring guilt beyond the shadow of a doubt. Does this evidence, as well as the above argument from Primoratz, affect your stance in any way? Are you more or less in favor of retention, abolition, or reform?

13. In a correspondence with me, Eric Gentes explained that DNA evidence is available in a minority of cases, and that without it, it is nearly impossible to prove that a person was wrongly convicted. Thus, the number of people exonerated by the *Innocence Project* may only represent the tip of the iceberg.

11.5 The Value of Human Life and *Dead Man Walking*

Dead Man Walking presents the argument that it is easy to kill a monster, but hard to kill a human being. Therefore, dehumanization is required in order to implement the death penalty. The film conveys the message that every person deserves respect, even someone like Poncelet. When he expresses to Sr. Prejean (Susan Sarandon) at the end of the film that no one had ever called him a son of God before, he simultaneously acknowledges the profound effect that her respect for his life has on him as well as the effect that his mistreatment by others throughout his life has had on him. He clearly expresses regret and remorse as a result of Sr. Prejean's relationship with him; as a result of her being "the face of love" for him.

QUESTIONS FOR CONSIDERATION

a. Is Poncelet's racism and violence excusable at all given the fact that he was poor, uneducated, and was seemingly never treated with the human dignity that Sr. Prejean displayed toward him?
b. Do you think Poncelet would have apologized for his crimes sooner if he had met Sr. Prejean sooner? Is it possible that he never would have committed his crimes if he had a relationship with someone like her sooner?
c. Does a racist murderer like Poncelet deserve respect at all?
d. Do your answers to these questions affect your stance on whether or not he received the death penalty justly?

11.6 Brutalization, "Cruel and Unusual Punishment," and Satisfaction: Seneca and *Dead Man Walking,* Including Excerpts from Letter Seven

As discussed in Chapter Six, the ancient Roman Stoic, Seneca, wrote a series of now-famous letters, many of which deal with the topic of death. The following treats the death penalty in particular, replete with Seneca's reflections on some of the Roman methods for capital punishment, and some of Seneca's negative thoughts about crowds.

Excerpts from Letter Seven:[29]

> [. . .] But nothing is so damaging to good character as the habit of lounging at the games; for then it is that vice steals subtly upon one through the avenue of pleasure.
>
> What do you think I mean? I mean that I come home more greedy, more ambitious, more voluptuous,[14] and even more cruel and inhuman, because I

14. One possible meaning of this word is "acclimated to luxury or sensual pleasure."

> have been among human beings. By chance I attended a mid-day exhibition, expecting some fun, wit, and relaxation—an exhibition at which men's eyes have respite from the slaughter of their fellow-men. But it was quite the reverse. The previous combats were the essence of compassion; but now all the trifling is put aside and it is pure murder. The men have no defensive armour. They are exposed to blows at all points, and no one ever strikes in vain.
>
> Many persons prefer this programme to the usual pairs and to the bouts "by request." Of course they do; there is no helmet or shield to deflect the weapon. What is the need of defensive armour, or of skill? All these mean delaying death. In the morning they throw men to the lions and the bears; at noon, they throw them to the spectators. The spectators demand that the slayer shall face the man who is to slay him in his turn; and they always reserve the latest conqueror for another butchering. The outcome of every fight is death, and the means fire and sword. This sort of thing goes on while the arena is empty.
>
> You may retort: 'But he was a highway robber: he killed a man!' And what of it? Granted that, as a murderer, he deserved this punishment, what crime have you committed, poor fellow, that you should deserve to sit and see this show?

APPEAL TO THE PEOPLE
The informal fallacy that occurs when one offers popular assent or popular opinion as a supporting premise for one's conclusion. For example, "90% of parents prefer corporal punishment, therefore it is right." Not only is the premise false, but it does not logically support the conclusion. Another example (at a political rally): "Everyone in this country knows that murderers deserve what's coming to them! Don't be a defender of murderers. Support the death penalty" (followed by cheers). In this case, the first premise is false and also does not logically support the conclusion. Many people thinking something does not make that thing true. In this example, the atmosphere functions essentially as another premise resting on popular support. The cheering crowd psychologically compels one to accept the arguer's claims, yet the opinions of those present are not an adequate reason for supporting such a conclusion.

> He's implying here that the spectator, who hasn't committed a crime, is punished by seeing the executions.

> In the morning they cried 'Kill him! Lash him! Burn him! Why does he meet the sword in so cowardly a way? Why does he strike so feebly? Why doesn't he die game? Whip him to meet his wounds! Let them receive blow for blow, with chests bare and exposed to the stroke!' And when the games stop for the intermission, they announce: 'A little throatcutting in the meantime, so that there may still be something going on!'
>
> Come now; do you not understand even this truth, that a bad example reacts on the agent? Thank the immortal gods that you are teaching cruelty to a person who cannot learn to be cruel.[15]
>
> The young character, which cannot hold fast to righteousness, must be rescued from the mob; it is too easy to side with the majority. Even Socrates, Cato, and Laelius[16] might have been shaken in their moral strength by a crowd that was unlike them. . .[30]

Clearly, the Roman methods of execution that Seneca describes are no longer in practice, at least in the US. However, the use of crowds to influence people's opinions is still widespread. The fallacy of **appeal to the people** occurs when one attempts to support a claim simply by arguing that because many people believe it, it must be true. This regularly occurs at political rallies and in advertisements. Questions remain (see below) about whether or not the spectacle of modern executions has a similar effect on those in attendance, and possibly society at large.

---

15. Do you think he means that he himself cannot be taught to be cruel?

16. See the appendix of biographies for Socrates's background. Seneca is probably referring to Cato the Younger here, who was a Roman statesman and Stoic. For more about his life, including his involvement with Spartacus, see: *Encyclopedia Britannica*, s.v. "Marcus Porcius Cato," accessed October 16, 2020, https://www.britannica.com/biography/Marcus-Porcius-Cato-Roman-senator-95-46-BC. Laelius was a Roman general and politician. See *Encyclopedia Britannica*, s.v., "Gaius Laelius," accessed October 16, 2020, https://www.britannica.com/biography/Gaius-Laelius.

Reiman argues that the satisfaction granted to victims by their perpetrators' executions is primitive. He adds that adhering strictly to the principle of an "eye for an eye" means that we must allow criminals to dictate our behavior in punishing. He points out that there are some crimes, like rape and torture, that humanity clearly should not try to duplicate. Just because something is deserved, does not mean we should do it, writes Reiman. By refusing to torture those who tortured, rape those who raped, or kill those who killed, we as a society clearly state that we think these things are too horrible to do to others even if someone seems to deserve it.[31] He says, ". . . Publicly refusing to do horrible things to our fellows both signals the level of our civilization *and, by our example, continues the work of civilizing*."[32] Agreeing with Nietzsche in *The Geneology of Morals*, Reiman states that "progress in civilization is characterized by a lower tolerance for one's own pain and that suffered by others."[33] Human beings allow themselves to regress into an uncivilized state when they implement the death penalty, according to Reiman. We make progress as a society when we refuse to impose this ultimate punishment.

© David Wayne Buck/Shutterstock.com

The Roman Colosseum, where many executions took place.

Another consideration in the debate about the brutalizing effects of capital punishment is as follows: Bedau points out that psychologists present compelling evidence that some people commit murders because they are afraid or unable to kill themselves, and prefer to have the legal system do it. Imprisonment, according to the evidence, does not incite murder or other violent crime in comparable fashion.[34] In this way, then, capital punishment makes criminals more savage.

QUESTIONS FOR CONSIDERATION

a. Was anyone benefited by Poncelet's execution? Perhaps the victims' loved ones? Was anyone, besides Poncelet, harmed?
b. Do the differences between the modern methods of capital punishment (lethal injection in the US) and Roman methods lead to the conclusion that modern executions don't have the same brutalizing effects on people as ancient methods did?
c. Were the Romans using "cruel and unusual punishment"? What about US states who use lethal injection?
d. Consider the scene of Poncelet's death and the various reactions of those in attendance. Does a phenomenon like the appeal to the people fallacy occur when people watch an execution alongside the victim's loved ones who presumably are there to derive some satisfaction? In other words, by joining in with them, are other spectators liable to agree with them about the rectitude of the punishment? Are all attendees being desensitized to murder by being there? What about the members of the society that sanctioned the killing? Are all affected in some way?
e. Do you agree with Reiman that capital punishment is a step back in civilization? Why or why not? Does this affect your overall stance on the death penalty?

11.7 Other Considerations: Costs and Race

Bedau addresses the financial costs of the death penalty, and though he is an abolitionist, he admits that it is very difficult to establish whether abolition or retention saves taxpayers and/or governments money.[35]

In *Dead Man Walking*, Poncelet remarks about the poverty of the population on death row. Bedau argues that legal systems disproportionately give the death penalty to the poor as well as racial minorities.[36] Primoratz admits that such findings are convincing, but that it is not relevant to the argument against capital punishment. This is because there are inequities in other punishments as well, and if such injustice implied the abolition of the death penalty, it would logically imply the abolition of other penalties as well. Instead of arguing against capital punishment, then, Primoratz argues, one must determine what reforms are needed to the criminal justice system as a whole.[37]

QUESTIONS FOR CONSIDERATION

a. Is the death penalty debate more complex than just a dichotomy between retentionists and abolitionists? Should a third category of "reformers" receive equal consideration?
b. Consider the statistics from The Innocence Project, the above thoughts of Bedau and Primoratz about vulnerable populations, and the high-profile killings of African Americans by law enforcement in recent years. Should the US reconsider the death penalty? Should it reconsider other aspects of the entire criminal justice system? Is the former question necessarily implied by the latter?
c. Should those with mental illness receive the death penalty for committing murder? Consider the difficulties involved in deeming someone either sane or mentally ill. Consider the articles linked to below about this topic.

11.8 Resources for Further Learning

11.8.1 Other Relevant Film

The Green Mile (1999), *Bundy* (2002), *Monster* (2003), and *Conviction* (2010)

TV Shows: *Dexter* (2006–2013), *The Walking Dead* (2010–present): Season 9, ep. 1.

11.8.2 Books

Cesare Beccaria, *On Crimes and Punishment*, trans. Henry Paolucci (Indianapolis: Bobbs-Merrill, 1963).

Hugo Adam Bedau, *The Death Penalty in America* (Oxford: Oxford University Press, 1982).

Helen Prejean, *Dead Man Walking* (Vintage, New York: 1994).
Tom Regan, ed. *Matters of Life and Death: New Introductory Essays in Moral Philosophy*, 2nd ed. (New York, Random House, 1986).

11.8.3 Freely Available Online Resources

11.8.3.1 History of Capital Punishment

Michael H. Reggio, "History of the Death Penalty," *PBS Frontline*, February 9, 1999, https://www.pbs.org/wgbh/frontline/article/history-of-the-death-penalty/.

11.8.3.2 Capital Punishment and Mental Health

"Death Penalty and Mental Illness," Amnesty International, May 18, 2017, https://www.amnestyusa.org/issues/death-penalty/death-penalty-facts/death-penalty-and-mental-illness/.
"Death Penalty," National Alliance on Mental Illness, accessed October 16, 2020, https://www.nami.org/Advocacy/Policy-Priorities/Divert-from-Justice-Involvement/Death-Penalty.
Shaila Dewan, "Does the U.S. Execute People with Mental Illness? It's Complicated," *The New York Times*, April 11, 2017, https://www.nytimes.com/interactive/2017/us/mental-illness-death-penalty.html.
"USA: The Execution of Mentally Ill Offenders," Amnesty International, January 31, 2006, https://www.amnesty.org/en/documents/AMR51/003/2006/en/.

11.8.3.3 The Catholic Church's Stance on the Death Penalty

Merrit Kennedy, "Catholic Church Now Formally Opposes Death Penalty in All Cases," *NPR*, August 2, 2018, https://www.npr.org/2018/08/02/634864608/catholic-church-now-formally-opposes-death-penalty-in-all cases#:~:text=The%20Catholic%20Church%20now%20formally%20considers%20the%20death,the%20common%20good%22%20in%20response%20to%20%22certain%20crimes.%22.
James Martin, "Pope Francis closes the door on the death penalty in 'Fratelli Tutti,'" *America*, October 4, 2020, https://www.americamagazine.org/politics-society/2020/10/04/pope-francis-closes-door-death-penalty-fratelli-tutti?fbclid=IwAR0PmLAj8KpiczOQLm0qfFRUpWM2UJ8NTwUrVmyaHaSyeJU9hq2WtC2TK5M.
John Nichols, "Pope's Influence on Death Penalty," *CBS News*, April 4, 2005, https://www.cbsnews.com/news/popes-influence-on-death-penalty/.
Carol S. Steiker and Jordan M. Steiker, "The Pope Changed the Catholic Church's Position on the Death Penalty. Will the Supreme Court Follow?," *Time*, August 15, 2018, https://time.com/5359690/pope-death-penalty-supreme-court-united-states/.

Endnotes

1. *Dead Man Walking*, written by Helen Prejean and Tim Robbins; directed by Tim Robbins (Havoc, Polygram Filmed Entertainment, Working Title Films, 1996). *Making a Murderer*, written and directed by Moira Demos and Laura Ricciardi (Synthesis Films, 2015, 2018).
2. Ernest van den Haag, "The Ultimate Punishment: A Defense," *Harvard Law Review* 99: 1662–1669.
3. Immanuel Kant, *The Philosophy of Law: An Exposition of the Fundamental Principles of Jurisprudence as the Science of Right* [1796], trans. William Hastie (Edinburgh: T & T Clark, 1887). Accessed here: https://oll.libertyfund.org/titles/kant-the-philosophy-of-law.
4. Primoratz, *Justifying Legal Punishment* (New Jersey: Humanities Press International, Inc., 1989).
5. See "Reflections on the Guillotine," 1957.
6. See Letter Seven, excerpted in this chapter.
7. See Merrit Kennedy, "Catholic Church Now Formally Opposes Death Penalty in All Cases," *NPR*, August 2, 2018, https://www.npr.org/2018/08/02/634864608/catholic-church-now-formally-opposes-death-penalty-in-all-cases#:~:text=The%20Catholic%20Church%20now%20formally%20considers%20the%20death,the%20common%20good%22%20in%20response%20to%20%22certain%20crimes.%22; and James Martin, "Pope Francis closes the door on the death penalty in 'Fratelli Tutti," *America*, October 4, 2020, https://www.americamagazine.org/politics-society/2020/10/04/pope-francis-closes-door-death-penalty-fratelli-tutti?fbclid=IwAR0PmLAj8KpiczOQLm0qfFRUpWM2UJ8NTwUrVmyaHaSyeJU9hq2WtC2TK5M.
8. Bedau, "The Case Against the Death Penalty," in *Matters of Life and Death*, 3rd ed. (New York: McGraw-Hill, 1992).
9. Reiman, "Justice, Civilization, and the Death Penalty: Answering van den Haag," *Philosophy and Public Affairs* 14 (1985): 115–148.
10. Primoratz, 159–164.
11. Written and directed by Moira Demos and Laura Ricciardi.
12. Bedau, 179.
13. Reiman, 134–142.
14. Lewis Vaughn's work was extremely helpful in selecting the authors and arguments on which to focus in this chapter. See Vaughn, *Doing Ethics*, 5th ed. (New York: Norton, 2019).
15. John Locke, *Second Treatise of Government*, 1690, https://www.gutenberg.org/files/7370/7370-h/7370-h.htm.
16. See John Stuart Mill, *The Collected Works of John Stuart Mill*, Volume XXVIII (Toronto: University of Toronto Press, 2006), https://oll.libertyfund.org/titles/mill-the-collected-works-of-john-stuart-mill-volume-xxviii-public-and-parliamentary-speeches-part-i.
17. Ibid.
18. Van den Haag, 1665–1666.
19. Ibid., 1666.
20. Kant, 196.
21. Ibid., 197–198.
22. Bedau, 174–175.
23. Van den Haag, 1664–1665.
24. See http://www.kathleentzellner.com/wrongful-conviction/.
25. N'dea Yancey-Bragg, "DNA is cracking mysteries and cold cases. But is genome sleuthing the 'unregulated wild west?'" *USA Today*, May 14, 2019, https://www.usatoday.com/story/news/nation/2019/05/14/heres-how-dna-cracking-cold-cases-and-exonerating-innocent/1159571001/.
26. "DNA Exonerations in the United States," Innocence Project, July 29, 2020, https://www.innocenceproject.org/dna-exonerations-in-the-united-states/.
27. Primoratz, 164.
28. Ibid., 165.
29. From *The Tao of Seneca*, Volume 1, 35–38, https://fhww.files.wordpress.com/2017/07/taoofseneca_vol1-1.pdf. This volume includes full excerpts from the Loeb Classical Library Edition: *Moral Letters to Lucilius by Seneca*, trans. Richard Mott Gummere (Cambridge, MA: Harvard University Press, 1917).
30. *The Tao of Seneca*, vol. 1, 36–37.
31. Reiman, 134–142.
32. Ibid., 136.
33. Ibid., 135.
34. Bedau, 172.
35. Ibid., 172.
36. Ibid., 177–179.
37. Ibid., 165.

Appendix of Context

Essential Background for Understanding the Philosophers, Texts, and Time Periods Discussed in This Book

The Ancient Period

Before diving into reading Plato and Aristotle, it's helpful to keep in mind some important background information. Both authors regularly reference the Greek literary tradition, including poets, political figures, accounts of historical events, and the philosophers of nature who preceded Socrates. The epic poet, Homer, the great tragedians, Sophocles, Euripides, and Aeschylus, and other notables like Hesiod and Pindar come up frequently. The great comedic playwright Aristophanes gets a mention here and there too. Lycurgus and Solon were prominent political figures. The Trojan, Persian, and Peloponnesian wars are examples of significant historical events. Notable Pre-Socratic philosophers whom Plato and Aristotle mention include Heraclitus, Empedocles, and Anaxagoras, among others. The sophists were a group of men who taught the art of rhetoric, or winning arguments through persuasion. Plato and Aristotle generally refer to them negatively. Prominent examples are Thrasymachus, Gorgias, and Protagoras. Many of these figures are discussed in the videos below.

Greek city-states often come under discussion, especially Athens and Sparta, including their laws, customs, and their most revered gods. The Greeks had a very rich set of cultural traditions, many of which were highly localized, which is foreign to many modern-day readers. And of course, all Platonic and Aristotelian texts were written in ancient Greek, which is a highly challenging and complex language to learn. The gods and traditions of the Greeks are treated in the videos below.

It's impossible for even the most advanced ancient Greek scholars to know every single background detail that's relevant to understanding Plato and Aristotle. It's probably also unlikely that students using this textbook are familiar with all of the people and places mentioned above. However, it is possible to begin to understand these great Greek thinkers without knowing *every* relevant piece of context. It's important to keep all of this in mind when approaching the texts of the ancient Greeks.

The Greeks did not conceive of the human person as moderns do today. The notion of inalienable rights based on human rationality, for instance, is not present in ancient Greek thought. The modern sense of individuality—the way in which moderns conceive of individuals as distinct from their race, gender, and culture—is foreign to ancient Greek thought. As a result, Plato and Aristotle sometimes make statements that would be politically incorrect in the twenty-first century. Though some criticism may be warranted nonetheless, treating them as harshly as we would a global citizen in our own century who make such statements would be anachronistic.

It's important to try to understand all authors on their own terms. This means that the reader ought to attempt to remove, as much as possible, their modern "spectacles," or present-day "lenses." Try to conceive of the author's perspective, with all of the human history they could not have experienced, removed. Try as much as possible to "stand in their shoes" while reading their work.

Videos on the Ancient Greeks

A basic, introductory-level overview:

> Emily Knapman, "Introduction to Ancient Greece," February 1, 2015, YouTube video, 2:31, https://www.youtube.com/watch?v=-9keQHIG_EQ#.

On the Greek gods:

> The Life Guide, "Greek Gods Explained in 12 Minutes," September 29, 2017, YouTube video, 12:23, https://www.youtube.com/watch?v=Ri-AoKE42rw#.

Fairly comprehensive Ancient Greek history:

> Arzamas, "Ancient Greece in 18 Minutes," May 30, 2017, YouTube video, 17:38, https://www.youtube.com/watch?v=gFRxmi4uCGo&feature=youtu.be.

Socrates

Socrates (469–399 BCE) was an ancient Greek philosopher who lived in Athens. He was a stonemason and a soldier, and though many referred to him as a teacher, there's good reason to think he did not consider himself to be one. He was not wealthy, though he was famous (infamous to some) for spending time with the youth of Athens—especially the well-off young men—in the *agora*, or marketplace. According to Plato's *Apology*, a dialogue about Socrates's trial, Socrates was showing the young men the value of rigorous questioning and critical thinking for the sake of seeking the truth. According to the same dialogue, those who misunderstood Socrates saw him as corrupting the youth by teaching them sophistry or rhetoric for the sake of manipulating others. He was famously arrested and executed for such

Vector illustration of Socrates in cartoon style.

corruption, and for not believing in the Greek gods. Many consider him to be a sort of martyr for philosophy because of the way he maintained his values while facing death. He initiated a unique way of thinking and conversing widely referred to as "Socratic Method." It inspired, influenced, and informed many people throughout the ages, including but not limited to educators, politicians, and authors. It is also plausible to consider Socrates to be the founder of ethics, perhaps alongside Plato and Aristotle. Socrates accomplished all of this without writing or publishing anything. He did all of his philosophical work in spoken form, usually with individuals or small groups. Many consider him to be a father figure for Western philosophy. This honor is undoubtedly due in part to the fact that he was Plato's mentor and most significant influence. The vast majority of what we know about Socrates originates from Plato and Xenophon. The former only wrote dialogues, in which Socrates is often a main character. Plato himself never explicitly indicated whether, and to what extent, readers are to associate the character Socrates with the real Socrates. Because of this, much of what we know about Socrates is somewhat unreliable, including the extent to which he really influenced Plato's thought.

Videos on Socrates

Joseph M. Forte and Maria Jacobs, "Who Was Socrates?" June 17, 2017, YouTube video, 3:06, https://www.youtube.com/watch?v=uPl6fAXiak8&t=2s.

Joseph M. Forte and Maria Jacobs, "Why is Socrates so Famous?" September 8, 2018, YouTube video, 5:26, https://www.youtube.com/watch?v=qCYf44AuxC0&t=10s.

Plato

Plato portrait in line art.

Plato was an ancient Greek philosopher who lived in Athens from 427 to 347 BCE. He was fairly wealthy, had Socrates for a mentor, and taught Aristotle. He founded the Academy, which had such an impact on Western intellectual culture that everything we refer to as "academic" derives its name from Plato's famous school. He wrote and published a great deal, all in dialogue form, possibly with the exception of a number of letters. The topics of his dialogues include every major subdiscipline of philosophy. Many of his dialogues, like the *Apology*, *Gorgias*, *Meno*,

Phaedo, and *Republic*, focus on ethics alongside other topics. His dialogues' characters often resemble real people, like Socrates, though there are also some fictitious characters. Plato's influence on the history of thought is not limited to the Academy and those educated in it. Platonism was the philosophy that clearly dominated Western intellectual culture into the 1200s, until Aristotelianism challenged it for prominence. Plato's dialogues thoroughly and rigorously treat so many foundational topics, that the famous twentieth-century philosopher Alfred North Whitehead said that all philosophy consists of footnotes to Plato.

Video on Plato's Life and the Seventh Letter

Includes many details about his brief and eventful political career:

Joseph M. Forte and Maria Jacobs, "Plato's 7th Letter: Interesting Stories About a Great Philosopher," October 24, 2020, YouTube video, 7:51, https://youtu.be/i2f_KMNh1R4.

Aristotle

Vector illustration of Aristotle in cartoon style.

Originally from Stagira, in ancient Greece, Aristotle was born in 385 BCE and died in 323 BCE. He established his own school, the Lyceum, and his work defined several subfields or subdisciplines of philosophy: For instance, he is often called the "Father of Logic." He's also a father figure to biology, which he wrote a great deal about. He was so highly regarded by the medieval philosopher/theologian Thomas Aquinas, that the latter called him "the Philosopher."

Aristotle remains the most famous student to emerge from Plato's Academy, after which modern academics gets its name. He was Plato's student there for about two decades. Aristotle was highly regarded in his time, and not just afterward—evidenced by his being selected to serve as tutor for Alexander the Great. He clearly had the educational pedigree and academic fame needed to begin his own school, the Lyceum, known also as the Peripatetic School,, lasting for about 500 years.

Though Socrates, Plato, and their followers were engaged in the study of what philosophers now refer to as subdisciplines of philosophy (like logic, metaphysics, ethics, and politics), these areas became clearly defined in large part because Aristotle devoted specific works to each of them.

Aristotle's work on metaphysics spans more than just the text with "Metaphysics" as its name. The fact that Aristotle devoted that substantial text to his study of that which is "after physics" or "beyond the physical," situating it in relation to logic and the study of nature, played a substantial role in defining metaphysics as a specific subfield or subdiscipline of philosophy. Many followed Aristotle in studying metaphysics in its own right for centuries after.

Aristotle devoted at least two works to the study of ethics: the study of the good life, and good actions. The *Nicomachean Ethics* is the most highly-regarded work of his on the topic—indeed it is recognized as Aristotle's most authoritative and complete work on ethics today, such that it is often simply called "the *Ethics*." Ethics is now one of the most—indeed perhaps THE most—important area among the growing number of philosophical subfields, and we have Aristotle to thank for delimiting it and situating it as a study of its own.

The *Politics* contains Aristotle's political theory, spanning the role of the family in the city-state, to the relation of the city-state to foreign entities. In *Nicomachean Ethics*, Aristotle defines the role of politics, especially as it relates to ethics, explaining what a good political scientist needs to do in order to create a good city that forms good people.

Aristotle's work on biology includes a now-famous text on the *Parts of Animals*, and his extensive biological research shows up in his other works as well, like his argument in *Nicomachean Ethics* Book One that the proper function of a human being, in contrast to all other natural creatures, is reason.

In the 1200s, there was a revival of research into, and scholarship based on, Aristotle's work. This took place not only among Christian intellectuals, but others as well—especially Islamic thinkers.[1]

Videos on Aristotle

Joseph M. Forte and Maria Jacobs, "What's the Big Deal About Aristotle?" January 10, 2020, YouTube video, 6:20, https://www.youtube.com/watch?v=xNWM79FwdHI&t.

Joseph M. Forte and Maria Jacobs, "Aristotle on Friendship," February 6, 2019, YouTube video, 19:07, https://www.youtube.com/watch?v=wmEfxtre6HA&t.

1. Articles about canceling Aristotle:
Agnes Callard, "Should We Cancel Aristotle?" *The New York Times*: "The Stone," July 21, 2020, https://www.nytimes.com/2020/07/21/opinion/should-we-cancel-aristotle.html.
Bryan W. Van Norden, "Who Is Canceling Aristotle?" *Medium*, July 21, 2020, https://medium.com/@bryanvannorden_14478/i-am-puzzled-by-agnes-callards-article-should-we-cancel-aristotle-92a08a4ec6de.

Epicurus

2019 Greek postage stamp depicting a bust of Epicurus.

Line art portrait of Epicurus.

Founder of Epicureanism, Epicurus lived from 341–271 BCE in the ancient Greek world. He was born in Samos, which is an island in the Mediterranean Sea, and he founded schools in Mytilene, Lampsacus, and finally Athens (the "Garden," ca. 306 BCE). Almost none of his work has survived, so scholars rely on other sources for information about Epicurus's ideas, most notably Diogenes Laertius, Lucretius, Cicero, and Plutarch. The *Letter to Menoecus* is a summary of Epicurus's ethics composed by Diogenes Laertius.[1] Epicurean ethics focuses on the attainment of happiness as pleasure, specifically long-term pleasures. It is not to be confused with crude hedonism, which seeks immediate gratification. Epicurus's physics and metaphysics reveal that he was a materialist.

Video on Ancient Rome

Arzamas, "Ancient Rome in 20 Minutes," May 30, 2017, YouTube video, https://youtu.be/46ZXl-V4qwY.

Seneca

Bronze statue of Seneca in Cordoba, Spain.

Portrait of Seneca in line art illustration.

Seneca (Lucius Annaeus Seneca, ca. 4 BCE–65 CE) was a Roman Stoic philosopher most famous for his Letters to Lucilius, in which he advances Stoic views about a life well-lived. He lauds self-control, not fearing death, and avoiding crowds, among other things. His relationships with Roman emperors include being exiled, then recalled, by Claudius, being a friend and tutor of Nero, and then being ordered by Nero to commit suicide.[2]

Epictetus

A Stoic philosopher who lived from 55–135 CE, he was born in Heirapolis in Phrygia (modern-day Turkey). He came to Rome as a slave when he was a boy. He was banished from Rome by the Emperor Domitian (ca. 89) and opened his own school in Nicopolis (in Greece). His school gained a good reputation and many followers. He seems to have written nothing. All of his extant works were composed by his student, Flavius Arrian.[3] Like other Stoics, his philosophy focuses on attaining a state of calm or tranquility through self-control.

Artist's rendering of Epictetus; engraved vector portrait with ink contours.

Videos on the Decline and Fall of Rome and Church History

History Matters, "Ten Minute History—The Fall of Rome (Short Documentary)," September 9, 2018, YouTube video, https://youtu.be/EIkeRBP5nDg.

TrueTube, "Church History in Ten Minutes," October 16, 2019, YouTube video, https://youtu.be/RQjS6NGvlQ0.

Augustine of Hippo

Augustine of Hippo (354–430 CE), an African philosopher and theologian, lived at the cusp of the early medieval period, and is referred to as both an ancient and medieval thinker. According to the Catholic Church, he is a saint, a Father of the Church, and a Doctor of the Church. These titles are due, in part, to his significant contributions to Christian philosophy and theology, which were highly influential on subsequent Christian thinkers, especially Thomas Aquinas. Scholars credit Augustine for using the philosophy of Plato to aid in the conception of God as immaterial, for instance. His work on the Holy Trinity (the Christian conception of God as three entities) is another major contribution to the Western understanding of divinity (see *On the Trinity*). His contributions to ethics include *On Free Choice of the Will* and *Confessions*, both of which also treat other topics besides ethics. His *City of God Against the Pagans* includes his contributions to political philosophy, among other subfields. His notable influences include Christian Scripture (especially Paul), Plato, the Neoplatonists, and the Stoics.

Baroque statue of Augustine on the Charles's bridge in Prague, Czech Republic.

His mentor was Ambrose, whom Augustine credits for leading him to Platonism, which had an effect on his worldview second only to the Christian faith. Augustine died in Hippo, which is in modern-day Algeria.

Video on Augustine's Life

Joseph M. Forte and Maria Jacobs, "Augustine's Life in His Own Words," October 26, 2020, YouTube video, 3:47, https://youtube/7Ex2pZULSzs.

The Medieval Period

The medieval period in the West typically refers to the time between the fall of Rome (400s CE) and the beginning of the Renaissance (1300s–1400s CE). The medieval period before 1000 is usually labeled "The Dark Ages," followed by what many call "The High Middle Ages," because historically, the former was seen as a time of economic, cultural, and intellectual decline, unlike the latter. Recent scholars, however, provide reasons to doubt this account of the so-called "Dark Ages."

Video on the "Dark" Ages

History Matters, "How 'Dark' were the Dark Ages? (Short Animated Documentary)," August 10, 2019, YouTube video, https://youtu.be/gnTMu4Ba17o.

By the 1200s, nonetheless, intellectual activity was booming, especially in and around Paris. The Roman Catholic Church had a great deal of power, was in the midst of the Crusades, had begun the Inquisition, and included many thriving religious orders. The Benedictine monks were the most highly regarded at the time, though the newly-formed Franciscans and Dominicans gained substantial traction.

Playlist on the Literature, Philosophy, Music, and Religion of the High Middle Ages

Joseph M. Forte, "The High Middles Ages in the West, Helpful Background," last updated September 4, 2020, YouTube playlist, https://www.youtube.com/playlist?list=PL8QcMfC1fvaBwFutSLep4OxszcAzqRKhH.

The scholars of the High Middle Ages inherited previous philosophy, most notably Platonism, and the work of Aristotle experienced a massive revival. The Platonism of the medievals, however, was not the same as that of today. The only Platonic dialogue that was widely available was the *Timaeus*, so most of their knowledge of Plato came through his followers. Latin was the language of scholarship. The disputation rose to prominence as a method of teaching and of publicly conveying ideas, as opposed to lectures. In a medieval disputation, an argument for a particular viewpoint is offered only after opposing viewpoints have received due consideration.

Video on Medieval Disputations

PhiLife Team, "What is Philosophical Disputatio?" April 1, 2019, YouTube video, https://youtu.be/2uuANFScjh0.

Thomas Aquinas

© Renata Sedmakova/Shutterstock.com

Painting of Aquinas from 1900 in St. Stephen's Church, Jerusalem, Israel, by Joseph Aubert.

Thomas Aquinas (1225–1274) was from Aquino, Italy, but spent much of his life in Paris because of his work at the University of Paris—the epicenter of Western intellectual life in the thirteenth century. He was born to a moderately wealthy family of Spanish descent and was educated by the Benedictines at a very early age, though he spent most of his life as a Dominican monk. As a child, he was called the "Dumb Ox" in part because of his stature, and though history has never forgotten that unfortunate nickname, Aquinas is mainly now remembered as one of the greatest minds of the Western intellectual tradition and possibly the single most influential author on Catholic teaching. He wrote numerous volumes, including commentaries on Aristotle that he spent about a decade working on. Through Islamic philosophers and his mentor Albert the Great, Aquinas learned about Aristotle, to whom he refers simply as "The Philosopher." Aquinas's work now remains as one of the most significant factors in the medieval rise of appreciation for Aristotle, and probably THE most significant factor in the use of Aristotle to benefit Christian philosophy and theology. Aquinas wrote commentaries on authors besides Aristotle and is most famous for his *Summa Theologiae* (aka *Summa Theologica*), a four-volume Latin treatise intended to be a concise introduction of all matters theological. He wrote in a style highly influenced by the practice of disputation. Other works, like the *Summa Contra Gentiles*, expand upon many of the topics in the *Summa Theologiae*. Since philosophy is the foundation for theology according to Aquinas, both "*Summas*" also contain a great deal of philosophy. Because of his work on angels, and because of his title as a "Doctor" of the Catholic Church, he is known as "The Angelic Doctor." Catholics also consider him to be a saint. Besides Aristotle, his notable influences include Plato, the Bible (esp. Paul, whom he calls simple "the Apostle"), Stoics, Augustine, and many others. Islamic philosophers like Averroes also influenced him, though Aquinas also famously argued against them. His work on ethics mainly involves incorporating Aristotle into Christianity—using aspects of the Aristotelian corpus that harmonized with Christian dogma and adjusting or arguing against what did not. Besides ethics and his work on angels, he's famous for his proofs for God's existence, his articulation of God's nature, his treatises on law and epistemology, and many other topics.[2]

2. Recommended biographies of Aquinas:
G. K. Chesterton, *Saint Thomas Aquinas* (New York: Image Books Doubleday, 1933, 1956); also Josef Pieper, *Guide to Thomas Aquinas*, trans. Richard and Clara Winston (San Francisco: Ignatius Press, 1962, 1991).

Videos on Aquinas's Life and Work

Joseph M. Forte and Maria Jacobs, "Aquinas: 'The Dumb Ox,'" October 24, 2020, YouTube video, 3:33, https://www.youtube.com/watch?v=Dj9-Z5MUHhc&feature=youtu.be.

For a very brief explanation of the Five Ways, or "proofs" for God's existence, see:

Joseph M. Forte, "Aquinas' Five Ways or Proofs for God's Existence," May 15, 2014, YouTube video, https://www.youtube.com/watch?v=SQlro0PlVg0&t.

For more stories about Aquinas, see:

Greg Aitchison, "12 Stories About St. Thomas Aquinas-by Peter Kreeft," April 13, 2012, YouTube video, https://www.youtube.com/watch?v=k-Pdo1avQHa0&list=PL8QcMfC1fvaBwFutSLep4OxszcAzqRKhH&index=11.

The Modern Period

Modernity begins with the Renaissance, and philosophy scholars usually label the beginning of modern, as opposed to medieval, philosophy as the "modern turn." The thinker responsible for this "turn" is under debate, with some pointing to the political thought of Machiavelli, others giving Descartes credit because of his famous "I think, therefore, I am," and others crediting late medieval thinkers like Ockham or even later modern thinkers like Kant. Modern philosophers before Kant are categorized as "early modern."

Major Renaissance Events	
1347	Black Death begins in Europe
1374	Francesco Petrarch, "father of the Renaissance," dies
1397	Giovanni de Medici founds the Medici Bank in Florence
1452	Birth of Leonardo da Vinci
1454	Johannes Gutenberg uses new printing press to publish the Gutenberg Bible
1475	Michelangelo Buonarroti born
1492	Columbus arrives in the Bahamas
1497	John Cabot sets sail to Newfoundland
1498	Vasco da Gama arrives in India
1509	Henry VIII crowned King of England
1513	Niccolo Machiavelli finishes writing *The Prince*
1517	Publication of Luther's Theses, beginning of Protestant Reformation
1531	Henry VIII is "Supreme Head of the Church in England"
1543	Nicolaus Copernicus's *Revolutions of the Celestial Orbits published*
1603	William Shakespeare wrote Hamlet[4]

Video on the Enlightenment

PragmaticMotion, "The Enlightenment and The Age of Reason including Francis Bacon, Rene Descartes, and Isaac Newton," July 29, 2013, YouTube video, https://www.youtube.com/watch?v=QXw7DFuqzzc&list=PL8QcMfC1fvaBf-9QZS-3A_PcORIlwjGsu&index=6.

Francis Bacon

Engraving of Bacon from 1738, via the Everett Collection.

Not to be confused with the medieval philosopher, Roger Bacon, Sir Francis Bacon (1561–1626) was an Englishman with a rather tumultuous legal and political career. He attended Trinity College, Cambridge beginning at *age twelve*, and was seriously lacking in financial support in 1579 after his father's death. Yet, in 1582, he completed a law degree, rose to great political power by 1618, and then suffered a fall from grace due to bribery charges in 1621, after which he had much more time for philosophical writing. His famous contributions to the history of thought include the novel the *New Atlantis*, a work of literary fiction, and the *New Organon*, or "True Directions Concerning the Interpretation of Nature" (1620). The latter is a work of science and philosophy written in an aphoristic style.[5]

Videos on the Thirty Years' War

(Which substantially affected Descartes):

Jabzy, "30 Years War. 3 Minute History," October 28, 2015, YouTube video, 4:28, https://www.youtube.com/watch?v=6hoPGiClufk&list=PL8QcMfC1fvaBf-9QZS-3A_PcORIlwjGsu&index=6&t=111s.

History Matters, "Ten Minute History—The Thirty Years' War (Short Documentary)," September 30, 2018, YouTube video, 9:59, https://www.youtube.com/watch?v=EBLVzdvp8qE&list=PL8QcMfC1fvaBf-9QZS-3A_PcORIlwjGsu&index=4.

Rene Descartes

Portrait of Descartes.

© Naci Yavuz/Shutterstock.com

Descartes (1596–1650) was a French, Jesuit-educated Catholic famous not only for philosophy, but also mathematics and natural science. The town of his birth (La Haye) has been renamed Descartes. His father was a lawyer and his mother died when he was just a year old. He was subsequently raised by his grandmother and his great uncle, who also was a lawyer. His collegiate education followed an Aristotelian curriculum, though he was also probably exposed to the Pre-Socratics, Plato, the Stoics, and the skeptics. While he served in the Bavarian army (allied with France) in 1619, he had three dreams that he interpreted as signs that he must re-establish the foundations of all knowledge, beginning with philosophy. For a time, he lived in Italy, followed by Paris, then the Dutch Netherlands in 1628, and finally Sweden in 1649. He had a daughter with his housekeeper in 1635, and they lived with him for a time. He contributed a dowry for his daughter's marriage in 1644. He moved to Sweden at the invitation of Queen Cristina, to join her court. He became ill the day he delivered the Statutes of the Swedish Royal Academy to her, which he composed for her. He succumbed to his illness and died in 1650.[6] His most famous works are the *Meditations on First Philosophy* and the *Discourse on the Method*, which both attempt to re-establish the basis of all knowledge on the "clear and distinct" premise: "I think, therefore, I am." Descartes argued that empirical philosophy really rested on this truth, a much firmer foundation than anything that can be obtained through the senses or imagination. He also uses his famous premise as a foundation for proofs for God's existence in those treatises.

Videos on the Glorious Revolution

(Which relate significantly to John Locke's life):

Jabzy, "Glorious Revolution. 3 Minute History," July 21, 2015, YouTube video, 3:55, https://www.youtube.com/watch?v=g77WJU3aQEA&list=PL8QcMfC1fvaBf-9QZS-3A_PcORIlwjGsu&index=7.

The Exploration with William C. Fox, "England's 'Glorious Revolution' Explained," March 2, 2018, YouTube video, 12:28, https://www.youtube.com/watch?v=Gx9N0mrTPtw&list=PL8QcMfC1fvaBf-9QZS-3A_PcORIlwjGsu&index=8.

John Locke

Vector illustration of Locke in cartoon style.

© Naci Yavuz/Shutterstock.com

Locke (1632–1704), from England, was well-connected and respected not only as a philosopher, but as a physician. His philosophical approach was empirical, meaning that it took as its starting point observations of the physical world. This is in contrast to Descartes (a "rationalist") who argued that the indubitable truth of our own existence as thinking beings must be the foundation of philosophy and all of the other disciplines. Locke wrote about political philosophy, philosophy of education, epistemology (study of knowledge), and other topics. His most famous work is *The Second Treatise on Government* (1690), which, along with some of his other political writings, influenced the US founders, other democracies that formed during the Enlightenment, and liberalism as a whole. He argued for equality and the protection of basic rights, and against absolute monarchy (the "divine right of kings") and slavery.

He was a Protestant (Church of England) and an avowed opponent to Catholicism. He in fact states that just as atheists cannot be trusted, neither can Catholics because of their allegiance to the Pope. A significant influence on his position was the controversial relationship between church and state in Europe, especially Britain, at the time.

Locke's relationship with slavery is controversial, because he participated in the slave trade, but argues vehemently against slavery in the *Second Treatise of Government*. Though he does not attempt to justify the legal slavery fueled by the slave trade, he does justify the enslavement of captives taken in war.[3]

Videos on the Rise of Prussia and the French Revolution

History Matters, "Ten Minute History- Frederick the Great and the Rise of Prussia (Short Documentary)," January 14, 2019, YouTube video, 9:59, https://www.youtube.com/watch?v=wzYfkezHp3k&list=PL8QcMfC1fvaBf-9QZS-3A_PcORIlwjGsu&index=11.

Videos on the French Revolution

(One of the most historically significant events of the Enlightenment):

The Infographics Show, "The French Revolution In a Nutshell," July 3, 2019, YouTube video, 9:26, https://www.youtube.com/watch?v=XmWc5BIhZHY&list=PL8QcMfC1fvaBf-9QZS-3A_PcORIlwjGsu&index=10.

3. For more about Locke's confusing position on slavery, see: William Uzgalis, "John Locke, Racism, Slavery, and Indian Lands," in Naomi Zack, ed., *The Oxford Handbook of Philosophy and Race* (Oxford: Oxford University Press, 2017), https://www.oxfordhandbooks.com/view/10.1093/oxfordhb/9780190236953.001.0001/oxfordhb-9780190236953-e-41.

John D Ruddy, "French Revolution in 9 Minutes—Manny Man Does History," January 12, 2015, YouTube video, 10:16, https://www.youtube.com/watch?v=X1_2NwmIobU&list=PL8QcMfC1fvaBf-9QZS-3A_PcORIlwjGsu&index=9.

Immanuel Kant

Vector portrait of Kant.

Kant (1724–1804), a Protestant (a Pietist), spent most of his life in Koenigsberg, Prussia, which is now in modern-day Russia. He spoke and wrote in German, and contributed to the fields of physics, metaphysics, epistemology, ethics, political philosophy, philosophy of religion, as well as others. His most famous works are the *Critique of Pure Reason* (1781, also known as the "First Critique") and the *Grounding for the Metaphysics of Morals* (1785, also known as the *Foundation of the Metaphysics of Morals*, or simply the "Groundwork" or "Grounding").[7] He built on the rationalist thinking that Descartes initiated by means of his philosophy of the noumena and phenomena, in which noumena, or "things-in-themselves," cannot be fully known. All that rational beings know—phenomena—is through our minds. This radical contribution to philosophy is known as Kant's "Copernican Turn," or the "Copernican Revolution in Philosophy." Kant's ethics takes this as its foundation. Many famous philosophers followed Kant and built on his work, including Fichte, Schelling, and Hegel.

Kant is famous for the daily schedule he kept. It was said that he was so punctual and routinized that his neighbors could set their clocks to Kant's comings and goings. He spent most of his day engaged in intellectual pursuits, including his own philosophy, his teaching, and his leisurely intellectual activity.

Though he famously argued against well-known proofs for God's existence, he went to great lengths to preserve religion using philosophy.

Video on the Industrial Revolution

Simple History, "The Industrial Revolution (18th–19th century)," October 1, 2017, YouTube video, 3:58, https://www.youtube.com/watch?v=xLhNP0qp38Q&list=PL8QcMfC1fvaBf-9QZS-3A_PcORIlwjGsu&index=12.

Jeremy Bentham

© Morphart Creation/Shutterstock.com

A British empiricist, Bentham (1748–1832) is typically credited as the founder of modern utilitarianism. He began reading at age four, when he also began studying Latin. Besides being a philosopher, he was also an economist. He was both a disciple and critic of Adam Smith. His most famous work is *An Introduction to the Principles of Morals and Legislation* (1789), where he defines the principle of utility. He contributed to the fields of political philosophy, ethics, philosophy of law, and others. He advocated for elections with secret ballots as well as women's suffrage. He was friends with James Mill, John Stuart Mill's father.[8]

John Stuart Mill

© Everett Collection/Shutterstock.com

Mill (1806–1873), who was British, also employed an empirical approach to philosophy. He argued against Kant, he built on and refined Bentham's utilitarianism, and his work contributed not only to the field of ethics, but to political philosophy, logic, economics, and other fields. He was highly influential in British politics. His most famous works include *A System of Logic* (1843), *On Liberty* (1859), *Utilitarianism* (1861), and *The Subjection of Women* (1869). In the latter, he argues for women's equality. He greatly respected, worked closely with, and was influenced by, his wife Harriet Taylor.

He began studying Greek at age three and Latin at eight, due mainly to the influence of his father. He spent 1820 in France and became fluent in French. He explains his mental crisis of 1826 in his *Autobiography* (1873), explaining that his mental issues mainly stemmed from his father. He highlights the poetry of Wordsworth as a factor that helped him emerge from his depression.

Mill, an agnostic, was critical of Christianity though he thought it could harmonize well with ethics.[9]

Karl Marx

© Everett Collection/Shutterstock.com

Marx (1818–1883) was a philosopher who inspired the political revolutions of Communism throughout the world. He contributed not only to the field of political philosophy, but also to economics and the philosophy of history. Marx was a materialist, meaning that he thought only the physical world existed, and he philosophized that class struggle would ultimately lead to Communism. Suffice it to say he was highly critical of capitalism, the breakdown of which he thought was inevitable.

He was born and raised in Germany, and converted from Judaism to Christianity with his family at a young age. His PhD thesis focused on Democritus and Epicurus. His most famous works include *The German Ideology* (1845) and *The Communist Manifesto* (1848), both co-written with Engels. His famous work on economics is the three-volume *Capital* (1867–1894), of which Engels edited the last volume. One of his best-known quotes, that "religion is the 'opiate of the people,'" occurs in his *Contribution to a Critique of Hegel's Philosophy of Right, Introduction* (1844).[10]

Video on Marxism

The Curious Classroom, "A Brief Introduction to Marxism," August 2, 2013, YouTube video, 4:26, https://www.youtube.com/watch?v=W0GFSUu5UzA&list=PL8QcMfC1fvaBf-9QZS-3A_PcORIlwjGsu&index=13.

Video on the Rise of Communism

Formosa, "History of Communism (Every Year)," November 7, 2017, 4:29, https://www.youtube.com/watch?v=8tOL-f_KsaA&list=PL8QcMfC1fvaBf-9QZS-3A_PcORIlwjGsu&index=14.

Aldo Leopold

Born and raised in Burlington, Iowa, Leopold (1887–1948) is often referred to as "father of wildlife ecology and the United States' wilderness system." He graduated from the Yale Forest School in 1909 and worked for the US Forest Service in Arizona and New Mexico afterward. By 1922, he played a significant role in the development of managing the Gila National Forest as the country's first official wilderness area. In 1933, he published the first textbook in the new field of wildlife management. That year, he also became chair of game management, which was the first position of its kind at the University of Wisconsin and the US. He wrote many articles, as well as a collection of essays published posthumously: *A Sand County Almanac*.[11]

Information about the Influence of Phenomenology and World War II on Twentieth-Century Thought

Followers of Kant dominated much of the intellectual landscape in the nineteenth century on the European continent. Phenomenology developed out of Kantian philosophy as a result of Hegel, Husserl, and Heidegger. It largely dominated European continental philosophy in the twentieth century. In highly simplified terms, the philosophical foundation of phenomenology is a particular conception of the human person. The subject, "ego," or "I" limits and defines our experience of the observable world in Kantian philosophical investigation. For Heidegger, the human person as "Dasein," or "being there" is a starting point and framer of philosophy. Phenomenological investigation is shaped and limited by the experiential capabilities of a certain conception of the human person.

Levinas and Arendt, discussed below, were part of twentieth-century phenomenological intellectual culture. They were both also greatly influenced by the events of World War II, as were many other philosophers, such as Theodor Adorno and Max Horkheimer, who were both notable thinkers of the Frankfurt School.

Some Notable Events of World War II	
1933	Hitler becomes chancellor of Germany, Dachau concentration camp opens
1934	von Hindenburg dies and Hitler becomes President of Germany; subsequently declares himself "Fuehrer"; becomes absolute dictator
1935	Anti-Jewish laws enacted in Germany
1936–1937	More concentration camps open
1938	Adolf Eichmann steps up the enforcement of Jewish emigration; Kristallnacht occurs
1939	Hitler invades Poland, Britain and France declare war on Germany
1939	Stalin and the Soviet Union invade Poland
1940	Nazis occupy Paris; Auschwitz concentration camp set up
1941	Japanese attack on Pearl Harbor: US enters the war; Germany invades Soviet Union
1944	Russians begin liberating concentration camps; D-Day occurs; Paris liberated
1945	Other concentration camps liberated[12]; victory in Europe declared, atomic bombs dropped in Japan, Japan surrenders

Emmanuel Levinas

Levinas (1905–1995) was a Lithuanian Jew whose family was murdered in the Holocaust. Unlike the famous phenomenologists Edmund Husserl and Martin Heidegger, in whose footsteps Levinas followed, Levinas developed an ethics rooted in phenomenological metaphysics.

Levinas saw ethics as fundamental—as "first philosophy"—unlike his many predecessors who reserved this place of privilege for metaphysics. Whether Levinas's ethics counts as a "theory" is doubtful for a number of reasons, including the fact that it might be better characterized as "meta-ethics."[13]

In 1923, Levinas left Lithuania to study philosophy in Strasbourg, France, and in 1928–29, he moved to Freiburg, Germany, to study with Husserl. While there, he attended a seminar Heidegger (a self-professed Nazi) gave. In 1939, he was naturalized as French and enlisted in the French officer corps, after which he was captured by the Nazis in 1940 and imprisoned in a labor camp. His family was murdered, except for his wife and daughter who were hidden by nuns in France. He began writing *Existence and Existents* while imprisoned. One of his most famous works is *Totality and Infinity: An Essay on Exteriority* (1965), and another is *Humanism of the Other* (1972). He became a professor, and a colleague of Paul Ricoeur, at the University of Paris in 1967.[14]

Hannah Arendt

1986 German stamp bearing Arendt's image.

Hannah Arendt (1906–1975), who was Jewish, was born in Hanover, Germany. In 1924, she traveled to Marbourg University to study with Martin Heidegger, who became a full-fledged member of the Nazi party and one of the most influential philosophers of the twentieth century. After a year, she moved to Freiburg University to study with Edmund Husserl for a semester. She worked at Heidelberg University with Karl Jaspers on her doctoral dissertation, which she completed in 1929. She was forced to leave Germany in 1933, and eventually relocated to Paris where she worked as an advocate for Jewish refugees. She was forced to move yet again in 1941 and came to New York City. While in the US, she taught at several institutions, including Princeton, Berkeley, and The University of Chicago, but was mainly based in New York at The New School for Social Research in Manhattan where she was a professor of political philosophy. Her most famous works are *The Origins of Totalitarianism* (1951) and *The Human Condition* (1958). She published *Eichmann in Jerusalem* by attending the trial of Adolf Eichmann in 1961 as a magazine reporter for *The New Yorker*.[15] She stands out among contemporary philosophers not only because of her impressive and highly influential body of work, but also because she was not just a professor and author: she worked with refugee organizations for six years and also had a brief stint as a journalist.

Endnotes

1. Tim O'Keefe, "Epicurus (341–271 BCE)," *Internet Encyclopedia of Philosophy*, accessed October 24, 2020, https://iep.utm.edu/epicur/#H1.
2. Robert Wagoner, "Lucius Annaeus Seneca (ca. 4 BCE–65 CE)," *Internet Encyclopedia of Philosophy*, accessed October 24, 2020, https://iep.utm.edu/seneca/.
3. Keith H. Seddon, "Epictetus (55–135 CE)," *Internet Encyclopedia of Philosophy*, https://iep.utm.edu/epictetu/#H1.
4. From "Key Dates in Renaissance Philosophy, Politics, Religion, and Science," ThoughtCo., updated July 14, 2019, https://www.thoughtco.com/renaissance-timeline-4158077, and "A timeline of contemporary European events, 1400–1550," British Library, accessed October 24, 2020, https://www.bl.uk/onlinegallery/features/flemish/timeline.html.
5. See David Simpson, "Francis Bacon (1561–1626)," *Internet Encyclopedia of Philosophy*, accessed October 24, 2020, https://iep.utm.edu/bacon/.
6. Gary Hatfield, "Rene Descartes," *Stanford Encyclopedia of Philosophy*, last updated January 16, 2014, https://plato.stanford.edu/entries/descartes/#EarLifEdu.
7. Specific dates obtained from *Encyclopedia Britannica*, s.v., "Immanuel Kant," accessed October 24, 2020, https://www.britannica.com/biography/Immanuel-Kant/The-Critique-of-Practical-Reason.
8. See *Encyclopedia Britannica*, s.v., "Jeremy Bentham," accessed October 24, 2020, https://www.britannica.com/biography/Jeremy-Bentham.
9. Colin Heydt, "John Stuart Mill (1806–1873)," *Internet Encyclopedia of Philosophy*, accessed October 24, 2020, https://iep.utm.edu/milljs/.
10. Jonathan Wolff, "Karl Marx," *Stanford Encyclopedia of Philosophy*, last revised April 12, 2017, https://plato.stanford.edu/entries/marx/.
11. "Aldo Leopold," The Aldo Leopold Foundation, accessed October 24, 2020, https://www.aldoleopold.org/about/aldo-leopold/.
12. From "Holocaust Timeline," Holocaust Museum Learning Center, accessed October 24, 2020, https://hmlc.org/holocaust-history/timeline/, "World War II Major Events Timeline," PBS, accessed October 24, 2020, https://www.pbs.org/wgbh/masterpiece/specialfeatures/world-war-ii-major-events-timeline/#, and "Timeline of World War II," PBS, accessed October 24, 2020, https://www.pbs.org/thewar/at_war_timeline_1945.htm.
13. Bettina Bergo, "Emmanuel Levinas," *Stanford Encyclopedia of Philosophy*, last revised August 7, 2019, https://plato.stanford.edu/entries/levinas/#LifeCare.
14. Ibid., https://plato.stanford.edu/entries/levinas/#LifeCare.
15. Maurizio Passerin d'Entreves, "Hannah Arendt," last revised January 11, 2019, https://plato.stanford.edu/entries/arendt/#BioSke.

ıformation can be obtained
CGtesting.com
ın the USA
061643120821
?7LV00002B/2

9 781792 433122